Improvised Continent

THE ARTS AND INTELLECTUAL LIFE
IN MODERN AMERICA

Casey Nelson Blake, Series Editor

Volumes in the series explore questions at the intersection of the history of expressive culture and the history of ideas in modern America. The series is meant as a bold intervention in two fields of cultural inquiry. It challenges scholars in American studies and cultural studies to move beyond sociological categories of analysis to consider the ideas that have informed and given form to artistic expression—whether architecture and the visual arts or music, dance, theater, and literature. The series also expands the domain of intellectual history by examining how artistic works, and aesthetic experience more generally, participate in the discussion of truth and value, civic purpose and personal meaning that have engaged scholars since the late nineteenth century.

IMPROVISED CONTINENT

Pan-Americanism and Cultural Exchange

Richard Cándida Smith

PENN

UNIVERSITY OF PENNSYLVANIA PRESS

PHILADELPHIA

Published by
University of Pennsylvania Press
Philadelphia, Pennsylvania 19104-4112
www.upenn.edu/pennpress

Printed in the United States of America on acid-free paper
10 9 8 7 6 5 4 3 2 1

A catalogue record for this book is available from the
Library of Congress.
ISBN 978-0-8122-4942-2

Ya que no hablamos para ser escuchados
Sino para que los demás hablen
—Nicanor Parra

Now that we do not speak solely to be heard
But so that others may speak
—translation by William Carlos Williams

Contents

Introduction

In March 1945, Brazilian novelist Érico Veríssimo stopped in Abilene, Texas, as part of a three-week tour of Texas, Oklahoma, Kansas, and Kentucky, where he spoke at nineteen locations about the place of pan-American unity in the global fight against fascism and militarism.[1] Abilene was then a medium-sized town of fifty thousand in the middle of the cattle and petroleum country of northwest Texas. Some six hundred people showed up for an afternoon's activities at Abilene Christian College. The meeting ground was decorated with U.S. and Brazilian flags, as well as cowboy gear from Texas and Brazil. After singing the "Star Spangled Banner," the audience was led in singing the Brazilian national anthem in English translation. A program of North American and Brazilian folk songs followed. Once again the audience sang along with translated lyrics projected onto a screen. Two songs were performed in Portuguese, so the audience could hear how they sounded in the original language.

After the cultural program, Érico Veríssimo presented a fifty-minute talk with slides entitled "Brazil, the Gentle Giant."[2] Veríssimo's talks were humorous, but he also used the opportunity and the goodwill he seemed to generate from his listeners to present them with his friendly criticisms of the United States. He insisted on talking about the country's long history of racial hatred and the damage that segregation laws did to the quality of human relationships within the United States. He confessed that he always had trouble filling out official forms in North America that required him to check the appropriate box for his race. He told his U.S. audiences, "In a melting pot like Brazil (and let it be said in passing, the same is true for the United States), none of us know for sure the lines of blood running in our veins." He decided to respond to such questions by writing in the only reply that he could say with certainty: "I am a human being."[3] He compared the situation in the United States with his own country's legacy of racial mingling, though he frankly admitted, unlike official representatives of his government, that Brazil needed to do much more to assure that all citizens enjoyed full equality. He also talked about misinformation in the U.S. media about Latin America, using examples of recent portrayals of Brazil in movies and the press. He hoped that communication between the two countries, such as represented by the day's event, would increase, and

Americans would quickly become as familiar with Brazil as they were with England or France.

At the end of his talk he received a thundering ovation from the crowd. The event concluded with a buffet of "typical Brazilian food" (menu not identified, but *churrascaria*, Brazilian barbecue typical of the southern region that was Veríssimo's home, would have been comfortably similar to Texas barbecue), and a chance for conversation with the speaker. The president of the college rushed up to him after the talk with an invitation to spend a year in Abilene as a visiting professor. It was a proposal that other academic hosts across the United States often made him after his appearances. The success of Veríssimo's first English-language publication, the novel *Crossroads*, had made him the most widely read Latin American writer in the United States, a position he maintained for the next two decades as eight more books appeared to critical and commercial success. Like many other writers and artists from Latin America, he had accepted a proposal from the U.S. State Department that he live in the United States "for the duration" and contribute to the wartime alliance by giving average U.S. citizens a sense of personal connection with Brazil, a country about which most knew very little.

Veríssimo's talks were part of a massive program the federal government sponsored through the course of the war utilizing speakers and media to introduce U.S. citizens to the many countries in the United Nations alliance. Latin Americans were, by far, the most frequently employed allied speakers because, for the previous thirty years, private organizations in the United States had already been promoting closer cultural interaction between the United States and the twenty other countries in the Pan American Union. The first formal cultural exchange programs between the United States and Latin American countries were launched in 1912 with pilot funding from the Carnegie Corporation, and then significantly expanded in 1916. Other philanthropies joined in, as did educational institutions, museums, libraries, and commercial publishing and media companies, plus of course the government, for which both pan-Americanism and cultural exchange had important roles to play in the country's broadest foreign policy objectives. An extensive network of personal and institutional relations took shape before World War II that allowed a select group of Latin American writers and artists to enter U.S. cultural markets and speak directly to the U.S. public.[4] For a few, like Érico Veríssimo or the Chilean poet Gabriela Mistral, participation in U.S. cultural life was a critical turning point in their careers. For most, the connection was secondary or momentary. Some, like the Mexican painter Diego Rivera or Colombian historian and essayist Germán Arciniegas, embraced the goal of pan-American unity with enthusiasm, tempered with reasonable skepticism about how committed U.S. leaders were to international equality. Others, like Mexican painter David Alfaro Siqueiros or Brazilian historian Sérgio Buarque de Holanda, wondered how a country as deeply racist as the United States could have become the leader of a global alliance fighting to end racism. Many more were like Argentinean writer María Rosa Oliver, who thought that the United States, like most places, was a mix of things positive and negative. The international responsibilities the United States had assumed made it imperative that any writer or artist who could address the U.S. public take advantage of the opportunities pan-Americanism offered. The writers and artists featured in this book were a diverse group, whose differences and disagreements were more important than the commonality they shared within the United States as representatives of a region. Even so, they understood that their ability to speak directly to people in the United States was a privilege that came with obligations to help whoever encountered their work see inter-American, and ultimately global, relations from the perspective of an intellectual from another country. What they had to say was often critical, but like Érico Veríssimo's public appearances, generally aimed to help people in the United States become better global citizens.

This would never be an easy task, given that both pan-Americanism and cultural exchange rested on an unstable synthesis of utopian ideals and the rise of the United States as a world power. The Pan American Union, founded in 1890, was the first institutional expression of a new vision of global organization that the United States vigorously promoted throughout the twentieth century. For the next seventy-five years, pan-Americanism provided U.S. leaders with a test case for developing an international system consonant with their country's distinctive institutions.[5] However much driven by considerations inside the United States of how to expand the nation's international power and influence, pan-Americanism as a policy linking twenty-one sovereign nations could not have endured if it had not expressed an idealistic, in many ways utopian vision of nations, big and small, rich and poor, equally submitting to a formal system of international law that resolved disputes through fair and disinterested procedures.[6] In particular, pan-Americanism drew upon preexisting liberal ideas that the American nations had a special place in history as the home of liberty.[7]

The union appealed to many across the western hemisphere because it addressed widespread hopes that international relations could be reformed around enforceable principles of equality, mutuality, and community. Given the discrepancy in resources and wealth, none of the other twenty republics in the Pan American Union could enjoy anything more than formal equality. Whenever joint action occurred, somebody from the United States organized it and provided money, at times the government, very frequently philanthropies and other private institutions. Equality often felt in practice very much like genteel servitude. A resistant understanding of pan-Americanism was ready at hand: it was the Trojan horse by which the United States delegated the administration of its empire to dependent but notionally sovereign governments. Private citizens involved in pan-American activities were being seduced into taking for granted that U.S. ways of doing things were always the best. Pan-Americanism invoked, and continues to invoke for many, a project for world domination that began with a campaign to absorb Latin America into a U.S. empire without borders. The noted Argentinean historian Tulio Halperín Donghi stressed that a distinctive feature of U.S. dominance was reliance on cultural conversion, with the assumptions of the more powerful partner presumed to reflect a "natural law" that the weaker had to respect, even if they did not particularly like the consequences for their countries. Integration required implementing the logic of the U.S. approach to business, politics, and culture, which forced the elites of client states to operate more like their counterparts to the north did. Even when disagreements arose, rupture was unthinkable, which tended to make ruptures that did occur particularly violent.[8] Halperín Donghi's astute analysis of the contradiction underlying the multilateral international organizations that the United States preferred during the twentieth century explains why in fact resistance was very thinkable and acted on continuously, a major factor in the continuing international instability that has marked the U.S. rise to global leadership.

If the confusion of power and ideals has been a defining feature of the U.S. relationship with other countries, activities where the two have been most inseparable offer particularly important entry points. As part of a formal commitment to reimagining international relations on republican and democratic principles, the American nations pledged to increase cultural interaction and promote a new pan-American identity that in an ideal world could transform state-to-state relations. Regularized citizen-to-citizen contacts, including increased exchange of intellectual and cultural work, would lead to the citizens of American nations forming a shared public opinion monitoring and guiding their governments' foreign policy choices as effectively as opinion within each nation shaped domestic politics. Programs organized under the rubric of "cultural exchange" had the formal charge of exposing citizens of other countries to U.S. writers, artists, and composers, while introducing foreign creative figures to the citizens of the United States. Interpretations of what these two broad goals meant shifted dramatically across the period covered in the book as the international situation and domestic politics within the United States changed.

"Cultural exchange," no less than pan-Americanism, invokes equally contradictory abstractions. Culture that has become an instrument of official policy cannot, by definition, offer critical frameworks for experiencing the complexities of the world in new, possibly uncomfortable ways. Even if the form appears innovative, as say with abstract expressionistic painting that the State Department exhibited abroad in the early years of the Cold War, the work is reduced to a form of propaganda, intended to extract conformist consent to policies serving the interests of those in power.[9] Participating artists, however, many enthusiastic to contribute to the cause of global understanding, brought their own concerns and causes to the program. They offered foreign publics messages about life in the United States that went far beyond what diplomatic patrons wanted. One of the most compelling examples of how difficult it has been for official cultural exchange programs to control the contributions of participating artists can be found in Penny Von Eschen's landmark study of African American jazz musicians whom the State Department recruited as cultural ambassadors during the Cold War. Forced to confront the absurdity of their touring the world as representatives of American freedom when they were second-class citizens at home, many of the musicians Von Eschen studied became more vocal activists for civil rights and black liberation.[10] The State Department often found that the political independence of U.S. artists, writers, musicians, and performers it drafted into foreign tours embroiled it in domestic political disputes. Anti–New Deal conservatives, in alliance with southern Democrats anxious to limit criticism of racial segregation from any source, foreign as well as domestic, argued that cultural exchange programs invited international public opinion to interfere in the internal affairs of the United States. However, even if domestic politics made many international programs unstable, cultural exchange staff had learned that outspoken cultural figures generated positive results overseas. Foreign audiences liked what they heard, and criticisms of the United States from U.S. artists on tour effectively countered widespread claims on the left and the right that the world's wealthiest power was materialist, machine driven, and conformist. Jazz musicians, as well as beat poets, rock musicians, and method actors, reinforced the image of the United States as a place where many social and cultural movements challenged entrenched custom and authority.[11]

"Exchange" is a word that logically implies two-way interaction. In principle, the impact of cultural exchange programs within the United States should be a topic of importance, but previous studies have primarily focused on how the U.S. government deployed cultural programs to influence public opinion in other countries.[12] As the evidence presented in this book suggests, the story within the United States may even be of paramount importance. How does a society in the process of becoming a world power prepare its citizens for the responsibilities and often-exorbitant costs of global leadership? Can they develop a sense of connection with the citizens of other countries independent from the strategic considerations guiding their government's foreign policy? Do they have the insight they need to ensure that government foreign actions are accountable to democratic oversight?

The mixture of ideals and the exercise of power made both pan-Americanism and cultural exchange "fields of opportunities," to borrow German historian Reinhart Koselleck's term, that attracted social democrats and liberals who saw possibilities for realizing their ideals. Koselleck noted that beckoning utopias and the dystopias they simultaneously invoke provide crucial evidence of "hope and memory" shaping the forms and possibilities of action. Koselleck added that hope and memory, or in more abstract and generalized language expectation and experience, "simultaneously constitute history and its cognition," that is, what people did and then the debates that follow over how to interpret those actions, their sources, and their consequences.[13] Both pan-Americanism and cultural exchange expressed an effort across the twentieth century to reconcile profound change with liberal, democratic ideals. Peoples thrown together in a tragic history of invasion, genocide, and slavery promised to work together to achieve a peaceful, stable, and prosperous future. As a result, pan-Americanism can still be an object for nostalgia, surprisingly to a greater extent outside the United States than within. It recalls a past when the power of the United States appeared as if it would be used for the common good of all peoples. There was as well a hope that a regard for opinion in other countries might keep a tendency toward unilateral action in check. During that brief moment, ideals associated with the United States could be and often were emblematic of popular aspirations internationally even though they were inseparable from the growth of U.S. national power.

If pan-Americanism was the trial run for a specifically U.S. vision of global governance, it is equally true that liberal ideas had deep roots in the Latin American struggle for independence, roots that explain the generally positive response given to U.S. proposals for greater hemispheric cooperation. When in the first decades of the twentieth century, the Uruguayan José Enrique Rodó, the Dominican Pedro Henríquez Ureña, the Brazilian Oswald de Andrade, the Chilean Gabriela Mistral, or the Mexican Carlos Pellicer each spoke of an "American ideal," they invoked images of opportunity, openness to change, personal freedom, individuality, and self-governance that many U.S. citizens may think of as uniquely belonging to their own country. The Americanism of these and other writers proclaiming America's mission in the world did not derive from U.S. ideas or U.S. practices. Indeed each of these figures wrote of the United States as a threat to the "American ideal," even if on other occasions, they also wrote of the United States as a caretaker of humanity's hopes. What U.S. journalists and historians have often described as nationalist resistance to imperialism might in other countries be viewed as a defense of "universal" values that people in the United States have not understood deeply enough and have often betrayed.[14]

Consistent with Koselleck's model, pan-Americanism acted as a "horizon of expectation," within which hopes and fears jostled as Americans from many nations tried to envision what the future would bring their peoples. Expressions of expectation take shape within the practical "spaces of experience" that develop within societies over time. For writers, artists, filmmakers, and their patrons, those spaces were not determined by geopolitics, nor even by national politics. Political goals helped establish an expectation of a future community of nations, while providing resources for promoting cultural interaction between the United States and other American nations. The people who had to do the work, however, followed their personal interests and the requirements of the institutions that made it possible for them to reach a public.[15] The practical conditions shaping what any cultural worker can say or do are a central part of the story that follows, for they clarify the restraints, both external and internal, shaping the production and distribution of cultural work.[16] Writing and art are meaningful when they can be scheduled into the practices that institutions foster to assure the continuity of their activities. The everyday practices of book publishing, of organizing exhibits and tours, or of releasing subtitled or dubbed films involve thousands of discrete activities requiring an experienced support staff. The availability of material presupposes volume, routines, and schedules that are comfortable for the people who must do the work. Satisfying the demands of organizational routine is a minimal requirement for any given work creating or finding its public. The practical disjunctions between how different countries organized the production and distribution of culture continuously proved to be among the most difficult obstacles to broadening cultural exchange. One of the key conclusions I have drawn in the course of this study is that practical "necessities" (which might better be thought of as organized routines that create a set of habits for everybody involved, including creative personnel) often lead to significant ideological results, which, however, cannot be understood, much less explained, by recourse to the ideological predispositions of the people involved.[17] By insisting that ideology is only one element in any given historically situated practice, we can escape the teleologies inherent to polemics and clarify the fractures that accompany any ostensibly utopian project without being trapped inside the emotionally intense political debates of the past.

Despite the importance given to practical matters, the narrative that follows does not utilize the methods of sociology of culture. Instead, the book presents a series of exemplary characters who took on the role of cultural ambassador, many (though not all) operating from a conviction that if citizens of different countries better understood each other, they would act to limit the evil their governments do. Érico Veríssimo has a particularly important role in the story of pan-American cultural exchange. The State Department brought him to the United States in 1941 because cultural affairs staff believed that he had a special talent for communication across cultures. They introduced him to publishers and provided funds for the translation of his first book. Their hunch that he could reach the reading public in the United States proved correct. After nearly three decades of cultural exchange efforts to promote interest within the United States in Latin American writers, Veríssimo was the first to enjoy both critical and commercial success in the United States, with nine titles published between 1943 and 1967. During this time, his only peer in the United States was the Chilean poet Pablo Neruda, whose work early gained a stellar position in the smaller but intensely committed poetry market. Today, Veríssimo is unknown in the United States to anyone who is not a specialist in Brazilian literature, though in the Portuguese-language world, he is considered among the most important novelists of the modern era. Veríssimo's personal trajectory made him an exemplary figure for this study. In the 1940s, he was an enthusiastic and popular spokesperson for the Good Neighbor Policy; during the Cold War, he was staunchly anticommunist and worked as director of cultural affairs for the Pan American Union in the mid-1950s; by the 1960s, he had turned critical of U.S. militarism and the propensity of the nation's leaders to respond to political problems with military solutions. In 1967 he published a novel whose central characters were U.S. soldiers fighting in Vietnam, a book that was not, and has not yet been, translated into English. His next and last novel, published in 1971, also never published in an English-language version, addressed the use of torture as an instrument of policy in Brazil. Veríssimo analyzed the social conflicts in the country that culminated in the military seizing control of Brazil in 1964 with the support and blessing of the U.S. government. That Veríssimo was once well known in the United States but has been forgotten raises a historical puzzle central to understanding how and why publishers, critics, and readers in the United States selected the foreign writers they absorbed into their own culture. For the writers and artists discussed in this book, a passionate effort to make a difference and leave the world a better place for the next generation is the heart of each story. The bodies of work produced vary in quality and effectiveness, reflecting the limitations of the creator's imagination and skill as well as the ideological and practical restrictions he or she faced on what could be said. The lives glimpsed inevitably were tragic as hopes collided with the fissures deeply rooted in the times and places in which they operated. Nonetheless, moving across borders often proved liberating because for a brief period routines were broken and new ways of understanding the world emerged in work that traveling made possible.[18]

The contradictions inherent to the emergence of pan-Americanism exemplify the political definition of community formation that Hannah Arendt developed in *The Human Condition*.[19] "Community" suggests ideas of sharing and cooperation, but Arendt offered her readers a darker vision, stripped of the illusions that ideals provide but more consistent with the historical lessons to be found in the experiences of people living and acting together. Arendt contended that political community forms primarily through the contention of different groups and individuals vying to recreate the world around one's "sovereign mastery." A clear example of what she meant can be found in U.S. secretary of state Richard Olney's declaration to the British government in 1895 that no other power was in a position to challenge U.S. interests in the western hemisphere. In fact, Olney presented an expectation as already accomplished fact. A determination to make the wish reality quickened the efforts of successive U.S. administrations to convince and coerce others into an international community based on U.S. ideas of a well-run society. But even if U.S. leaders assumed their own values were universal, they operated within a highly partisan, competitive political world. As practical politicians, they knew that communities do not grow from "shared values" but from an often reluctantly embraced necessity to understand what opponents are trying to say and then search for a way to reconcile disagreements—with weaker parties having to decide the balance of adaptation and resistance most realistic for the given situation. The goal of communication in a situation of potential violence is not the promotion of "good will," but to put opposing parties into a relationship that requires both to change as a result of interaction. Communication always raises fundamental existential issues. In the process of trying to decode and interpret what an opponent demands, an inward process that opens as recognition of differences leads to questions central to self-understanding: who am I, what do I want, how should I act now, how might *we* act if we were to act in concert, what conditions allow groups that historically encountered each other as opponents to become a "we"?

Arendt, in her discussion of the political, conflict-based nature of community, proposed a model for understanding the critical role that cultural work can play. The results of actions are often unpredictable, Arendt noted, and in many situations losses are irreversible, particularly once opponents turn to violence to achieve their goals in preference to dialogue. Cultural work, perhaps particularly fictional work or the visual arts because they present worlds of "as if," offers a domain where issues can be addressed with relative safety because the ideas and feelings to be exchanged and examined do not require public action of any sort. Nothing is asked of the recipient beyond reflection on what one has seen. Writing, art, and other cultural products can play an important role in community-formation processes because solitude, Arendt insisted, is necessary for communication to be digested. Communication must include moments when retreat into one's own interiority is an appropriate response, a situation that corresponds well with the anonymity of twentieth-century mass media. But although reading a novel, viewing a film, or walking through an art exhibit provide relatively safe spaces for absorbing different points of view, the process remains uncomfortable, even if not directly threatening. For there to be an exchange that can be called communication, change must remain a possible outcome. Pondering what they have seen or heard, recipients evaluate the differences revealed and what they require. A successful communication makes recipients vulnerable, potentially aware of their own failings (typical absences in perspectives) and of their own failures (specific acts). In the process of self-recognition growing from communication across differences comes an availability to change. Whether the end result is some form of cooperation or more sharply defined hostility, repertoires of identity and collectivity are thrown into play. This was the possibility that motivated the men and women whose hopes constitute the narrative of this book.[20]

Diego Rivera in 1943 wrote an article for a Mexican journal in which he explained why he remained convinced that pan-Americanism would eventually overcome national chauvinism and convince the people of the United States to enter into a fuller political community with the citizens of other American countries. The logic of their own national ideals projected into hemispheric and, as a result of the war with Germany and Japan, global arenas would lead U.S. citizens to abide by the will of the world's majority if decisions emerged from free, open debate, rather than the dictates of corrupt leaders. Rivera was not so naïve as to believe that the time had arrived for equality between citizens of rich countries and those of much poorer countries. Mexicans still needed to be vigilant in protecting their interests. One of the best ways to do that, however, was to leap across the border and engage people in the United States, as he had done with great success. He took a leap of faith, typical of many who found the opportunities that pan-Americanism provided them mysteriously exciting. Rivera argued that pan-Americanism made U.S. society more available to the logic of international engagement, but only to the degree that it was connected to an international movement to expand democratic participation in governance. The desire to prevent another war potentially more horrifying than World War II might push the citizens of rich countries like the United States to broaden their understanding of fellowship. As long as pan-Americanism remained limited to negotiating over trade and security issues, the countries would be trapped in what made them most unequal. Equality would emerge only to the degree that developing a shared imagination had priority, and toward that aspiration, not surprisingly Rivera thought that creative workers such as he had an indispens-able role. To explore the foundations and the possibilities of Rivera's expecta-tion, let us turn now to the beginning of the twentieth century as efforts to create a new pan-American culture got under way.

Chapter 1

Pan-American Culture

In the autumn of 1889, delegates representing the independent republics of America assembled in Washington, D.C., to discuss proposals from the Congress of the United States to establish a hemispheric customs union and a permanent arbitration court for settling inter-American disputes. Both ideas were controversial, and the twenty delegations agreed only to form the International Bureau of the American Republics, a small office headquartered in Washington charged with coordinating exchange of information between the member countries. The bureau connected politicians, businessmen, journalists, and intellectuals from throughout the Americas who were interested in closer interaction with the United States, establishing in the most practical terms that if there were to be a greater American union, the United States would be its hub. From 1890 until the late 1930s, the population of the United States was greater than that of all other American nations combined.[1] While deep poverty characterized the South and other primarily rural areas, in general the U.S. population enjoyed considerably higher median incomes, along with greater levels of literacy and property ownership, than the citizens of any other member of the Pan American Union. At the beginning of the twentieth century, Argentina had per capita income levels comparable to the United States, but with higher levels of income inequality and political disenfranchisement. To a degree, the centrality of the United States to the Pan American Union grew from its development as a manufacturing nation with technologically advanced if high-cost finished goods to exchange for agricultural products and natural resources. The dollar value of U.S. exports to the rest of the hemisphere rose quickly through the 1890s and the first decades of the twentieth century. As an aid to communication, the bureau published directories for each of the American countries with names and addresses of government officials, leading bankers, and owners and managers of import-export firms, as well as other prominent figures in agriculture, business, and the professions.[2]

The guiding principle underlying the bureau's activities was that private initiative could best determine which inter-American connections were beneficial. That the purposes of the bureau were nebulous was inevitable for it had no models to follow. The International Bureau of the American Republics was the first of the many regional and global organizations that would develop across the twentieth century, providing a new structure for international governance. The responsibilities of the bureau grew, and in 1910 the member states meeting in Buenos Aires replaced the bureau with a new organization with enhanced responsibilities, the Pan American Union. Steel magnate Andrew Carnegie, personally committed to developing international government, funded the construction of an imposing neoclassical palace in Washington to serve as the organization's headquarters.[3]

In addition to its diplomatic and commercial functions, the Pan American Union sponsored conferences addressing a broad range of topics, financial, political, and cultural. In December 1908, the first Pan-American Scientific Congress convened in Santiago, Chile, bringing together over four hundred scholars from the United States and Latin America.[4] The congress ended with a resolution calling for an ongoing bibliography of books published in each country. The delegates also urged that the governments of the hemisphere establish a translation fund in order that the most important works written in the American nations would be equally available in English, French, Spanish, and Portuguese.

Expanded cultural exchange remained on the agenda in December 1915, when 2,566 delegates assembled in Washington for the Pan American Union's Second Scientific Conference. War in Europe added an unexpected political face to a conference with sessions discussing agronomy, particle physics, the principles of international law, telephone exchange and relay systems, the effects of tax policy on economic growth, and preservation of Native American languages, among many, many other topics featured in several hundred sessions. U.S. president Woodrow Wilson accentuated the political overtones when he welcomed conference delegates with a speech outlining his proposal for an American collective security agreement, which he dubbed the "Pan-American Peace Pact."[5] Planning for the congress had started well before the outbreak of World War I in 1914, but the war increased its symbolic importance. The American nations were suddenly on their own, not only the heirs of "Western civilization" but also its caretakers by default, or so many speakers at the congress proclaimed. Throughout the hemisphere, the press gave close attention to the proceedings, particularly debates over how the American nations might best preserve their neutrality while working for an end to the European war.

Jane Addams (1860–1935), speaking at a session organized by the Women's Auxiliary of the Pan American Union, argued that internationalism in the hands of diplomats stymied meaningful ties between the citizens of different nations. For the previous generation, conference after conference had gathered together the leaders of Europe, but good intentions failed to prevent the outbreak of the continent's most brutal war ever. The vision of international cooperation, she insisted, had been entirely formalistic: "People would say, 'Come together, let us be international,' and then they would pass resolutions and found a constitution, and so forth and so on." If the Pan American Union were to succeed where Europe had failed, a dramatically different understanding of global governance was needed to replace a system based on balance of power. Leadership had to come directly from the people and not from governments. To those who thought this was naïve idealism, Addams protested that in her hometown of Chicago, people of many different national backgrounds, speaking dozens of languages at home, worshipping in many different ways, regularly worked together to solve the city's problems. She was certain that similar collaboration was found in any large city in the hemisphere, São Paulo no less than Chicago: "These immigrants, as we call them, who have lived all over the world, find it quite possible to make friends with each other. They find it quite possible after a few months, and better still after a few years, to understand each other and to live together, not only in amenity, but with mutual interest and mutual undertakings [of] people who become international through this perfectly natural and spontaneous process."[6]

Addams was deeply skeptical that the Pan American Union, bound by the political needs of the member governments, could develop citizen-to-citizen communication. If there were to be a breakthrough it would have to come from groups like the Women's Auxiliary of the Pan American Union. Women, divorced from power in all nations, she asserted, had little stake in concepts such as "national honor." Women more readily understood what she had learned in the slums of Chicago: put people who are worrying about the same problems into close contact, get them talking and listening to each other, and they will overcome their differences to develop a community of interest. She did not speculate on how the face-to-face contact experienced in a densely packed urban neighborhood might be replicated on a continental level, much less across the globe.

The larger goal of the Pan American Union's conferences was the building of a common culture among the educated elites of the continent; their conversations both technical and general could be the foundation for a shared inter-American "public opinion."[7] Addams's question whether the Pan American Union could create a space across national borders for meaningful, effective debate confronted the asymmetry between the United States, with its industrialized dissemination of opinion through the mass media, and many Latin American countries, where low literacy rates kept the market for books and magazines small.[8]

After the congress's conclusion, the Carnegie Endowment for International Peace organized a tour around the United States for several prominent Latin American participants to speak at universities, civic and women's clubs, and business groups.[9] The delegates invited included a vocal critic of the United States, Manuel Ugarte of Argentina, who had previously declared that Pan American Union congresses were nothing more than gatherings "of mice chaired by a cat."[10] The speaker most in demand after the congress concluded was Ernesto Quesada (1858–1934), rector of the University of Buenos Aires and head of the Argentinean delegation. Quesada, having spent part of his child-hood in the United States, was fluent in colloquial American English, and he knew the U.S. education system firsthand as a student and a teacher.

The standard talk that Quesada gave on his tour began with the proposition that, since independence, the idea of the continent forming a political union was deeply rooted in the American imagination, perhaps inherited from the ambition of each of the colonial empires to eliminate its rivals and seize control of the entire hemisphere.[11] Nonetheless, he argued that pan-Americanism rested on a fiction that peoples living close to each other shared the same ideals, and thus it was easily turned to serving the narrow interests of the biggest member states, a polite way of suggesting as Ugarte did that the organization primarily served U.S. political and economic domination of the hemisphere. Quesada warned that, as a concept, pan-Americanism was idealistic but divorced from the historical realities of each nation. In normal political situations, this would be a fatal weakness, but with Europe in crisis, the potential idealism of pan-Americanism offered an alternative to the tragic realities of history. Because the pan-American ideal existed in a realm apart from everyday life in any coun-try, it provoked Americans to think about how they might live in new, possibly better ways. Pan-American unity was therefore, he concluded, a concept most at home in universities and other cultural institutions. Academics and students had the responsibility of demonstrating to their fellow citizens how the creation of a hemispheric body superior to national governments might actually improve their lives.

Quesada asserted that any future world community was likely to begin in the Americas precisely because each nation had been a laboratory for how people of radically different backgrounds could live together productively. Not always in peace, he acknowledged, but more so than in any other part of the world. In its most idealistic aspect, pan-Americanism was the most impor-tant experiment yet tried preparing the way for world unity. The responsibility of scholars in America's universities was to synthesize the experience and de-termine what was productive and what proved to be an obstacle to progress. He concluded his presentation by reporting that the major achievement of the scientific congress had been the formation of a new organization for coordinating exchange between universities, libraries, and museums across the hemisphere. The Carnegie Endowment for International Peace provided the new group's start-up funds. The war might be uppermost on everybody's mind, forcing all to think about the organization of the world in new ways. Long-term results, however, looked past the war to ask how people in many walks of life could more regularly collaborate with similarly situated people in other nations.

From the arguments already in motion by 1915, we can see a singular, even strange phenomenon developing: national leaders were encouraging a utopian vision of the future relations of the world's peoples, a vision distinctly in conflict with the historical concept of the nation as the most natural, indivisible source of collective identity. As soon as citizens were growing accustomed to the proposition that they did in fact belong, as if naturally, to the nations where they had been born or immigrated, the increasingly horrific carnage attending conflict between modern nations suggested that nation-states could not in fact provide the security they promised. Additional connections were needed that went beyond nationalism, connections that, if people-to-people communication and international decision making were central to the process, logically led to curtailing national sovereignty. The conflict between national identity and a desire for a more far-reaching union of peoples and cultures was a powerful theme recurring in the poetry of Rubén Darío (1867–1916), arguably the most important Spanish-language American poet of the early twentieth century. For many North Americans, his most famous poem, perhaps the only poem by Darío that they might have encountered, remains "A Roosevelt" ("To Roosevelt"), an angry protest against President Theodore Roosevelt's theft of Panama from Colombia in 1903.

> Eres los Estados Unidos,
> eres el futuro invasor. . . .
> Crees que la vida es incendio,
> que el progreso es erupción;
> en donde pones la bala
> el porvenir pones. . . .
> Se necesitaría, Roosevelt, ser por Dios mismo,
> el Riflero terrible y el fuerte Cazador,
> para poder tenernos en vuestras férreas garras.

> You are the United States,
> you are the future invader. . . .

You believe that life is fire,
that progress is eruption;
that wherever you put a bullet
you make the future. . . .
Roosevelt, for you to hold us in your iron claws,
you will need God Himself to make you
the terrible Rifleman and the mighty Hunter.

Because God stands by the faithful, Darío believed his "naïve" America of mixed Spanish and Indian ancestry could defeat an enemy reemerging in new guise out of the ancient, bitter conflicts between Catholic faith and Protestant heresy, between law-bringing Spain and piratical England.[12] A prominent figure in the growing cultural nationalism sweeping Latin American intellectuals at the beginning of the twentieth century, Darío, only two years later, tentatively shifted his thinking about the future of inter-American relations after he heard U.S. secretary of state Elihu Root address a conference of the hemisphere's political leaders, held in Rio de Janeiro in 1906. Root affirmed that he and President Roosevelt desired a hemisphere where all nations, big and small, were equal. He pledged that the U.S. road to prosperity was not to profit from the ruin of others but "to help all friends to a common prosperity and growth."[13] Root's speech received a standing ovation and inspired Darío, attending the conference as the head of the Nicaraguan delegation, to write "Salutación al águila" ("Greetings to the Eagle"), which reversed the caustic criticisms he had made two years earlier in "A Roosevelt." Darío began his new poem,

Bien vengas, mágica Águila de alas enormes y fuertes
a extender sobre el Sur tu gran sombra continental,
a traer en tus garras, anilladas de rojos brillantes,
una palma de Gloria, del color de la inmensa esperanza,
y en tu pico la oliva de una vasta y fecunda paz.[14]

Welcome, magical Eagle with enormous and powerful wings
as you spread your great continental shadow across the South,
carrying in your ruby-ringed claws,
a palm leaf of Glory, the color of unlimited hope,
and in your beak the olive branch of a long and prosperous peace.

The phrase *E pluribus unum* provided the explanation for the extraordinary success of the United States, Darío declared. He predicted that the miracle of uniting the one and the many would be the secret of the future greatness of America, as the races of the hemisphere shared their respective secrets of industry and of poetry. If the United States remained committed to the pluralist but universal vision that Root presented to his listeners in Rio, Darío concluded, the country would truly become the instrument of God's beneficence for the modern world, a genuine miracle showing how complex were God's plans because the world's largest Protestant country would accomplish the unity of humanity that the universal Catholic church had sought for two millennia but failed to achieve. Even the figure of Theodore Roosevelt merited revision in 1907, when in the preface to a new book of poems, *El canto errante* ("The Wandering Song"), Darío observed that he had read an essay on poetry that Roosevelt had written and found it to be among the most intelligent, sensitive discussions of the social functions of poetry that Darío had ever encountered. He concluded, "For this, you must grant that the terrible hunter is a wise man."[15]

The unexpected brutality of the European war shattered the world in which American elites had lived comfortably for several generations. The war proved how illusory had been the hallowed liberal tenet that hearty commercial ties fostered peace, progress, and the expansion of civilization. The United States, however vulgar, mechanical, or ugly it might be, was suddenly the most credible protection against the spread of war. In 1915, Rubén Darío returned to the subject of the United States and its relation to the rest of America. In "Pax," a poem Darío first read publicly at Columbia University in New York City, he uttered a prayer for peace that took for granted that, aside from divine intervention, only U.S. power could protect him and his Latin race from the conflagration threatening the globe. Another poem written at the same time, "La gran cosmópolis" ("The Great Cosmopolis"), contemplates New York as a city of incomparable speed, size, and power. The vision of the future that the largest city of the United States presented was awe inspiring, but Darío saw the city's denizens trapped in a materialist nightmare crying out in sorrow for divine charity. Yet despite the bitter evocation of the ugliness of life in the spiritual capital of Yanquilandia, Darío's conclusion discerns a glimmer of a sheer animal force that gave him hope for the future:

> . . . el yanqui ama sus hierros,
> sus caballos y sus perros,
> y su yacht, y su foot-ball;
> pero adora la alegría,
> con la fuerza, la armonía:
> un muchacho que se ría
> y una niña como un sol.[16]

... the Yankee loves his golf clubs,
his horses and his dogs,
and his yacht, and football;
but he lives to be happy,
to capture the harmony
of a laughing young man
and a girl who looks like a sun.

Darío struggled with conflicting feelings about the future of the world modeled after the United States. Still, he saw the brutality of life in the United States as evidence of a force capable of protecting the weak precisely because its power caused so much devastating hurt. Darío hoped that a harmony between the aspirations of the founding fathers of the continent's nations might bring all Americans together to face a world turning more dangerous than ever before imaginable.

Rubén Darío and Jane Addams, in their very different ways, struggled with the impossibilities of uniting history and utopian aspiration. Only something simultaneously spiritual and physical made sense, something based in the immediacy of *touch*, the touch of a neighbor, the touch of God. But how could either connection conceivably scale up to a global level? How could people actually *touch* each other across national boundaries? To be a visionary working toward a new system of global governance required practical experience in international affairs.

The guiding figure behind the Second Scientific Congress was Elihu Root (1845–1937), a Wall Street lawyer who, having served as U.S. secretary of war from 1899 to 1904 and secretary of state from 1905 to 1909, was one of the most influential architects of U.S. international power. In 1910, Andrew Carnegie asked Root to serve as president of the Carnegie Corporation, the group of twenty philanthropies that Carnegie, one of Root's closest personal friends, had established to direct his vast personal wealth into public causes. Root also served as president of the Carnegie Endowment for International Peace, the Carnegie philanthropy closest to Root's personal interests. Having left the executive branch for private life, Root continued to think of the Pan American Union as a showcase for his ideas of an alternative international order based on republican principles.[17] The Carnegie philanthropies provided more money for the costs of the Second Pan- American Scientific Conference than the member states of the Pan American Union put together. Root intended the Washington conference to rival in attendance and scope of presentations comparable international scholarly congresses held in prewar Europe. At the end of the congress, the Carnegie Endowment boasted that its efforts "extended at a critical point in the preparatory arrangements" had been vital to the success of the venture.[18]

Elihu Root understood that compulsion, both legal and psychological, played a central role in the implementation of any visionary plan. Theorists had discussed and debated principles of world government for centuries, but their arguments, however logically or morally attractive, were consigned to a world of make-believe. The problem with every utopian vision was its radically antihistorical foundation. To implement a workable system of governance required translating utopian values into historical time, which is to say into institutionally situated practices. Andrew Carnegie's wealth provided Root and his colleagues the means to change how people and governments behaved. Though the president of a philanthropic organization dedicated to promoting international peace, Root was no pacifist. He took as self-evident that war was often the only just solution available when existing formal institutions failed to resolve political disputes. As an advocate of U.S. imperialism, he had had no compunction when he was secretary of war or secretary of state to use military force against Filipino rebels or Caribbean countries he decided had fallen into a state of "anarchy." The two-tier strategy he envisioned for reducing the likelihood of war was codifying international law to provide clear procedures for dispute arbitration while simultaneously expanding intellectual and cultural exchange between nations.[19]

Root took it as self-evident that neither political theory nor moral principles ever solved political problems. Increasing the likelihood of international conflicts ending in peaceful resolution required creating new "facts" to which all governments and the most powerful interests in each nation had to respond. National leaders would seek peaceful rather than bellicose solutions as they adjusted to a growing body of law that international public opinion insisted be respected. Limits on force would grow firmer, more difficult to evade. Nonstate actors, what at the end of the twentieth century were commonly called NGOs (nongovernmental organizations) or INGOs (international nongovernmental organizations), would become active participants in the international balance of power as, previously, they had become actors shaping governments' domestic policies. In the process, interest-group politics would be internationalized as coalitions formed across national boundaries to work on shared material interests or for shared philosophical values. Over time, international organizations with the resources to make their opinions heard would make both international law and public opinion increasingly powerful within each country.[20]

Root accepted that national publics seldom had identical perspectives on any particular question; in the same way, the public within a single country such as the United States itself almost never formed a unitary national opinion.

International publics would be divided on many issues, but exchange presumed concern for the respect of other publics, whose perspectives would become active forces in national debates. Determination to maintain international exchange would become more important than prevailing on any given point. Countries that excluded, or even attempted to limit, the influence of international public opinion were by definition enemies of international order, law, and accountability, hence subject to isolation and if necessary military retribution. Root saw no contradiction in pursuing a utopian plan for international peace while simultaneously advocating firm military action against Germany after the outbreak of war in Europe in 1914. He subsequently took a leading role in organizing international efforts to suppress the 1917 Bolshevik revolution in Russia. On the other hand, he argued for U.S. neutrality in the Mexican revolution. He introduced legislation into the U.S. Senate to ban all sales of arms to Mexico until a stable government had formed.

The issue for him was not establishing a regime of universal peace, an impossible goal given the intractability of many disputes within and between nations, but transforming the existing state of international anarchy into a manageable order based on principles and procedures that people around the world understood, valued, and wanted to maintain. Global governance inevitably required limiting national sovereignty, but he opposed creating international executive bodies possessing independent police powers. As a man of state, Root took for granted that national governments would be the primary organizers of global institutions to which they surrendered a portion of their sovereignty, but public opinion formed in regular exchange of perspectives would shape the goals politicians pursued and ultimately coerce them into surrendering as much national sovereignty as any national public was comfortable allowing because of the increased security the new arrangements provided. In rejecting the workability of an elaborate global government with executive and legislative bodies, Root assumed that most important decisions remained at the national level, and national governments would have primary responsibility for implementing and enforcing international court decisions. Creating formal structures beyond a system of international tribunals would have the effect of lessening the pressure on national political leaders to assure that global governance functioned according to their own public's preferences.[21]

Root did not believe that citizens of democracies were inherently peace loving. The citizens of nations on the brink of war, he had written while secretary of state, generally adopt an "uncompromising and belligerent attitude" that works against peaceful settlement of differences. Congresses bringing together the educated of many nations were an essential preliminary step for raising the consciousness of national citizens about their responsibilities in the international order, given that educated professionals were a group to whom the public turned when it needed information on a subject. The challenge was to develop ongoing popular interest in topics important for global governance, as well as curiosity about the concerns and values of citizens in other nations.[22] A self-conscious historical understanding guided Root's vision of how to achieve what he believed would be a more peaceful and prosperous world than that created by the European powers since the seventeenth century, but his synthesis rested on an arbitrary selection of positive elements, such as an independent judiciary or a strong civil society organized around a free press and many active voluntary associations, for generalization from his nation's experience of how the world at large might work. Root and his many followers took for granted that a necessary condition of a better global order was North American leadership. In effect the new global order would be an informal empire the structure of which echoed the historical experience of the United States. Within that framework, international cultural programs ought not to be run by government but be organized, funded, and executed by private associations, philanthropies, and educational, cultural, and religious institutions expressing the long-term interests of the American people.

European culture retained a high level of prestige for most middle-class Americans. Before World War I, many educated Americans sought advanced training in European schools, while the wealthy took regular visits across the Atlantic, with the result that wealthy and educated Americans often had personal relationships with counterparts across the Atlantic. Not so for either Asia or Latin America, the two areas of the world that Root thought were most important for the U.S. strategic vision, but areas where the U.S. public knew little beyond stereotypes. As a result, Root's most ambitious cultural exchange efforts were directed toward Latin America and East Asia, where he was convinced the United States would find its most likely allies for initiatives to limit European hegemony. In 1929, after retiring as president of the Carnegie Corporation, Root observed in the course of a letter to his successor, Frederick P. Keppel, urging support for a project bringing Mexican art to the United States and another project studying the lives of Japanese in the United States, "We need in this country to think a little more about other people, and to do that we must learn a little more about them. We are too self-centered; we lack humility; we unconsciously feel as if we stood alone in the universe. We feel under no obligation to consider the rights or interests of other peoples. This condition of things among a great and powerful people soon becomes national arrogance, and that is something which the high Gods always punish soon or late."[23] Root was particularly keen to develop a program for mutual cultural understanding within the Americas, a requirement if the Pan American Union were to provide a model for a new international regime grounded in principles of international law. Root understood well that the leaders of the Latin American nations remained suspicious of U.S. objectives and participated in the Pan American Union primarily because their fears of the European powers, or of their regional enemies, were greater than their distrust of the United States. Root did not expect dramatic transformation of such attitudes. The path to increased international collaboration among citizens and the ability of global public opinion to shape how governments developed international policies would require many generations. The pragmatic utopian understood that people's better aspirations needed institutions and regulations if the hope that international disputes should be resolved peacefully were to become unchallenged practical common sense.[24]

In 1912 the endowment launched a pilot cultural exchange program between the United States and Latin America. Endowment staff and consultants selected two people a year from the United States to travel in Latin America and meet counterparts, while two scholars from member states of the Pan American Union were to come to the United States. Given the university training of the primary participants in pan-American cultural exchange, humanist dialogue across national boundaries was a feasible goal, an extension within the Americas of the kinds of conversations that American scholars and intellectuals had had with their European counterparts throughout the nineteenth century, discussion typically normative and rationalist, organized around efforts to define basic principles. But while scholars from the United States, Brazil, or Chile looked forward to their exchanges with colleagues in Britain, France, or Germany, they took for granted that the "other America" was so devoid of culture and science that inter-American intellectual exchange could offer little of value. The first task of events such as Pan American Union congresses was to foster the kind of personal encounters that could overwhelm stereotypes and preconceptions.

Developing a constituency within the U.S. public that would be more knowledgeable about Latin America and supportive of developing a shared cultural space was the second priority that the Carnegie Endowment pursued after the close of the Second Pan-American Scientific Congress. Through 1916, the endowment coordinated a discussion among "a number of important women's clubs throughout the United States" to host member discussions on topics like "The United States as a World Power," "Pan-Americanism and Its Relation to Universal Peace," and "A New Era in the History of the American Nations." The endowment supplied materials to assist the discussion. Similar discussions were sponsored in summer schools and summer sessions at seventy-eight colleges and universities located in thirty-eight states. Over four hundred thousand people attended 550 Carnegie Endowment–sponsored events on Latin America in the summer of 1916. Cultural exchange programs sending U.S. citizens to Latin America grew, with the endowment deciding to focus on locating men "for the most part, comparatively young, having their future before them, yet with training and experience sufficient . . . to enable them to derive the greatest profit from the trip."[25] Carnegie publications stressed that cultural exchange was not a good in and of itself. Over the long term, such programs would increase "an understanding and dissemination of just principles of law and their application to disputes which are bound to arise among members of one and the same family. How can this law be developed? How can these principles, when found and formulated, be best disseminated? These are questions which must be answered and upon the correct answer depends in large part the future relations of the American nations. It needs no argument that a law to affect all must be made by all, that is to say, it must be the result of cooperation."[26]

In addition to convincing elite public opinion in Latin America that the United States was a trustworthy partner, cultural exchange had goals related to debates within the United States over the country's potential place in the world. Root's conception of the U.S. international role required an educated populace capable of understanding debates in other countries, whether they were allies or potential enemies. If the United States as a society were concerned only with itself, the nation would never develop the perspectives needed for responsible, authoritative international leadership—a situation he viewed as particularly dangerous because he knew that the executive branch would increasingly act unilaterally while U.S. businesses operating abroad sought every advantage that they could, often colluding with corrupt foreign leaders. Without a robust cultural exchange program, there would be no counterbalance in the U.S. public to correct the mistakes of the powerful, mistakes that sooner or later led to war. The deeper purposes of cultural exchange within Root's framework were internal, to develop a domestic public opinion with the inclination and the power to force the executive branch and U.S. business to reform their overseas dealings. At the same time, public interest in international affairs was an essential foundation for successful expansionary and interventionist policies.[27] The goal of developing expertise on Latin America quickly conflicted with the goal of an informed, engaged public developing connections across national boundaries with citizens in other countries with like interests. As we shall see, experts within the United States questioned the very premise that citizens, even educated citizens, could understand foreign societies, particularly in countries viewed as radically different. Expert doubts notwithstanding, through the first half of the twentieth century, the best-funded programs operated on an assumption that a broad range of citizens could and would develop a sense of personal connection to other American countries as they learned more about their history and culture.

As a result of Carnegie funding, instruction in both Spanish and Portuguese exploded throughout the United States. By 1925 Spanish had leaped ahead of French and German as the most studied foreign language in the United States.[28] Portuguese instruction remained largely confined to colleges and universities, but the number of schools offering courses grew from three to over 700.[29] The growth in students studying the languages of the hemisphere was not the result of random changes in the priorities of students, but the product of a concerted and well-funded effort to promote a larger, continental American consciousness within the United States, in which it became "natural" for Americans to learn the main languages of the region. U.S. national identity was being closely wedded to construction of American regional identity, one in which the "New World" stood in opposition to an "Old World" destroying itself through war, imperialism, decadence, and Bolshevism. Lecture series on Latin American culture and society became a common feature in the public programming of U.S. civic associations. As Carnegie efforts succeeded in stimulating public interest in the languages and cultures of the Pan American Union member states, the Carnegie shifted its efforts to increasing the work available that U.S. citizens could read in either the original language or English translation.

Gabriela Mistral (1889–1957, born Lucila Godoy Alcayaga), one of Chile's most famous poets and the first Latin American author to win the Nobel Prize in Literature, was one of the writers whose careers benefited from a growing enthusiasm in the United States for pan-Americanism (Figure 1). Federico de

Figure 1. Gabriela Mistral. With the collaboration of Gabriela Mistral Foundation, Inc., New York, 2015 (www.gabrielamistralfoundation.org).

Onís, professor of Spanish at Columbia University, introduced Mistral's work to a group of high school teachers working to expand Spanish-language classes in New York City. Mistral was a schoolteacher, and many of her poems sprang from her experiences in the classroom. The teachers group thought that Mistral's themes would interest students, and her language was accessible to readers learning Spanish. At the time, however, her work was available only in mimeographed chapbooks or in hard-to-get small journals. A committee formed to produce a book of her poetry that could be used in schools throughout the United States. The New York–based Instituto de las Españas, assisted by a grant from the Carnegie Endowment for International Peace, agreed to act as publisher. Mistral responded to the committee's request with seventy-three poems and eighteen prose pieces. *Desolación* ("Desolation"), which appeared in 1922, was Mistral's first book, and unlike most first books by relatively unknown poets it had international distribution.[30]

Mistral organized the collection around her experiences as a schoolteacher in rural Chile. She used family ties allegorically to represent the bonds Americans had with a nurturing, maternal earth as the source of their freedom and their prosperity. She presented the history of the Americas as the story of humanity's struggle to return to a balanced relationship with the elements, their many rhythms, and the resources they provided. In the process, immigrants from many countries merged with the continent's first inhabitants to form a new people united through faithful obedience to divine will. Schools around the country adopted the book, a success that encouraged the New York teachers group to prepare companion volumes of poems by Amado Nervo from Mexico and Rubén Darío from Nicaragua.

At the invitation of the publishers of *Desolación*, Mistral traveled to the United States in 1924. She was a featured speaker at the Pan American Union headquarters in Washington, D.C. Discussing, in the context of the story of Ruth, the need for a deeper, spiritual union of the hemisphere, she asserted, "I believe that difference in the case of humanity, as well as in nature, is merely another form of enrichment. In this way what is Latin, even in its sharpest contrast, when face to face with Anglo-Saxonism, is a kind of strength through different virtues, through other modes of living, but in no sense the occasion of inevitable discord. . . . Friendship of the different peoples sought by the Pan American Union would be easily attained if we were all imbued, to the farthest limit of consciousness, with the concept of *dissimilarity without inferiority.*"[31]

In 1931, the Pan American Union commissioned Mistral to write a Pan-American Pledge for students to recite in classrooms in all the member states. The pledge opened with the simple declaration: "We Americans of North and South America have accepted with our heritage of geographic unity a certain common destiny that should find a threefold fulfillment on our continent in an adequate standard of living, perfect democracy, and ample liberty." The pledge continued with the claim that North Americans and South Americans, despite superficial differences, were united by a common Christian heritage, while their efforts to create new societies meant that they had been fated to give "a new democratic interpretation" to the culture, customs, art, education, and science all Americans had inherited from Europe, "blending them all into a harmony of greater beauty and greater sweetness." The conclusion promised that unlike Europe, the American peoples sought to solve their differences without violence or the desire to take away the independence of any people.[32]

Mistral was an odd symbol for pan-American unity. She was a lesbian, an aspect of her life never publicly discussed but not hidden from friends and acquaintances. She was devoutly Catholic, and she shared the feeling of many Latin American Catholics that the United States had developed a culture that encouraged people to satisfy individual desires instead of submitting in faithful obedience to natural and divine law. Nonetheless, she was fascinated with and increasingly seduced by life in the United States, which she found both a comfortable and surprisingly moral place. If the American people exceeded her expectations, the government almost always disappointed her with the policies it developed for Latin America. She was a vocal anti-imperialist frequently criticizing U.S. actions in the hemisphere and elsewhere. She wrote articles attacking President Calvin Coolidge's military occupation of Nicaragua in 1926 to end a civil war and the subsequent campaign to suppress the revolutionary forces of Augusto César Sandino, fighting to restore their country's independence. Nonetheless, she also frequently told her Latin American readers that the United States had a special role to play in protecting peace and bringing together the peoples of the world, a role that it would fulfill at a time when Latin Americans least expected.

The aspect of her career that most made her an unlikely symbol in the United States for an emerging hemispheric culture was entirely practical: despite the attention she received as a public figure, very little of her poetry was available in English. Her friend Langston Hughes (1902–1967) prepared the first volume of Mistral's poetry translated into English, but the book was published in 1957, shortly following her death at her home on Long Island.[33] Mistral wanted to publish more journalistic work in North American newspapers and magazines, but editors seldom turned to her. She had not developed the necessary personal connections with U.S. editors, difficult to explain given her celebrity, and the Pan American Union, which occasionally published her work in its journals, did not actively work to place her pieces in the country's commercial press, perhaps because attention to positions she took on specific policy issues could turn her into a controversial figure and diminish her value as a symbol of American unity. As a result, Mistral's voice in the United States appeared primarily in the words of others invoking her name and image.[34]

Her case demonstrates how practical realities frequently frustrated the pan-American project, evidence of Elihu Root's basic proposition that aspirations count for little if new institutional realities do not emerge and mature. The failure of either her journalism or her poetry to appear regularly in English, despite her own wishes, was symptomatic of a major problem subverting the stated purposes of pan-American cultural exchange: editors preferred to publish U.S. authors interpreting other countries rather than translate authors from those countries. An analogous situation was true in Latin America, where readers seeking deeper understanding of the "great republic to the north" turned to books and articles by authors from their own countries. If translation were in fact to link the publics of the various American nations, writers crossing national borders, and their editors as well, had to figure out who their new readers were likely to be, what readers already knew, what the expectations and desires of those readers were. Publishers of course had to worry about how to pay for books they wanted to publish.

To the degree that cultural exchange was reserved for the most highly educated, it would never be self-sustaining in purely market terms, but it could have a core audience with a shared formation in classical and humanist culture, though only in a small number of modern languages. Even in the universities, language barriers necessarily limited access to the most intense debates in other nations. A sizable majority of professors in all countries of the hemisphere could read English, French, or German, and often more than one of the three languages. In the United States, during the 1920s, professors who were not specialists in Romance languages and literatures were not likely to work in either Spanish or Portuguese, nor did they have incentives to spend the time acquiring skills in those languages. Probably only a small minority could read comfortably in any foreign language, even French or German. Translation was required if opinions were to be shared across borders, and if books by Latin American authors were to be assigned in undergraduate classes, commercial presses had to supplement what university presses could do. Commercial presses were seldom interested in academic studies, but the translation of literature that was popular in other countries might be attractive, particularly if authors were good storytellers.

The Pan American Union and the Carnegie Endowment for International Peace worked to increase access to opinion across the western hemisphere by subsidizing the publication of three monthly magazines, *Pan-American Magazine*, *Pan American Review*, and *Inter-America*, all of which offered English translations of articles published in the leading Latin American newspapers and magazines, while *Inter-América* offered Spanish translations of articles published in the U.S. press. The *Bulletin of the Pan American Union* reprinted short stories, literary essays, and poetry by authors from the member nations, each piece published simultaneously in the four official languages of the union.[35] The effort did lead to a increase in the translation of Latin American books into English that was significant if only because what had been virtually nonexistent became a regular, if still limited occurrence. Between 1800 and 1915, thirty-four Latin American books were translated into English, published either in the United States or Britain. Between 1916 and 1940, eighty-eight books were translated into English, all but two of them published first by U.S. presses, with English publishers typically reprinting the translation for markets in Britain and the British Empire (see Table 1 in the Appendix).

There were significant obstacles to publishing nonfiction works that foreign authors had written about their own countries. To explain another country to North Americans, writers had to have a well-developed sense of what readers in the United States and Canada knew. A book about another country required considerable contextualization, particularly for books dealing with regions about which little previously had been written for general readers. Writers who were not from the United States could provide adequate background to U.S. readers only with difficulty. Given that their books were usually written for readers in their own country, translation generally required substantial additions or footnoting to make an author's comments about, say, Brazil or Mexico comprehensible to U.S. readers. Despite these obstacles, in the mid-1920s, the University of Chicago published books in English by José Vasconcelos, Manuel Gamio, and Moisés Sáenz, three of the most important intellectuals of revolutionary and postrevolutionary Mexico. Each of them spent time at Chicago, invited by Robert E. Park, chair of the Sociology Department, to work with students, give public lectures, and develop a research project. Manuel Gamio, an anthropologist, used his time at Chicago to conduct the first field research on Mexican migrant laborers in the United States, with two books appearing on the topic in 1930 and 1931. In 1926, his lectures *The Indian Basis of Mexican Civilization* appeared, along with Vasconcelos's lectures, *Aspects of Mexican Civilization*, and Sáenz's *Some Mexican Problems*. The three men were opposed politically and philosophically, and the three works offered U.S. readers an opportunity to think about the differences of opinion within Mexico over how to build a modern state and a modern citizenry.[36] Their books were particularly accessible to U.S. readers because all three authors had studied and lived in the United States. They were comfortable in English, and the books Chicago published were written for English-speaking U.S. readers who were not specialists on Mexico or Latin America.

Despite their differences on many issues, each of the three authors emphasized that Mexico had a diverse population, and that the Mexican people had
yet to overcome long-standing internal differences. U.S. authors writing on
Mexico argued instead that the country had a homogeneous indigenous culture
that developed over the millennia as humans adapted to the geography and climate of the country. Vasconcelos, Gamio, and Sáenz saw broad differences
within over fifty major Native American peoples who had resisted four centuries of colonial rule. Indian communities spoke different languages and were
firmly determined to protect their unique identities. Their dissimilarities with
each other and with mestizo and white Mexicans who were the majority in the
country's cities posed an obstacle to national unity that the policies the national
government developed for education, economic growth, and democratic institutions had to take into account if they were eventually to be overcome. The reviewer at the *New York Times* noted the differences that the three Mexican
authors brought to the discussion of U.S.-Mexican relations, but he also wondered how the average reader could determine whether the perspective of a
Mexican writer was more reliable than that of a U.S. author. He thought that
"racial antipathy" made communication across the border difficult, with each
side preferring to trust its own kind rather than give credence to the arguments
that foreigners made. To the degree that the reviewer's attitude was typical of
his generation, the project to encourage inter-American dialogue among the
educated sectors of different countries faced considerable resistance.[37] The emphasis that Carnegie programs put on introducing inter-American material into
the schools suggests that the endowment looked to a new generation with a
broader understanding of the U.S. place in the world to have greater openness
to what writers from Latin America or Asia had to say. The books that Vasconcelos, Gamio, or Sáenz produced for Chicago were unusual. They were dedicated
men whose primary interests lay in Mexico, not the United States. Vasconcelos
ran for president of the country in 1929. He lost against the preferred candidate
of the revolutionary generals, and he spent the 1930s building a new conservative
opposition movement. Gamio became the director of the national anthropology
museum in Mexico City, while Sáenz led the country's ambitious rural education
program.

Fiction also required contextualization, but translators had more leeway in
modifying the text to help a reader understand unfamiliar situations. In general, however, bookstore owners preferred nonfiction titles, which consistently
had wider sales than most fiction books. Of the seven most commercially successful books in the 1920s, two were fiction and five were nonfiction, closely
matching the general division of books published during that decade. Public libraries, however, wanted lots of fiction books, and 75 percent of fiction sales

were to libraries rather than in bookstores or through book clubs. The more than fifteen thousand libraries in the country supported publication of a wide range of fiction titles, but only a few fiction books achieved the very high sales volume of a successful nonfiction book.[38]

Given the difficulties foreign nonfiction writers had in understanding their potential U.S. public and given the limits on fiction sales, the repeated calls after 1915 for greater access in English to books *by* Latin American authors would likely not have influenced U.S. publishers one bit were it not for the extraordinary and accidental success of Spanish novelist Vicente Blasco Ibáñez, the most widely read foreign author in the United States in the 1920s writing in a language other than English. In 1918, E. P. Dutton released an English translation of Blasco Ibáñez's *Four Horsemen of the Apocalypse,* prepared by a high school Spanish teacher in New York City. The book, about an Argentinean playboy who impulsively joins the French army to fight the Germans, was a runaway best seller, perhaps because its release coincided with U.S. armed forces entering into combat in France. Competition among publishers for translation rights to other books by the author followed, and over the next five years, twenty more books by Blasco Ibáñez appeared in the United States, nineteen novels along with the author's interpretation of the Mexican revolution. In 1921 Rudolph Valentino starred in the first of four Hollywood productions of *The Four Horsemen of the Apocalypse.* Blasco Ibáñez attended the world premiere in New York City, and his subsequent tour of the United States consolidated his reputation as a celebrity author, whose books regularly became Hollywood films featuring the biggest stars.

Publishers and film producers looked for other authors whose combination of romantic Latin characters with more broadly human-interest situations might regenerate the avid passion readers had shown for Blasco Ibáñez. Several of the Latin American novels chosen, particularly *The Man of Gold* by Venezuelan Rufino Blanco Fombona (Brentano's, 1920) and *Amalia: A Romance of the Argentine*, a classic work by José Mármol first published in 1851 that told the story of the eventually successful resistance against the brutal Rosas dictatorship (Dutton, 1919), received superlative reviews, but failed to break out of the pack of two thousand novels published annually in the United States during the 1920s. Publishers' enthusiasm for "Latin" authors declined, but they remained open to proposals. Novels published in the 1920s and 1930s reflected the personal interests of enthusiasts of Latin American culture, interests that tended to reinforce ideas that identified the United States with "mechanical progress" and Latin America with "virgin nature."

The critic and novelist Waldo Frank (1889–1967), for example, sponsored a collection of short fiction, *Tales from the Argentine* (Farrar and Rinehart, 1930), as well as the translation of the novel *Don Segundo Sombra* (released in English as *Don Segundo Sombra: Shadows on the Pampas*, Farrar and Rinehart, 1935), the most famous work by Argentinean novelist Ricardo Güiraldes (1886–1927). Both books stressed the pampas and the gaucho as the defining features of Argentinean identity, with the rich urban culture of the country an ominous, but still distant threat. The publisher's abstract described the novel as a "tale of the wandering life of the cowboys on the pampas . . . told by a boy who gets a job on a ranch, and then rides with his hero, Don Segundo, from one ranch job to another. Horse races, cock fights, dances, round-ups and fiestas make up the pattern of their everyday, roaming life."[39] The reviewer for the *Boston Transcript* reiterated this aspect of the book, while praising Güiraldes's poetic vision of American nature as "ageless and unchanging," offering a life so difficult that the land in the New World brings out the heroic potential of every American. Other reviewers also noted the timelessness of the characters' lives, and like the *Boston Transcript* reviewer praised the work as a "little classic" (F. T. Marsh in the *New York Times*), "lovable" (Lewis Gannett in the *New York Herald Tribune*), "unmistakably an American book . . . endless and generous [with] the vigor and nobility of youth, the casual ruthlessness, the horseplay, and the enormous hopefulness of the primitive" (Anita Brenner in the *Nation*).[40]

Frank's introduction to *Don Segundo Sombra: Shadows on the Pampas* contrasted Güiraldes's book with *Huckleberry Finn*. Both books were stories of adolescent boys who ran away from elderly women into whose care they had been put. The boys were products of a "frontier" already vanishing at the time the books were written. Frank argued that the differences in what happened on the two frontiers were more profound than the similarities. In the United States, the frontier had been a "barbarous, anarchic world," where traditions inherited from England had little relevance and survived only in parodied forms, offering great opportunities for Twain's comic genius. But given the poverty of human relations on the U.S. frontier, Frank noted, Huck Finn discovered that the only person he could trust was a fugitive slave. Finn's path to maturity required him to reject the institutions that his country bequeathed him. Twain's satiric imagination was unable to imagine alternatives to the radical dehumanization that slavery had brought the United States, and the author could respond only with rowdy, anarchic humor. The Spanish Catholic heritage of Argentina proved both more enduring and "humane." The boy of Güiraldes's novel finds a teacher who gets him a job as a ranch hand. He learns the skills of roping cows, but the deeper truths he discovers involve the unspoken spiritual connections between men working in an unforgiving environment, and above all the psychic unity that must be formed with the land if humans are to prosper. Frank concluded, "In all the rough work, a real culture lives in the pampa. . . . Huck sees mainly the outside of events and is moved only by simple human feelings. The Argentinian lad, quite as naturally, is alive to the nuances in his adventures of color and emotion. . . . The order of Argentina is more inward, it is cultural rather than institutional. It is an order of human values, much more than of business and of public affairs."[41] The contrast between how the books end could not be more striking. Huck Finn remains an outcast, escaping into "Indian country" at the end of the novel to continue his wandering life. The hero of *Don Segundo Sombra* inherits a fortune from his natural father. He becomes a property owner responsible for the men working for him, perhaps more just because he has lived as a gaucho.

A distinct genre of Latin American novel published in English translation during the interwar years told stories of the Mexican revolution of the 1910s. The civil war in Mexico was likely the single most deeply reported foreign event that the U.S. press had ever covered up to that time. Even small-town newspapers sent correspondents to determine why Mexico had fallen into chaos. The *Seattle Republican* summarized a widely held opinion on the causes of the political turmoil that had proven such an embarrassment to the U.S. government's pan-American policy: the Mexican dictator, Porfirio Díaz, in power since 1876, was "the most heartless wretch that has directed the destinies of any nation since the death of Nero"; that he had opened Mexico to foreign investment served the financial powers of the United States, who gave no thought to the legitimate needs of the oppressed Mexican people.[42] The political turmoil that led to Díaz resigning and the first free elections in the country since 1871 captured public attention in the United States as a sterling example of the good outcomes can happen when an aroused people stand up against politicians and capital to demand the rights of self-government. Optimism on either side of the border was unwarranted. The opponents of popular democracy hated the new government and looked to the military to restore order to a country conservatives claimed was sliding into anarchy. In 1913, a junta of generals led by Victoriano Huerta seized power with the blessing of the U.S. ambassador to Mexico. The first act of the Huerta dictatorship was to murder the democratically elected president, along with his vice president, instead of sending them into exile. The brutal act clarified for most Mexicans the nature of the new regime. People who had previously had no interest in politics chose to fight instead of accepting a new dictator. Neither side was prepared to give quarter, and the political turmoil of the early 1910s transformed overnight into the first great social revolution of the twentieth century, covered in detail by U.S. journalists and the object of considerable debate among U.S. opinion makers. By 1920, Mexico, a country of 15 million in 1910, had lost nearly a million people as a result of civil war. Half had died in the fighting, the other half had fled to the United States.

After 1917, when revolutionary forces triumphantly formed a new government committed to defending the political and economic sovereignty of the
people, Mexicans began to write about their personal experiences during the
war using both the memoir and the novel form. The single most successful book
of revolutionary-era recollection was Mariano Azuela's *Los de abajo* (literally,
"those from below"). Azuela (1873–1952) had been a medical doctor practicing
in a small town in the state of Jalisco when the revolution erupted. He volun-
teered for the forces fighting to overthrow the dictatorship and served as a field
doctor in the army of Julián Medina, a follower of Pancho Villa. Disenchanted
with the anarchy of Villa's forces, Azuela escaped to El Paso, Texas, where he
wrote and self-published *Los de abajo* in 1916. The following year, he returned
to Mexico, where he set up a medical practice in a poor neighborhood in Mexico City. Azuela continued writing, self-publishing his books to very limited
distribution. *Los de abajo* remained unknown to most Spanish-language readers until a commercial press in Spain republished it in 1926. Critics in Mexico,
discovering the novel for the first time, praised the story of a group of peasants
drawn into Pancho Villa's army as the most important novel yet written of the
Mexican revolution.

Enrique Munguía, Jr., a Mexican diplomat living in the United States, prepared an English translation, published by Brentano's in 1929, with the title *The
Underdogs*.[43] Even if Munguía lacked an ear for idiomatic English, *The Underdogs* made a powerful impression on reviewers in the United States. The "first
real account of that volcanic epoch" declared the reviewer for the *Boston
Transcript*. The reviewer for the *New York Herald Tribune* declared that he had
learned more from Azuela's novel about the revolution than any book he
had read previously. Azuela, the reviewer continued, "writes with the cold realism of a heart broken by a decade of continuous revolution." The characters are
desperate men but neither heroes nor villains. A war fought with the rule of kill
or be killed broke them along with the revolutionary ideals that had spurred
them in the first place. Waldo Frank, reviewing the book for the *New Republic,*
highlighted the formal inventiveness unifying Azuela's account of an inherently
chaotic experience. Frank concluded with an argument central to *América
Hispana*, his interpretation of Latin American culture that he published in 1931.
Azuela's brilliant retelling of the "ignorance and horror" of the revolution spoke
with the power of Homeric epics, and in so doing the novel revealed the spiritual depth of Mexico's revolt against modernity and the country's return to "an
organic world . . . of wisdom and revelation." The book brought a truth that
people in the modern, machine-driven United States needed to learn: "no man
could record so low a story and make it beautiful who was not a great man who
did not belong to a potentially great people."[44]

Had the Spanish publisher not reprinted Azuela's novel, it may well never have appeared in English. Perhaps the most serious difficulty in promoting literary cultural exchange in the 1920s and 1930s was the asymmetry between how publishing operated in the United States and in Latin American countries. In the United States, publishing had grown into a major industry producing twenty thousand titles annually. Bookstores, book clubs, and libraries operated in every part of the country. Sales were brisk, and, even if only a handful of books each year turned into megasellers, overall sales were robust enough for publishing to be a profitable business. Book publishing had a long history in Latin America, extending back to the sixteenth century, but print runs were always small, if only because literacy was the privilege of a very few. Even at the beginning of the twentieth century, books were special projects that circulated as gifts among a network of friends rather than as merchandise. In January 1900, for example, the Uruguayan publishing firm of Dornaleche y Reyes released José Enrique Rodó's *Ariel, a la juventud de América* ("Ariel, to the Youth of America"), in a limited edition of seven hundred copies. At that time, very few books published in Spanish-speaking America reached bookstores outside the borders of the country where the book first appeared. Authors maintained contact by sending each other copies of their new books as gifts, and Rodó, a young man of twenty-nine working as a librarian at the national university, sent packages of books to writers and professors in other countries asking them to distribute the complementary copies as they saw fit to people who might appreciate the volume's message.[45] Favorable reviews appeared in journals across the continent and in Spain as a result. The news that an important work had appeared in Uruguay spread through word of mouth. The widespread response was unusual, for most books simply disappeared shortly after their limited run appeared.

Given the undeveloped state of the Latin American publishing and book-distribution market, good press did not make it easier for readers to find copies. Over the next decade, new editions of *Ariel* were printed, without Rodó's authorization, in Mexico, Cuba, the Dominican Republic, Venezuela, and Spain. In 1908, a Spanish press published a commercial edition that it distributed widely across the Spanish-speaking world, and Rodó finally gained readers in large numbers. Spanish presses were successful business enterprises, but their model was to produce relatively expensive, quality books for elite readers across the Spanish-speaking world. Literacy was low in all countries, but somewhat higher in Spain, Argentina, and Uruguay, the three countries with mandatory school attendance laws. Spanish authors dominated the titles that Spanish presses produced, but publishers did look for Latin American writers who could provide local-color stories with rough-hewn dramas of life in the pampas or other parts of the American wilderness. It was unusual for a sophisticated writer like Rodó to find an international publisher. When Rodó was elected to his country's national legislature, he helped pass laws to promote publishing in Uruguay, but the first presses in Spanish-speaking America to operate successfully on a commercial basis were Fondo de Cultura Económica, which opened in Mexico City in 1934, and Editorial Porrúa, a small firm operating out of a book store in Mexico City that during the 1930s started producing more popular books, including translations of U.S. best-sellers. In 1935, Ediciones Botas, a co-venture of Mexican editors working with the U.S. publisher Henry Holt, produced Latin America's first best-seller, *Ulises criollo* (translated into English as *A Mexican Ulysses*), the first volume of José Vasconcelos's memoirs. Nearly fifty thousand copies sold, a remarkable achievement in a region where no book had ever previously sold more than seven thousand copies.[46] Vasconcelos had been a major intellectual figure who had led the development of Mexico's national educational system in the 1920s. In 1929, Vasconcelos's quixotic but doomed campaign for president inspired many in the educated middle class who were disenchanted with pervasive government corruption. His book's surprising sales figures reflected the rapid growth of the urban middle class after the revolution, as well as the country's success in expanding public education in every part of the nation, though adult illiteracy remained high. Nonetheless, even though a modern book business was beginning to take shape, the book market remained small until the 1960s, when book sales multiplied across Latin America.

In 1948, Daniel Cosío Villegas, the founding director of Fondo de Cultura Económica, prepared a report for UNESCO (the United Nations Educational, Scientific, and Cultural Organization) on the state of the publishing business in Mexico.[47] Over the previous fourteen years, he had led the most successful press based in Mexico, an enterprise with branch offices across the continent. Fondo de Cultura Económica had started with an initial investment from the Mexican government to produce textbooks on economics and the other social sciences for use in Mexico's universities. The firm expanded into textbooks for the natural sciences and the humanities, and developed a list of journals, many primarily for academic specialists, but *México Moderno* ("Modern Mexico") was a popular magazine that introduced Mexican citizens to new developments in science and scholarship. The press created a list of children's books that proved particularly profitable, and in the 1940s, the Fondo de Cultura Económica began publishing fiction, poetry, and other literary works.

Despite his firm's relative success and the emergence of commercially viable publishers in Argentina and Chile, Cosío Villegas's report emphasized the obstacles he and every other publisher faced. He noted that no Spanish-language publisher could survive without being able to sell in every Spanish-speaking country without exception. Forty percent of Spanish-language books were sold in Spain, 30 percent in Argentina, 20 percent in Mexico, and the remaining 10 percent elsewhere, including the United States, which had already become the fourth largest market for Spanish-language books in the world. In addition to high illiteracy rates—65 percent of Mexico's population was still illiterate in 1948—the weakness of individual national markets was due to the small number of bookstores. Mexico City had only 37 bookstores, with another 50 stores selling some books along with other merchandise. In the entire country, there were only 159 dedicated bookstores. Twelve states had no bookstore whatsoever, and another dozen states had only one. Cosío Villegas noted that even Argentina, the Latin American country with the highest literacy rate, shared the problem, with 227 bookstores in the entire country. Any large city in the United States or western Europe, he claimed, had at least 250 bookstores.

Cosío Villegas identified two problems in the relationships that Mexican publishers had with their Spanish and U.S. counterparts. First, because Spain was the single largest market for Spanish-language books, access to the country's bookstores and libraries was essential. The fascist dictatorship in power since 1939 prohibited the introduction of books with topics that would be offensive either to the regime's political perspectives or to the Catholic Church. Even books produced in Latin America that spoke positively of the continent's nineteenth-century independence struggles were automatically banned. The need to produce books that Spanish censors would approve skewed publication choices in ways that made many books less interesting to Latin American readers. The need to placate Spanish censors had the effect of depressing the potential growth of the American market.

The second problem facing Mexican publishers was finding a way to increase the number of U.S. best-sellers they had on their lists, if only because those were books that middle-class Latin American readers wanted most. A steady stream of U.S. books in Spanish he believed would help Mexicans develop the habit, already well developed in the United States, of buying books regularly. Cosío Villegas was certain that Mexican readers, and readers in other Latin American countries, would then start demanding more popular books by Mexican writers. U.S. publishers had offered Latin American presses the rights for books that sold hundreds of thousands of copies in the United States for less than $1,000, and with generous terms for royalty remittances. Cosío Villegas concluded that U.S. publishers understood that there was, as yet, no money to be made for them in Latin America. Their motivations were political, in that editors supported the principle of pan-American unity and the long-term goal of developing a robust book market in Latin America.

Even though U.S. publishers had offered their most valuable books on terms that were advantageous to Mexican publishers, editors could afford to release only a fraction of the translations that Cosío Villegas was convinced Mexican readers were likely to buy. Given the anemic market for books in Spanish-speaking countries, even a successful book needed a minimum of two years to pay back the publisher's initial investment. In most cases, publishers waited even longer to realize the profit needed to pay salaries, operating expenses, or the rights to new titles. The government could offer publishers loans and grants, as it did with textbooks, but the departments involved in supporting the expansion of Mexico's book trade refused on the grounds that subsidies should be available only for national work. A sensible policy, Cosío Villegas agreed, when the question of how to build a national enterprise was viewed in the abstract, but not when the actual result was the continuing secondary status of the Mexican publishing industry and a paucity of opportunities for talented Mexican writers to publish. Cosío Villegas then discussed the difficulties the writers he published typically had. All needed jobs because no one could count on living on royalties. Most worked for newspapers or universities, or they were in government service. Some like Mariano Azuela, who was a medical doctor, had fulltime professional careers. Working conditions limited the time they had free to write, as well as the time they could spend promoting their work.

Cosío Villegas noted in passing that one of the effects of the difficult situation that both publishers and writers faced was continuing international invisibility for Mexican literature. His conclusions pointed to an ongoing problem facing those in the United States who, like Elihu Root, made two-way cultural exchange a priority. It was difficult for publishers to discover who were the most compelling writers, the ones whose perspectives U.S. readers would find interesting. Few writers in Latin America had the profile that could catch and hold the attention of U.S. editors, whose experiences publishing Latin American authors tended to be disappointing. Critical response was often strongly positive, but still no book translated from a Latin American writer had sales large enough to warrant a second printing. Editors recognized that there was a fast-growing demand within the United States for books on pan-Americanism and inter-American relations. They turned to U.S. authors to fill it.

Chapter 2

National Ways of Looking

The project to develop a greater sense of connection in the United States with other American nations succeeded in increasing publication of books and articles by U.S. authors on nations to the south. Several books sold very well and contributed to national discussions of foreign policy and, more philosophically, of the place that the United States occupied in the world. However, a style of writing developed in which, even as authors acknowledged the complexity of the countries they discussed, the narratives proceeded as if a nation's innate "character" could be easily defined. Typically countries were reduced to a handful of predictable stereotypes such as "mechanical civilization," "virgin nature," "an organic world," the same generalizations generally guiding which Latin American books were translated into English. A tendency to think of Latin America as a single region that served as the cultural, economic, and political foil to the United States guaranteed that most books relied on oversimplification to convey their most important arguments. Radical difference between the United States and other American societies was the most important lesson U.S. authors wanted to convey to their readers about Latin America. Authors challenged models of progress that smugly envisioned people in other countries wanting to become like the United States in most ways. They argued that U.S. leaders did not grasp what made Latin American countries a unique cultural zone, that U.S. government and business played consistently negative roles within most countries. The emphasis given to difference in many interpretive books offered a not so subtle challenge to the hope that expanded cultural exchange could lead to better understanding. U.S. authors consistently pointed out that urban elites, those who could communicate most easily with U.S. audiences, were unrepresentative of their countries. The difficulties of understanding other countries where everyday life had little to no correspondence with how most people in the United States operated required experts to act as mediators who could explain and interpret deeply rooted differences.

The limitations of these books are more obvious eighty years later than they were when originally published. Reviewers responded positively to the symbolic and abstract character of much of this work, and readers bought the books, several titles in large numbers. The posing of radical, possibly innate differences may have provided a familiar and comfortable map for understanding the complexities of the growing power of popular movements in many countries. Generalizations about Latin Americans abound, but cheek by jowl with assertions about the United States every bit as stereotypical. According to these authors, nations big and small acted the ways they did because of environment, history, or biology, foundations that if not absolutely immutable, as with pseudobiological conceptions of race, changed slowly. If the assumptions were true, the behavior of individuals, families, communities, and even nations followed predictable patterns. Finding the deterministic key might be elusive, but the faith that it could be found and then used to understand complex social phenomena in a systematic manner affirmed that humanity could shape its future. Progress was credible, even if difficult to ascertain. Critics, and presumably most readers, understood that authors offered partial answers at best, that few works were equal to the classics of the genre, Alexis de Tocqueville's *Democracy in America*, Lord Bryce's *The American Commonwealth*, or Samuel Brownell's *French Traits*. Nonetheless, assumptions that national identities were relatively stable helped build confidence that the forces at play within the social world could be understood.

John Reed's *Insurgent Mexico*, published in 1914, was the first book on Latin America to become a best-seller. *Metropolitan* magazine sent Reed, then twenty-five years old, to northern Mexico to interview Pancho Villa, the charismatic leader of the northern revolutionary armies, and to report on the civil war. His dispatches attracted strong public interest, which the magazine's publicists worked to augment by promoting the brilliance and bravado of the young author. Reed organized his reports into a book that required multiple printings to keep up with reader demand. At the age of twenty-six, Reed found himself a highly paid superstar journalist sought after by editors to bring his lively perspective to other topics.[1] It is likely that, for the next decade, editors in the United States viewed Reed's work as the best available model for what other books on related topics could do. *Insurgent Mexico* is a fast-paced, personal account of the journalist's encounters with revolutionary leaders and soldiers, supporters of the federal forces, and ordinary Mexican men and women. The timeliness of the subject matter contributed to the book's success. More important were the personalities that filled the book, starting with the first-person narrator, a cocky, young American continually discovering that no matter how jaded he might think himself, the people he met in Mexico never stopped surprising him with their intense faith that, if they overcame their fear of death, they could improve their lives.

Reed avoided presenting any explicit arguments, relying instead on a flow of lively impressions to hold his readers, but his selection of incidents and characters conveyed the conclusions that Reed had formed about U.S.-Mexican relations. The U.S. government and press wanted a strong leader to take charge of Mexico and keep its economy open to foreign investment and trade. U.S. officials hoped that the leader of Mexico would be a reformer pushing his people into democratic, market-driven society, an authority figure but ideally not a dictator. Initially, the U.S. media idolized Pancho Villa, presented to their readers as a Robin Hood character committed to democratic and entrepreneurial values. Reed's interview with Villa, however, stressed that the general rejected any political role for himself after the civil war ended. A leader should be an educated man, Villa told Reed, because his sole responsibility was to represent the country in its dealings with other nations. The people wanted to control their own lives and their own communities with no outside interference. Reed stated simply that as a man of the people, Villa knew he led a movement to destroy the institutions that had oppressed the poor in Mexico since the Spanish conquest. The strong central authority that U.S. leaders wanted for Mexico was at the top of the list of what ordinary Mexicans wanted most to annihilate. Villa became a leader because he shared the desire of working people to take control of their lives back from an oppressive government, large landowners, and foreign investors. Reed organized the final chapter around a holiday presentation of a play that the women of a small village perform telling the story of Lucifer, fallen angel but the bringer of light. Reed ended his book on a poetic note removed from the war and politics that consumed U.S. news accounts of Mexico. He saw himself observing with wonder and delight a culture that was still in its "medieval stage." Someday the creative energy in Mexico might produce another "Elizabethan Golden Age," he thought, but only if the country somehow avoided being dragged into the consumer and industrial culture of its northern neighbor.

Reed's reporting provided an initial statement of a position that became a dominant theme in later writing on Mexico and insurgencies in other American countries: popular hopes were in fundamental conflict with how U.S. business and politics operated. Reed showed fighters who were undisciplined and impulsive; he highlighted the pervasive graft and corruption found at all levels of society. These weaknesses attracted Americans into Mexico, Reed insisted, but if popular confusion provided opportunities for predatory gringos, it also meant that the country would resist and frustrate the systemic reforms that Americans wanted in order to make exploitation of the country more efficient. The chaos of war had released village culture from the chains that had silenced people for generations. Now that the poorest Mexicans were moving to assert their interests, they were not likely to put down their arms or go along with U.S. preferences.

At the other end of the political spectrum, the most prominent probusiness and prointerventionist author on inter-American affairs between 1910 and 1940 was Wallace Thompson, a journalist who had moved to Mexico City several years before the 1910 revolution to work as an editor for a commercial journal for U.S. businessmen in Mexico. After the revolution, Thompson returned to Mexico as U.S. consul in the northern city of Monterey, a commercial center for U.S. mining and petroleum interests. In addition to his diplomatic duties, he was a paid consultant for the Doheny Foundation, a philanthropy run by the family that owned Union Oil, with extensive operations in Mexico's oil fields. Thompson dismissed Mexican peasants and workingmen as racially inferior. They were incapable of building a modern nation, but they lived in bitter resentment of wealth their betters had created. "The Indian culture," he asserted, "if we may so use the term, is perhaps the most sinister threat against the civilization of the white man which exists in the world today."[2] More U.S. investment was needed, he claimed, if Mexico and countries like it were to progress, and they needed massive immigration of European and North American skilled workers and professionals to develop a robust middle class and to do the jobs that involved more than brute strength. Above all, U.S., Canadian, and Mexican elites needed to form an alliance to restrain the self-destructive impulses of racially inferior workers. Thompson promoted paternalistic pan-Americanism that would impose modern industry on peoples who otherwise were doomed to live in poverty. He advocated revising the Monroe Doctrine to assert an explicit right of the U.S. government to protect the rights of U.S. businesses to develop Latin American resources, by force if necessary.[3]

As he extended his arguments to other Latin American countries, Thompson evaluated the potential for a country to progress largely by the racial composition of the population.[4] One might assume that views aligned with contemporary racial prejudices and so congenial to U.S. business's overseas ambitions received wide distribution. However, reviewers in the popular, academic, and business press, with very few exceptions, dismissed Thompson's work as uninformed and ungenerous. One reviewer surveying recent publications on U.S.-Latin American relations stated baldly of *The Mexican Mind*, "The book as a whole is bad. While the author has lived in Mexico many years, he has evidently never sympathized—suffered with—the Mexicans. As a foreigner and a newspaperman he has met the governing classes and the serving classes in the capital city and probably been entertained in some large haciendas and Indian villages. But he would hardly have written this book if he had really lived with the people."[5] The reviewer for the *New York Times* observed that Thompson overestimated the virtues of U.S. society as much as he underestimated the qualities of the Mexican people.[6] Tellingly, the most successful writers on U.S.-Latin American relations ignored him, as well as other authors with similar views, suggesting that they saw no need to argue with writers whose influence on the general public was nil.

The most prolific contributor to the commercial niche for books *on* the Americas was Carleton Beals (1893–1979), a journalist whose eighteen books and over two hundred articles on aspects of Latin American political and social life published between 1923 and 1949 gained him the distinction of being the most widely read U.S. commentator on contemporary affairs in the hemisphere.[7] In 1917, Beals quit a desk job in the accounting department at Standard Oil of California to become a wanderer. His "invisible assets," he thought, "consisted of youth, a good physique, two university degrees, one of them *cum laude,* and—as in the story books—a will to get somewhere."[8] He wound up in Mexico City just as a new revolutionary government was consolidating its authority and ending years of civil war. Beals was penniless when he arrived, but well educated and filled with abundant self-confidence. Within a few weeks, friends he had made in the new government arranged a job for him teaching English to officers in the Mexican army. Beals, whose parents had been radical agrarian populists, became an advocate for revolutionary populism, exploring the backstories to "popular uprisings," "charismatic leaders," and "instability" to reveal the persistent role of U.S. business and government in fanning deeply rooted anti-U.S. attitudes. During his first stay in Mexico, from 1918 to 1921, he decided to write a "sociological study" of the country to be published in the United States. The sociological ambition shaped the first chapters of *Mexico: An Interpretation* (1923), but the effort to explain to Americans how Mexican society had changed as a result of the revolution became instead a detailed description of pervasive political corruption and continuing inequality.[9] The situation in Mexico convinced him that revolutionary movements did not necessarily lead to popular empowerment or democratic rule. The regime established at the conclusion of the civil war rested, at least as presented in his articles and books, on an unstable coalition of peasant groups, labor unions, middle-class professionals, and officers from the various revolutionary armies. Those with political power acquired property while also satisfying the demands of groups allied with them. Ideological debates were intense and pointed to real divisions within the new government, but political conflicts were often only superficially about contending visions for Mexico's future.

Rhetoric, Beals argued, generally masked competition for limited resources as well as the unstable balance of power among different forces. When American officials used their own country's experience to interpret what they saw in Mexico, they made things worse, as happened between 1910 and 1913, when the U.S. Embassy's continuing efforts to find a group inside Mexico that could restore stability after the fall of the dictator Porfirio Díaz contributed to the country's slide into full-scale civil war. The incommensurability of political realities in the United States and most Latin American countries meant that when the United States became a party to internal conflicts in another country, the U.S. government's agents inevitably violated their own country's norms and values. To protect themselves from exposure and criticism, they tried to keep their activities secret. They lied to the press, and even more troubling for Beals, U.S. officials became increasingly divorced from difficult realities on the ground. Having insisted that everything was improving because of U.S. involvement when in fact conflicts were growing more intense, the U.S. government leaders found themselves trapped in quagmires that they, refusing to look at their own contribution to the crisis, could explain only by recourse to conspiracy theories.

In 1926, Beals succeeded in exposing the central role that the U.S. ambassador to Mexico had played in the overthrow and murder in 1912 of Francisco Madero, the country's first democratically elected president since the 1870s. Madero's death triggered a popular uprising against the military junta that had seized control of the country. The public in the United States had been unaware of U.S. responsibility for what happened in Mexico because the retired ambassador, Henry Lane Wilson, with strong support from the State Department and friends in the Republican Party establishment, had successfully used libel suits to silence authors attempting to publish what they had discovered. Beals evaded that obstacle by presenting his findings at a conference funded by the Carnegie Endowment for International Peace. When Wilson attempted to pressure the Carnegie into removing Beals's contribution from the conference proceedings, the affair attracted national attention in the press. The Carnegie edited Beals's contribution to the published proceedings to remove the material Wilson wanted to keep secret, but Beals's most important arguments had already been widely reported as news, information exempt from legal intimidation.[10] Beals's pugnacious style propelled him back into public attention the following year when he showed that documents the Hearst newspapers claimed proved that the Mexican government had attempted to bribe two U.S. senators and was supplying secret military aid to rebels in Nicaragua were forged. William Randolph Hearst, summoned to testify before a congressional committee, had to confess publicly that the documents were not genuine.[11]

In early 1928, Beals secured his most impressive reporting coup when the *Nation* magazine sent him to Nicaragua to interview revolutionary leader Augusto César Sandino (1895–1934). The fighter's band of 150 men had successfully held off over 2,000 U.S. marines sent to destroy him while an envoy from Washington oversaw forthcoming Nicaraguan elections.[12] Beals's journey took four days by pack mule to reach the secret camp where Sandino had his headquarters, surprisingly only yards away from a marine base. The interview was widely reported in U.S. newspapers, reprinted in full by over two hundred.[13] For U.S. readers, this was the first look at a mysterious figure that the government described as a ruthless bandit who came from Mexico to start a new revolution. Beals confirmed that Sandino had been in Mexico, where he worked for a Standard Oil refinery until 1926 when he returned home. He had fought for the Liberal Party in the recent civil war because he viewed its Conservative Party opponents as agents of foreign banana companies in his country. Sandino rejected U.S. mediation to end the civil war because the U.S. government was not and could not be a neutral party. Beals's report questioned many of Sandino's claims about his resistance movement, which looked to the reporter to be small and poorly armed. The evident weakness of the Sandino force made the failure of the marines to capture or kill Sandino puzzling, but Beals suggested that the revolutionary's survival was evidence that local peasants were doing what they could to protect him. At the end of his final report from Central America, Beals stated simply and directly: "My personal opinion is that if Sandino had arms he could raise an army of ten thousand men by snapping his fingers; that if he marched into Managua, the capital, tomorrow, he would receive the greatest ovation in Nicaraguan history. America's friends in Nicaragua are the politicians who have bled the country for so many decades, they are the politicians who wish to stay in power or to get into power with our help. I would not advise any American marine to walk lonely roads at night in Nicaragua."[14]

U.S. intervention in Nicaragua was unpopular in the United States and even more so in Latin America, and Beals's interview helped refocus debate away from claims of shadowy left-wing networks financing Sandino to President Coolidge's decision that U.S. military force could solve Nicaragua's internal political disputes.[15] The State Department attacked Beals for offering oversimplified interpretations of U.S. policy, but the intensity of official protests pushed mainstream leaders like Walter A. Jessup, Frederick P. Keppel's adjunct at the Carnegie Corporation and eventually his successor as president of the Carnegie, to speak out in defense of the journalist's honesty and objectivity.[16] Beals had excellent contacts inside the State Department and other U.S. agencies, contacts with information he used to develop well-grounded arguments whose common sense appealed to average readers. His writing rests on straightforward presentation of facts, from which he derived conclusions that appeared to be independent of his otherwise obvious sympathy for the "underdog." The evidence showed that the contests between political elites had little to do with the priorities of the majority, even in Mexico where the bloody revolution had thrown forward a new class of leaders, some of whom came from humble backgrounds. The evidence also showed that U.S. intervention in Latin America failed to resolve political divisions or improve how people lived, a conclusion that a State Department report from 1928 on the status of Nicaragua after sixteen years of U.S. occupation and tutelage noted with considerable chagrin: "In its contact with backward peoples the United States stands for roads, schools, public health facilities and those other material improvements which are reflected in security, wealth, literacy, health and progress. Our record in Nicaragua is not up to the mark. [It is] humiliating to see such countries as Salvador and Costa Rica, in which American political control does not exist, surpass in real achievement, Nicaragua, in which we have intervened for many years."[17]

Beals's self-proclaimed political independence made him a popular writer in Latin America as well, where his articles and books were regularly translated into Spanish and Portuguese. That Beals was not personally allied with any of the many socialist and anti-imperialist groups in Latin America underscored his reputation as an honest observer. Beals's critics in the United States and Latin America routinely accused him of being a communist sympathizer. He was an independent socialist generally unsympathetic to the Soviet Union, or for that matter to any efforts to impose modernization on peasant societies, including most of the policies of the nationalist government in Mexico. Beals stressed that peasants in most Latin American countries were largely indigenous peoples who had never stopped fighting to preserve their land and communal independence since the arrival of the Spanish in the sixteenth century. He argued that the best way for the United States to support democracy and economic justice was to limit its involvement. Underlying his advice on how to respond to ongoing internal conflict in other American nations was his conviction that the interests of the general public in the United States diverged from the priorities of U.S. businesses investing abroad. The demands of indigenous communities for inalienable land rights and the liberty to live according to their own cultural values conflicted with the goals of U.S. investors and a determination in Washington to develop Latin America into a stable market for U.S-produced goods. U.S. society itself had an unresolved question to settle in its relations with other countries: did visions of the United States leading a world united around market principles trump the principle of "government for the people, by the people, and of the people"?

If Carleton Beals was the most prolific U.S. journalist working in Latin America, the single most widely discussed book on Mexico of the interwar years was *Mexico: A Study of Two Americas* by economist Stuart Chase (1888–1985), published in 1931, after the author spent two years in Mexico studying the emerging postrevolutionary society.[18] The book echoed many of the arguments that Beals and other experts had already made about the nature of peasant life in Mexico, but Chase did not focus on political or social movements. He proposed to analyze Mexico as a distinctive culture that had survived centuries of political turmoil, a culture that would continue to endure regardless of whatever happened in the national political realm because it grew out of the country's geographic and climatic realities.

Mexico: A Study of Two Americas presented Mexico as an indigenous country grounded in artisanal, handicraft culture, strikingly in contrast to the machine-driven United States. Comparing the small town of Tepoztlán, some sixty miles outside Mexico City, with Muncie, Indiana, Chase developed the ironic argument that the people of Muncie, hence the people of the United States, had lost the foundations for personal independence and economic security, while the residents of Tepoztlán remained small, self-sufficient producers, who could survive comfortably on what they grew and made for themselves. The machine age had promoted a complex, interdependent society in the United States that made everybody vulnerable to the unpredictability of global markets. Indigenous Mexico was a place where paradoxically the conditions for Jeffersonian democracy survived. Chase warned his readers in his introduction that he had nothing to say about Mexico City, as he had wanted to understand life in a small town that he believed was typical of towns and villages of central and southern Mexico, where Aztec and Maya "prevail[ed] with least corruption."[19] Diego Rivera, already a well-known name in the United States, provided fourteen drawings as illustrations.

The preservation of ancient traditions, Chase argued, was due primarily to the topography of the country. The first chapter surveys the geography and climate of Mexico, followed by a hundred-page summary of Mexican history from prehistoric settlement to the 1920s. Chase underscored that everyday life in ancient Mexico had developed on the basis of cultivating maize as the main food source and maguey as the primary source of cloth. Worship of the sun and rain had developed from this economic base to offer Mexicans a unified philosophical system that survived Spanish conquest, independence, and the growing influence of the United States. Mexican society had grown around communal ownership of land. The inequities that foreigners introduced were the primary cause of poverty. Efforts to modernize and mechanize were bound to fail given a "stubborn" commitment to handicraft economy in the countryside. The Mexican revolution had started out as a political contest among elites, but became a popular movement as average Mexicans took up arms to defend an artisanal economy from the threats inherent to producing for global markets. That the common people of Mexico supposedly preferred to be machineless made a startling contrast to the United States, and it also explained why the revolution had broken out in 1910 after forty years of statistically impressive growth. Postrevolutionary Mexico, Chase insisted, did not want the types of development that most people in the United States took for granted as necessary for a good life.

The third section of the book compares everyday life in Tepoztlán with Muncie. The people of Tepoztlán were poor, but "free," because every household had its own plot, where families grew the basic crops they used to feed themselves and make their own clothing. In Tepoztlán, "people do not go [to the market] to make a profit; they go to deliver what they have made [their surplus], get what they need, and pass the time of day."[20] Cooperation governed community relations. Mexicans came together to help each other, whenever there were projects beyond the capabilities of any single household, such as digging an irrigation ditch or erecting a new home. Chase noted that given the prevalence of wage labor in the United States and the need of entrepreneurs to produce for investors, he and his fellow citizens had "no conception of our basic biological and psychological needs."[21] The people of the United States had more to gain from their association with Mexico than Mexicans gained from trading with the United States, though he assumed that since Americans were fundamentally products of a machine-based economy, they could never regain the basic understanding of their environment or their own place in it that the revolutionary founders of the United States had had and which the vast majority of Mexicans retained.

Postrevolutionary political leaders, Chase argued, were attuned to the deep resistance of the rural population to anything that could put their communal self-sufficiency at risk. Urban elites, while fully incorporated into the modern machine age, were developing master plans to keep the development of the economy under control and to reduce U.S. dominance. This would be to the good of Mexico, and in the long run, to the good of the United States, particularly if its people could adapt over time to the reality that most of the world rejected the equation of continuous growth with prosperity. Chase's book was first and foremost a message for the Depression-era United States in the early 1930s, when a quarter of the labor force was out of work. Subsistence with dignity might be a better solution to the problem of "overproduction" than oscillating between boom and bust. Chase's study of Mexico was his second study of a revolutionary society. He had previously written about the new society that the communists were building in Soviet Russia. The Russians were building a modern, industrial society, but Chase preferred the greater personal freedoms that the Mexican approach to revolution protected.[22]

Reviews were overwhelmingly positive, even when a critic noted Chase's inherently romantic assumptions. The book provided food for thought, especially

Chase's argument about a radical difference that had to be faced if there were ever to be shared understanding between the peoples of the Americas. Chase observed that elites across the continent could speak with each other because they shared a common cultural heritage that included reasonably similar conceptions of modernity. When average citizens were brought into the discussion, as they had to be if international exchange were to have any semblance of democracy to it, the differences between the everyday circumstances and values of ordinary people had to be understood, by the people themselves perhaps, but certainly by the men and women responsible for national and international governance. To make the claim of radical difference credible, Chase had of necessity to avoid discussion of Mexican cities or, beyond a brief section on postrevolutionary politics, trade union movements. If Mexican rural society were indeed as resistant to change as Chase believed, then the gap between the countries was unbridgeable and it would usually be difficult for Americans and Mexicans to grasp what people on the other side of the border wanted and why. Like Beals, Chase came to the conclusion that the most effective way to prevent conflict was to limit contact.

* * *

The same year that Chase's book on Mexico appeared, novelist Waldo Frank published *América Hispana*, a broader study of the cultural divide between English-speaking America and Latin America. He developed themes he had introduced five years earlier in his tribute to Spanish culture, *Virgin Spain*, a book successful both critically and commercially. Frank argued that Latin societies retained "mutualistic" mores and customs that the competitive, technologically driven United States had lost but needed to regain. "The average Spaniard was an integrated person," Frank asserted, while in the United States, "the immense pressures and invasions of modern science . . . have alienated man from his instinctual counterpoint with his earth, his group, and his self."[23] Unlike Chase, Frank assumed that the two "halves" of the Americas profoundly needed each other. Contact did need to be limited, but could proceed successfully to the degree that both sides identified areas of mutual benefit.

América Hispana opens in Panama, at the site of the Panama Canal, a technological triumph but built on land that the United States had stolen from Colombia. Panama allowed Frank to meditate on the two forms of Americanism that had emerged in the early nineteenth century, characterized through the contrasting figures of Henry Clay and Simón Bolívar. Frank discussed Clay's vision more briefly because it was "less of mind, more of body." The United States had a brutal urge to expand; it had no values beyond "faith in its own destiny." The U.S. vision of Americanism was one of unlimited expansion and extraction of wealth, in the process permanently transforming the environment. The Panama Canal, literally cut into the land, perfectly symbolized an immutable Anglo American desire that technology triumph over nature.[24]

Bolívar too had wanted to build a canal across the Panama isthmus, in the process making the country the hub of the Americas, an international zone that connected sovereign peoples, each living "harmoniously" in their lands, but sharing material products others could not produce. The most important aspect of American unity was to be a continuous sharing of ideas, cultural and scientific, and Bolívar's America would be one based on creative imagination becoming increasingly conscious of its capabilities. The United States had tools, and its political and business leaders had the force to accomplish almost anything they wanted. Anybody who resisted U.S. ambitions paid a heavy price for trying to preserve their independence. Latin America had dreams and a faith in a transcendent future. The Latin American vision was necessary if international relations were to be based on voluntary union rather than domination. The United States was not ready for that path yet, but by embracing pan-Americanism for a variety of strategic reasons, its leaders had adopted a policy that required the sharing of ideas across borders. Over time, Frank was sure that the people of the United States would change, adopting the spiritual values of those who resisted a technologically driven vision of the good life. Frank's utopian vision required radical difference, though he had little to say about how in practice the two halves of the Americas would reconcile their differences to form a more harmonious union.

The bulk of what comes after the utopian promise is a strangely abstract form of travelogue. Frank very seldom described what he saw during his journeys across the Americas, and he discussed people that he encountered even less. The book is divided into a sequence of zones—the Andean nations, Argentina, Brazil, Chile, the Caribbean basin, Mexico—each of which is defined as a geographical, topographical, climatological entity. Environment is destiny, and the culture of each nation is defined by its adaptation to the specifics of its land. Echoing the ideas of his friend Gabriela Mistral, he wrote of Latin American culture as rooted in the environment, while machines govern the United States, alienating its people from nature. (Mistral, at least, believed that the technological civilization of the United States was also rooted in the particularities of the nation's topography and climate.) In Peru and Mexico, connection with the environment endured in cultures that had existed for millennia. Even in Argentina or Brazil, two countries like the United States formed primarily through waves of immigrant settlement, national life is circumscribed by the realities of the pampas (extensive grass plains) in Argentina or the "jungle" in Brazil. Nature itself, however, is ineffable; no mere physical description can convey its essence. The pampas region, Frank states bluntly, "is a quality; it cannot be pictured except by the substantial form of things within it [people, buildings, animals, plant life] . . . [the] pampa itself has no surface and no body."[25]

His descriptions of Buenos Aires, São Paulo, Rio de Janeiro, and Santiago de Chile emphasize the conformity of these cities with an overwhelming natural environment. The buildings are extensions of grasslands, coffee farms, thickly forested mountains, or the rocky and dangerous Pacific coastline. To the degree that these cities have unique characteristics, it is the quality of the land from which they grew, and here again, he wrote of cities in the United States as divorced from, existing in opposition to, the land where they sit.

When Frank mentioned people, he reported only a conversation and that briefly. The Latin Americans presented to his readers function in the book as additional symbols of the harmonious unification of humanity into the environment that Frank argued was the core of Latin American civilization. At Victoria Ocampo's home in Buenos Aires, the interior and the exterior flowed into each other to form an inseparable union. Ocampo (1890–1979), a distinguished writer and editor, is presented as a "woman of Argentina and America, in her cult of light, in her work of structure within the chaos of the pampa motion." She "has learned that she must clasp the bitter cactus in her hand, clasp it against her breast. She has prophesied for her country."[26] Few readers in the United States outside literary circles knew her name, and Ocampo serves as a private symbol that perhaps only those already in personal conversation with Frank could decipher. In Ocampo's case, his description of her negated her well-developed position in Argentinean letters as a cosmopolitan who did not view herself or her nation as predetermined by the pampas.

The reviewer for the *Nation*, while sympathetic to Frank's goals, complained of the abstract character of a book that continually replaced observation with overt symbols.[27] Mary Austin, a well-known novelist of the U.S. Southwest reviewing Frank's book for the *New York Herald Tribune*, observed that Frank conveyed his own personality instead of the character of the countries he visited, but she still found the argument "profitable and stimulating."[28] Most reviewers praised the book, and the reviewer for the *Yale Review* wrote that *América Hispana* was difficult but ultimately a more satisfying study of the U.S. relation to Latin America than Chase's *Mexico: A Study of Two Americas*.[29] Latin American writers and critics also praised the book, which was released simultaneously in Spanish translation, the sales of which were brisk enough to warrant additional printings. José Carlos Mariátegui, a Marxist social critic and editor of the Peruvian journal *Amauta*, speculated that Jews in the Americas, like Frank, might enjoy a unique responsibility in "formulat[ing] the hope and ideal of America" because secure in their own ancient culture they were freed from limitations of a narrow national perspective and could see more clearly the ways different cultures expressed humanity's ancient fascination with the eternal puzzles of existence, while other authors remarked on Frank's ability to speak with "the emotive accent of the Old Testament Prophets."[30]

Frank imagined literary exchange as the critical initial step in uniting the two "half-worlds" of the western hemisphere. Contemporary Latin American writers could provide North American readers with a vision of societies more closely attuned to the "elements" and the soil. Gabriela Mistral, he wrote on her death, "came from the mineral mountains and deserts of Northern Chile. . . . Gabriela made one think of her Andes in all their immobile composure."[31] Casey Nelson Blake has noted that Frank's views rested on a mystical recuperation of "buried memories of maternal love."[32] Men who used business, science, and engineering to tame nature governed U.S. society. Divorced from nature, they were divorced from their own inner lives, unable to reflect on the spiritual consequences of their choices. They strove to integrate themselves into the logic of the problems they solved. They transformed into mere functions of the mechanical processes they directed instead of being self-conscious creators of a new world.[33] Iberia and the American societies that sprang from Spain and Portugal retained a connection to the soil that allowed a full balance between imagination and purpose to unfold. Men could develop their emotional capacities more completely than an industrial society based on scientific management could allow. The conclusion to *América Hispana* called for "an *integral* socialism which would transfigure the present industrial body on the basis of the true concept of the person."[34] Land and climate would defeat any effort to imitate the acquisitive individualism of "Birmingham, Berlin, and Chicago," and the "go-getter" of Brazil will never be the equal in business or politics of the imperial powers "although he study the technique of aggression in the best law schools of the United States and the best Chancelleries of Europe. If Brazil becomes finally keyed to a civilization of the go-getter, it will be a hinterland for alien powers." Brazil's power must come from its "tropic waters" and from its forest wilderness. Only by being in harmony with the soil will humans achieve the spiritual wisdom that is the flower of any true civilization.[35]

Frank left the practicalities of the exchange at an aspirational level. Latin Americans would teach North Americans how to enjoy life and to understand the soil on which they lived. North Americans would share their technology so that standards of living could rise more quickly. The entire framework required postulating an absolute difference between Anglo American and Latin American civilizations, with the latter succeeding in everything where Anglo Americans had failed and thus providing a secret path to redemption when U.S. capitalism no longer could work its magic.

Frank received an extraordinarily enthusiastic response from Latin American intellectuals, but at least one who had lived in the United States was skeptical of the mystical symbolism that Frank's message required. Moisés Sáenz (1888–1941), who had studied at Columbia University and, as noted in Chapter 1, returned to Mexico to lead its rural education programs, told Frank in 1929 that he was "a fraud, a cheat, a second-rater. Your visit will accomplish nothing and will bring nothing about."[36] We do not know what Sáenz actually said or what his motivations might have been. Sáenz in his capacity as assistant secretary of public education had invited Frank to give six lectures in Mexico City, offering the writer a handsome honorarium. They had gone to Sáenz's home in Taxco for the weekend. Frank reported the event in his memoirs, which remained unpublished during his lifetime, as a counterpoint to the success of his talks in the capital. Sáenz's attack came as Frank contemplated the view of Cuernavaca from the veranda of Sáenz's villa. The "enchantment" of the view merged with the "enchantment" of his reception in Mexico, where his ideas seemed to excite all but the politicians. "I did not understand the success," he noted. "I simply drank it in, hardly tasting it, as a very thirsty man takes in a glass of water." And then this sudden personal assault from a man he considered a friend and a comrade in arms for the campaign to build a new world. In his account, Frank protested, "Fraud! But the United States no less a fraud, equating progress with refrigerators, prophesy with profits."[37]

In more practical terms, Frank's approach to inter-American community was antithetical to the modern development Sáenz was working to bring to his own country—children learning practical skills that would allow the country to develop its agricultural resources more effectively, that would expand the number of trained mechanics and artisans present in every community. The national goal was indeed to industrialize to the degree that the nation could produce most of its basic goods, just as the United States did, and to mechanize agriculture to the degree the topography of the land allowed. To become self-sufficient might well mean developing the capacity of the Mexican people to grow their agricultural products as efficiently as U.S. farmers did. For all the raw emotional intensity driving Frank's critique of how the United States had developed, Sáenz was in a good position to know that Frank was an outsider in his own country and his passion for things Hispanic signified nothing for long-term U.S.-Mexican or U.S.–Latin American relations.[38]

Frank helped convince Victoria Ocampo that she should use her wealth to start her journal *Sur*, one of the most important expressions of modernism and cosmopolitanism in Spanish-speaking America between 1930 and 1960. Frank sat on the editorial board and periodically contributed articles even though he seldom agreed with Ocampo's tastes. She refused to follow Frank's recommendations that the magazine publish work that represented "typical" Latin America.[39] *Sur* was the personal project of an unusual woman whose income from the vast land holdings of her family allowed her to develop a cultural project independent of the considerations of profit that surrounded the decisions successful U.S. publishers made. Ocampo presented her readers with a range of North American writers who might not otherwise have been translated into Spanish, but she criticized writers who presented the various parts of the Americas as inherently opposed.[40] She viewed the traditional Argentina of her family as a prison for women, or for that matter for any man with a streak of curiosity. She married young to escape the constant supervision of her family, but her husband, charming and witty when he courted her, became her new prison guard. She left him, but Argentinean law prohibited divorce. When she met the man with whom she wanted to spend the rest of her life, their relationship had to remain clandestine, not only because for her to have a lover would have shocked Buenos Aires society but because she risked arrest for breaking laws that made adultery a criminal offense. When she published her first book, a study of Dante's *Divine Comedy*, society mocked her for having the ambition of a man. If she must write, one critic told her, why not write about the "personal themes" that women understood. She determined that she would make no concessions to a society determined to remain mediocre. "Work as if nothing happened, as if nothing had been said to you, numb to this type of criticism" became the motto for both her professional and her personal life.[41] *Sur* had to attack the prejudices of her America. Ocampo had to attack the very assumption that the cultures of her America could not change, perhaps need not change, because they represented a unity of land and spirit. She had to alert her readers to the most interesting new ideas in Europe and North America; she had to identify and publish cosmopolitan Latin American writers who could easily feel at home anywhere in the world. *Sur* provided Jorge Luis Borges with a place where he could explore the intellectual foundations of his ideas as he developed a body of literary work that would seize the world's attention after 1945. Frank detested Borges because the writer's commitment to imagination and literary play was at odds with Frank's understanding of genuine culture arising from a people's unity with the land where they lived. Frank discouraged the publication of Borges in the United States on the grounds that he was a derivative writer unduly influenced by European thought who turned his back on Argentinean reality. Frank, like Ocampo, pursued a project of cultural criticism and spiritual redemption, but his vision required a timeless Latin America whose magical reality could reverse the mistakes of the North. Committed to building bridges between the United States and Latin America, he brought a focus, however odd it might have been, to the project of cultural exchange that eluded most others before the State Department launched its Division of Cultural Affairs in July 1938.

If private initiative were to drive the building of a transnational culture, the contours would follow the heartfelt passions of those few individuals ready to commit the time and resources to achieve their goals. While the Carnegie Endowment for International Peace had tried to fund projects that could normalize relations, the strategy of private initiative meant that the exchange developed in a shape that accentuated difference instead of seeking the building blocks of common sentiment. The irony in Frank's case was that his efforts aimed at reigniting a sense of compassionate fellowship in the United States by exposing North Americans to the primarily spiritual and earthy temperament he argued characterized everyday life in Latin America. The task required expertise in seeing and decoding difference, or else Americans in love with their own gadgetry would fail to see the profundity of the values that were most important to Latin Americans.

This was not a question of outdated stereotypes persisting. Writers like Frank and Chase were actively inventing a fantasy history that escaped time. Given that radical difference stood outside time as most humans experienced it, the challenge was to learn from the other America without imagining that new social relations could emerge that might ultimately dissolve current differences or in the process create new ones. In that sense, the most widely read books that appeared in the 1920s and 1930s exploring the possibilities for inter-American relations contradicted the idea that America, the "New World," was a place of unlimited potential where even brutal raw experience could be redeemed in new, more honest ways of representing the world. For at least one writer, the open-ended nature of the New World experience was too important to sacrifice to the elusive certainties provided by "national character." William Carlos Williams's *In the American Grain*, published in 1925, is the only book of the genre that became a classic of national literature, offering a vision of American identity that is still read and discussed as relevant for the twenty-first century.

Chapter 3

"In the American Grain"

As publishing interest in books on the Americas grew, the modernist poet William Carlos Williams (1883–1963) proposed to a small commercial publisher in New York that he write a two-volume history of "America" as told through the stories of men and women who had created the New World. The first volume appeared in 1925 under the title *In the American Grain*. Williams's history began with Eric the Red and Christopher Columbus, then moved into stories of Spanish, French, and British invaders competing with Native Americans for control of what would eventually become British North America and the United States. The volume ended with the assassination of Abraham Lincoln. He had intended to end with Edgar Allan Poe, but his publisher insisted on a more conventional conclusion. In most chapters, Williams built his stories around extensive quotations from his subjects or documents of the period. Williams explained later, "The plan was to try to get inside the heads of some of the American founders or 'heroes,' if you will, by examining their original records. I wanted nothing to get between me and what they themselves had recorded."[1]

At the time Williams was forty-two. His first book of verse had appeared in 1913, followed by three others. Williams had contributed to a number of small presses, and he was an active participant in the underground theater movement in Manhattan. Most of his time, however, was spent working as a medical doctor in Rutherford, a factory town in New Jersey eight miles west of Manhattan where he had lived for most of his life. His parents had immigrated to the United States from the Caribbean after their marriage. His mother was Puerto Rican, and his father while born in England had grown up in the Dominican Republic. Williams grew up hearing Spanish spoken at home between his parents and the "steady stream of West Indians, South Americans, and other speakers of the Spanish language [who] came to visit us, to stay sometimes the entire winter."[2] Beyond impressions formed during many years of family conversations, Williams had no direct familiarity with the societies of the Caribbean or Latin America, nor any knowledge beyond what he read in the newspapers of how the

United States was working to reshape the continent in its image. Nonetheless, his contribution fit into an effort to rethink the United States by placing the country's origins and development in a truly American, that is, transnational, context that could redefine the supposedly distinctive conditions of national life.

Williams's conclusions about what was "distinctive" and "essential" ran counter to the prevailing search found in the work of other U.S. writers for root cultures and races, for expressions of national identity that were considered "pure" because grounded in soil, blood, or a romantic conception of language as the crystallized expression of a people who had developed together in harmony with the land where they and their ancestors had lived. The types of explanation of national character found in most of the books published on inter-American relations in the 1920s Williams dismissed with the observation that history "portrays us in generic patterns, like effigies or the carvings on sarcophagi, which say nothing save, of such and such a man, that he is dead. That's history. It is concerned only with the one thing: to say everything is dead. Then it fixes up the effigy: there that's finished. Not at all. History must stay open, it is all humanity. Are lives to be twisted forcibly about events, the mere accidents of geography and climate? It is an obscenity which few escape—save at the hands of the stylist, literature, in which alone humanity is protected against tyrannous designs."[3] Given Williams's choice to base most of the book on his subjects' own words, the "stylists" in *In the American Grain* might be thought of as anyone who struggled to talk about their own past actions or those of their neighbors. As divergent, idiosyncratic characters, their adventures cannot easily fit a conception of national character reflecting an intersection of race and geography. Nor, given that very few of his subjects were writers in the conventional sense, did the documents he selected correspond with the texts students in the United States were reading as the canon of "national literature." He presented documents of everyday speech, not literature. Much of what his characters say is banal, but their struggle to express their feelings about life in what became America says much more about the formation of country than classics of literature with their affirmations of well-known truths can ever say.

Despite the many peculiarities of the book, Williams's *In the American Grain* remains the only U.S. book still read today that responded to pan-Americanism, although his approach disregarded entirely any idea of American uniqueness. The book has become a classic of national literature, while Williams has long been a monument of U.S. literature and more recently has entered the canon of Latino literature. His canonization is ironic in that Williams rejected ideas of purity and he thought that the labels that could be applied to him had only relative value. He was a U.S. writer because he was born and worked in the United States, but his background and his experience gave him no ability to summarize the national experience. Nor did he think that the "pure products of America," the root cultures that had shaped each nation, have any better ability. He understood the local community in which he had lived. He had an idea about how it reflected the larger problematic of the "New World," of which America was itself only one expression. The book identifies patriotism and vague ideals such as pan-Americanism as repressive mechanisms that block confronting a hidden history of how American societies had formed. More than reciting platitudes imagining a future world where all nations were equal, the peoples of the western hemisphere needed to dig into how the past the American peoples shared continued to shape everyday experience.

In the twentieth century, white Americans across the hemisphere talked of the settlement of the New World as an expansion of Liberty, in the English-speaking countries, or of Civilization, in the countries derived from the Spanish, Portuguese, and French Empires. Williams viewed the conquest as an act of nature, meaning to him that the urge to dominate sprang from lusts, fears, and ambitions common to human psyche and then channeled into particular encounters with other people as the historical circumstances demand, or, in some cases, allow. Invasion requires violence, and thus demands from both intruders and resisters a psychological need for violence that displaces the victors' tensions and confusions onto the bodies of those they brutalize. Williams started *In the American Grain* with the story of Eric the Red in part because the Norse incursion into eastern Canada had by the 1920s become an important part of how the "discovery" of America was narrated in the United States. More importantly for Williams's purposes, the dark violence behind the Norse move west in the tenth century fit a pattern Williams wanted to emphasize. Eric was an outlaw who had left Norway for Iceland because he was a murderer fleeing justice. He fled Iceland to what would become the Americas because he killed anew and needed an even more distant hiding place. The Native peoples sensed the chaotic evil that Eric brought with him. Instead of welcoming a stranger in need, they understood that the newcomer knew no law other than satisfying his desires. Sensibly, they rose up to drive the interloper away.

Turning to Columbus, Williams reminded his readers that the great discoverer had failed to find what he had promised the Spanish Crown, a direct route to India. His enemies in Spain had him arrested, and he returned from his last voyage in chains charged with treason and corruption. "There is no need to argue Columbus' special worth," Williams stated simply. "Let it have been as a genius that he made his first great voyage, possessed of that streamlike human purity of purpose called by that name—it was still as a man that he would bite the bitter fruit that Nature would offer him. He was poisoned and his fellows turned against him like wild beasts."[4] "Nature" in this case, and in much of the book, meaning the deadly competition for power coursing through most of humanity's known history, a force continuing throughout the move across the Atlantic. Underlying conquistadores like Hernán Cortez was "the evil of the whole world; it was the perennial disappointment that follows, like smoke, the bursting of ideas. It was the spirit of malice which underlies men's lives and against which nothing offers resistance."[5]

Long before it was common for Americans of European ancestry to do so, Williams insisted that conquest by its very nature requires horrific crimes. The history of America, Williams insisted, began "with murder and enslavement, not with discovery."[6] The motivations for Europeans to cross the Atlantic were many, including "the pursuit of beauty." Nonetheless, "the husk that remains" grew out of "perversions and mistakes," murder, lies, trickery, rape, theft.[7] The Native peoples had been surprised when the intruders arrived, unsure of their motives or how to respond. Native societies learned quickly, and as they did, their resistance grew more determined, making the European conquest of what became the United States a protracted, three-century-long oscillation of war, negotiation, trade, fear, and curiosity. Williams insisted that even if the motives of some involved in taking the land away from Native peoples and turning it into "America" had been noble, the process was without exception brutal. For Americans to accept who they were as a people, what their legacies actually were, they needed to put aside ideals and face the fear and violence of national origins without an effort to disguise, or rationalize, what had happened. The failure to acknowledge the horrific scale of the crimes underlying the formation of new societies generated frantic efforts to substitute pretty-sounding words for actual experience, and the languages available to Americans to describe their own world abetted continuing violence. Insisting on the need of Americans to face the brutal facts of their national origins, Williams declared in one of the more tendentious sections of the book, "It is an extraordinary phenomenon that Americans have lost the sense, being made up as we are, that what we are has its origin in what *the nation* in the past has been; that there is a source in AMERICA for everything we think or do . . . that, in fine, we have no conception at all of what is meant by moral . . . and that if we will not pay heed to our own affairs, we are nothing but an unconscious porkyard and oilhole for those, more able, who will fasten themselves upon us."[8]

Williams the medical doctor approached the nation as "a closed system" based on false premises, which he noted function by "shutting those who confine themselves to it from the rest of the world." The languages nations provided their citizens stymied communication, left people struggling with clichés that rendered them "unable to say the simplest thing of importance to one another."[9] Looking at the words that had been used to describe conquest and the formation of a new society was required to uncover fears and desires deposited within national culture over many generations. Williams offered stories rather than explanations in a book that he may well have considered a therapeutic effort to help modern Americans see how the words available to them to describe their identities as Americans shaped their feelings and perceptions of their immediate surroundings as well as of the people with whom they had to live. In listening to the voices of men and women who had been important in founding America, one could hear the symptoms left over from the fever of conquest. That Americans of any nationality might not know what they were saying, that they might have been inarticulate and self-deceiving, was hardly the point. Most of his patients in Rutherford, New Jersey, could not describe what was going on within them. He, the doctor, had to listen carefully to move backward from their raw but naïve descriptions to any apparent physical symptoms to developing a theory about what the underlying systemic problem might be.

Williams rejected any assumption that language ever easily expresses who we are or where we have been. He dismissed national literature as a "dead layer" smothering experience.[10] National languages were artificial and learned for a few official circumstances. They were false because they provided ready-to-hand patterns for responding to the world, and "a fog of words" replaced lived experience. In the United States, Williams asserted in *In the American Grain*, the pervasive fear that the pattern might be false had led directly to racial segregation and ostracism of the poor: "Do not serve another for you might have to TOUCH him and he might be a JEW or a NIGGER. . . . Be careful whom you marry! Be careful for you can NEVER know."[11] A war within the heart of Americans appeared in public life as a clash of civilizations or as competition between races, two ideas that he thought expressed fear of the unpredictable complexities of life, not enduring historical realities.

His family's experience had been different, and he emphasized that the absence of strict racial separation found in the Caribbean was clear evidence that U.S. racial practices were radically un-American. He noted in a later book about his mother, "In the West Indies, in Martinique, St. Thomas, Puerto Rico, Santo Domingo, in those days, the races of the world mingled and intermarried— imparting their traits one to another and forgetting the orthodoxy of their ancient and medieval ways. It was a good thing. It is in the best spirit of the New World. That it is good and that my mother is good by virtue of these things that she had taught me, I live largely to exemplify as best I may."[12] Her stories of peasants, some white and others black, however, pointed to class barriers that people in her West Indies took for granted. Peasants came down from the hills and performed their dances and songs for religious and patriotic festivals. Their music and energy delighted the comfortable classes, but no one invited the peasants inside to join their family celebrations. There was no shared social life between the rich and the poor. "Many rigidities were perpetuated," he acknowledged, "many stupidities of classic proportions were entrenched."[13] Williams nonetheless insisted that merchants and professionals in the West Indies had a better understanding of how their society worked because they knew that divisions based on money and education did not originate in racial or color differences. The inheritors of a great revolution, people in the United States were uncomfortable with social divisions and needed to believe that immutable laws of nature must determine the relative success and failure of different groups.

Williams's history of America zeroed in on the fear of TOUCH (one of the words Williams set in small caps to emphasize their taboo quality) reinforcing Anglo-American insularity. The question has many dimensions in the course of the book but resolves quickly to race, which Williams viewed as barring the social interaction necessary to create one people out of many. The English arrived refusing "close contact" with the original inhabitants of America. They had refused to TOUCH the indigenous people they conquered, and those who succumbed to curiosity, desire, or sentiments of fellowship were quickly punished. The approach embedded in Anglo American culture went well beyond recognition of difference. It required enforced separation.

Apartness was the nub and the essence of the English legacy the people Williams called "United Statesers" inherited, regardless of actual racial or ethnic ancestry. They believed that Liberty was inherent to the "American experience," an idea requiring formal respect for individual rights, at least to the degree that everybody ought in principle to find their chance to show what they can do. But, on the other hand, no one could avoid an ever-present command: don't TOUCH, which meant, Williams thought, don't be curious about the lives of others, don't talk to anybody about anything except immediate business or irrelevant chit-chat, keep relations at a superficial level, don't get involved, and above all, don't develop a sense of mutual responsibility with anybody outside your immediate circle. Any natural interest you might have in another person was always potentially dangerous.

The rebels he chose to celebrate form an odd assortment: the French Jesuit missionary Sebastian Rasles; Daniel Boone, portrayed not as an Indian fighter but as a pioneer ready to live with and learn from Native peoples; Abraham Lincoln, presented as a maternal figure trying to nurture his people into accepting themselves for who they were; Edgar Allan Poe, whom Williams declared the most original of U.S. writers; and a completely fictionalized character, Jacatacqua, an eighteen-year-old woman leading an Abenaki band in Maine at the time of the Revolutionary War. Each overcame, to some degree, his or her fear of the new and, for the Anglo American characters, the prohibition against TOUCH.

They promoted a counterculture of creativity, hybridity, cross-pollination, a North American counterpart to ideas of *mestizaje* then coming to define twentieth-century Latin American ideas of their America's racial identity.[14]

Jacatacqua avoided a battle with U.S. military forces that Aaron Burr was leading into Quebec by inviting them to join her troops in a hunt. Burr, driven by the sexual desire he felt for the Indian leader, reflected an openness to experience that Americans needed to get past their tragic origins. The New World "democracy" that Williams celebrated was found primarily in small personal choices, such as choosing to go on a hunt together instead of fighting, decisions made on the basis of affection, desire, want, or immediate need rather than religious dogma, constitutional system, or intellectual propositions, a clear counterpart to Williams's motto "no ideas but in things," used in his poem "A Sort of a Song" (1944).

The villains in the book insisted on limiting experience and thus surrendered their impressive talents to the service of smallness. The colonial-era theologian Cotton Mather turned his logical powers to providing scientific evidence for the vast extent of Satan's conspiracy against Puritan New England; he ensured that fear of others would be central to the Anglo American psyche and the command not to "TOUCH" never challenged. The most insidious villain in the book is Alexander Hamilton. His program for central government and capitalist enterprise chained Americans to their treadmills and transformed the Passaic valley, where Williams had lived all his life, from a natural paradise to "the vilest swillhole in Christendom."[15] The result was control and wealth for a few, but for the majority, the growth of fear and "striving the while to pull off pieces to themselves from the fat of the new bounty."[16] Hamilton's country was one of closed windows, locks, fences, walls, mean, narrow, and provincial, not the great liberty-loving country affirmed in national creed. "Who are we?" he asked of who Anglo Americans had become, "degraded whites riding our fears to market where everything is by accident and only one thing sure: the fatter we get the duller we grow."[17] The end result: a nation of men, women, and children suffering from alienation and various forms of mental illness. Alienation he understood as a poet to mean the barriers between experience and language that prevent an accurate feeling for one's reality. Mental illness he understood as a doctor whose patients came from working-class families; many among them simply could no longer make sense of the stresses pressing down upon them, a recurrent theme frequently explored in Williams's fiction. "The pure products of America go crazy," Williams had written in 1923 in his poem "To Elsie."[18]

Williams's vision was every bit as romantic as that of Waldo Frank or Stuart Chase, but he interjected a gap between social action and underlying biological impulses that could not be bridged with appeals to "harmonious" unity with the landscape of one's ancestors. Williams presented existing social hierarchies as the products of earlier crimes. He savored the possibilities emerging from more open-ended connections growing through mutual exploration of "delight," "fancy," and "a mounting desire that makes [a human being] seem . . . like a bird in flight" and not a two-legged beast of burden chained to a harness.[19]

Williams's "place" in much of his writing was neither the United States of America as such nor the Americas, nor an ancestral homeland in the West Indies. These names referenced abstract ideas laden with emotional power but divorced from the realities of touch. His standpoint was and remained throughout his career the very particular location of the Passaic River valley in northeast New Jersey. In an unpublished poem, "A Democratic Party Poem," drafted around 1928, Williams argued for decentralized government with local control allowing people to decide how they want to live by arguing out their disagreements with each other face to face.[20] Like Jane Addams, he could envision a successful democracy bringing together people of very different backgrounds if only they had to communicate with each other in order to solve their problems. His inclination, however, was to imagine community as much a result of surrender to shared pleasures as of bringing people together to solve problems. If people could go hunting, fall in love, compete in games, share their songs, dances, stories, inherited barrier ideas would lose their power, and possibilities increased that people of different backgrounds might discover solutions to shared problems.

Williams in most respects was a backward-looking figure, trying to synthesize U.S. ideas of self-governing communities with his conviction that his family's Caribbean reality had been more open to the variety of heritages and experiences that exist within any community. Diversity of local customs could, he thought, provide a secure basis for recognizing individuality and thus for the expansion of humanity's knowledge and capabilities. Immediacy provided the antidote to a central, arbitrary authority that required an abstract set of ideas to be able to rule.[21] He ignored the ways in which violence against immigrants and people of color in the United States was securely rooted in local relations, with, at the time, the primary hope for a release lying in the potential of the federal government to protect minorities based on the essentially abstract idea of "constitutional rights." The immediacy of power in the local situation, in the microworld that he valued as the source of freedom, remains one of the gaps in his vision of democracy, even if his accounts of national history underscored the chaotic violence of immediate situations. In a review of Logan Clendening's book *The Human Body* that Williams wrote for the *New York Post*, he noted, "And, since there is a lust in us all today to get back to a basis of power, if we take this to be the body, as a whole, a light is cast upon many of the seemingly base phenomena with which we are surrounded and we shall quickly understand them in their simple normality."[22] If central power rested its power on abstractions that could be applied in a variety of situations, local power rested on the physical proximity that made raw violence a quick, efficient way of settling disputes.

The "local" can have different connotations, with many institutions creating real if virtual "local" spaces where one acts and affects others. Williams worked locally as a doctor, largely because he had limited his ambitions in medicine to serving his patients and earning a living. As a poet, Williams had grander ambitions. He looked to an international network to advance his reputation, his ideas, and his publications, all of which connected fragments of many local physical environments into a social locality focused on a particular kind of work that stretched across different places. The way in which Williams posed the immediate against the abstract was part of a strategy of literary self-positioning that necessarily obscured the ambiguities of the "local," even in his personal life, much less in the national history he analyzed.

His insistence that the crimes upon which American societies had been built be squarely acknowledged was forward looking when *In the American Grain* appeared, a position that grew more widely accepted across the second half of the twentieth century, even if still fiercely resisted by many whose patriotism requires no doubts about the essential goodness of one's forebears. Williams's focus on the global and the local as the most important sites of political and cultural life keeps him a relevant figure for the twenty-first century. For Williams, the local was the place of experience with actual other people and with actual physical environments. The local was the place where touch occurred and desire became a practical political point. People who did not reflect on their locality had nothing to exchange in either the national or the international arenas. Desire broke down barriers between people, but the stories he told in *In the American Grain* made clear as well that desire easily resulted in cruel violence.

Despite his ambition to celebrate the political importance of direct connection, to fight the taboos preventing TOUCH, Williams evaded looking directly at slavery and its aftermath. The four-page chapter "The Advent of the Slave," among the shortest in the book, juxtaposes the voyage of the *Mayflower* to Massachusetts with the simultaneous arrival of the first slave ships in Virginia. Williams told his readers that the descendants of slaves were the most genuinely American and the most deeply Christian people living in the United States. The observations are in passing. He did not turn to any of the many narratives that slaves and former slaves had written, nor to any documents of slave revolts. Instead, he proclaimed that "the special virtue" of the slaves and their descendants was that they were "nothing" in the United States. Barred from the most basic right, they had, supposedly, not developed the lust for power that defined Anglo-American society. To illustrate his point, Williams turned to two African American patients he had treated in Rutherford. Like most of his patients, they were poor working people who drank too much. They arrived in his office in the final stages of serious illnesses that were too far advanced to treat. They hoped that the doctor could provide a miraculous cure, but they assumed already that their cases were hopeless. Williams recounts their problems with ironic humor, liberally quoting their garbled efforts to explain their lives in language that Williams reduces to stereotyped dialect. The brief account is a clear example of where immediate, local relations, particularly when the relationship is inherently unequal in terms of race, social standing, and education, do not lead even to understanding, much less empathy.

Slavery and the relation whites developed with blacks were topics that Williams did not feel comfortable folding into his history of American experience. He did not return to the topic, even when it would have been an obvious connection. As a result, the book's vision of building a healthy American identity by confronting the history of conquest, genocide, and slavery remained an aspiration. His emphasis on the fear of TOUCH reflected Williams's imagination of Spanish-speaking America as a place of more genuine person-to-person interaction that provided an antidote to the failings of an advanced capitalist society, including the country's deepening racial divisions.

*   *   *

Although Waldo Frank was enthusiastic about the book, *In the American Grain* failed to capture the public imagination when it first appeared.[23] Reviewers acknowledged that Williams was a poet, not a historian or a journalist, and the book was very different from most others of its kind. The critic for the *New York Times* found much of it "remarkably lucid and pregnant," even if some sections were "remarkably turgid and inconsequential." The language that Williams brought to recounting the founding of U.S. society was unusually beautiful and passionate, a point underscored by other reviewers.[24] Most reviewers praised Williams's ambition to combat nativist parochialism.[25] The thrust of Williams's argument was clear enough, but he did not provide his readers with a checklist of conclusions. Were he already a famous author, like T. S. Eliot or Ezra Pound, Williams's roommate at the University of Pennsylvania, one might have bought the book to find out what a celebrity poet had to say about his country's history. Williams, however, was still unknown to the general public, and his opinions had no particular authority. The book sat unsold on bookstore shelves.

Williams's publisher remaindered the title and had copies still in the warehouse pulped to reuse the paper for the company's next set of publications.

Williams did not write a planned second volume that was to cover the pioneer settlement of the West, U.S. involvement with Mexico and the Caribbean, the building of the Panama Canal, opposition to imperialism, the industrial revolution, and the rise of Hollywood. The disaster of World War I and pan-Americanism as an antidote to European tutelage were to bring the second volume to a close, though he also considered ending with Pancho Villa and the Mexican revolution.[26] While the interpretive emphases of the project are clear in the initial volume, the second volume would likely have developed more explicit arguments related to practical choices the United States faced in the mid-1920s.

Williams's critical evaluation of U.S. culture in itself was certainly not the cause of the book's failure. Waldo Frank and Stuart Chase had found Anglo culture wanting in comparison to Latin American authenticity, and they received critical praise and reasonable sales. Repudiation of the country's Puritan origins as the source of religious fundamentalism, crass commercialism, and nativist racism was commonplace in modernist circles.[27] Criticizing the United States for being *over*reliant on technology, for being *overly* influenced by market values assumed that the citizens of the wealthiest nation in the world ought also to be the happiest, the most spiritually enlightened. Learning from "premodern" Latin America about the importance of humanistic values could further perfect the nation, and thus fit well within the mainstream of progressive expression before World War II.

The failure of *In the American Grain* when it first appeared may rest on Williams's unrelentingly tragic assessment of the origins of the United States. Most of his subjects failed in the goals that they had set for themselves, and successful figures, like George Washington or Benjamin Franklin, achieved greatness only by stepping back from their desires and fancies. Williams's insistent linking of fear of TOUCH to fear of interracial sexual relations broke a basic taboo for white Americans during the period, as did his repeated demand that Americans acknowledge that conquest, genocide, and slavery shaped everything their country had become. His message stressed that modern nationalism posed a deep threat to psychological wholeness, a message more meaningful to readers after the horrors of World War II and the unprecedented threat to human existence that marked the Cold War.[28]

After 1925, Williams spent more time writing fiction, primarily exploring the lives of neighbors and patients in the Passaic valley. He also translated poetry from Spain and Spanish-speaking Latin America. Williams published most frequently in the *New Masses* and *Blast*, two left-identified, "proletarian" literary journals, but he also developed a good working relationship with James Laughlin, a steel-industry heir whose press, New Directions, developed into the most successful and most important avant-garde publishing venture in the post–World War II United States.[29] In 1939, after New Directions reissued *In the American Grain*, Williams began to receive invitations to visit various countries as part of the Good Neighbor cultural exchange program. He declined most requests, but in 1941 he accepted an offer to attend the Inter-American Writers Conference, held in Puerto Rico.[30] During this trip, he visited his mother's hometown and reunited with his many cousins still on the island.

The explanation he provided for declining most invitations to promote U.S.-Latin American unity was his heavy professional responsibility as head of the pediatrics service at two hospitals and as president of the local medical society. It was difficult for him to get away, and time traveling inevitably took away from the relatively limited time he had for his literary work. Octavio Paz noted that Williams was unusual among writers in being so fully engaged with the everyday life of his country. He was not an expatriate, nor was he an internal exile locked away in the countryside, a university, or a bohemian enclave.[31]

Paz visited Williams after reading "Hymn among the Ruins," a translation Williams had published of one of Paz's most famous poems. Paz thought it the most impressive translation of his work he had yet seen. He traveled to Rutherford expecting to meet a highly refined sophisticate, but instead he discovered that Williams was a modest suburban doctor knowledgeable on many literary topics but also well aware of the limitations of his learning and of his experience. Paz made a succinct assessment of *In the American Grain* in an essay he published on Williams: "America [Williams says] is not a given reality but something we all make together with our hands, our eyes, our brain, and our lips. The reality of America is material, mental, visual, and, above all, verbal—whether speaking in Spanish, English, Portuguese, or French, the American speaks a language different from the European original. . . . American is a reality that we say."[32]

Victoria Ocampo made a similar point when she compared Williams to one of his Latin American contemporaries, Argentinean poet Leopoldo Lugones. She noted that modern poetry put literary language in confrontation with the language spoken in the streets, leading to violent, erotic images often juxtaposing the dual absurdity of much of the modern world: either pursue an alienated but relatively free existence in the world's big cities or try to return to a more natural life closer to the soil and movement of the four seasons, but always in localities deformed, she thought, because they were organized solely for the purpose of making as much money as possible for landowners.[33]

The originality of Williams's contribution to debates in the 1920s within the United States over American identity and what that meant for the relationship of people in the United States to other Americans stemmed in part from his being divorced from discussions in Spanish-speaking countries at the time. In the 1920s, his work as a poet was not yet known in Latin America, nor did he travel there.[34] Frank, Chase, and Beals developed their ideas in extensive conversations with Latin American intellectuals, who praised what their North American friends published. Ideological and professional affinities brought together people whose agreement transcended national borders and thereby reinforced the passion of their convictions. William Carlos Williams was an outsider to the conversations U.S. radicals had with their counterparts to the south. He was, at best, on the margins of conversations between U.S. and European modernists. He was neither a metropolitan nor a peripheral intellectual.

If Williams was an outsider to conversations in Spanish-speaking America, there was nonetheless a curious overlap in his way of analyzing nations and cultures with how contemporary Brazilian modernists had begun in the 1920s to redefine the relationship of Brazil to Western civilization. "Originality or death!" the poet Cassiano Ricardo declared in 1927 of the effort to discover genuinely national form.[35] Modernist writers shocked the sensibilities of Brazilian elites by celebrating racial mixture as the defining feature of the country. Oswald de Andrade's "Cannibalist Manifesto," published in 1928, declared that the country had grown out of ancient Native American rituals of eating each other. The Brazilian neither imitated nor resisted European culture, he "devoured" it, along with everything else that entered the country. "Only cannibalism unites us. Socially. Economically. Philosophically. The only law in this world. . . . I am interested only in what is not mine. The law of men. The law of the cannibal. . . . Only the pure elites were able to perform carnal cannibalism, which brings with it the highest understanding of life. . . . The carnal becomes elective and creates friendship. Affectionately, love. Speculatively, science. Deviation and transference."[36] De Andrade's arguments spread widely in Brazilian intellectual circles, particularly the point that there was nothing to learn from Europe, which should no longer be viewed by elites as a place to be imitated. Whatever useful things originated in the north, Brazilians could absorb, but they would have to transform whatever they adopted to fit the particular circumstances of life in their country. The movement led to radical reevaluation of every aspect of Brazilian history, particularly the legacies of conquest and slavery. What made Brazil a distinct society, the young modernists of the 1920s asserted, was the centrality of Native and African customs in the formation of the national culture. If Williams emphasized the walls dividing Anglo American society, his Brazilian counterparts celebrated how their nation had emerged through an underground history of exchange that colonial governors had condemned but could not frustrate.

In his masterly study of Brazilian colonial culture, *Casa Grande e Senzala* (translated into English as *The Masters and the Slaves*), published in 1933, Gilberto Freyre identified sexual desire as the force that had guided Brazilians toward a culture in which not even the brutality of slavery could entirely eradicate possibilities for mutual "enjoyment." Freyre described the Portuguese colonists, "enjoying mixing themselves with women of color right after the first contact and multiplying themselves with mixed-blood children."[37] All young men in the slave-owning class developed from infancy to adulthood always touching the bodies of those their fathers owned: "Many a Brazilian boy in the time of slavery was raised entirely by slave nannies. Rare was the child who was not nursed by a black woman. Who did not learn to talk more from the slave than from his father or mother. Who did not grow up among slave children. Playing with slave children. Learning how to be naughty with them and young black serving girls. And soon losing their virginity. Virginity of the body. Virginity of the spirit."[38] Freyre's celebration contrasts sharply with Williams's assertions about the fear of TOUCH dominant in English-speaking America. For North Americans, sexual liaisons between masters and slaves was something shameful to be condemned, for conservatives as an example of white men too often being unable to control their lusts, for progressives as a key example of how slavery had affirmed dehumanizing coercion as the center of social relations, replacing mutual affection with rape. In Brazil, emotional connections developing between people living together in isolated communities were seen as complex, nuanced, and powerful enough to bridge the abyss separating masters and slaves.

Whether slavery in Brazil was less brutal or less driven by the determination to extract as much wealth as owners could from the people they owned than in the United States is doubtful. Nonetheless, in both countries, a conviction that Brazil had developed racial relations that encouraged blacks and whites to recognize each other as fellow Brazilians took on mythic importance. For Brazilians, an imagined history of "racial democracy" identified one area of difference from the United States where Brazilians were more advanced in their thinking and practices. For critics of racial segregation in the United States, Brazil showed that racial prejudice could be overcome. The prevalence of racial mixture was a reality of modern Brazilian society, but the country was hardly a democracy, racial or otherwise. Nonetheless, the effort to imagine that Brazil, unlike the United States, had transcended race, however unreal the proposition was, helped put class relations in sharp focus, particularly after 1930 when the Great Depression plunged Brazil into deep social and political crisis.

There is no evidence of contact between Williams and writers in Brazil. Williams did not speak Portuguese, nor did he translate Portuguese-language writers at any point in his life. One might be tempted to put Williams in relationship to what Édouard Glissant called "Caribbean discourse."[39] In tracing the influence of Williams's Puerto Rican background on his work, Julio Marzán has shown a number of areas where Williams's writing resonates with elements of folk culture that he may have learned from his mother and her family.[40] If we stick to the more immediate conditions of Williams's life, there was little to no opportunity for Williams to refresh his connections with popular culture in his mother's home beyond what he heard from his relatives, who all were somewhat privileged professionals observing popular life but not directly part of it. Beyond that, Williams's fluency in Spanish allowed him to keep track of writing that most readers in the United States never saw. If his direct interactions with the Caribbean were weak, Williams nonetheless shared the belief that for Americans to discover who they might be, they had to stop turning to Europe for inspiration. In the middle of *In the American Grain*, Williams digresses from his historical framework to discuss a six-month-long stay in Europe that he and his wife made in 1923. At the climax of the chapter, Williams retells his awkward visit in Paris with Valéry Larbaud, a French poet who was also his country's leading specialist in U.S. literature and a translator into French of both classic and contemporary work.[41] Williams reported that Larbaud prattled on about how much he "liked the way the Spaniards 'moved in' to the New World, bringing *lares, penates,* and Olympus too with them. . . . I stammered a word about admiring something of the Maya culture." Williams's stammering responses to Larbaud's facile comments reflected the embarrassment of the moment. He was meeting an honored figure, an eminence who had singled Williams out as among the most interesting of the younger poets of America. Larbaud, famous in France for his interpretation of American realities, had not the slightest interest in American realities or listening to Williams's perspective on the "New World."[42]

Williams used the meeting to underscore that he had returned home from Europe convinced that there was *absolutely nothing* to be learned from the giants of European culture. Why, he asked, had Americans celebrated the freedom that they claimed came from living in a "New World" but still looked to Europe as the ultimate source of universal values? Why did they rely on patriotic platitudes instead of digging more deeply into their own history and natural environment to understand what it meant to live as a "new people"? Americans of every background did not understand that being "new" was an inescapable, fundamental existential challenge that, for the previous five hundred years, America had symbolized, not because the continent was inherently a better place but because the cruel destruction of older cultures and the chaotic emergence of new societies offered a paradigmatic illustration of people facing unimaginable challenges and developing in surprising ways, but not the only ones possible. The "New World" is also, Williams reminded his readers, the domain of infants and children; it could be seen in the experience of adolescents turning into a new generation of adults facing challenges their parents can understand only imperfectly. A "new world" appears every time people try to describe and explain experiences that do not fit what society has taught them. The constant changes at work in the natural environment throw living creatures into a "new world" that forces them to discover their potential for adaptation, an idea that Williams explored in the poems he collected into *Spring and All* published in 1923, two years before *In the American Grain*:

> They enter the new world naked,
> cold, uncertain of all
> save that they enter. All about them
> the cold, familiar wind—[43]

Williams was speaking in this passage of plants reappearing at the beginning of spring, while winter weather still blows, but the image pointed to larger processes uniting a variety of phenomena.

In any "new world," instincts do their work with less interference. In human life, new situations lead to intensified conflict between the social and the instinctual. Society responds by inventing new types of controls on people and their environments; the effort is never truly successful because leaders seldom understand what is happening and rely on imperfect lessons learned from past events with only partial relevance for current crises. The continuing tug of war between society and nature leads to violence and resentment becoming normal parts of everyday life. Official language atrophies. Williams thought poetry, meaning language that expresses immediate experience, however confused it might be, might reopen the locks Americans have created for themselves by overpowering the thinness of official language with new words that circulated widely because they refreshed people's sense of wonder and contact. Only the "stylists" of American life could reveal the promise of the new world, that is to say, any person struggling to make the forms available for expressing shared experiences say more than they usually do. A poet interested understanding the "new world" within which every generation lived should dig into and enjoy the stereotypes filling popular language and customs. The people might have no inherent wisdom, but their inventive if awkward ways of expressing themselves illuminate experiences that official culture deemed too lowly to acknowledge.

The limitations of communitarian liberalism permeated Williams's screed on American identity. Democracy, he was convinced, functioned only in self-contained and self-governing localities where citizens had to confront and "touch" each other. Analogous arguments were implicit in the writings of John Reed, Carleton Beals, Stuart Chase, and Waldo Frank. Chase and Frank saw indigenous communitarian solidarity as a seedbed for a new type of democracy that would be totally contrary to the organization of everyday life in their homeland. Reed and Beals shared this anticipation as well, but as journalists they were alert to the violence endemic in human relations and the degree to which the weakness of national structures contributed to contests quickly turning bloody. Beals in particular saw a plethora of obstacles to the successful institution of democratic practices, among them the hostility of the U.S. government and business. In any event, the kind of democracy possibly emerging out of Latin American movements for popular sovereignty had no relevance for a society as overdeveloped as the United States. The conviction that the United States was radically different from the other countries in the Pan American Union served to downplay in their writing the existential questions at the center of Williams's book. Williams's answers were confused, for he was unable to imagine a way to reconcile communitarian democracy with the national structures that had pushed the country to prosperity and world leadership. The other writers interpreting the U.S.-American relation fully shared his failure of imagination. All they hoped was that pan-Americanism potentially could moderate the U.S. relationship with the world, with luck buying time for a more radical change.

The politics of interpretation had reached a limit that no U.S. writer seemed able to transcend. Latin American writers had distinct, often more complex perspectives on the basic questions with which their U.S. counterparts struggled. The publishing business stumbled on the question of how to identify interesting writers who could capture the attention of U.S. readers. By the end of the 1920s, however, curators at museums and galleries in the United States were very excited about the work of important contemporary artists in Mexico, many of whom were working on large state-funded mural projects in easily accessible, prominent public buildings. Leaders in the U.S. art world invited artists north. Exhibitions attracted sizable numbers of the public. Interest in the Mexican mural movement led to commissions north of the border, and visual artists creating works in the United States captured the public attention. Muralists in particular operated in the United States as symbols exemplifying cultural exchange and pan-American unity. As socialists who had just witnessed one of the century's great revolutions, muralists from Mexico were convinced that a mobilized citizenry possessed the power to reconcile democracy and industrial organization. That faith no doubt played a part in their popularity in the United States, for their message, even if often critical of modern capitalism, was positive and, in Diego Rivera's case, admiring of U.S. industry. As they became more deeply embedded in U.S. cultural life, however, they confronted the political and practical limitations of the structures that allowed them to communicate with the public of another country.

Chapter 4

The Muralists Arrive

In his memoirs, Diego Rivera (1886–1957) observed that, when he received an invitation in 1927 to work in the United States, the proposition excited him because, "unlike Mexico, the United States was a truly industrial country such as I had originally envisioned as the ideal place for modern mural art."[1] Between the need to complete his murals for the Department of Public Education and overcoming unexpected difficulties in getting a visa for working in the United States, Rivera and his wife, Frida Kahlo, did not arrive in San Francisco until late 1930. He had two mural commissions, one for the California School of Fine Arts (later renamed the San Francisco Art Institute) and the second for the lunchroom at the Pacific Coast Stock Exchange. For the latter, Rivera's theme was the "bounty of California." He chose to center the mural around two figures, tennis champion and fashion designer Helen Wills Moody and a boy playing with a model airplane, respectively representing the spirit of California as a place and its future as a center of science and technology.[2] Agricultural, industrial, and mining workers surround the central figures, along with historical representations of James Marshall discovering gold in 1848 and botanical experimenter Luther Burbank examining plants. Despite vocal critics questioning why a foreign artist, well known as a communist critic of life in the United States, received the commission, response to the completed mural was enthusiastic. The review in *Arts and Architecture*, the leading journal of the visual arts on the West Coast, praised Rivera for having captured "the splendor and the opulence of California" in a way that surpassed all previous efforts.[3]

For the California School of Fine Arts (Figure 2), Rivera decided to design a mural that illustrated "how a mural is actually painted: the tiered scaffold, the assistants plastering, sketching, and painting; myself resting at midpoint; and the actual mural subject, a worker whose hand is turning a valve so placed as to seem part of a mechanism of the building. Since I was facing and leaning toward my work, the portrait of myself was a rear view with my buttocks protruding over the edge of the scaffold."[4] Some thought the design revolved around an of-

Figure 2. Diego Rivera. *The Making of a Fresco Showing the Building of the City*, 1931. Image Copyright © San Francisco Art Institute.

fensive visual joke intended as an insult to his U.S. admirers, but every controversy contributed to the success of Rivera's U.S. début in San Francisco. More
commissions followed in other parts of the country, while growing U.S. interest
in contemporary art from Mexico led to invitations for other Mexican artists to
design public art projects in locations all across the United States. José Clemente
Orozco produced large-scale murals at three U.S. schools, Pomona College, the
New School for Social Research in New York City, and Dartmouth College (Figure 3). David Alfaro Siqueiros worked in both Los Angeles and New York City.
In addition, more than a dozen other Mexican painters came to work in the

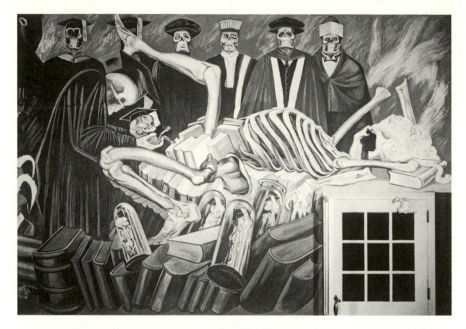

Figure 3. José Clemente Orozco, *Gods of the Modern World*, from *The Epic of American Civilization*, Baker Memorial Library, Dartmouth College, 1932–1934. Courtesy Hood Museum of Art, Dartmouth College.

United States. Some like Jean Charlot or Alfredo Ramos Martínez spent many years working and teaching in the United States. Rufino Tamayo, a figurative painter who turned to abstraction in the 1940s and 1950s, spent a semester annually teaching painting at the Dalton School in New York City, where he had a gallery that provided him regular exhibitions of his paintings.[5]

The selection and presentation of artists to a U.S. public followed patterns similar to the publication of Latin American authors in the United States. Individual patrons took up the cause of artists they particularly liked and used their connections to make the work better known. The major difference between support for literature and patronage of art was that the promoters of visual artists were wealthier and more closely integrated into networks of economic and political power. Many factors underlay the ability of visual artists to address the U.S. public more directly than writers, but among the most important reasons was the willingness of patrons with significant resources to publicize work that they had funded. Additionally, contemporary art fit more clearly into a deeper historical context as survey shows featuring masterpieces from the preconquest and colonial periods proved to be very popular with the U.S. public. In 1930 the Metropolitan Museum of Art in New York opened *Mexican Arts*, a blockbuster exhibition attracting several hundred thousand visitors to look at work largely drawn from collections owned by the Mexican government. The following year, the Museum of Modern Art (MoMA) opened the first one-artist show of Diego Rivera in the United States, publicizing the artist as a modern expression of the ancient traditions New Yorkers had delighted in the previous year. With over fifty-seven thousand visitors to the exhibition, attendance at the Rivera show surpassed the Henri Matisse exhibition earlier that year.[6] Rivera's outsized personality captured as much attention as his work. He was the first Latin American creative figure who figured out how to break down the barriers obstructing direct communication with the U.S. public.

Throughout the 1930s, Rivera continued to capture public attention. His success as a mythmaker of his country's revolution brought him to the United States, where he designed murals dramatizing his hosts' myths of science, industry, and commerce combining to revolutionize human life. Political messages consistent with his well-known radical views were muted, but not entirely absent. The juxtaposition of workers surrounding the central figures of Rivera's mural for the Pacific Coast Stock Exchange conceivably suggests that underlying U.S. prosperity remains the disjunction between labor and leisure, a contradiction demanding further revolutionary change. The sites of his murals in the United States were not as public as his work in Mexico, but given well-illustrated press reports, Rivera's U.S. murals nonetheless reached large numbers of people, particularly when his sponsors found ways to publicize their presence by focusing on Rivera's controversial views, both political and personal.[7] "I should say that his [Rivera's] predominant characteristic is a conscious showmanship," wrote San Francisco artist Rudolf Hess. "He is the P. T. Barnum of Mexico. Possessed of tremendous poise, he approaches his painting scaffold as a statesman would approach a platform from which to deliver an oration. He dominates his audience and his 'stage' with the easy confidence of an experienced actor. His oration he delivers by translating it into terms of form and color, and stating it on the walls."[8] But Frances Flynn Paine, writing in the catalogue for his 1931 one-artist show in New York, reassured visitors to the Museum of Modern Art that Rivera's oratory was about art itself primarily: "Diego's very spinal column is painting, not politics. . . . Contact with the people and the earth of his native land had brought back again his sensitivity and his joy in painting."[9]

While Rivera primarily selected paintings of Mexican peasant life for his show at MoMA, he included a new mural with a contemporary U.S. subject that he painted after he arrived in New York. The work, *Frozen Assets* (Figure 4), has three horizontal panels. A bank vault overflowing with money fills the bottom panel. A woman deposits her jewels, while other wealthy people wait in line to

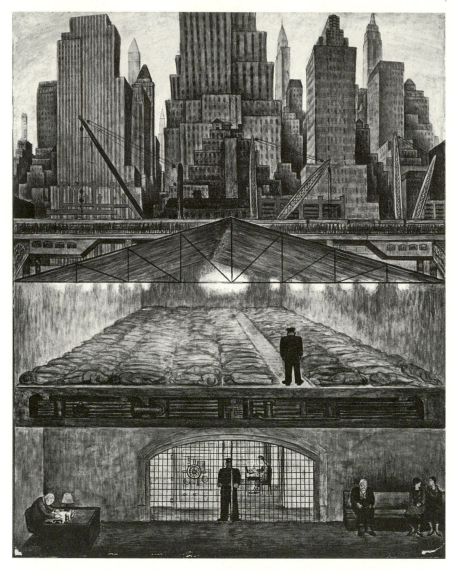

Figure 4. Diego Rivera, *Frozen Assets*, 1931. Fresco, 2.39×1.88 m. Museo
Dolores Olmedo Patino. © 2016 Banco de México Diego Rivera Frida Kahlo
Museums Trust, Mexico, D.F./ Artists Rights Society (ARS), New York.
Photo credit: Schalkwijk/ Art Resource, NY.

Figure 5. William Valentiner, Frida Kahlo, and Diego Rivera at the Detroit Institute of Arts, 1932. Courtesy The Detroit Institute of Arts/Bridgeman Images.

enter the vault. The middle panel shows the interior of a cavernous shed, a space that *Fortune* magazine identified as the Municipal Pier on East 125th Street, used as a shelter for homeless men. Dozens of sketchily painted supine figures lie on flimsy mats. A single but ominous police guard watches over them. "At the top," according to Rivera's description in his autobiography, "loomed skyscrapers like mausoleums reaching up into the cold night. Underneath them were people going home, miserably crushed together in the subway trains."[10] Unlike the California murals that celebrated the industry and wealth of the United States, *Frozen Assets* underscored a well-known, deeply controversial fact during the early years of the Great Depression—while unemployment soared, industry came to a standstill, and the incomes of those with jobs fell, as did the value of most property, the country's wealth remained intact and protected. The painting responded to the misery increasingly evident in the world's wealthiest nation.

Rivera's biggest and most successfully realized project in the United States was for the Detroit Institute of Arts (Figure 5), where he was given a large hall to create his *Detroit Industry* on all four walls. Nelson Rockefeller then commissioned Rivera's most famous U.S. mural, *Man at the Crossroads*, a celebration of the scientific, industrial, and social possibilities of modern life planned to be the centerpiece of the main lobby at the new Rockefeller Center in Manhattan. Rockefeller fired Rivera when the painter refused to remove a portrait of Lenin, the deceased but revered/reviled leader of the communist revolution in Russia. The management company in charge of renting office space in the building ordered the mural destroyed instead of sending it to the Museum of Modern Art, which wanted to acquire the work. Rivera returned to Mexico, where he created a somewhat smaller version of the mural with the title *Man, Controller of the Universe*, for permanent display at the Museo de Bellas Artes in Mexico City.

The controversy that had done so much to keep him in the spotlight finally turned against him. General Motors canceled the mural commission the company had given Rivera for its pavilion at the 1933 Century of Progress Exposition in Chicago. Other potential projects in the United States disappeared as well, except for a mural for a workers education center in New York City. Rivera's defense of his rights as an artist to express a personal vision generated widespread admiration in the United States, especially among progressive intellectuals, many of whom had been uncomfortable with the world's most famous communist artist working so intensively for the leading figures of U.S. capitalism. His reputation as Mexico's most important living artist, perhaps the country's most important artist ever, survived and grew. Museums continued to collect his work, assisted by the wealthy collectors across the country who already owned his work. Nelson Rockefeller sought to distance himself from the controversy by insisting that the management company had been solely responsible for all decisions about Rivera's mural, and that he, Rockefeller, still admired Rivera's achievement as an artist. In 1935, the Rockefeller family began donating its Mexican work to the Museum of Modern Art. The first donation was *Subway*, a painting by José Clemente Orozco (1883–1949) done in 1928 when he first arrived in the United States. Orozco found in New York City's subway system an ominous symbol for the anonymity of modern, capitalist life. In 1937, the Rockefellers gave the museum their extensive collection of Rivera paintings, drawings, and prints, while other donors donated additional work by Orozco as well as work by David Alfaro Siqueiros (1896–1974). In 1940, as part of a major exhibition of the museum's recent Latin American acquisitions, Abby Aldrich Rockefeller, Nelson Rockefeller's mother and one of the founders of MoMA, gave the museum funding to commission Orozco to do the experimental mural *Dive Bomber*, a six-panel vision of warfare in the industrial age. Orozco planned the work so that the panels could be organized in any order, with each variation revealing a new dimension to his interpretation of modern war.[11]

U.S. patronage of contemporary Mexican art expanded dramatically when Dwight Morrow, U.S. ambassador to Mexico from 1927 to 1930, and his wife, Elizabeth Cutter Morrow, developed a passion for Mexican art from all periods. Their collection, formed while Morrow worked to repair frayed relations with Mexico, became the basis for exhibits in the United States and then was donated to several museums and universities.[12] Rivera's patrons from

San Francisco, the first group in the United States that commissioned work from him, were an assortment of local artists and business leaders who had become friends while working together in local cultural organizations. Sculptor Ralph Stackpole had met Rivera when they were both students studying art in Paris in the 1910s. Stackpole and Ray Boynton, a fellow faculty member from the California School of Fine Arts who specialized in mural painting, visited Mexico in 1926 to see for themselves what Rivera and other muralists in Mexico were doing. They brought back several paintings, which wound up in the collections of William Gerstle, the owner of a shipping line, and Albert Bender, an insurance broker, both active in the San Francisco Art Association. Gerstle and Bender arrange for the first showing of Rivera's work in the United States, in the 1926 San Francisco Art Association annual exhibition. In 1935, thanks to donations from the two collectors, the largest collection of work by Rivera and other contemporary Mexican artists in the United States gave the new San Francisco Museum of Art (later renamed the San Francisco Museum of Modern Art) an international collection that extended beyond European modernism. In 1927, the two businessmen sent Rivera an invitation to come to San Francisco for the purpose of creating a public mural about life in California. This first effort failed, however, when the State Department refused to give Rivera the visa he needed to work in the United States. At the time, Rivera sat on the central committee of the Mexican Communist Party, and the United States and Mexican governments were at loggerheads over U.S. efforts to suppress the Sandinista revolution in Nicaragua, a revolution that the Coolidge administration claimed the Mexican government was sponsoring in order to undermine U.S. influence in Central America.[13]

Bender and Gerstle continued to fight the State Department decision. Timothy Pflueger offered Rivera the commission to decorate the walls of the new Pacific Coast Stock Exchange that Pflueger was designing.[14] The Californians received assistance from Dwight Morrow, a partner at J. P. Morgan before he became ambassador to Mexico. When Morrow and his wife began collecting work by contemporary artists in Mexico, they commissioned Rivera to do the murals for their vacation home in Cuernavaca. The Morrows introduced Rivera's work to their friends in eastern and midwestern business circles, and by 1930, the artist had powerful supporters from across the United States. Rivera's cause may have been helped as well by his expulsion from the Mexican Communist Party in 1929. The State Department relented and gave him a visa to work in the United States. Rivera's continuing communist sympathies and activities seemed not to disturb his U.S. patrons, though American artists associated with the U.S. Communist Party were not happy with Rivera's success, given that he had become a vocal critic of Joseph Stalin.[15]

Figure 6. David Alfaro
Siqueiros at the Experimental
Workshop, New York City,
1936. Courtesy Acervo
INBA-Sala de Arte Público
Siqueiros, Mexico City.

Unlike Rivera, David Alfaro Siqueiros arrived in California unexpected and uninvited (Figure 6). Shortly after being released from prison in Mexico, Siqueiros escaped to Los Angeles in 1932 after hearing that the government planned to arrest and imprison him again for his political activities. Alerted by painters Alfredo Ramos Martínez and Luis Arenal, the arts communities of Los Angeles welcomed Siqueiros as a hero, but he never found the kind of plutocratic patrons from the business community who sponsored Rivera's work in San Francisco. Film director Josef von Sternberg commissioned a portrait, and Jake Zeitlin hosted a small show of Siqueiros's lithographs at Zeitlin's bookstore in downtown Los Angeles, a favorite gathering spot for the city's artists, writers, musicians, and actors. A second exhibition at another local gallery followed. Millard Sheets from Chouinard Art School arranged for Siqueiros to teach a class in fresco mural technique. Siqueiros designed *Street Meeting*, a mural for the school's sculpture court, which the students in his class helped him execute.[16]

Siqueiros then received a commission to paint a mural, with the title *Tropical America*, on the side of a building above the Olvera Street plaza near the downtown business district. The location was in the center of what was then the main Mexican neighborhood in Los Angeles. Developers were turning the plaza, adjacent to the city's main railroad station, into a Mexican-themed tourist attraction. Siqueiros's mural hardly fit his patrons' commercial purposes. He organized the design around a central figure, the crucified body of an Indian, surrounded by the ruins of pre-Columbian buildings and sculptures of ancient deities. Snipers identified with revolutionary movements in Mexico and Peru took aim at an eagle hovering menacingly over the scene. The Los Angeles art community responded to the mural with enthusiasm. A huge crowd attended the unveiling, and *Tropical America* generated critical approval in both the United States and Mexico as one of the most important works ever produced by the Mexican mural movement.[17] Lorser Feitelson, a local artist who was one of the most vocal proponents of modern art in the city, exclaimed, "It had guts in it! It made everything else of the time look like candy box illustrations."[18] The developers promoting the Olvera Street Plaza project, however, did not like the work. They insisted that the painting be whitewashed so Siqueiros's disturbing images would not conflict with the festive feeling they planned for Olvera Street shops and restaurants. As the mural faced erasure, the immigration service arrested and deported Siqueiros for working in the United States without the necessary visa.[19]

The fate of Rivera's Rockefeller Center mural and Siqueiros's Olvera Plaza mural was not typical of the dozens of murals that Mexican artists created across the United States, but it underscored the problems that arose when politically charged themes collided with commercial priorities. To the degree that the art Latin Americans created could remain within a museum and gallery context, work could be fit more easily within a formalist and modernist framework even if it had overt political content. Siqueiros was the most militant of the three great Mexican muralists. He spent much of his life in prison for his political and labor activism, yet, ironically, the paintings he produced for MoMA during his stay in New York City in 1936 and 1937 may well have adhered most closely to the formalist ethos that the museum promoted, even, as in his famous painting *Collective Suicide*, when he worked with as brutal a subject as the Spanish conquest of ancient Mexico (Figure 7). The workshops Siqueiros led for younger painters were well attended and introduced many artists who would be important in the 1940s turns to abstraction to the Mexican artist's revolutionary ideas about the use of industrial materials and nontraditional techniques in painting.[20]

Alfred H. Barr, Jr. (1902–1981), began collecting Latin American art for the Museum of Modern Art in 1935, after the Rockefeller family made its first donation of contemporary Mexican work. Barr focused on a small group of artists he thought merited international attention because they were major contributors to the international modern arts movement. The collection at MoMA held only eleven artists, and four artists created over 80 percent of the work MoMA acquired—Diego Rivera, José Clemente Orozco, David Alfaro Siqueiros, "los tres grandes" of the Mexican mural movement, plus the Brazilian painter Cândido Portinari (1903–1962).[21]

Other museums, particularly the Detroit Institute of Arts and the San Francisco Museum of Art, cast a broader net across the continent looking for artists unknown in the United States. William Valentiner (1880–1958), director of the Detroit Institute of Arts, had an active program to give Latin Americans

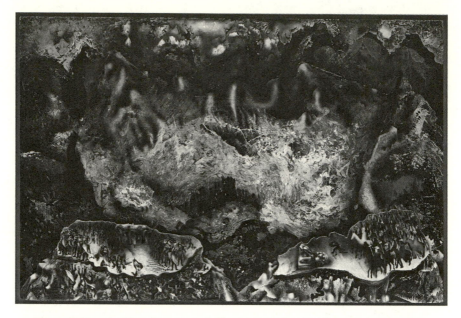

Figure 7. David Alfaro Siqueiros, *Collective Suicide*, 1936. Lacquer on wood in applied sections, 49 in. × 6 ft. (124.5 × 182.9 cm). Gift of Dr. Gregory Zilboorg. © ARS, NY. Digital image © The Museum of Modern Art/ Licensed by SCALA/ Art Resource, NY.

one-artist shows, and many of the exhibitions he or his staff organized traveled around the country to other institutions.[22] Grace McCann Morley (1900–1985), the founding director of the San Francisco Museum of Art, served as the primary museum specialist advising the U.S. government on how best to expand exhibitions of U.S. art in Latin America and Latin American art in the United States. Morley's collecting strategy, typical for regional museums with small budgets, was to focus on artists who were still establishing their reputations. The work was relatively inexpensive, and a museum could acquire a broad, representative collection showing the state of visual thought in any given period. Some artists would never realize the potential suggested in their early work, but many of the artists she collected, Morley believed, would eventually achieve great fame. The result, she observed later, was "quite a nice collection of Latin American painting, not nearly as complete as I'd like to see it, but there were acquired a good [Pedro] Figari [from Uruguay, 1861–1938] and a good [Joaquín] Torres-García [from Uruguay, 1874–1971]. We already had excellent Mexican examples."[23] Morley organized the first U.S. one-artist exhibition of the Argentinean painter Emilio Pettoruti (1892–1971), who she thought was the single most important pioneer of modernism in South America. The exhibit led her into an unpleasant dispute with Barr, who dismissed Pettoruti as an untalented imitator of French neocubism. Barr would not allow the Museum of Modern Art to accept the exhibit. Morley asked René d'Harnoncourt, a MoMA curator who disagreed with the decision, to get Barr to relent. D'Harnoncourt could not convince his boss to change his mind, but he secured the National Academy of Design as the New York host for Pettoruti's first show in the United States. Pettoruti was insulted, and so was Morley, as MoMA's refusal of the show pegged the Argentinean artist as of inferior quality.[24]

Morley preferred art that expressed "a locality," as she put it, art that challenged the identification of great art with a main line of European masterpieces that American artists were then encouraged to imitate.[25] Latin American art supported her conception of art as innate problem-solving activity that all humans shared to greater or lesser degree. The most successful art expressed most clearly the unique characteristics of how humans responded to particular natural and social environments. Morley's interest in contemporary Latin American art complemented her commitment to regionalist art in the United States. Across the western hemisphere, artists were exploring how to represent the specifics of local experience without being beholden to European models. Her conception of pan-Americanism was consistent with a type of U.S. nationalism that stressed that popular democracy was rooted in local traditions. But even though the desire to achieve a genuinely national art might be similar, because U.S. art was not known in Latin America at all, the work that Latin American artists produced looked startlingly different. Thus expanded exhibition of art from other American countries was valuable to artists and art lovers in the United States because the work offered additional models for how to escape the domination of European modernism.

Morley took a leadership role in promoting Latin American art because of her personal positions on the politics of modern art, but her ability to shape what Americans saw reflected the expanding role the federal government played in cultural exchange after 1938, a role that allowed greater voice for curators whose perspectives differed from those of Alfred Barr. Nonetheless, selection of artists to present to the U.S. public relied on personal, often idiosyncratic enthusiasms of collectors, curators, and artists. Painter Rockwell Kent (1882–1971) was the first North American who wanted to bring the work of Brazilian painter Cândido Portinari to the United States. Kent was a leading figure in the American scene movement and a successful commercial illustrator, working in both advertising and book illustration. His talents as a writer and speaker made him a much sought after public figure with strongly expressed opinions about culture and politics. When he first traveled to Brazil in November 1937, he arrived not as an artist, but as a left-wing activist leading a delegation that the

National Committee for People's Rights and the Joint Committee for the Defense of the Brazilian People sent to report on the recent coup and its effects on trade unions and communist activists. Kent's friendship with Osvaldo Aranha, the Brazilian ambassador to the United States, provided him an introduction into the highest circles of Brazilian society and government that most communists lacked, but the secret police still briefly arrested him shortly after his arrival. Kent viewed the arrest as insignificant, given that the police themselves knew that Kent's international status shielded him from the reprisals that other procommunist foreign visitors experienced. The police confiscated his papers, but otherwise wished to assure him that they only wanted to help him learn more about the current state of affairs in Brazil. Kent reported that he immediately provided his interrogators with a list of Brazilian political prisoners whom he wished to interview; at the top of the list was Luiz Carlos Prestes, the leader of the Brazilian Communist Party. Kent then invited the police officers out for a drink. Aside from the largely comical account of his encounter with the Brazilian police, Kent's report contained little about the political situation in Brazil beyond what an assiduous reader could learn from a careful reading of English-language newspapers and magazines.[26]

Kent had no abilities in Portuguese, and he relied on the English-speaking Brazilians he met while in Rio de Janeiro to provide him the information he needed for his political report. Among them was the Brazilian painter Cândido Portinari, and the two artists developed a professional friendship. Both were left militants, and their ideological bonds augmented appreciation for the work the other was doing.[27] Kent returned home with the idea of promoting Portinari's work in the United States, a project that Gustavo Campanema, the Brazilian minister of education, actively encouraged, providing Kent with high-quality photographs of murals Portinari had done for the new ministry building. The minister offered to pay for shipping a selection of Portinari's paintings and drawings if Kent could arrange an exhibition.[28] Given Kent's prominence at the time as one of the country's most highly regarded painters and illustrators, he was in an excellent position to promote his friend.[29]

Portinari quickly achieved unusual visibility in the U.S. art world. Museums across the country clamored for exhibitions of his work and began purchasing his paintings, prints, and drawings. He had been poor, living in humble circumstances, supported by occasional commissions to do murals for one Brazilian government agency or another, in addition to portraits he did for Brazilian business and cultural leaders. His sales to the United States brought a new, elevated level of income that was unusual for most Brazilian artists, even those who were much older. As he explained to Kent, he had a large extended family still living in the coffee region of the state of São Paulo that depended on him for help, and the money coming to him from the United States had paid for several opera-

tions, dental work, school expenses, and home repairs that his relatives otherwise would have been unable to afford.[30]

Portinari's success coincided with the U.S. federal government's assuming a
greater role in coordinating and promoting cultural exchange. Building a strategic alliance with Brazil was central to Roosevelt administration plans to unify the
Pan American Union into an alliance against Nazi Germany. Yet global politics
alone cannot explain Portinari's stunning, if temporary achievement. His paintings had to speak to critics, curators, and collectors. Their concern was Portinari's
contribution to the modern movement in painting. They had to believe that he
used image, line, and color to say something unusually compelling about the
human condition as Brazilians experienced it. His national way of looking could
be valued because he reinforced humanist traditions that art revealed fundamental truths about humanity's place in the world and that a world united under liberal values could build a common culture that nonetheless respected local
idiosyncrasies as expressions of underlying universal principles. Portinari's technical but experimental sophistication, as well as his abundant, if ironic references
to Italian Renaissance old masters—precisely what marked him as a modernist
working in a distinct national idiom—established him as an emerging artist of
special interest.[31] None of his sponsors could or would have supported him as pas-
sionately as they did for geopolitical reasons. Nor did Rockwell Kent work assidu-
ously on Portinari's behalf solely because they were comrades in arms enlisted in
the fight for a global communist society. In the letters they sent each other, Kent
and Portinari primarily explored their shared ideas about art, not politics. As we
shall see, Kent the consummate public intellectual was particularly adept in introducing Portinari to Americans by stressing the Brazilian's humanist and modernist credentials, helping establish Portinari's value as a symbol for distinctively U.S.
conceptions of a global liberal society. Kent knew as well that the people who
could make things happen had to be centrally placed in the country's major cultural institutions, and only appeals to Portinari's potential contribution to a liberal humanist heritage would move them to act on the Brazilian's behalf.

On the basis of Kent's strong recommendation, Florence Horn, art critic for
Fortune magazine, visited Portinari during her tour of South America in 1938.
She decided to write about him and reproduced two Portinari paintings for an
article in what was then the leading business magazine in the United States.[32]
Alfred Barr came to Horn's offices to look at three paintings by Portinari she
had brought back to the United States in addition to photographs of other work
still in Brazil. Barr decided to buy a painting, *Morro*, a large oil canvas depict-
ing a favela on the hills above Rio de Janeiro, the first of numerous MoMA acquisitions (Figure 8). Horn wrote Portinari that he should arrange a visit to the
United States as soon as he could to take advantage of Barr's interest.[33]

Figure 8. Cândido Portinari, *Morro*, 1933. Oil on canvas, 44 7/8×57 3/8 in. (114×145.7 cm). Abby Aldrich Rockefeller Fund. Digital image © The Museum of Modern Art/ Licensed by SCALA/ Art Resource, NY. Right to reproduce kindly provided by João Candido Portinari.

Portinari did not yet have money for what was at the time a prohibitively expensive journey for most Brazilians. He did not disappear from sight, because the Brazilian government chose Portinari to create the murals for the Brazilian pavilion at the 1939 New York World's Fair. Horn and others in the press singled out Portinari's work in the pavilion as the single most interesting contribution to the fair's visual art program. In 1940, Portinari contributed thirty-five works to the second Latin American Exhibition of Fine Arts held at the Riverside Museum in New York City. Critical response to the exhibit once again identified Portinari as the most interesting artist in the show. Doris Brian, writing in the *Art News*, claimed that Portinari's work "eclipsed" even the paintings that the Mexican masters had contributed.[34] Portinari's work was strong, but also new and different, while the work of Rivera, Orozco, and other Mexican artists was already well known. That Portinari could be related to surrealism helped critics write about his work, as was his obvious debt to Pablo Picasso and to nineteenth-century caricaturists like Honoré Daumier. Yet he still could be seen as an American artist innovating new ways of thinking about painting that grew out of his country's particularities.

As a result of the Riverside Museum show, Portinari received requests to contribute work to two shows surveying contemporary Latin American art organized in Washington and New York City. Growing interest led to a single-artist show at the Museum of Modern Art in 1940, as well as shows in commercial art galleries. Milton Brown, reviewing the MoMA show for *Parnassus*, observed that the show elevated the stakes: "It is no longer a question of whether Candido Portinari is a good painter, but whether Portinari of Brazil is a great modern artist." Brown understood that Portinari's exhibit had everything to do with regional politics, but in this case, Brown argued, geopolitical stratagem introduced into the United States painters like Portinari who were exceptionally good and whose work art lovers should know even if the United States did not need to build a hemispheric alliance against Germany.[35]

More single-artist shows followed in Detroit, Pittsburgh, Minneapolis, Chicago, Saint Louis, San Francisco, and a dozen other cities, while Portinari's work became virtually a requirement for any survey of contemporary Latin American painting exhibited in the United States. Howard University organized an exhibition because Alonzo Aden, the curator of the university's art gallery, was particularly impressed by Portinari's renditions of Afro-Brazilian life.[36] That the United States had much to learn from Brazil on the organization of racial relations increasingly became an important element in Brazilian-U.S. cultural relations, and Portinari's paintings were taken as evidence of the recognition that Afro-Brazilian labor had built and continued to build the country.

Articles on Portinari and his work appeared in several dozen newspapers and magazines, going well beyond art magazines with major articles in *Fortune*, *Time*, *Harper's*, the *New York Times*, and the *Washington Post*. The MoMA show allowed Portinari to come to the United States, along with his wife and son and one hundred additional canvases (Figure 9). He had a modest but wry sense of humor that delighted the journalists assigned to write about him. On arriving in New York City, he told the reporter for the *New York Herald Tribune* that he was surprised by how quiet and orderly the world's largest city was. "Everyone told me it would be so noisy you couldn't hear yourself think," he said. He liked cafeterias because they were efficient and beautiful, and the food in the United States was tasty and well prepared.[37]

Portinari was the son of Italian immigrants who worked as laborers on coffee farms in the state of São Paulo. Portinari, unlike the Mexican muralists, had a personal story that appealed to themes of upward mobility due to personal discipline, themes that were meaningful to readers in the United States. Florence Horn wrote of his family background that his parents "as coffee workers . . .

Figure 9. Cândido Portinari in New York City with his son, 1940 ("Brazilian Artist Is Here for His One-Man Show," *New York Herald Tribune* 18 September 1940, p. 16). Courtesy New York Public Library, General Research Division, Astor, Lenox and Tilden Foundations. Right to reproduce kindly provided by João Candido Portinari.

were assigned by the plantation owner a certain number of coffee trees to tend for a whole year. The number of trees depended on the size of the family and the ages of the children. In return for keeping the earth clean around the trees and harvesting the berries they got a small primitive dwelling, credit at the plantation store and, at harvest time, some cash." His parents were illiterate, and schooling for working-class children in rural São Paulo was "irregular and brief." When he was eight years old, an itinerant painter arrived in his small town to decorate the local church. The boy apprenticed himself to the painter and began learning his craft. Local community leaders recognized that the child had talent and provided him with the supplies he needed to continue working. When Portinari turned fifteen, he left home to study at the National School of Fine Arts in Rio de Janeiro. He worked his way through school with a job at a restaurant doing home delivery of meals that customers had ordered. By the time he turned twenty, he was winning prizes in competitions, and eventually a traveling fellowship allowed him to study in France.[38]

That he was a communist, to the degree that it was mentioned, seemed only natural given his background and the inequality and the depth of poverty throughout Brazil. He downplayed his political ideas while in the United States. "Politics is always changing," he told reporters, "but art remains the same. If we build our ties on art, we build on a firm foundation."[39] His images of everyday life in Brazil, however, eschewed realism for a colorful style that echoed Daumier and Francisco de Goya at times, Italian old masters at other times, while often referencing surrealism and other contemporary movements. The union of classical and contemporary in order to express social reality struck a deep chord with U.S. critics. His politics were never hidden, but his work seemed more motivated by humor than by revolutionary anger. Horn observed that, when he spoke of the long, hard path behind him, Portinari "never makes himself pitiful. He is wryly humorous about his own life, but out of the hard poverty have come Portinari's warm interest in and sympathy for the very people from which he came . . . apparent in his pictures."[40]

In 1940, the University of Chicago Press released a book on Portinari and his work with an introduction by Rockwell Kent.[41] The book repeated the by then well known biographical details that made the artist's life so unusual. "A sweet story," Rockwell Kent called it, "the rise of Portinari from the coffee plantations of Brazil. It is a story of the devotion, confidence, and self-sacrifice of parents. Of a youth's adventuring into the great world. Of persistence against the stress of poverty, of unremitting work, of talent, of strong will."[42] Portinari's paintings impressed most who saw them, Kent insisted, because the man who made them had overcome his many handicaps to see "the beauty of life and the essential goodness of mankind." His work expressed the life of everyday

Brazilians, a life he had shared in every way. Kent concluded that Portinari's journey reflected a larger, more important story of common working people around the world discovering their innate talents. This, Kent intoned, was part of a revolution that had begun with "our North American Declaration of Independence." Portinari's art was "concerned with people" because it came from the life of the people. As a result there was nothing abstract in the images. His work affirmed "decent Christian hopes for peace on earth," hopes that would overcome the "barriers and smoke screens to understanding, which those *things*—the nations, *interests*, war—erect."[43]

Perhaps the most surprising aspect of Portinari's U.S. career was how easily Americans incorporated him into their own national patriotic project. His work seemed to affirm the global aspiration for what President Franklin D. Roosevelt called the Four Freedoms: freedom of speech, freedom of worship, freedom from want, freedom from fear—a vision that equated U.S. liberal institutions with popular desires in poor countries like Brazil for prosperity, democracy, and peace.[44] Norman Rockwell illustrated Roosevelt's freedoms in four paintings published on the covers of successive issues of the *Saturday Evening Post*.[45] Many other artists took up the theme of the four freedoms in the early 1940s, either through personal enthusiasm for Roosevelt's vision of the postwar world or as a result of commissions. Additionally, there needed to be images that showed that the values Roosevelt promoted spoke to universal human aspirations found in every country. Archibald MacLeish, a poet and playwright whom President Roosevelt asked to serve as Librarian of Congress through the war crisis, wrote Portinari at the end of 1940 hoping that the artist would agree to do four murals for the Hispanic Reading Room at the library.[46] The Brazilian government contributed the commission for Portinari's work, while the U.S. government paid for expenses, including his travel to the United States to finish the work in site. The murals opened to the public in January 1942, a month after the Japanese attack on Pearl Harbor, and the press discussed Portinari's work in the context of a common American heritage that Brazil and the United States shared, a heritage that was taken to mean that the two nations would stand together during the global crisis. The patriotic fervor that Americans could project onto Portinari's otherwise very Brazilian images contributed to his reputation as one of the most important contemporary artists the general public should know.[47]

Portinari said nothing that encouraged this reading of his work. Nor did the paintings for the Library of Congress have content that related directly to the United States. The commission from MacLeish specified that the murals should present historical scenes that could have occurred anywhere in Latin America: the first encounters of Spanish or Portuguese sailors with the tropical forest, Catholic missionaries working with indigenous peoples, the discovery of gold. The overall narrative could apply to the French and English conquest of North America as well, but the imagery was supposed to express the history of the lands invaded by the Spanish and Portuguese. Portinari's images underscore the racial variety of his America. Blacks are as prominent as whites, and the encounter with Native Americans points to the American nations as a synthesis of Europeans, Africans, and the indigenous peoples of the hemisphere. In discussing the murals, Portinari insisted that art was an independent visual experience and not a way of expressing political ideas. He was all in favor of the American countries being "good neighbors," but that was a matter unrelated to the murals.[48] He said similar things about his murals for Brazilian government buildings. His murals spoke for themselves and had nothing to do one way or another with the policies of the government that had hired him, nor with his own politics as an activist who twice ran for the Brazilian Congress on the Communist Party ticket. Even so, his success in the United States was inseparable from the federal government's responding to the increasing likelihood of a new world war by actively seeking to expand the cultural integration of the western hemisphere, in hopes that "good neighbors" in the New World would stand firmly together to repel aggressors from the Old World.

Chapter 5

Responding to Global Crisis

German intervention in the Spanish Civil War in 1936 and Japan's invasion of China in 1937 signaled that a second world war was imminent. The leading figures in Franklin Delano Roosevelt's administration understood that the United States would be drawn into the war and likely play a decisive role in its outcome. Public opinion, however, remained adamantly opposed to involvement, and Congress responded to the international threat by cutting military spending and passing legislation barring the U.S. government and private citizens from assisting any belligerent. In July 1938, the State Department created a Division of Cultural Relations, the primary purpose of which was not to influence public opinion abroad but to change domestic public opinion along the lines that Elihu Root had earlier warned were necessary if the United States were to become a world power.[1] Richard Pattee, a professor of Latin American history at the University of Puerto Rico, who left his home institution to serve in Washington as deputy chief of the new division, insisted, "Not only must channels be opened for the free flow of our ideas and cultural production to other countries, but, just as important, channels must also be opened for the flow of cultural production from other countries to the United States. Intellectual co-operation would be a vain and meaningless term if only a unilateral policy were carried out."[2]

Born in Arizona in 1906, Pattee studied at the University of Arizona and the Catholic University of America, where he taught after leaving his State Department post in 1945. In his writings on colonial-era Ecuador, Haiti, and Brazil, Pattee focused on the role of the Catholic Church in fostering the development of new societies with distinctive cultures. He was a friend of the Cuban anthropologist Fernando Ortiz and influenced by Ortiz's concept of "transculturation," through which Ortiz argued that American national cultures developed as initially diasporic cultures adapted to the topography and climate of their new homes. Ortiz's theories provided a template for thinking about how to support the future of pan-American culture. The key challenge was breaking open the intellectual isolation of the United States. In a memo written in January 1939,

Pattee argued that the single most important objective of the division was to bring Latin American intellectuals to the United States and support their developing long-term personal friendships and institutional connections.[3] State Department assistance should focus on introducing Latin American authors into the U.S. national book and magazine markets, and when possible into Hollywood. Bringing Latin American literature and journalism to the attention of the U.S. public was essential given that many of the histories of the region available in English focused on government leaders and formal constitutional arrangements without consideration of everyday lived experience. Stereotypes of every kind prevailed, and would continue to do so as long as readers in the United States had no way of comparing what U.S. writers produced about Latin America with what their counterparts in other American nations were doing. In a review of a book by a Haitian historian published as Pattee assumed his role in developing cultural exchange programs between the United States and the other members of the Pan American Union, he asserted that U.S. writers on Latin America too often highlighted the "spectacular and the grotesque" to such an extent that countries like Haiti appeared to be "little else than a chamber of horrors." Pattee observed that "no people could live for any length of time at a level of psychic tension" attributed to many communities in Latin America. Understanding the opinions of Latin Americans, Pattee declared, was more important to the United States, as it developed a new relationship with the region, than publishing yet more suppositions from North American writers about "what Latin America is."[4] The new division set out to identify contemporary Latin American authors who might be of interest to U.S. readers.[5]

Federalization of cultural exchange was not to substitute for private action. Philanthropies and educational institutions provided 95 percent of the funding for exchange programs. The office took responsibility for coordinating activities, helping private groups avoid duplicate efforts and reach a broader audience. For example, with assistance from the new division, the federal Office of Education, the National Education Association, and the Heath publishing firm prepared a series of books, New World Neighbors, for use by older primary-school children to learn about the history and geography of other American nations. The National Council of Teachers of English prepared curriculum guides for teaching Latin American literature in English translation for primary and secondary courses.[6] Waldo Frank's edition of Argentinean short fiction was strongly recommended, as was Ricardo Güiraldes's *Don Segundo Sombra/ Shadow on the Pampas*.

Following the goals Pattee had outlined, the division also worked to increase the number of Latin American intellectuals and artists visiting the United States and to assure that they had greater public visibility during their stay. Often, this involved collaborating with other government agencies charged with promoting the president's pan-American objectives. The division organized conferences that brought together publishers, museum directors, university administrators, writers, and artists to discuss how to develop more coordinated exchange programs.[7] With the aid of Pattee's cultural division, enthusiasts for the pan-American cause increased their efforts in hopes that federal assistance would overcome the obstacles that had limited what cultural exchange could do.

With the outbreak of war in Europe in September 1939, the primary goal of U.S. policy shifted to building support, domestically as well as internationally, for an international alliance to oppose extension of the war into the western hemisphere. This policy increasingly rested on overt opposition to dictatorship and racism, with the goal of the U.S. government to put itself at the forefront of an international alliance distinct from the belligerents but also from the other major neutral country, the Soviet Union. Official U.S. policy had two aspects, potentially contradictory depending on how the global conflict unfolded. The first was to unite the western hemisphere under U.S. leadership to create a united front that could inhibit incursion from Germany or its allies. That required doubling down on pan-Americanism as the logical extension of the national principles of each nation and emphasizing what the United States shared with its American neighbors. The second aspect involved laying the foundations for a new international system consistent with U.S. republican principles, a goal that would ultimately culminate in the formation of the United Nations as a permanent organization.[8] The first aspect provided the foundation of strength for the United States to extend its power around the world, while establishing the perimeters of what the United States considered its zone of influence, a semicolonial region where U.S. dominance was undisputed, in case German victory over Britain (and after the summer of 1941, Russia) could not be prevented.

Before U.S. entry into the war and then during the first two years of U.S. participation, outcomes remained a matter of conjecture, and the two aspects of U.S. policy overlapped closely. As long as the outcome of the war remained unsure, retreat into a hemispheric security zone under unquestionable U.S. leadership remained an ever-present option. German, Italian, and Japanese influence had to be ejected, while the influence of the British and French was to be reduced. A robust "American" identity was an essential ingredient, in which the "New World" experience was to be foregrounded as the foundation for a closely linked community.

The possibility of German victory seemed highest in June 1940 when German forces quickly defeated and occupied France. Throughout Latin America, some intellectuals, along with leaders in business, government, and society, supported Germany. In any event, accepting the new order the Nazis were creating seemed to many leaders a necessity to preserve access to European markets. They were confident that the United States would eventually arrive at its own accommodation with Germany, and, above all, U.S. leaders had neither the resources nor the will to defend the entire hemisphere.[9] For liberals, as well as leftists like Diego Rivera, a world organized on German principles was a nightmare. Jorge Luis Borges, reviewing a new book of Ellery Queen detective stories, commented, "I am writing in July 1940; each morning reality seems more like a nightmare. All I can do is read pages that have no connection to that reality [such as] the frivolous problems that Queen poses."[10] Cultural exchange programs that the United States had already launched were to discover many men and women ready, even eager, to work closely with the United States.

Victoria Ocampo and the writers working with her on the Argentinean literary journal *Sur* had long avoided political topics, in part because Ocampo's interests were aesthetic, in part because appearing to be socially irrelevant avoided problems with the conservative, authoritarian-tending government in Argentina. A review of *Sur* issues published in the second half of 1940 reveals how an influential group of liberal intellectuals responded to the collapse of France, the country whose culture had guided their personal formation, by turning to the United States. In the first issue that appeared after the German occupation of France, Benjamin Fondane, a Franco-Romanian poet who had been a frequent contributor through the 1930s, sent a reflection from his hiding place in the south of France on the necessity of intellectuals to struggle against confusing appearances with reality. He insisted that even with the swastika flying over Paris, German triumph in the war was not inevitable if intellectuals around the world continued to believe in humanity's unlimited potential to resist. Fondane acknowledged that German power was a fact: "I am *forced* to accept it. But nobody, ever, will be able to *persuade* me that this fact has the dignity of what we call the truth."[11] The refusal to obey apparent facts, Fondane continued, was the foundation of dignity.

For many Latin American intellectuals in 1940, the turn to the United States was necessary as the first practical step in asserting that Germany was not invincible. Freedom required imagination, as always, and after June 1940, the imagination of the United States as a society capable of defeating fascism demanded an act of faith. The United States, logically speaking, was a bastion of freedom only to the degree that people around the world perceived its ideal side as more fundamental than the country's messy, contradictory aspects. Ocampo insisted on this point in her review of the film adaptation of *The Grapes of Wrath*, released in Buenos Aires in the summer of 1940. The film itself became, in her interpretation, a symbol of the spiritual leap that the collapse of France demanded from her and her friends. "What it gives us," Ocampo concluded, "merits more than admiration for its director John Ford and his collaborators (cinematography and acting magnificent at moments, never less than good). It awakens a deeply moving respect for a nation sufficiently strong, free, and secure in itself to permit this film to be shown in its own territory and sent overseas, such a sad and humiliating social document, humiliating for the systems (or the men?) who are not yet ready to correct such injustice. . . . What nation, other than a great democratic nation, would allow the exhibition of a *mea culpa* like *The Grapes of Wrath*?" Ocampo concluded with a meditation on the benevolence and generosity in the United States that she and other foreigners traveling there noticed. No doubt, she thought, episodes in the film exaggerated the levels of poverty and violence in the country by concentrating them into an epic story. Paying attention and publicizing the miseries and horrors affecting others less fortunate reflected a deep-set generosity, especially when so many people, among them those with the power to change society, prefer to keep such facts hidden. The new masters of Europe celebrated their culture and their greatness. The United States had become the last line of defense because its culture, with all the flaws of everyday life in any society, celebrated the ability to see past the logic of the present. Its creative figures reaffirmed that the greatest power on earth retained imaginative ability to see alternatives and to act on them.[12]

Richard Pattee's Division of Cultural Relations focused its programs on responding to the distress that the collapse of France caused among Latin American intellectuals. Archibald MacLeish, in his capacity as librarian of Congress from 1939, worked closely with the division to reach out to intellectuals in other American nations. In February 1940, he published a brief article, "The Art of the Good Neighbor,"[13] which was translated and published in literary and cultural periodicals around the western hemisphere. MacLeish's article began with an apology for using the term "cultural relations," which he admitted was a bureaucratic policy most serious thinkers disliked, especially those who assumed that cultural exchange was another ploy for assuring U.S. domination of their countries. He acknowledged that the U.S. search for resources and markets had led to exploitation, but he insisted that, despite this history, the current battle over Latin America was over something larger than markets. German propaganda disseminated around the world focused on the cultural deficits of the United States, not on economic issues. It was easy to say that the United States and Germany were fighting over control of natural resources both nations needed, and for Latin Americans it did not matter which country prevailed. He acknowledged that some powerful political forces across the hemisphere openly advocated alliance with Germany as a way of escaping U.S. hegemony. MacLeish countered ideas that the global conflict was one more instance of interimperial competition with a few images that he knew would resonate with the majority of intellectuals: "Events in distant parts suggested that the purposes of those who bombed the Spanish towns and shot the Czechoslovak students were not economic purposes alone but purposes of a more ambitious character. What was under attack was not merely the present title to the riches of the world. What was under attack was the entire moral and intellectual and artistic order which, by accident or otherwise, was associated with that title. Which meant, first, that the flank attack on the culture of the North Atlantic democracies in Latin America was perhaps not a flank attack at all but the principal engagement."[14]

To declare that culture was the leading element of any society, the ultimate standard available to judge a nation, flattered the ambitions and the self-image of his readers, divided in ideology, but united around a conviction that humanist values were necessary for any decent life, whether individual or collective. MacLeish asserted that for most citizens of the United States, the current war, in which they were still officially neutral, could no longer be seen as interimperial competition between England and Germany. If the question was which European country exploited the people of India or dominated Africa, the only sensible policy was to stay out of a conflict that could bring no good to the world. However, MacLeish insisted, which country triumphed could determine whether Thomas Mann's books were taken out of American libraries and burned, whether Shostakovich's music would be censored as it was in Moscow, whether poets would be executed in New York as Federico García Lorca had been in Spain, or whether the natural sciences would have to be organized in the western hemisphere along the same party-line criteria required in Siberia. The threat MacLeish invoked came from left and right, both challenging the commitment to finding truth through investigation and open debate that, MacLeish argued, defined the humanist tradition he shared with his readers.

Turning to Good Neighbor Policy programs, MacLeish challenged his readers to find evidence that cultural exchange was a form of "missionary work" designed to enlighten backward peoples south of the border to the glories of U.S. civilization. The goal of programs that introduced U.S. art, music, and literature to Latin Americans was simply, he insisted, to show the small minority of critics, artists, and professions "with a refined critical sense" that there was serious culture in the United States and that much of it was worthy of admiration and not to be confused with the popular fiction and Hollywood movies that Latin Americans consumed in large quantities. Most Latin American intellectuals, MacLeish observed, knew U.S. culture only to the degree that French intellectuals had commented on it. As a result, Latin Americans knew nothing of contemporary concert music in the United States or of contemporary painting and sculpture.

They knew a bit more but still very little of U.S. novels beyond detective fiction. The only poets known were Walt Whitman and Edgar Allan Poe.

Many of MacLeish's claims were simply not correct. The same literary magazines in which MacLeish's appeal was published frequently ran reviews of U.S. fiction and poetry, including work that was not translated into Spanish or Portuguese. Latin American presses had increased translation of U.S. authors they thought would be of interest to middle-class readers, while books analyzing life in the United States were common. If translated fiction tended to follow U.S. best-seller lists, preferences for which poets to translate diverged dramatically from those of most U.S. literary editors. Langston Hughes was the U.S. poet most widely translated in Latin America during the 1930s, well before critics in the United States outside the African American community recognized the importance of his work. In the second issue of *Sur*, Ocampo had published three poems by Hughes translated by Jorge Luis Borges.[15] The claim that Latin Americans were ignorant of North American culture was a truism that no doubt appealed to the vanity of those who knew a little and took an interest in new developments to the north. In that way, flirtation with pan-Americanism could become a sign of distinction.

As MacLeish's article made its way around Latin American journals, the Division of Cultural Relations provided help for groups interested in hosting public forums on inter-American relations. For example the *Sur* editorial board sponsored a public debate in Buenos Aires in August 1940 on what the collapse of France meant for pan-American unity. Sociologist Carlos Alberto Erro chaired the discussion, which featured three principal speakers: Edith Helman, professor of art history at Simmons College in Boston, a specialist on Goya but at the time working on a book on colonial Peruvian art; Germán Arciniegas, a Colombian historian who had served his country as minister of education and was a vocal advocate for more robust pan-American unity; and Pedro Henríquez Ureña, a literary historian and critic, originally from the Dominican Republic, who had been teaching at the University of La Plata in Argentina for the previous decade.[16] Henríquez Ureña had earned his Ph.D. at the University of Minnesota. In addition to writing on Latin American literature, he was the foremost writer on U.S. literature working in the Spanish language.

Helman began the program with vigorous criticism of U.S. corporations operating in Latin America that failed to treat their workers with dignity. She spoke of conditions she had seen at U.S.-owned mines in Peru that shocked her. She noted that U.S. companies failed to act decently primarily because corrupt national leaders did not enforce the country's laws. Economic exchange brought out the worst sides of both the United States and Latin America. Invoking a platitude that by 1940 already had a long history, she insisted that intellectual and cultural pan-Americanism was needed to create a hemispheric public able to insist on civic rights, social justice, and democratic government in all American nations. Helman wanted to see many more students and professors from Latin America spending time in the United States, and she stressed that participation had to expand beyond the capital cities to include talented people from the interior. She spoke about the difficulty in many countries of writers getting anything published, and she hoped that the Pan American Union would make it a priority to provide support for increased publication opportunities.

Arciniegas returned to a theme on which he had already written extensively. He thought many writers exaggerated the distinctions between North and South. The most important division within the Americas crossed all the linguistic zones. Major cities like Boston, New York, Havana, Rio de Janeiro, and Buenos Aires, located on the Atlantic coast, were oriented primarily to Europe, while to the west the centers of American life had developed a more "autochthonous culture." English-speaking California shared Colombia's isolation from the Eurocentric Atlantic, but neither California nor Colombia were for that reason less cosmopolitan. Only after he began traveling across the United States was he able to discover that most of the country had developed, like his own Colombia, on its own terms. Between New York and San Francisco, there were greater differences in outlook than between New York and Buenos Aires. He wanted pan-American exchange to allow others like him to know the United States that was not simply an extension of Europe but nonetheless was not "barbaric." Travelers from the United States to Latin America also needed to get far beyond the capital cities. Exchange would fail if it united only the most privileged sectors. Arciniegas's most important point was one that he had made many times since the outbreak of the war in Europe. Europeans, he reiterated, believed that all American countries were primitive and dismissed evidence that they could function as modern nations. This prejudice governed how they viewed the United States as well, whose undeniable wealth offended most European intellectuals. Reviewing the histories of the two continents, he argued that fascism and war were direct products of a history of colonialism. The American nations emerged in resistance to colonial rule. They had been forced, despite the poverty of their circumstances, to develop principles of universal justice. All the American nations, the United States included, had trouble implementing those principles, but they could not repudiate them as the fascists in Europe had for do so would repudiate as well the independence movements that had brought American nations into being as modern societies. Whether prepared for the challenge or not, the Americas had become the bastion from which a war for democracy and liberty could be waged in Europe and Asia. He concluded, "For the first time, the voices of the poor of all races, white and colored, are being heard in all their intensity."[17]

The discussion period after the presentations focused first on whether the U.S. Good Neighbor Policy would become so deeply rooted that it would last beyond the present war crisis. The U.S. response to Mexico's nationalizing its petroleum industry in 1938 struck the audience as an excellent sign that a potentially profound and positive change was under way. The *Sur* roundtable in Buenos Aires and other forums led to the formation of Acción Argentina, a committee chaired by Victoria Ocampo that worked with the newly formed U.S. agency, the Office of Inter-American Affairs, to promote U.S.-Argentinean cooperation and to combat Nazi and fascist influence.[18] The committee produced radio shows that were among the most widely popular programming in the country. When the United States became a full participant in the war in December 1941, *Sur* published a special issue, "Guerra en América" ("War in America"), in which the editorial board declared its full support for the U.S. war effort and for pan-Americanism.[19]

The Argentinean government was deeply divided over how to respond to the European war, and the government resisted U.S. pressure to fall in line with its pan-American strategy. When the United States entered the war, Argentinean leaders began censoring U.S.-funded radio programming, eventually driving it off the air. In August 1942, when Brazil declared war on Germany, the Argentinean government claimed that the United States and Brazil were planning to invade Argentina. *Sur* responded by publishing, in its September 1942 issue, the full text of Brazilian president Getúlio Vargas's speech announcing his country's entry into war. Vargas had stressed the need for increased cooperation between all American countries, particularly between Brazil and Argentina, which he described as naturally friendly neighbors separated temporarily by unfounded suspicions. Later that year, when Waldo Frank toured South America to build support for the war effort, five men broke into the apartment where Frank was staying in Buenos Aires. Shouting anti-Semitic slurs, the intruders beat him severely, but fled when people in neighboring apartments heard screaming and came to Frank's assistance. Frank left the country as soon as he received medical treatment. The Argentinean press condemned the attack, but the government suggested that U.S. agents staged the event to provoke an incident. In 1943, the police briefly arrested and interrogated Victoria Ocampo on her return from a trip to United States to study women's participation in the war effort. They released her after a few hours, but she remained under surveillance for the remainder of the war as a result of her activities advocating Argentina join the alliance against the Nazis.[20]

The U.S. government interpreted the Argentinean position on the war as evidence of the growing strength of pro-German military officers and wealthy landowners in Argentina. The Argentinean government, for its part, repressed pro-Allied activities within Argentina and limited the ability of the U.S. government to influence public debate as part of its policy of strict neutrality. Throughout the war, even after the military coup of 1943, Argentinean newspapers were overwhelmingly sympathetic to the Allies and hostile to the Germans and Japanese. Richard Pattee, along with other experts on Latin America, insisted that Argentina retained a lively liberal public culture, with considerable influence on the government. He argued that U.S. funding, whether open or covert, undermined the efforts of anti-fascist Argentineans to shape public opinion. Spruille Braden, U.S. ambassador to Argentina, dismissed Pattee's argument as too idealistic. Braden developed into a staunch opponent of open-ended cultural exchange programs, favoring instead making U.S. geopolitical interests the center of international exchange, a position that came to dominate thinking at the highest levels of government by the end of World War II.[21]

Indeed, the intersection of government policymaking with rapidly expanding people-to-people cultural exchange proved inherently fraught throughout the war. Building visibility for aspects of U.S. culture that remained largely unknown in Latin America developed as a secondary, but nonetheless important goal. For example, shows of U.S. art began touring Latin America only at the end of the 1930s, when the State Department invited proposals for projects to fund. The first exhibition of U.S. art ever to reach Brazil arrived at the end of 1941, when *Pintura Contemporânea Norte-Americana* ("Contemporary North American Painting") opened at the Museu Nacional das Belas Artes in Rio de Janeiro, days before the Japanese attack on Pearl Harbor. The exhibition featured the work of Charles Demuth, Max Weber, Edward Hopper, and Georgia O'Keeffe.[22] With this and other traveling exhibitions, the U.S. government stressed the independent development of U.S. art as a form for exploring the unique conditions of national life, a form that offered a robustly democratic alternative to the barbarism engulfing Europe.[23]

Diego Rivera, back in the United States in 1940 after a seven-year absence, used his mural for the San Francisco World's Fair, *Pan-American Unity*, the formal title of which was *The Marriage of the Artistic Expression of the North and of the South on This Continent*, to speak to the war crisis engulfing the world after the outbreak of war in September 1939. Rivera started working on the mural in June 1940, just as France collapsed. Rivera's mural struggled to reconcile contradictions within pan-Americanism so that the American nations could unite in defense of democracy (Figure 10).

"My mural," he said, "will picture the fusion between the great past of the Latin American lands, as it is deeply rooted in the soil, and the high mechanical developments of the United States." The basis for pan-American unity would be a "marriage of artistic expression" that would culminate with the "blending

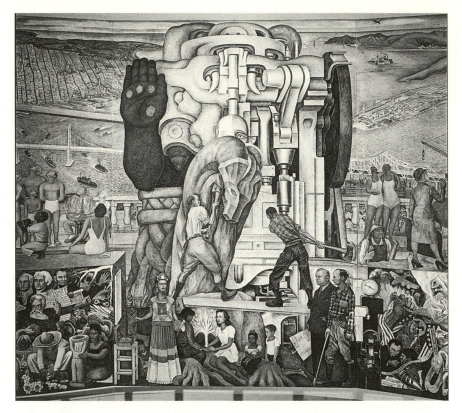

Figure 10. Diego Rivera, *Pan-American Unity*, section 3: *The Plastification of Creative Power of the Northern Mechanism by Union with the Plastic Tradition of the South*, 1940. Courtesy San Francisco City College. © 2016 Banco de México Diego Rivera Frida Kahlo Museums Trust, Mexico, D.F. / Artists Rights Society (ARS), New York.

of Indian, the Mexican, the Eskimo, with the kind of urge which makes the machine, the invention in the material side of life, which is also an artistic urge, the same urge primarily but in a different form of expression."[24] The discrepancies between the two societies shown in the mural have to do with level of technology, not energy or organization. The technological wonders of contemporary California blend into scenes from the Valley of Mexico before the Spanish conquest. In both societies, large groups work together to erect massive structures. In the center is a figure made of machinery merging into the Mexican goddess Coatlicue, the deity of death and the earth. Rivera explained: "On one side of this figure there is the northern culture, on the other the southern art, the art of the emotions. People are working on this figure, artists of the

North and South, Mexican and North American. I have also Fulton and Morse, artists who, as well as being painters, invented the tools for the industrial revolution, the telegraph and the steamboat, the means of transporting ideas and materials. From the South comes the plumed serpent, from the North the conveyor belt. So that is my idea which I am trying to express in this mural."[25]

Along the bottom of *Pan-American Unity*, Rivera portrayed Adolf Hitler, Benito Mussolini, and Joseph Stalin as three dictators threatening the peaceful productivity of the Americas, along with scenes of war and Nazi brutality drawn from two recent motion pictures, Charlie Chaplin's *The Great Dictator*, released in 1940, and *Confessions of a Nazi Spy*, Anatole Litvak's film from 1939. In the central bottom panel, Rivera showed himself holding hands with Hollywood movie star Paulette Goddard planting a Maya tree of life. At the time Goddard and Rivera were romantically involved, and the image he described as a personal symbol of his hopes for "closer pan-Americanism" through the collaboration of artists.

In 1943, Rivera published an article in Mexico, "El arte, base del Panamericanismo" ("Art, the Foundation of Pan-Americanism"), which elaborated his thinking on the need for continental unity but clarified what he viewed as the limitations crippling the alliance between the United States and Latin America in the war against fascism.[26] According to Rivera, European civilization since its earliest days had been based on slavery. The dictatorships in Germany and Italy manifested the contemporary form these slave societies assumed. The only part of Europe that had escaped slavery was the Soviet Union, and the redemption of European culture would come only through merger with the Soviet Union once it had been purified of Stalinism and returned to the goal of democratic socialism.[27] The United States had also had a successful democratic revolution, the basis for the country's unique role in the global struggle against fascism. U.S. democracy, however, was incomplete since its Constitution accepted the continuation of slavery and gave the president powers that "in reality Augustus Caesar never possessed."[28] Latin American democracy, on the other hand, had failed entirely in the aftermath of the revolutions against Spain and Portugal. Elites established police dictatorships to suppress the popular majority and invariably turned to European and North American capitalists to provide the economic development that would come naturally after a people was unleashed from slavery. The dialectical relationship of North and South in the American continent pointed to the way out of the impasse created by deformed democracy in the United States and aborted democracy in Latin America.

For Rivera, the unification of the Americas was necessary to restore democratic ideals that inspired independence movements both north and south. Neither side could move forward without the other. The first step toward the unification of the American nations was the elimination of racial prejudice and discrimination, overt in North America, but equally present in Latin America even if denied. Embracing the principle of racial equality would allow the peoples of America to recognize the "magnificent indigenous culture" that had existed in close contact with the land for thousands for years. This was a culture, Rivera insisted, that all Americans already were unconsciously adopting regardless of their ethnographic diversity. The food Americans ate had indigenous roots, as did their homes. Art was another "indispensable biological function" that helped people adopt emotions appropriate to their relationships with each other and with the land that fed and sheltered them. Therefore, he concluded, art "is a factor of the first order in the necessary, indispensable work ahead of constructing the Pan-American Union, a task we must complete if we do not want to perish."[29]

Rivera's framework shared the geographic determinism of his U.S. contemporaries writing on the unbridgeable divisions separating the cultures of people who were indigenous from those descended from immigrants. Rivera did not accept, however, that because many Mexicans lived in an ancient culture already at one with its environment, they lacked interest in the improvements that the modern United States hoped to export. Rivera looked for democratically chosen leaders to control how foreign developments were imported into Mexico. If modernization followed democratic principles, indigenous traditions would inform popular understanding of what Mexicans wanted from international organizations like the Pan American Union or, after 1945 the United Nations. In the most utopian sense, he wanted the United States to purify its deformed democratic life by uniting with other American nations, largely populated by very poor working people of color. The Pan American Union would be democratic to the degree that North Americans were willing to debate the vital issues with all other Americans and join with them in accepting the will of the majority as the best way to move forward. Once the political process had become truly democratic, very quickly, he predicted, the peoples of America would no longer be thinking in terms of their national citizenship, their race, or their ancestral homelands. Divisions and debate would continue, but as people spoke from their experience and hopes, instead of the privileges and fears, they would find their allies in every nation and in every social group.

The formal structures of *Pan-American Unity* reiterate analogies between Anglo and Latin American history. In the upper left panel, Indian sculptors work on a Toltecan column; in the upper right panel, Anglo American artisans build a wine press. In the lower left, the Aztec poet-king Netzahualcoyotl develops an early, if primitive flying machine; in the lower right, Robert Fulton completes the steamboat. Rivera's wife, the painter Frida Kahlo, is juxtaposed with Rivera's friend and patron Timothy Pflueger as kindred creative spirits. Charlie Chaplin is posed against Rivera himself, both presented as the creative figures needed to redeem the world from the nightmare of militarism and dictatorship. Mexican peasants create the folk art that had recently become so popular in the North, while opposite them an Anglo American folk artist carves a cigar store Indian. The heroes of national independence movements are juxtaposed: Simón Bolívar and George Washington, Miguel Hidalgo and Thomas Jefferson, Benito Juárez and Abraham Lincoln. Mesoamerican religious ceremonies parallel Protestant church meetings in the English-speaking part of America. Religion, engineering, art synthesize into Rivera's prayer that creativity as a basic human urge could, in an America still sheltered by U.S. power from the holocaust of world war, be a force capable of defeating the nihilism dominating the Old World whether it was formally democratic, fascist, or communist. Rivera insisted that the creative urge so important to the development of American societies belonged to all who lived in the New World.

In contrast to Diego Rivera, Cândido Portinari had a more apparently diffident attitude toward his relationship with the United States. He responded with alacrity to interest that Americans showed for his work. He made sure that a representative sample of his best work got to the United States. He accepted commissions, and he traveled to the United States to complete work begun at his studio at home. His focus, however, remained on representing Brazil. He did not have the ambition to imagine a dramatic narrative of human history that would allow his images to operate as critiques of the past and signposts to a better future. Portinari's work was social, but without being political. He interpreted the life around him without using the images to develop an argument about the causes of misery or the role of art in redeeming humanity, ambitions that Rivera, Orozco, and Siqueiros shared in equal measure.[30] In one of his few addresses on the social responsibilities of art, given in 1947 in Buenos Aires, Portinari insisted that he was a craftsman who thought with his hands: "The technical side records artists' knowledge and the development of their sensibilities. Technique is the medium with which artists transmit their sensibilities."[31]

Nonetheless, to represent the impoverished, but hardworking Brazilians whom Portinari knew intimately pointed to realities found in every country, to miseries that preceded the war and would continue after the fight between the world's imperialist powers ended. World War II brought new, previously unheard of horrors, but the suffering that the war caused was part and parcel of a larger picture of desolation stretching across the world. His *Retirantes* ("Migrants") series focused on the thousands of desperately poor farmers of Brazil's northeastern states who, through the first half of the twentieth century, abandoned their homes to trek to the cities in search of jobs (see Figure 22).[32] Many walked over fifteen hundred miles from Ceará in the far north to São Paulo or another of the rapidly industrializing cities of the south, where northeastern migrants took up the most poorly paid jobs. For a few years at the beginning of the 1940s, U.S. military bases in the northeast opened up a new source of employment, but U.S. spending declined after the surrender of German forces in North Africa in 1943 and the subsequent Allied invasion of Italy made the threat of a German attack across the Atlantic unlikely. The holocaust of the war was ending, but the daily holocaust of a world that accepted deep poverty would not.

In Brazil, many critics talked of Portinari as a "sentimental humanist" who dug deep into his feelings about Brazil's most pressing problem, the suffering of the poor.[33] Most of his U.S. admirers appreciated his new work, which they understood as articulating important humanitarian aspirations for the postwar war in a modern style. Critics who wrote about Portinari did not see his affiliation with the Brazilian Communist Party as particularly important for the work he did as a painter. Others outside the art world, however, did. In 1947 when Portinari wished to visit the United States, the State Department refused to give him a visa. In 1954, it again refused him entry when he needed to supervise the installation of two murals he had painted for the United Nations headquarters in New York. He had problems as well within Brazil, and the attitudes of Brazilian authorities may have affected State Department decisions. Following the banning of the Communist Party, the national security police marked Portinari as a person to be kept under surveillance and whose public activities were to be severely restricted. Portinari and his family moved to Uruguay, his wife's native home, and they stayed there a year until emissaries from the Brazilian government encouraged him to return home.[34] Portinari's public reputation in the United States remained high, and there was no mention in the U.S. press of the activities that made him unwelcome to the State Department. His longtime supporters writing in *Time* and *Life* magazines and for newspapers and art journals continued to speak of Portinari as one of the most important artists of the mid-twentieth century. In 1954, with the installation of *War* and *Peace*, his murals designed for the entryway to the General Assembly hall at the United Nations, the art critic for the *New York Times* proclaimed that, finally, the international organization had public art worthy of its mission. Nonetheless, given that he was unable to enter the United States, Portinari's relations with critics and dealers turned sporadic and distant. He remained an artist of special note, but increasingly at the fringes of attention.[35] Portinari was not happy about his inability to enter the United States, but his priorities had always been to his home, while he deepened relations with the broader South American arts communities as well as with critics in France and elsewhere in Europe. His international reputation continued growing, even as his ability to communicate with his U.S. public diminished.

The program for increased cultural exchange launched in 1915 presupposed that an informed public was necessary for the United States to play a responsible role in world affairs. However, the degree of popular input U.S. leaders wanted from their own citizens on matters of foreign policy or national security was an open question throughout the 1940s, even if popular support was essential for U.S. leaders to develop strategies for global governance. That pan-Americanism had, for many reasons, to be the test case situation for developing a new U.S. position on international organization added stresses that might have been lessened had the North Atlantic relation been central from the beginning. To believe that U.S. citizens could ever respect the peoples and cultures of nations that were poorer and inhabited by people of color required faith that egalitarian traditions existed in the United States with deep enough roots to combat and overcome the structures of racial separation found in every aspect of society.

The war crisis required nations, with good reasons to suspect U.S. intentions, to hope for the best, while leaders in the United States understood that their citizens needed to see other Americans as virtuous allies, if only because they were the only allies ready to hand. A mutual need to build more reliable ties led to the expanded cultural exchange that facilitated the extensive publicity given Portinari at the end of the 1930s and beginning of the 1940s. Between 1938 and the end of World War II, efforts intensified to give pan-American cultural exchange deeper institutional roots. The Museum of Modern Art significantly expanded its Latin American collection in 1942 after an anonymous private donor provided money targeted for that purpose. The results of two years' effort to develop a broader program were exhibited to the public in spring 1943 with an omnibus show that presented the museum's understanding of contemporary art in Latin America, along with historical work over a three-century period that was intended to provide viewers with a sense of the historical roots of modernism in the Americas.[36] The expanded collecting program led to sixteen other exhibitions, featuring art primarily from Mexico, Cuba, Brazil, and Argentina. MoMA shows traveled to other museums across the country.[37] More aggressive interest from museums was a direct result of the war, and political considerations drove the activities of donors and curators alike, in large part because, after 1938, the federal government took an aggressive role in promoting cultural exchange. The resulting expansion in museum exhibitions organized and books published was impressive, but government guidance caused its own problems. From the perspective originally pursued through the Carnegie Endowment for International Peace, citizen-to-citizen encounters served the vital function of counterbalancing the spasmodic fluctuations inherent to politics, whether domestic or international.

Policymakers, on the other hand, wanted specific results; they viewed programs with an open-ended goal of linking diverse national publics sometime in the future as naïvely idealistic; they resented independent thinking, whether it came from other governments, various national coordination committees organized and funded to promote the Allied cause, Americans who were experts on Latin America, or federal staff in the State Department and other agencies who took the goal of people-to-people contact too seriously. In the first years of the global crisis, the need to pull together against fascism overcame a wide variety of suspicions that otherwise were well grounded. The cause of convincing U.S. citizens that they were part of a global alliance that they needed for their own security sponsored movements of artists and writers north and south at a rate previously unmatched. Their work responded to the global challenge with results occasionally impressive, at other times inconsequential if not outright silly. Overall the war crisis stimulated serious reevaluations of "American" identity from hemispheric perspectives. The task required making Latin American allies visible to the U.S. public. That goal required English-speaking Americans traveling south, but also Spanish- and Portuguese-speaking Americans traveling north. In either event, the primary target was a U.S. public that policymakers presumed to be ignorant of, and largely indifferent to, the rest of world. Perhaps, above all else, the U.S. public was deeply committed to staying out of the global conflict if it was at all possible, and this resistance interfered with the flexibility leaders desired to craft a strategic response to a world at war.

Chapter 6

Making Latin American Allies Visible

Following the fall of France, the White House assumed direct supervision of relations with Latin America by creating the Office for the Coordination of Commercial and Cultural Relations between the American Republics (later renamed the Office of Inter-American Affairs).[1] The president appointed Nelson Rockefeller, the thirty-two-year-old scion of the Standard Oil dynasty, to lead the office. He and his staff enjoyed a sizable budget to spend on programs directly serving presidential priorities. (The Division of Cultural Relations continued within the State Department under its existing charge and considerably more limited budget to assist private groups active in cultural exchange.)

The OIAA had a broad, ambitious range of responsibilities, but its most important assignments were to facilitate U.S. military expansion into Latin America. One of the largest programs the new office undertook was the development of a network of airfields across the continent, linking the United States to Chile on the Pacific and Brazil on the Atlantic. Since the American republics, the United States included, were all officially neutral and popular opinion in every Latin American country without exception identified any U.S. military presence with intervention, development of the airfields needed to appear solely the result of private initiative. Pan-American Airlines received a secret contract to manage a massive multinational development project that the U.S. government funded in its entirety. For the airfields to function properly in the event of war, radio communications had to expand as well, and the Office of Inter-American Affairs funded work for a new U.S.-controlled radio network, ostensibly privately owned, that was to replace existing German and British systems.[2]

Rockefeller's office invested as well in medical care, clean water systems, and sewers in the communities where new facilities were built. Latin American governments were well aware that the airfield and radio network projects were not private investments, but the subterfuge served their needs to limit domestic criticism. In addition, each country had priorities unrelated to the war effort that entered into the negotiations over allowing the projects to move forward.

In Brazil, for example, development aid included funding for a massive new steel foundry complex outside Rio de Janeiro that the government had made a centerpiece of its economic development strategy.[3]

The rationale for cultural exchange funded by Rockefeller's office was consistent with the underlying purposes of putting the continent on a war footing, while simultaneously facilitating U.S. economic penetration of countries like Brazil that had previously had closer trade and investment ties with Europe. Governments had to be convinced that they wanted to be U.S. allies, and this often meant propaganda campaigns aimed at a much wider segment of the population than previous efforts, either private or governmental, had tried to reach. In defining its public relations objectives, staff at the OIAA, who were more likely to come from private industry rather than from universities as was the case with the Division of Cultural Affairs, developed a set of "credos" that the citizens of the Americas should accept as a result of having been the recipients of information about the importance of pan-Americanism in the fight against fascism. The "Credo for the Individual Citizen of Latin America" read:

I. I believe my best interests are linked with the U.S. . . .
II. I believe my best interests will be harmed by the Axis . . .
III. I believe that the U.S. is going to win the war, although it will be a
    difficult struggle . . .
IV. Therefore, I am supporting the U.S. and stand ready to cooperate
    with the Americas and to make additional personal sacrifices
    along with the American people so that I can help the U.S. win
    the war and establish a better world.

The U.S. public also had to understand that its country needed its Latin American allies. The "Credo for the Individual U.S. Citizen" had four parallel points that OIAA information and cultural programs were charged to "sell" on the home front:

I. I believe that Latin America has much to offer me not only economically; but also socially, esthetically, and spiritually.
II. I believe that the Axis wishes not only eventually to conquer Latin
    America but also more immediately to use certain of the
    Republics as bases from which to attack the U.S.
III. I believe that active cooperation from Latin America in all ways is
    essential if the U.S. is to win the war.
IV. I believe that, therefore, Latin America should be assisted by the
    U.S. in order to enable her to assist us and also herself.[4]

While the credos reflected the influence of advertising and public relations experts, practical applications usually reaffirmed the liberal, humanist perspectives that had motivated the Division of Cultural Affairs.[5] When programs related directly to U.S. strategic interests, the OIAA funded cultural exchange directly, including an ambitious film and radio show production program. The new office also suggested projects to universities, private philanthropies, and private companies while offering pilot funding or guarantees to compensate businesses for any losses they incurred. The bureaucratic relationship between the OIAA and the Division of Cultural Affairs in the State Department was often rocky as the OIAA's determination to focus on what was needed immediately to secure U.S. dominance in the western hemisphere conflicted with the division's longer-term vision of broader, deeper relations between institutions with shared interests developing over time.[6] The OIAA emphasis on cultural exchange programs more directly serving administration international priorities prefigured broader changes that would come at the end of the war when "exchange" gave way to a new "public information" approach educating foreigners about their relationship to U.S. society.

No country was unaffected by the campaign to solidify the pan-American alliance around U.S. goals, but Brazil was particularly important in the plans the Roosevelt administration developed for hemispheric defense.[7] Were the Germans to secure control over North Africa, northeast Brazil was the most probable location for a German incursion into the western hemisphere. Beyond the threat of a potential German invasion, which diminished significantly in May 1943 with the surrender of German and Italian forces in Tunisia, Brazil was a country with strategic economic importance. The United States imported most of its rubber from Southeast Asia, but those sources were expected to be lost if the war in Asia expanded. Brazil offered an alternative source for rubber and other resources imported from Africa and Asia.[8] How were people in the United States to be convinced that significant involvement and investment were required in a country few Americans knew? Articles in *Time*, *Life*, and other illustrated mass-circulation magazines were particularly important for introducing Brazil as a potential ally to readers in the United States. Funding from the OIAA assisted the publication and marketing of two books on Brazil with strong reviews and sales, Vera Kelsey's *Seven Keys to Brazil* (1940) and Stefan Zweig's *Brazil, Land of the Future* (1942).[9]

In late 1940, the Office of the Coordinator for Inter-American Affairs hired three photographers to travel to Brazil and send back images that could help Americans became more familiar with the country and its potential. Their photographs were used in government press releases and publications; the images were also distributed free of charge to U.S. newspapers and magazines.

George Kidder Smith, the most senior of the photographers, focused on architecture, both colonial and modern. The Museum of Modern Art curated a traveling exhibition of his work, *Brazil Builds*. Smith's photographs showed Brazil as a progressive, modern country with ambitious plans for the future already well under way.[10] Alan Fisher, a seasoned photojournalist on loan from the New York City daily newspaper *PM*, documented U.S.-funded projects across Brazil. Fisher was also responsible for photographing visits of U.S. officials and celebrities.[11] The youngest of the three, Genevieve Naylor, had just turned twenty-five when she arrived in Brazil. She had experience as a freelance photographer for *Time* and *Fortune* magazines, but her work as a staff photojournalist at the Associated Press news agency had brought her to the OIAA's attention, that and the fact that the OIAA had hired Naylor's fiancé, the painter Misha Reznikoff, to go to Rio de Janeiro to help the Brazilians found a new museum of modern art (Figure 11).[12] Her focus was capturing the everyday lives of Brazilians.[13] The couple found an apartment in Rio, where the dynamic literary and cultural communities welcomed them with enthusiasm. Poet and playwright Vinícius de Moraes noted in his column for the daily newspaper *A Manhã* ("Morning") that he recently had the pleasure of getting to know a photographer who had worked for *Life* magazine: "Genevieve is her name, the wife of the grand Misha who has conquered the artists of our city with his warm personality and educated eye. Genevieve looks like she's stepped out of the pages of a Robin Hood story, with her look of a young page, her colorful elegance, and a feather always stuck boldly in her hat. Nothing escapes our bewitching visitor's camera. She glimpses a possible photographic moment, and she makes it hers. Genevieve gives a little click, and she captures a fleeting bit of life on film."[14] Aníbal Machado, a prominent critic at the time in Rio de Janeiro, was also taken by the work: "More than her technical skill, what is most striking in Miss Genevieve's work is the sociological insight of how she uses the lens, revealing a brave and sincere spirit moved by what she has seen of Brazilian reality. . . . The humble places and activities of everyday life, framing the faces of our people, spill out of the images of this 'Good Neighbor' photographer. There is nothing monumental in the reality she captures. No waterfalls, no monumental buildings, no idyllic landscapes."[15]

As with Smith's more impersonal photographs, the Museum of Modern Art organized a traveling exhibition of fifty of Naylor's Brazilian pictures after she returned home, *Faces and Places in Brazil*. The critic at the *New York Times* praised the work and wrote that Naylor's eye revealed that Brazilians loved playing football, rode crowded streetcars, enjoyed lively holidays, and made sure that their children received a free lunch every day in school. Brazilian women seemed to be exceptionally beautiful, which made Naylor's photographs highly

Figure 11. Genevieve Naylor (right) with Misha Reznikoff, 1941. Courtesy Peter Reznikoff. © Reznikoff Artistic Partnership.

enjoyable, but beyond that, the critic found the most striking aspect of Naylor's pictures was how much everyday life in Brazil was remarkably familiar and ordinary. Naylor gave her American viewers a glimpse into the privileged lives of the glamorous and wealthy, but most of her pictures presented men and women with modest but pleasant lives that did not appear "burdened with too much drama." The scenery was different from the United States, the reviewer noted, the people dressed a little differently, but Naylor's scenes should help most people in the United States see Brazil as a country much like their own.[16] Both U.S. and Brazilian officials worried that she was taking too many pictures of working people. The OIAA wanted to show Latin American countries as modern nations, whose citizens were industrious and eager for progress. The

Figure 12. Genevieve Naylor, *Newspaper Vendor in Rio de Janeiro*, 1941–1943. Courtesy Peter Reznikoff. © Reznikoff Artistic Partnership.

Brazilian government wanted Naylor to highlight industry, its large urban planning projects, and life in more affluent neighborhoods. Naylor located her subjects in a variety of social landscapes that distinguished the Brazil of wealthy elites from that of the urban working class as well as from the very different life in the impoverished countryside.[17] Her photographs offered a more varied feel for Brazil than what was shown in *Life* magazine at the time, but her style overall was consistent with the cheerful, if sentimental populism of mass-circulation journals, particularly when magazines hired photographers to capture the struggles of working people during the Depression (Figure 12).

As a result, viewers and critics in the United States, like the critic for the *New York Times* reviewing her show at the Museum of Modern Art, could look at images of Brazilian life and feel that even with the differences, average Americans and Brazilians did have much in common. Naylor served the larger war effort by applying photographic principles with relatively clear meaning in the United States to the specific conditions in Brazil, showing Brazilians in everyday activities and poses that would be recognizable to most in the United States instead of being subjects of exotic or ethnographic fascination. Naylor succeeded in satisfying Good Neighbor goals of developing mutual understanding between allied peoples. Her decisions demonstrated good intuitive sense of the kinds of images needed for North Americans to feel a sympathetic connection with their Brazilian allies.

Citizenship can be seen as a pact for shared security. For citizens in the United States to imagine that there could be pan-American citizenship required belief that Latin American allies had the capacity to protect themselves, at least with the help of a richer country such as the United States. Citizens in Latin American countries would need to believe that the powerful ally with a long history of aggression in Mexico and the Caribbean basin would furnish assistance without undermining national sovereignty. As long as a German offensive into the western hemisphere remained a credible possibility, both the Brazilian and the U.S. governments were committed to promoting the confidence of their respective publics in the alliance. The U.S. government needed images of Brazil on the way to becoming a fully modern and progressive nation, whose likable citizenry was as fully capable of becoming global citizens as the people of the United States. Naylor's work, produced for publication primarily in the United States, is further evidence that interpretations of the Good Neighbor Policy as an effort by U.S. policymakers to influence the publics of other nations obscure deeply rooted conflicts within the United States. Influencing public opinion in Latin America was an important objective, but shaping public opinion in the United States had greater priority, particularly in 1940 and 1941, when sentiments against involvement in the European war were widespread. Given that Naylor's photographs from Brazil were produced for distribution in the United States, they served a government effort to convince average citizens in the United States that Brazil would be an important and reliable ally, well worth the expensive investments that some conservatives in Congress found questionable.[18] Naylor shot the lives of the poor as well as the rich, but she showed the poor as contemporary, urban people trying to better their lives.

To understand Naylor's success as an artist and as an advocate for a U.S.-Brazilian alliance against fascism, one needs to place her photographs within visual conventions pioneered by Lewis Hine during the first three decades of the twentieth century for representing the working class in the United States, an approach that a group of younger photographers in the 1930s—most prominently, Dorothea Lange, Walker Evans, Margaret Bourke-White, Ben Shahn, John Vachon, and Roy DeCarava—adapted and developed into a movement to use photography for social documentation. In the depths of the 1930s Depression, the federal government employed photographers to document the difficulties that the government was trying to address through New Deal programs. The Farm Security Administration developed the largest photography department, with

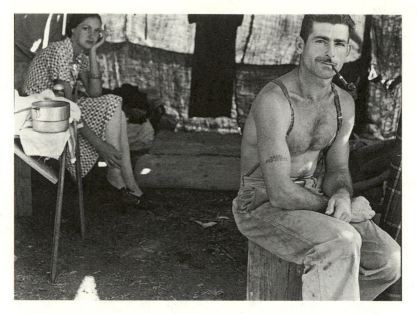

Figure 13. Dorothea Lange, *Lumber Worker and his Wife, Oregon*, 1939.
Courtesy Library of Congress, Prints and Photographs Division, Farm
Security Administration Collection.

several dozen men and women whose work became at the time the classic representation of the effects of the Great Depression on rural Americans (Figure 13).[19]
The codes to represent U.S. workers often stressed the disciplined masculine
independence that had developed for a cultural identity appropriate for a modern, industrial society that was also democratic. Subjects confronted the camera
full face and gazed directly into the lens, challenging the viewer to recognize the
person in the picture as a fully equal citizen, rather than as an indigent in need
of charity. The preferred attitude for seasoned male workers was daringly defiant. The superior worker was convinced of his own skills and knowledge; he
took pride in getting his job done well—if he had a job, which was the justification for government programs to get the nation moving again. The workingman
who has work and money gains self-sufficiency, as well as a respectability potentially more profound than that of the middle-class viewers who are, ostensibly,
the primary recipients of photographic documentation of fellow citizens whose
lives are not as comfortable or privileged. A defiant attitude was a sign of determination to prevail, a perspective that in nationalist terms could be the foundation of reimagining the United States as a workingman's republic. The Farm
Security Administration and other government agencies adopted the conventions of social documentation for extensive photographic projects commis-

Figure 14. Genevieve Naylor, *Men by Favela Restaurant*, 1941–1943. Courtesy Peter Reznikoff. © Reznikoff Artistic Partnership.

sioned to link New Deal programs to an idea of citizenship as a social compact. When the United States entered World War II, the self-confident defiance of the U.S. worker was applied to photographs and posters created for recruiting purposes and for building home front morale.

The photography program that the Office of Inter-American Affairs developed followed the model of the Farm Security Administration, shifting the focus to present free citizens in the western hemisphere uniting together in response to global political crisis. Social documentation conventions adapted to another country allowed Naylor to rise above the ethnographic presentation of Brazil as a land of curious differences. Instead, she represented Brazil as a fully contemporary society, somewhat poorer than the United States, but still a place where everyday life was understandable to North Americans because even if people and places were different from their U.S. counterparts in specifics, they were similar in kind. People in the United States understood that Brazil was a poorer nation. They often heard that a privileged elite with excessive, concentrated wealth had retarded the development of the country. The reality of social and income disparity was the basis for several of the most powerful stereotypes of Latin America common in the United States. The more immediate question, given the war and its demands, was whether the people of Brazil were in a position to overcome national poverty, whether like their counterparts in the Depression-era United States, they refused to let economic difficulties prevent them from acting as free men and women. The suits, neckties, and sporty hats Naylor presents in a photograph she took of working-class men in a favela responded to that concern with an affirmative answer (Figure 14). The men's clothing, relatively equivalent to what workingmen in the United States wore at the time, neutralized the poverty of the neighborhood where the photograph was taken. Instead of showing the favela as a place of exotic difference, the image functioned as a sign that Brazil was in the midst of a transformation that would make it a more progressive place, a message that the government of Getúlio Vargas wanted to convey to Brazilian citizens, many of whom were suspicious for good reason that the political system would never diminish the privileges that the national elites enjoyed.[20]

Photographs of packed streetcars and trains emphasized the daily discipline of Brazilian workers, confronting everyday situations that their peers in the United States knew only too well every rush hour, but in a form that underscored the somewhat earlier position of Brazil on a presumed ladder to progress (Figure 15). Determination to get to work revealed that Brazilian citizens merited the assistance their country needed to contribute to the defense of western civilization. The presence of so many men in uniform among the passengers showed as well that this ally was already, like the United States, building a citizen army for national self-defense. The iconicity of the image, however, derives from its synthesis of everyday routines and the carnivalesque.

In the United States, the symbol without equal of social progress was the image of the modern workingwoman, usually referred to in the press and movies as "working girls," female archetypes that moved through the world with effervescent freedom.[21] Images of women war workers expressed the defiant determination of the modern U.S. worker but with an additional touch of humor. Images of perky, self-sufficient women rely on stereotypes no less than images of women as passive. The particular stereotype authorizes women to act for themselves and for others, instead of accepting subordination. Nonetheless it rests on a reduction of complex social and psychological realities into a story that in this case is likable, perhaps especially likable because ideals of women as perky

Figure 15. Genevieve Naylor, *Streetcar in Rio de Janeiro*, 1941–1943. Courtesy Peter Reznikoff. © Reznikoff Artistic Partnership. Original caption from *Pittsburgh Sun Telegraph*, 29 January 1943: "*Fares, Please*—So you think Pittsburgh street cars and buses are crowded? Here is a street car during the rush hour in Rio, Brazil, another country in which President Roosevelt stopped on his return from Casablanca."

"companions" enhanced rather than challenged the institution of marriage. All stereotypes convey a sense of the world that gives structure and reduces ambiguity, and the recipients use stereotypes to help define themselves and their own capabilities, sometimes in contrast to negatively connoted images; but often more positive yet stereotypical images promote identification and even imitation. During the war, government and industry encouraged women to serve the nation by working, but women who took traditionally male jobs often faced deeply rooted prejudice and, no doubt at times, lack of self-confidence, both of

Figure 16. Genevieve
Naylor, *Women in the Door
of a Restaurant*, 1941–1943.
Courtesy Peter Reznikoff.
© Reznikoff Artistic
Partnership.

which were to be overcome. Naylor's images of poorer women in Brazil could suggest to U.S. readers that the status of Brazilian women was moving in the same direction as that of women in the United States.

The simple but well-groomed clothes and hair dressing express the dignity and independence of the women in a picture taken in a poor neighborhood (Figure 16). The expressions and postures of the women suggest that these Brazilian women enjoy a sense of self-sufficiency comparable to that of their North American counterparts. Naylor's photographs often emphasized the energy and the faith in one's own capacities that were signs of the fully modern citizen. A progressive democratic faith, as articulated in the photographic tradition within which Naylor worked, identified work as the source of progress and the diversity and continuous remixing of a pluralist society as the driving force for deeper democracy. Economic democracy had pushed the United States into global leadership, but its continuing failure to see a diverse citizenry as a source of national power remained a potentially fatal weakness. Photographs commissioned to develop support for a U.S.-led global alliance needed to go beyond the immediate goal of saying here are your allies. They had to help U.S. citizens accept that connections with citizens of other American countries were real and positive. Differences could not be avoided, but viewers needed to recognize themselves and see Brazilians occupying a world that was similar if not identical. The same longings moved Brazilians that moved Americans.

Naylor's photographs stand out among OIAA-funded work for their resistance to stereotypes, an accomplishment that may well be because of their sympathetic and at times romantic observation of what she saw in Brazil. They stood out because her sympathetic gaze at everyday life in an important ally did not avoid the difficulties many Brazilians faced. Naylor's pictures did not exaggerate the situation in Brazil, but her willingness to look at the difficult lives of the urban and rural poor made both OIAA and Brazilian government officials nervous, the latter probably because they did not want wartime alliance leading to U.S. meddling in Brazil's internal affairs.[22]

The OIAA did not want the programming it funded to antagonize allied governments, and in general the agency preferred simplistic presentations of allied countries, as if stereotypes could assure U.S. viewers that they remained in familiar, easily comprehensible territory. The short informational films on life in Latin America that the OIAA funded for showing in movie theaters as short subjects accompanying feature films provide a good example of genre formulas deployed to imbue a complex foreign social environment with a sense of familiarity that many in the audience must have intuited was false. In ten minutes, Julien Bryan's *Lima Family* (1944) offered American audiences a glimpse into the life of a surgeon in Peru and his family.[23] The doctor is seen as a benevolent master of a family of fourteen, but also as dutifully fulfilling his responsibilities to his patients. His sons, all studying professions, demonstrate affection for popular American culture, suggesting that Peru's conservative, patriarchal culture will change as the country absorbs U.S. mores. Looking at how Peru's support for the war was transforming the lives of the doctor's daughters reinforced the theme of convergence toward U.S.-defined gender norms. The narrator informs us that prior to the war, women were trained to run a house and manage a staff of servants. One of the doctor's daughters was somewhat "rebellious" and had taken a part-time job teaching ballet in a progressive girl's school run by nuns from the United States and Canada. After Peru joined the allied effort, however, the doctor's wife and her daughters started going to the presidential palace twice a week, where under the patronage of the president's wife, they and other society women roll bandages for the Red Cross. This kind of imagery was likely what the OIAA and the Brazilian government expected from Naylor. It is hard to imagine that U.S. audiences, most of whom were working people, would have found much in common with the privileged elites featured in *Lima Family*, or even have found it credible that the doctor and his family were on their way to lives more like their own.

Bryan's *São Paulo* (1943) presented a more impersonal if frenetic overview of "the fastest growing city in the world . . . the leading industrial city in South America," using language to describe Brazil's major industrial and financial center typical of patriotic, boosterist descriptions of Anytown, USA.[24] Founded by "hardy pioneers," São Paulo has long been a city "dedicated to freedom," and the city was even where Brazil declared its independence in 1822. With a temperate climate, its inhabitants are "highly energetic, enterprising, productive people." A quick succession of shots demonstrates the plenty Paulistanos produced: coffee, cotton, wire and cable, automobiles (made in modern factories "now totally devoted to making and assembling military vehicles"), tires, steel. And as in any city in the United States, the energetic citizens enjoy good public transportation, excellent schools for their children, and many parks.

Filmmakers from Latin America also worked for the OIAA. Their work more typically was shown in Latin America, but Agustín F. Delgado, a Mexican newsreel producer, made the first OIAA film for U.S. film audiences, *The Day Is New: Dawn to Darkness in Mexico City* (1940).[25] The film opens with a montage of Mexicans awakening in the morning as a milkman does his delivery rounds. Families have breakfast, some go to church, but soon the whole city is on its way to work or school. Mexico City transforms into a bustling metropolis of busy offices, factories, and stores. In the evening, as people get off work, the pace slows down. Young couples stroll in the park, mothers prepare dinner, families get ready for bed, and in the closing shots, a police officer patrols silent, empty streets. The narrator concludes the film with the declaration that "Mexico is an old country that is new, a poor country that is rich, a strong country that has more freedom than it has ever had before."

The OIAA sent Walt Disney on a tour of South America and subsidized a feature-length animated film, *Saludos, Amigos* (1942). Disney claimed he made the trip and the film solely to help his country win the war. He never expected the film to do well, but audiences in both the United States and Latin America loved it. He made a more expensive sequel, *The Three Caballeros*, featuring Donald Duck; José Carioca, a samba-dancing Brazilian parrot; and Panchito Pistoles, a Mexican rooster, who given his name always has his guns ready at hand to avenge insults to his honor. The Latin American friends have arrived to celebrate Donald's birthday. Panchito gives Donald a piñata and explains the Mexican custom of children breaking open piñatas at their birthday to discover their presents. The seven segments of the film explore different parts of America, leaping from Patagonia in the far south to the pampas of Argentina and Uruguay, to Brazil, and far north to Mexico. Carmen Miranda's sister Aurora introduces Donald to samba by teaching him Ary Barroso's "Bahia," which like Barroso's earlier "Aquarela do Brasil," recorded by Jimmy Dorsey and his orchestra, was a hit on U.S. record charts.

Orson Welles, fresh from his triumph with *Citizen Kane*, developed what was to be the OIAA's most ambitious and expensive film project, a commercial feature that Welles titled *It's All True*. The Brazilian government initially suggested to the OIAA that it would like Orson Welles, whose *Citizen Kane* had enjoyed enormous success in Brazil, to make a film set in the country's annual Carnival celebrations. The OIAA passed the suggestion onto Welles and RKO Studios, his employer, but the agency wanted the film set in several Pan American Union member states, not just Brazil. If RKO agreed to produce the film as a commercial project, the OIAA guaranteed to cover up to $300,000 of costs were the film to lose money. With Nelson Rockefeller one of the largest investors in RKO and an active member of the board of directors, the arrangement illustrated how during the war distinctions between government and private enterprise blurred. Welles proposed a film with four stories each based on actual events, hence the working title *It's All True*. One of the four segments was set in Mexico, two in Brazil. Welles had two ideas in mind for the fourth episode. He sketched out a story of New Orleans jazz roughly based on Louis Armstrong's career, a musical history that would complement the story of samba told in his episode on Carnival in Brazil. But he was also taken with having the fourth segment set during the Spanish conquest of Peru, a story that would foreground Native American perspectives on the meaning of liberty and equality. Both the OIAA and RKO were excited about the project. Welles went to Mexico to shoot the episode there, a sentimental story of a small boy in a rural village who raised a young bull, whose courage in the ring led the audience in Mexico City watching him fight to ask that his life be spared.[26]

In February 1942 Welles headed to Rio de Janeiro to begin planning how he would shoot the history of samba. He arrived in Brazil a celebrity. Government officials greeted him at the airport and escorted him to his hotel in the center of Rio de Janeiro in an official motorcade. His presence was important for presentations of the alliance in the United States. When Brazil declared war on Germany, Italy, and Japan in August 1942, Welles was placed next to Brazilian foreign minister Osvaldo Aranha for the minister's official signing of the declaration. His radio broadcasts from Brazil and other Latin American countries provided humorous and music-filled introductions to the other American nations that pleased the OIAA because they were so popular in the United States. He scripted and shot the film's longest episode, the re-creation of the voyage on a flimsy raft of four impoverished fisherman from the far northern city of Fortaleza over sixteen hundred miles south to Rio de Janeiro. They came to present the grievances of fishermen and farmworkers who had been excluded from the protections and benefits of labor and social security legislation that President Vargas had promulgated. The men became national heroes for their heroic effort, and the story about their journey and their cause that appeared in *Time* magazine inspired Welles to make their search for justice and equality the pivot of the film as a whole.[27] He re-created their journey, using the four men and their families as his actors. In the most tragic of the many problems plaguing the film, one of the four fishermen from Fortaleza drowned when an accident occurred during filming in the Rio de Janeiro harbor.

The film project fell apart in 1943, while Welles was still shooting. RKO canceled all of Welles's projects and ejected his company from the studio lot. Nelson Rockefeller had recently resigned from the RKO board of directors during a dispute over the direction of the studio. New management came on board with new priorities: instead of prestige films, the studio would produce a larger number of less expensive comedies and thrillers. RKO locked the raw footage for *It's All True* in its vaults. Welles tried to interest other studios in his pan-American project, without any success. The new RKO management complained that Welles's projects were all excessively over budget, though film historian Catherine Benamou has argued that this was not the case but a pretext used to justify the decision to terminate the studio's relation with Welles. There is evidence suggesting that Brazilian officials had also soured on Welles, in their case because he showed far too much interest in the lives of poor black Brazilians. The OIAA, for its part, no longer was prepared to guarantee that the project be protected against financial loss, and as U.S. troops began fighting in Italy and preparing for the invasion of France, Hollywood film executives must have thought that audiences no longer would be interested in a film focused on Latin America.[28]

During the course of the war, hundreds of writers, musicians, and artists worked to promote pan-American unity. Almost all of them were, like Genevieve Naylor, less well known than Orson Welles or Walt Disney. They served the pan-American cause by getting out the message one photograph, one newsreel, one radio broadcast, one concert, one magazine article at a time. The ability to communicate a message rested on satisfying the expectations within any given genre and medium. The immediate task for all involved was to help develop ties between the peoples of the United States and the member states of the Pan American Union so that governments could respond to the global crisis in concert with minimal internal dissent. In the process, progressive people could form transnational identities that were hemispheric in the pan-American context, but ultimately pointed toward the United Nations as the culmination of humanity's quest for democracy, justice, and prosperity. Naylor's activities bridged contemporary social realities with utopian ideals that perhaps in fact were vital primarily for liberal and progressive intellectuals, but the work served the interests of both governments, even with qualms that some functionaries expressed about some of Naylor's choices. For very different reasons, both the Roosevelt and the Vargas administrations wanted to project the image of a special relation that could be confused with the human condition in general. Progressive cultural workers in both countries were needed to tell that story, and in general they were allowed to do so in their own ways.

Naylor could synthesize Good Neighbor politics with her own cultural and intellectual priorities, in part because she was a superb photographer, but also because the genre of social documentation had an established place within photojournalism. Naylor's Brazilian photographs may have pushed against the boundaries of what her Brazilian and U.S. overseers preferred for the representation of one of the most important allies the United States had at the beginning of the war. Nonetheless, newspaper and magazine editors published her pictures, and the Museum of Modern Art curated a show, because her work fit its criteria for photography that should attract and hold the attention of the public. To that degree, her work relied on tried and true formulas that, in this particular genre, demanded photographers challenge stereotypes and politicize how people looked at the world.[29] In most other media and genres, whatever the artist's intentions, stereotypes were difficult, perhaps impossible, to avoid or to transform.

Not all photojournalists sent to Brazil worked within a social documentation framework. Before and during the war, *Life* magazine, whose editors were deeply committed to a more robust role for the United States around the world, also sent photographers to Brazil. In May 1939, a multipage spread devoted to the country focused on the country's economic potential and its growing importance on the world stage.[30] The magazine noted that the British, German, and Japanese governments were actively seeking to influence Brazilian society, but the United States had the advantage of having been Brazil's most important customer for its products since the middle of the nineteenth century. U.S. businessmen, *Life*'s writers complained, were more arrogant than their foreign competitors. Nonetheless, if they reflected on the determination in Brazil to industrialize, U.S. businesses had an important advantage because they were already investing in Brazil's industrial development while competitors remained interested only in importing agricultural commodities or raw natural resources such as rubber, lumber, or mineral ores. The photographs chosen to illustrate U.S. involvement in Brazil emphasized the massive automobile assembly plants that both the Ford Motor Company and General Motors built in São Paulo. The country wanted to modernize, the text emphasizes, but "without interfering too much with its leisure."[31] One photograph showed idle wealthy women on their way to the beach, an image that contrasts sharply with Naylor's more self-sufficient, hard-working women (Figure 17). While *Life* published a few photographs portraying the quaint backwardness of working conditions in some sectors, in general the images selected showed Brazilians as hard workers (Figure 18). In marked contrast to Naylor's, *Life* magazine images primarily focused on white Brazilians, nor did they foreground the everyday, casual mixture of Brazilians of different races at school, at work, or on the street. When Brazil entered the war as an ally in August 1942, *Life* emphasized

Figure 17. *Life* magazine, *Women on Their Way to Copacabana Beach*, 22
May 1939. Photograph by John Phillips, Getty Images. Original caption:
"Shapely Cariocas (citizens of Rio) walk down to the endless beaches that line
Rio's shore, in bathing suits. Cariocas are among the world's pleasantest,
gayest, friendliest, and most relaxed people. These girls are pure white and
proud of their blood. But they are careful to treat mulatto fellow citizens as
equals. The language and heritage of Brazil are Portuguese."

the determination of the people and its president, Getúlio Vargas, to work with
the United States for Hitler's defeat.

In most respects, *Life* repeated the preferred messages of the Vargas regime. In the magazine's discussion of Brazil as an important member of the
alliance for democracy, the fact that the country had been a dictatorship since
1937 was a detail that faded away lest it conflict with the strategic goals of
the economic and political alliance. Brazil was progressive because it was opening up to U.S. industrial investment and had signed up to help the United States
in the campaign against fascism. Vargas was in any event a popular president
whose policies, while authoritarian, were in line with the preferences of a majority of Brazilians, preferences that supposedly were found at all levels of society.
Brazilian productivity remained the theme *Life* magazine stressed about the
country throughout the war, but with increased emphasis on the importance of
the country's vast natural resources. The magazine saluted as well the valor of
Brazil's military forces during the Italian campaign, "who fought with a curi-
ously impromptu gallantry and gave the Allied armies a new piece of slang, 'the

Figure 18. *Life* magazine, *Stevedore in Santos*, 22 May 1939. Photograph by John Phillips, Getty Images. Original caption: "Brazil— A sweaty worker loading sacks onto the McCormack line boat."

snake is smoking,' meaning, 'things are getting rugged.'"[32] An article celebrating Brazil's contribution to victory published only a week before Germany surrendered veered into tropical exoticism with claims that Americans stationed in Brazil were typically seduced into adopting many Brazilian customs because of the sensuous way of life and the tradition of warm human relations linking everybody who worked together. Brazil was a place where people learn to avoid doing anything "the hard way." A handful of Americans hated being stationed there, the article conceded, but the large majority found it an extraordinarily comfortable place to live and work. Instead of illustrating the article with a photograph, the magazine reproduced a surrealist-inspired watercolor that painter Reginald Marsh created while he was stationed at the U.S. Navy's facilities in Recife. U.S. military personnel, out for a tour of the city, encounter workers carrying a piano and piano player, both improbably upside down (Figure 19).

Marsh's image seems more like the Brazil encountered in Carmen Miranda's Hollywood films *That Night in Rio* or *The Gang's All Here*. Nonetheless, his Brazil is consistent in tone, imagery, and style with paintings of New York City he had done prior to the war (Figure 20). Marsh was and remains famous for his tawdry but exciting pictures of working people out for a good time. The

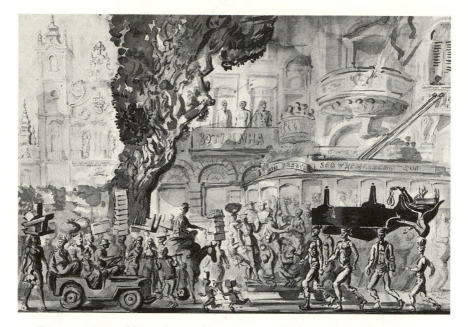

Figure 19. Reginald Marsh, *Heads Up*, watercolor on paper, 1943; published
in *Life* magazine, 30 April 1945. Life Collection of Art from World War II,
Courtesy of the Army Art Collection, U.S. Army Center of Military History.
Original caption: "In Recife, Brazil, the American Army (left) is equally
impressed by the universal glamour of the young Brazilian girls and the
Brazilian feat of transporting an inverted piano (right) on the heads of the
porters. Reginald Marsh has amused himself by adding a piano player, upside
down. Some sense of the indescribable Brazilian scene is given by this
combination of a baroque 17th Century Portuguese church, a monstrous
tropical tree and the three clothes dummies on the store balcony. Notice that
even a Brazilian army officer rides on the outside of the São Francisco trolley,
which was made in the U.S. a long time ago. Brazil's trolley cars are nearly
always terrible overcrowded. The charmed and bedazzled Americans came to
believe that little in Brazil was in dead earnest, that everything was for fun."

editors at *Life* knew what they would get when they published the Marsh watercolor: a crass, gaudy image, full of glee and sexual energy, focused on the working
poor and their cheap entertainments. Choppy brushwork and lightly saturated
color helped convey the agitation and fragility of the lives modern cities had
conjured. Stereotypes, without a question, but in Marsh's works applied to both
countries with an equivalent heaping of cruel affection.

As we have seen, Hollywood served the effort of pan-American unity, but
the mode of production established in the film industry had little capacity for
working outside simplistic and stereotypical images, even when the filmmaker

Figure 20. Reginald Marsh, *Twenty-Cent Movie*, 1936. Courtesy Whitney Museum of American Art.

was someone as gifted and idiosyncratic as Orson Welles. Carmen Miranda, who starred in eight Hollywood musicals and two Broadway musical shows between 1939 and 1944, captured public attention as the image without equal of Latin America. Every one of her productions was a box office success. Even though she was never the headliner and always performed as a supporting character actress, the press reported and the studios believed that the public went to her movies in very large numbers primarily to see her. Miranda was reportedly the highest paid female performer in the United States, and the money she earned for Twentieth Century-Fox stimulated other studios to seek their own "Latin bombshells"—Lina Romay at MGM, Lupe Vélez (most famous for her series of films as the "Mexican Spitfire") and Margo at RKO, María Móntez at Universal. None of them came close to Miranda's ability to excite the public, and their roles were limited to second-tier horror and adventure movies, or low-budget comedies. Stereotypes of Latin bombshells and spitfires were not in themselves sufficient to grab and hold popular attention.

Miranda's attraction rested on her ability to perform clichés so that they became funny and exciting. Which is to say, that in her hands, stereotypes turned into the opposite of clichés even if they never let go of familiar, predictable routines. The pattern of transfiguring stereotypes began when she was a young singer in Brazil, where in her rise to stardom, she, a young white woman, an immigrant from Portugal no less, adopted the clothes and mannerisms of black Bahian women. Her routines invoked stereotypes analogous to the Mammy and Aunt Jemima images in the United States, but somehow in the racial masquerade Miranda escaped ridiculing the symbols she performed. Intellectuals in both the United States and Brazil disapproved of her image, derided as ludicrous and, in Brazil after Miranda's success as a global star, as "Americanized."[33]

The critical accusations were accurate, but popular audiences in both countries nonetheless adored her, suggesting that they experienced something that the more refined did not, or that their interaction with stereotypes operated at a different level, perhaps because popular audiences in both countries experienced their own identities as already deeply stereotyped for reasons of race, gender, ethnicity, education, social position, or class. Miranda exemplified the ridiculous nature of self-images working people had to live with, while simultaneously skewering the pointlessness of the public language that elites used to maintain their power and privileges. Miranda performed her first successful record in the United States, "The South American Way," in Portuguese, except for the repeated choruses of the heavily accented title words. The lyrics of "Chica Chica Boom Chick" consisted solely of nonsense syllables sung over samba rhythms, a musical approach paralleling the simultaneous development of scat singing in U.S. jazz. As her motion picture career developed, humor surrounding her persona frequently involved her mangled English syntax and her mispronunciation of simple words. In the first feature written about her for a U.S. magazine, Miranda described her knowledge of English with self-deprecating phrases that can signal "I'm one with you, I've been through what you've been through" to readers who have shared her experience in being underestimated: "'I say monee, monee, monee,' she told an amazed group on the boat before a single question had been asked. 'I say twenty words of English. I say yes and no. I say hot dog! I say turkey sandwich and I say grapefruit. . . . I know tomato juice, apple pie and thank you,' she says brightly. 'De American mens is like potatoes.'"[34]

Criticisms of Miranda during her lifetime point to the limits constraining a humanist conception of cultural exchange. Once cultural exchange became democratic, the problematics of difference assumed new dimensions. Often, understanding differences is less important than maintaining that a shared "human condition" is what counts if people are to work together. Whether differences were superficial or fundamental need not be examined. For the purposes of the war, citizens of many countries were enlisted in the same cause, and they needed to know each other only to the degree that they actually had to work together. Cooperation need go no further. North Americans need not give up their stereotypes of Latin Americans as impulsive, sensuous, and unreflective. Nor did Latin Americans have to abandon assumptions that the United States was a place of human potatoes without an ounce of culture. Those who fell into the role of cultural bridges were likely to be locked into these images. Carmen Miranda could not expand the roles she played in the United States, and indeed her talents as a musician were sacrificed so that audiences could revel in her abilities as a comedian. At the same time, when she returned home in 1940, stony silence greeted her performance at the Urca Casino. She responded with a samba recording, "Disseram que eu voltei americanizada" ("They Say I Returned Americanized"), an angry song that rejected the charges against her in the Brazilian press, a song that quickly became a hit within Brazil with the working-class public that still loved her. "Americanized," she asked, because she returned home with money and was "very rich," because they said she ran around like a crazy woman with her hands waving, because she had "no sauce, no pace, no nothing, no magic"? No, no, no, she responded, those "above her, filled with so much poison," they wanted out of Brazil, they despised the thoughts and feelings of the Brazilian people. She who was born with the samba still lived with its rhythms, she still said "eu te amo" and never "I love you." As long as there was a Brazil, she would still look forward to eating the simple shrimp and vegetable stew that she loved as a child. Everyone knew that those who criticized her success abroad were also those who looked down on average Brazilians as uneducated children, and Miranda's response played with stereotypes to retain the affection of her fans who like her grew up in the slums.

Vinícius de Moraes in reviewing the Brazilian premiere of *That Night in Rio* took an understanding approach to the work that popular entertainers like Miranda did. The film, he noted, was "a friendly gesture from Hollywood in our direction." Brazilians liked slapstick, they liked looking at pretty images of Rio de Janeiro, they were eager to see Carmen Miranda. The music was agreeable, and American dancers performing samba as if it were a cabaret number were grotesquely fascinating to watch. In the end, of course, "the film as such is worthless." The story had been done before, on stage and in film, with Maurice Chevalier. The setting had been switched from Paris to Rio, but for all practical purposes Rio was a name for sets and situations that could be Paris. Miranda was the only part of the film that had anything Brazilian about it, and she jumped around like a schizophrenic. On second thought, de Moraes decided, Carmen Miranda looked more Hindu than Brazilian, with her succession of colorful turbans, her arms waving like snakes, her hands turning into hooded cobra heads. Had Hollywood made her a yoga adept, for whom imitating a snake is a sign of spiritual mastery? De Moraes had to conclude that *That Night in Rio* failed as publicity for Brazil, but was a personal success for its star.[35]

Consistent with Hollywood's efforts to incorporate inter-American relations into its highly reductive, if commercially successful conception of the human condition were the various Latin American fairs and fiestas that the OIAA encouraged department stores in the United States to organize. Tropical plants and booths designed to look like pre-Columbian temple ruins and Spanish colonial churches provided a "fun" environment for offering customers food and clothing with a "Latin" theme. In this case, in addition to promoting "understanding" of other American cultures, the fairs provided customers with imports of products not available from American producers because their facilities were dedicated to war production. Speaking at the opening of a Latin American fair at the Macy's store in midtown Manhattan, Nelson Rockefeller observed, "We in the United States, must, for a long time, devote ourselves militantly to the production of the weapons and munitions of war and we will need—and need increasingly—from our neighbors, not raw materials for war alone, but these products of their crafts and industries for our basic living requirements."[36] Latin American countries had lost their European markets, and stimulating consumer demand in the United States could compensate Latin American companies hurt by the war and solidify integration of the pan-American countries into a more unified, single market. The fairs became a major site for the exhibition of Latin American art, just as many U.S. department stores in the 1940s mounted shows of U.S. artists.[37]

That department stores and motion picture companies operated as commercial entities, even when acting to assist strategic government goals, should be no surprise. The worlds created in such activities had to conform to predictably limited frameworks for what would be interesting to customers. That they relied on iconic stereotypes should also not be surprising, as there were no representations independent of the well-developed repertoire of stereotypes and clichés that formed the "common sense" of consumers. Even with those limitations, at least one Hollywood film, Howard Hawks's *Only Angels Have Wings* (1939), starring Cary Grant and Jean Arthur, provides evidence that a commercial product unambiguously reliant on cultural stereotypes could successfully imagine a shared affective universe linking Americans from the United States with the people of a Spanish-speaking country. Set in an unnamed country roughly geographically equivalent to Colombia or Venezuela, the film depicts U.S. aviators who have started mail service into the Andes, connecting their headquarters at a coastal port to mining communities in the deep interior. The film treats jazz and Latino popular music as equivalent. Musicians from both cultures proficiently play the music from the "other America" and enjoy doing it, just as musicians were actually doing in clubs across the hemisphere.

Stereotypes abound, but the film at several points suddenly goes against the grain of a cliché. Perhaps, the best example is the small town's medical doctor, whose untranslated flowery speeches in Spanish provide a comic relief to the main story with a condescending stereotype of Latin men as blustery talkers, all hot air and no action. However, later in the story, the doctor is needed to fly into a mining community where there has been a serious accident. The flight is difficult, possibly very dangerous depending on unpredictable turns of weather. He replies to the request with his longest speech, which the other characters openly mock as an effort to get out of the trip. However, when his words are translated, they prove entirely apropos to the situation. The doctor has responded to the request with a quotation from Shakespeare's *Henry IV*—"a man can die but once; we owe God a death and let it go which way it will, he that dies this year is quit for the next." The Anglophone characters' mocking attitude disappears instantly. They grasp that what they assumed to be nonsense actually articulated the heart of their own code of honor. "He's no fool," one of them says simply. The filmmakers have acknowledged that they had deliberately set up the doctor to appear as a fool to the audience, but then turned the tables so that the audience would recognize their connection to a man historical convention told them to despise. Suddenly, the doctor has transformed into the pivot of the film's obligatory scene, the moment in a story that articulates in crystal-clear form the theme of the film. He proves to be the character who states the principle with which the characters must live if they are to be true to themselves. Stereotypes abound throughout the film, but that the treatment of the Yankee characters was no less dependent on clichéd conventions might remind us of the well-known fact that humor in the United States has long depended on self-deprecating stereotypes. Nobody is exempt because the defiant self-reliance of the American worker comes from not taking oneself too seriously, a theme noted by some of the Latin Americans who visited the United States during the Good Neighbor period.[38]

The irony of the pan-American moment, and a key theme of this book, is that the vision of a fuller intersubjective communication collided against the necessity of formulas, even of stereotypes, to present comprehensible social messages. They were needed by all, those seeking more agency as well as those maintaining power. Naylor did not escape the tyranny of stereotypes, but the social documentary tradition offered a complex mosaic of stereotypes, so complex that the ambiguities of social realities and the individuality of each situation could at times become visible in the excess of images produced and selected for distribution. It was only a stepping-stone to something further, but it marks a point at which the power of stereotypes begins to dissolve in the continuous flow of images that the mass media needed for the thousands of pages printed and the hundreds of hours of film produced every month. The culture industries wanted predictable effects and turned to stereotypes, but capturing the attention of audiences, however briefly, required novelty and therefore the presentation of variation after variation. A generous and thoughtful observer, Naylor produced images that revealed the ambiguities present in the scenes she represented but reaffirmed the liberal and humanist ideals for which the United States and its many allies claimed to defend. That the pan-American moment grew out of a colossal will to power, a movement to transform one nation into the cynosure of the world, should not surprise, for only such colossal hubris could overcome the resistance to complex thinking embedded in stereotypes.

The rediscovery of Naylor's Brazilian photographs came after the end of the Cold War. Renewed interest reflected a resurgence of liberal ideas that could neutralize the failed dichotomies that had molded most political utopias during the twentieth century. Liberal utopias were not as dramatic or heroic as those motivating Marxists, but they were often grounded in consideration of everyday life and supported faith that social divisions could heal without violent upheaval. The diversity of Brazil shown in Naylor's work offered valued clues of an older way of thinking about difference that could be resuscitated for the twenty-first century. It is necessary, however, to keep in mind that the defense of pluralism and the hope that the abysses that set different peoples against each other could be bridged helped justify the expansion of U.S. economic and military power to every part of the globe. For many of the artists and writers who dedicated their talents to the war effort, the project of people-to-people communication was not an illusion. Nor was the utopian dream that local, national, and global cultures could be harmonized without anybody having to abandon their own roots. Érico Veríssimo, whose participation in wartime cultural exchange programs led to him becoming the first Latin American author to enjoy commercial success in the United States, discovered how difficult global politics made it to remain in the dream, but it was global politics that provided him an opportunity to speak to North American readers, and through them to readers around the world. Within that inescapable contradiction, the liberal effort had yet to find a way to build a society where people could stand before each other face to face and recognize what they shared as the basis for working together to solve common problems.

Chapter 7

"Black Cat on a Field of Snow"

In late 1940, Érico Veríssimo (1905–1975), author of six novels, one collection of short stories, and seventeen children's books, received an unexpected invitation from the U.S. State Department to tour the United States, all expenses paid (Figure 21).[1] At thirty-five years old, he was one of Brazil's most popular younger writers, but none of his work had yet been translated into English. From January to April 1941, he traveled across the United States, meeting politicians, celebrities, business leaders, and a sprinkling of average citizens. During his odyssey, he gave twenty-four lectures on Brazilian literature and society to both civic groups and university classes. His book reporting his impressions, *Gato Preto em Campo de Neve* ("Black Cat on a Field of Snow"), remains in print, a classic in the field of travel literature. As an effort to influence public opinion in Brazil, the State Department considered its invitation to Veríssimo to have been exceptionally successful. *Gato Preto em Campo de Neve* was a "best-seller" of its kind, with a sale of fifteen thousand copies in the first two months, a sales figure that at the time was said to have exceeded any previous book published in the country.[2]

The book presented a positive account of a people Veríssimo described as fundamentally peaceful and inward looking but grappling with many questions, foremost among them in 1941, whether the United States would go to war against Hitler. The book generated extensive discussion within Brazil, generally in a positive tone. The questions of war and peace that the United States faced also pressed on Brazil, divided over its responsibilities in world affairs, unsure whether aligning with the United States against Germany would lead to U.S. culture flooding into the country and overwhelming everything distinctive about Brazilian society.[3] Veríssimo reminded his readers that Americans and Brazilians knew little of each other. Americans confused Brazil with Spanish-speaking America and often assumed that it was a primitive place where most people walked around without clothes. He noted that when he visited the Philadelphia Academy of Natural Sciences, his host "showed me graphics and instruments with a bit of a protective air as if he were revealing to a savage recently arrived to civilization the wonders

Figure 21. Érico Veríssimo, Mafalda Volpe Veríssimo, Clarissa Veríssimo Jaffe, and Luiz Fernando Veríssimo arriving at Miami International Airport, 1943, photographer unknown. Permission to reproduce the photograph kindly granted by Agência Riff on behalf of the Veríssimo family. Image courtesy of the Acervo de Érico Veríssimo, Instituto Moreira Salles, Rio de Janeiro.

that the privileged mind of the white man had produced. He acted surprised, even incredulous, when I told him that in Brazil we do know about electric lights, the microscope, and photography." Brazilians, for their part, often imagined that the United States was a place filled with gangsters, cowboys, and "fallen women."[4]

In either direction, formulas and prejudices substituted for real knowledge, but Veríssimo assumed that reliance on stereotypes reflected lack of knowledge rather than prejudice. Veríssimo continually insisted throughout the book that the United States was filled with marvels that were possible only when a people "have a feeling for beauty" and "are capable of poetry."[5] Veríssimo argued that attitudes toward life he encountered were similar to those of most Brazilians, who much like Americans were generous and open hearted, but also largely ignorant of the world outside their immediate lives. That the two countries, which Veríssimo assumed were to become allies, were both like adolescents excitedly searching for the poetry of existence gave him hope for the world's future. For peace to be restored, for there to be an end to dictators, for a new world where goodwill, poetry, fantasy, diversity, and tolerance flourished, Americans and Brazilians needed to know each other on a deeper level than they ever had in the past, even though neither people was particularly sophisticated or worldly. The bureaucratic formulas of the "Good Neighbor Policy" were largely silly, he added, repeating a phrase that had become commonplace for writers and artists involved in its programs, but, to the degree that the U.S. government pursued people-to-people contact, its actions encouraged hope.[6]

The United States had long been a place Veríssimo wanted to see firsthand, in part because of the many Hollywood movies he had seen since his childhood, in part because of the many short stories and novels by U.S. authors he had translated into Portuguese.[7] As a writer also working as an acquisitions editor for a Brazilian publisher, he was particularly interested in how U.S. publishing houses selected the books they released. During his stay in New York City, the State Department arranged for him to meet with editors of some of the biggest companies in the country. At Macmillan, Veríssimo learned that "to a certain degree, taking into account differences in size, our problems are the same as those with which North American editors must struggle."[8] Macmillan had discovered Margaret Mitchell and published her first novel, *Gone with the Wind*, a worldwide success that sold millions of copies. No Brazilian publisher could ever hope for sales of even a small fraction of that figure, but Theodore Purdy at Macmillan assured him that very few books sold more than one hundred thousand copies. A successful book sold between ten thousand and fifty thousand copies, each generating a small profit for the firm. Macmillan stayed in business by publishing a large list, most of which sold reasonably well, with a handful generating extremely large profits.[9] The "avalanche" of paper included many mediocre books, but the process also allowed editors room to publish books simply because they admired the quality of the author's writing. Veríssimo, who worked for Editora Globo, a small press that in the 1960s was bought by a media company based in Rio de Janeiro that has since become one of the largest and most important mass-media companies in the world, pondered the tension between quality and commerce that had become typical of U.S. culture. "A publisher that wants to have the material resources sufficient to gamble with the publication of books by authors like, for example, Thomas

Mann," Veríssimo wrote, "must find the resources by publishing an Agatha Christie." He doubted that the general public would ever prefer Marcel Proust to Margaret Mitchell, but he came away from the United States convinced that editors working at the scale he saw enjoyed the flexibility to take risks in what they produced. The bookstores he visited carried a wide range of work, inviting readers to explore difficult materials. An industrial-scale publishing business made it possible for public taste to evolve. To complain about the tawdriness of the U.S. mass media, as many writers and critics in Brazil did, struck Veríssimo as missing the point that, in his opinion, writers "who passively turn themselves over to the public, satisfying all the desires of readers in order always to make them feel good, run the risk of irremediable destruction; but whoever despises the public is likely to become inhuman, pretentious, and isolated from the simple truths of life."[10]

The cultural system that the United States produced gave Veríssimo hope as an author that he could conceivably reach the U.S. public, and the people he had met struck him as curious and eager to learn. At the same time, the U.S. publishing business was in a position to fulfill one of the basic conditions for Americans to know more about Brazil and its people. U.S. publishers were able to take financial risks, and the editors he met seemed genuinely interested in publishing Brazilian authors. Veríssimo personally agreed with one of the basic propositions behind the State Department's efforts at cultural exchange: when books from Latin America started appearing in the United States, when they found readers and generated informed criticism, the Good Neighbor Policy would move to a new stage. Instead of its being an alliance of convenience that suited the needs of the Roosevelt and Vargas administrations, Veríssimo believed, the people in both countries would start getting involved. They themselves would demand more contact. Stereotypes would linger, for, Veríssimo noted, the human mind seemed to need ready-to-hand formulas for looking at what was outside immediate personal experience, but, if contact increased, formulas would come into conflict with experience. The publics in both countries would demand more information once they began to learn more of the reality of the other country.[11]

Veríssimo came from a "traditional" landowning family based in Cruz Alta, a small town in the center of Rio Grande do Sul, the southernmost state of Brazil. His father, who in addition to owning land ran a pharmacy, went bankrupt in 1922 and lost everything. Veríssimo, studying at a private high school run by Episcopalians from the United States, had to leave school a year before he was to graduate and go to work. His mother left her husband and returned home to her parents, also "traditional" landowners who had lost most of their wealth when they could not pay off mortgages taken out to develop their land, but they had held onto a house and a small plot of land on the outskirts of the town. She supported herself and her two sons by running a small dressmaking business out of her parents' home, while Veríssimo worked, first in an uncle's warehouse, then in a bank. When he turned twenty, a relative bought a pharmacy that Veríssimo ran for three years. He augmented his income by teaching English and doing translations from English and French.[12]

In 1930, he moved from his hometown to Porto Alegre, the state capital, where, after publishing his first short story, the editors of a local magazine, the *Revista do Globo*, offered him a job. Veríssimo's primary responsibility was to scour newspapers and magazines from the United States, Britain, Germany, France, Italy, and Argentina to locate stories and articles that might interest the readers of the *Revista do Globo* and then translate them into Portuguese. Operating on a shoestring, the journal had no money for buying rights, and the editors simply pirated foreign content they wanted to publish.[13]

The job quickly educated Veríssimo in the standards of commercial literature published in Europe and North America. In the process, he developed a Portuguese-language style that effectively communicated the sentiments of global middle-class literature to Brazilian readers. In addition to his work for the *Revista do Globo*, Veríssimo worked on the Sunday literary pages of two newspapers, and he wrote a column, "A Mulher e o Lar" ("Woman's Home"). As his employer expanded into publishing books, also typically pirated, Veríssimo translated U.S. and English detective novels as well as more serious fiction by a wide variety of prominent authors, including Aldous Huxley, John Steinbeck, W. Somerset Maugham, and Katherine Mansfield. His employer put him in charge of the program to publish translations of classic and contemporary literature, with republication of U.S. books the highest priority for Veríssimo's employers. Veríssimo selected titles to be translated and supervised the translators he hired. In this capacity, Veríssimo introduced many North American writers to the Brazilian reading public for the first time.[14] He began publishing his own short stories in the *Revista do Globo*, and *Clarissa*, his first novel, appeared in 1933—a book Veríssimo later noted he modeled after the work of Katherine Mansfield and Francis Jammes, two authors he had translated.[15] Given everything he had to do, his own writing happened "in between everything else,"[16] but in 1938, his fifth novel, *Olhai os lírios do campo* ("Consider the Lilies of the Field"), turned without any expectation into Brazil's first bestseller, selling some forty thousand copies. He was one of three Brazilian writers at the end of the 1930s whose income as an author, while modest by standards in Europe and the United States, could conceivably support him and his family. He continued working as foreign book editor for Editora Globo, while he wrote a new novel every year.[17]

Around the time of his first visit to the United States, Veríssimo jotted down a note *in English* about himself and his goals as a writer:[18] "It is very difficult to be a professional writer. If you want to make a living from your writing you must publish at least one book per year. But you cannot do that without endangering the very quality of your books. Take my case, for instance. I mean my novels. I am able to turn out a novel each year. I am sure they may be very readable novels."[19] He did not continue his self-evaluation, but two years later, in a letter sent to a studio official at Warner Brothers, Veríssimo observed, "I am now starting a new novel. I hate to write a book each year, but I can't help it. Writing is my 'racket.' And moreover I don't believe in masterpieces. We are living in a mad and changing world. It is no use to polish and repolish what you write in order to cause the book to last. What is going to *last* of the thousands and thousands of books that are being published in these days of our years?"[20] Veríssimo was trying to interest producers in one of his books, and the letter accompanied a copy of *Consider the Lilies of the Field*.

Unlike that of most other writers of his generation, his formation, particularly his being thrown into the initial development of a mass media industry in his own country,[21] made him particularly well prepared to speak to the U.S. reading public; few other writers of his generation in Latin America had so thoroughly internalized the demands of modern consumer culture. Nonetheless, despite the apparent interest of many editors in his work and a commitment from the State Department to provide subsidies to help a publisher pay for the additional costs of translation, the path to publication in the United States proved difficult. The middle and late 1930s had been very good years for the book business, and competition to find the next potential best-seller intensified. The business model, however, remained uncertain since sales varied dramatically. In 1936, for example, to take two of the most famous books published in the United States that year: Margaret Mitchell's *Gone with the Wind* sold 1.7 million copies while William Faulkner's *Absalom, Absalom* sold six thousand. Mitchell's book was the only title that sold more than one hundred thousand copies that year, and it would not be until 1941 that another book broke the hundred thousand sales mark. Publishers did not require or expect large sales on every title, but operated on the assumption that the larger number of titles released increased the possibilities for success as long as most titles generated a steady if modest income. Publishers relied on the over fifteen thousand public libraries to provide a minimum number of sales for each title. Purchasers for libraries were not concerned with whether they personally liked a given book or not; they needed to serve a range of tastes within their given communities by providing readers with books that had gained attention in major newspapers and national magazines, while avoiding books that could be considered offensive to community values. Reviews in the general press and in specialized library journals provided libraries with the information they needed in order to know which books to buy.[22]

Publishers needed new manuscripts to maintain a volume of production that had proved overall profitable, but the number of submissions increased at a much faster rate than the increase in titles accepted. Any publisher's review process had to weed out the large majority of potential books hopeful authors or their agents sent in. Manuscripts were judged quickly, and the assumption was that a book would be rejected unless it leaped out and seized the imaginations of reviewers. In Veríssimo's case, there was additional confusion over how to assess what would make a Brazilian writer appealing to U.S. readers. Translations of classic novels by Machado de Assis and Aluísio Azevedo had previously appeared in English. A small press had published a translation of Mário de Andrade's experimental novel *Amar, verbo intranzitivo* ("To Love, an Intransitive Verb") under the title *Fräulein* in 1933, but in general, contemporary Brazilian fiction had no track record in the broader U.S. book market. The experts on Latin America whom publishers turned to for advice provided negative reports of Veríssimo's work. He heard from a writer friend he knew in New York that Ernesto Montenegro, a Chilean journalist living in the United States, had become the reviewer of Latin American books for Farrar and Rinehart, arguably the most important publisher of foreign literature in the United States at the time. Montenegro dismissed Veríssimo's novels as written for Latin ladies who like to weep, rather than for readers looking for serious literature. Veríssimo, Montenegro concluded, needed to learn more about the tastes of the U.S. reading public.[23] Greenberg Publisher, another press that the State Department was trying to interest in Latin American writers, declined Veríssimo's *Caminhos Cruzados* ("Crossroads") because "its technique is too discontinuous; its plot is thin; it has too many characters." The style would not be suitable for an American public.[24]

Farrar and Rinehart declined to publish Veríssimo, as did Harper and Brothers. Thornton Wilder had personally asked his editor at Harper and Brothers to look at *Saga*, Veríssimo's Spanish Civil War novel. Harper's initial response to the book was enthusiastic, but editors questioned whether given the new world war, readers were still interested in stories set during the Spanish Civil War. They thought *Saga* could do well if it were published after other books first appeared and Veríssimo's reputation was established in the United States. Knopf also decided against publishing Veríssimo. Knopf's editors provided no explanation for their decision. Blanche Knopf, who typically made the final choice of books the firm selected from Latin America, preferred work with plenty of folkloric or mythic elements in the storytelling. She had already rejected publishing the work of Jorge Luis Borges because his work was too urbane, too full of literary tricks, and divorced from the intersection of landscape and popular customs that many intellectuals in the United States took as the benchmark of Latin American culture. In 1941, the winner of the first annual prize for "best Latin American novel" to be translated into English was Peruvian Ciro Alegría's *Broad and Alien Is the World* (*El mundo es ancho y ajeno*), a strongly written story of a violent struggle between an indigenous community in the Andes and white politicians and businessmen who want to integrate a rural region into the national political and economic system. Veríssimo's novels generally lacked images of overpowering nature or popular folklore preserving a purer, premodern way of life, the trademarks of novels from Spanish-speaking America translated into English in the 1920s and 1930s.

The most positive response came from Macmillan, where Veríssimo had developed good personal relationships with Doris Patee, the children's book editor, and with Theodore Purdy, who, competent in eight languages, handled acquisitions of foreign books for the firm. Purdy was enthusiastic and hoped to shepherd one of Veríssimo's books through his firm's review process, but immediately after Pearl Harbor, he took a leave of absence to work in Washington with the Office of Strategic Services (OSS the precursor to the CIA). Macmillan turned to Lewis Hanke, a specialist in history of the Spanish colonial period and director of the Hispanic Foundation at the Library of Congress, for advice. Hanke's report was negative: Veríssimo's work was untypical of literature in South America and his picture of southern Brazilian society did not sufficiently distinguish Brazil from more developed countries.[25] Hanke's report underscores a point of division in how different groups within the United States defined authenticity and accessibility. What appealed to the State Department officials who discovered Veríssimo's work was his apparent similarity to popular U.S. writers of the time, authors like Edna Ferber, A. B. Guthrie, or John Steinbeck. His focus on contemporary Brazil made his work, in the State Department opinion, more accessible to U.S. readers, and that could contribute to securing popular support in the United States for an alliance with Brazil. Veríssimo had a talent for overcoming cultural differences, which would help his readers discover shared histories and shared interests. For reviewers like Lewis Hanke, literature published in the United States should help readers understand the profound differences that existed between the United States and Latin American nations, differences that required professional scholarship to elucidate. Robert E. Luckey, surveying Brazilian novels available in English, complained that Veríssimo's work was "less illustrative of a variety of Brazilian personalities."[26]

Negative readers' reports might have been the end of the story, but Veríssimo had several important advocates, fellow writers Thornton Wilder, John Dos Passos, and Robert Nathan, the author of an extraordinarily popular novel, *A Por-*

trait of Jenny. Wilder and Dos Passos used their prestige and Nathan his sales figures to write directly to publishers insisting that they give Veríssimo's work another reading. Additionally, Walter A. Jessup, the new president of the Carnegie Corporation, took up Veríssimo's case. In one letter, Jessup praised a children's book Veríssimo had written on the history of Brazil, *As Aventuras de Tipicuera* ("The Adventures of Tipicuera"): "It is an inspired little book. . . . [On] the last page . . . [he has] phrased most admirably the objectives of this Endowment, and indeed my own personal ambitions since I ended as a soldier in the last great war of 1914–18."[27] Endorsements from writers and public figures like Jessup were important to keeping interest alive, as in practical terms were the efforts of State Department officials to facilitate contacts, but ultimately, Veríssimo required an internal champion within a press, someone like Theodore Purdy at Macmillan, someone whose enthusiasm could override the hesitations of his colleagues.

Much of what Veríssimo experienced was par for the course in the publishing business. Personal connections have long been important for authors to receive full consideration of their work. In an industry where it is difficult to project the outcome of any given product, "gut reactions," not precise calculation, guided decision making. Hanke's report to Macmillan sapped the excitement that the editors had felt at first for a promising new author to add to their list. Now they were unsure whether the material could sell. Simultaneously, Macmillan pursued publication of a novel by Chilean writer Magdalena Petit Marfán, *La Quintrala*, published in 1942 and advertised by the press as a "tale of seventeenth century Chile, in which a beautiful and wealthy woman, known as La Quintrala, is the central character. Her career of evil and bloodshed, witchcraft and murder is based upon legend. Her fourteen crimes begin with the poisoning of her own father when she is sixteen, and continue thruout her long life. The powers of evil and good are represented on the one hand by her witchlike black nurse, on the other by her saintly confessor."[28] Macmillan's editors were looking for Latin American fiction that might fit into the popular fiction market of the United States, and Marfán's work, thoroughly escapist, fit the identification of Latin America with a folkloric, premodern world.

While Veríssimo's books were still in review at Macmillan, Doris Patee wrote Veríssimo: "Seldom do we find an author from another country writing in another language, who has such an understanding of American interests and problems as you have." But then she added, "My conviction about books from other lands is that they should be clearly representative of that land." She emphasized that Veríssimo's book on Joan of Arc would not be appropriate for translation, since in the U.S. book market the topic needed to be treated by a French, English, or American author. "What we do want are stories that really reflect your country." Then complicating the advice, Patee continued, "We also like stories of everyday life in Brazil, introducing of course incidents, back-grounds, customs, that would be new to our [readers]—but experiences which they can share because they are a part of the life of [people] who are quite like themselves except that they live in another land. This always seems a hard kind of book to get."[29] Stories from Brazil needed to be specific and unique to the coun-try, but at the same time they had to convey universal situations that average readers would recognize with pleasure. In a later letter, Patee asserted, "We often find that there is considerable difference in the appeal of books from other coun-tries . . . here and in their own land. There is certainly something universal about [readers'] interests and there ought to be books that we could exchange but in many cases they do seem too strange and different to meet the same response."[30]

The contradictions in Patee's advice suggest that editors often had no idea why one foreign author—say Thomas Mann or Vicente Blasco Ibáñez, two undisputed star writers in the U.S. book market between the two world wars—sold well, and another did not. Lacking that knowledge, they had no firm basis for predicting how any given book would fare, and editors had to (and have to) rely on their gut instincts whether the particular gamble is worth it or not. Patee was interested in getting Veríssimo to produce a book for Macmillan's children's department, which was one of the biggest in the country. A successful children's book could generate as much income for the publisher and the author as a successful novel, but with considerably smaller production, publicity, and marketing costs. As with his novel, Veríssimo failed to produce a proposal that Patee could endorse, and the idea of his writing children's books for the U.S. market evaporated, along appar-ently with Macmillan's interest in adding him to its author list.[31]

Shortly after Doris Patee sent her letters, Veríssimo received a more formal communication from Macmillan declining to offer him a contract. At this point, the University of New Mexico Press approached Veríssimo with a proposal that one of his books appear in its Inter-American Translation Series, subsidized by the Carnegie Corporation. The publisher admitted that there would be hardly any sales beyond university libraries, but at least the book would be available in English.[32] Hearing about this offer from his friends at the State Department, The-odore Purdy made a quick trip to New York to convince the publisher in chief to override the decision of the Macmillan editorial department. Purdy decided that *Caminhos Cruzados* would be the first book to appear, precisely because it had an urban setting. Purdy liked that Porto Alegre felt similar to many modern mid-sized cities in the United States. The book could be appreciated on its merits as a story, *not* as a symbol summarizing another country.[33]

Reviews of the book when it appeared in English in 1943 as *Crossroads* val-idated Purdy's judgment, as did the positive sales figures the book garnered. For the first time in the history of the U.S. publishing business, a book by a Latin

American author went into multiple printings. Critics appreciated the fact that while the characters and the settings were clearly Brazilian, overall situations described were easily accessible. Brazil was not an exotic foreign land, but a society where contemporary people were searching for love and security while struggling with poverty, unemployment, crime, and the persistent danger of war on the horizon. As the *New York Times* summarized it: "A story of life in a teeming modern city in Brazil, where a group of characters work out their crossed destinies amid problems not unlike our own."[34]

Veríssimo himself had expected the translation to fail, telling his translator that the lack "of the colorful things that most readers expect in a novel by a Brazilian author—palm trees, Indians, rumba, serenades, the Amazon jungle, and so forth" would doom the edition.[35] What was the appeal? The *Handbook of Latin American Studies*, published by the Library of Congress, identified the strength of Veríssimo's work in the author's ability to interweave "human destinies in the life of a provincial city, in this case Porto Alegre, set off by the author's unfailingly beautiful prose style and his deep fund of sympathy and human emotion." Another reviewer spoke of Veríssimo's writing as marked by "innate modesty, the absolute lack of any hint of pomposity [and an] invincible sense of humor, always ready to puncture any touch of self-importance."[36]

Veríssimo described an agricultural society in upheaval as industrialization and urbanization quickened. He presented the transformation through sets of personal relationships that dramatized the psychological stresses of sociological processes. Given the centrality of family to the older agricultural order, social stresses played out in the alienation of family members from each other (much as Veríssimo's parents had separated in 1922) and the development of new expectations in which women and children could claim greater autonomy. Happiness, depression, love affairs, divorces, family feuds were indicators of social states in transition.[37] In *Um Lugar ao Sol* ("A Place in the Sun"), a local political boss has the father of the main character killed. Her mother moves with her children to the city. The daughter emerges as the novel's central character as she is torn between her yearning for the solidarity of life in the countryside and the personal freedom she discovers in the city. This was a formula consistent with many a Hollywood film and many a middlebrow novel, most famously at the time Margaret Mitchell's *Gone with the Wind*. In his stories of families in stress, Veríssimo celebrated the lives of men and women forced to discover their latent possibilities. The mixture of utopian and sociological aspects supported what one of his reviewers in the United States called "a dream of the possible oneness of all humankind, united in the bonds of mutual comprehension, peaceful cooperation, and social labor, with the banishment of injustice and selfish ambition. In brief we here draw near to the vast problems confronting the world today; and these problems are treated in the spirit of that great-heartedness which Verissimo, the biographer, found so admirable in his Jeanne d'Arc."[38]

Macmillan released a new Veríssimo novel every two years, and agreed as well to publish a book by him on the history of Brazilian literature. It decided to forgo any further government assistance for translation as the bureaucratic requirements delayed publication, and the editors believed that, with the positive reception *Crossroads* had received, likely sales could easily cover translation costs.[39] A measure of Veríssimo's commercial success in the United States is that he was the only contemporary Latin American novelist with more than two titles published between 1940 and 1960, during which time Macmillan released seven separate books by him. Pablo Neruda was the only comparable contemporary writer, with five poetry books published in the United States before the explosion of interest in Latin American writing during the 1960s (see Table 3 in the Appendix).[40]

Reviewers, with occasional exceptions, praised the author for his storytelling abilities and his understanding of the "human condition." The reviewer for the *Chicago Tribune* praised the book for being "Brazilian in detail, universal in emotion."[41] Veríssimo, the reviewer noted, was said to be the most popular novelist in South America, and "*Crossroads* with its skillful weaving together of five stories showed why."[42] William Du Bois, reviewing the book for the *New York Times*, compared Veríssimo to Theodore Dreiser: "Both writers have the same super-abundant vitality, the same blunt approach; both pour out their story like over-charged dynamos, and let the pieces fall where they may." Du Bois praised Veríssimo for having greater control over form and content than Dreiser. Addressing the Brazilian setting, Du Bois noted that Porto Alegre was the capital city of the southernmost state of Brazil and lay as far south of the equator as Jacksonville, Florida, was to the north. Du Bois added,

> Érico Veríssimo's novel does more than burnish one's geography, far more than bring a strange corner in a strange land alive for us. Though his whirlwind tour of Porto Alegre lasts only five days, it covers the city from slum to boulevard. Senhor Veríssimo moves his characters with such practiced ease the reader forgets how much ground he takes in. But when he puts the book down, he will realize that Porto Alegre is not so different from Jacksonville. *Crossroads* is definitely a solid contribution to a good neighbor policy. . . . Without a single false climax, without rising above an artless reportorial style [Veríssimo] can focus one's interest from the start, and hold it fast, as he manipulates a teeming dramatis personae. The smallest character comes vibrantly alive under his hands,

though he does no more than sketch in an outline. . . . Though [Veríssimo] offers no salvation to ease man's burden, he understands man to the core; he is by turns profound as a saint in armor and cynical as a café wit; always, he is as easy to read as a child's primer. *Crossroads* is a long novel, but this reviewer only wishes it were longer. He is not ashamed to admit that he devoured it in a sitting.[43]

Du Bois's review was particularly auspicious for Veríssimo's debut as a novelist in the United States. The reviewer joined the *New York Times* staff in 1926 and quickly rose to become the editor in chief of the newspaper's book review section, a position he held for three decades. His review of *Crossroads* established a language for discussing Veríssimo's work that most other reviewers echoed and continued to use with subsequent translations of his books. Significantly, both *Library Journal* and *Booklist* recommended that libraries acquire the book, important for assuring a book's commercial success.[44] Reviewers' evaluations of Veríssimo's books over the next two decades again and again stressed his delightful writing style in excellent translation, his powerful understanding of the human condition, his clever ability to weave together several stories into a satisfying unity, his exploration of human frailties made sympathetic "by a deep feeling for the mystery of human existence."[45] While *Crossroads* and *The Rest Is Silence* had urban settings, *Consider the Lilies of the Field* took place in a fictional small town in the central agricultural region of Rio Grande do Sul, a town no doubt modeled on Cruz Alta, where Veríssimo had been born. This novel centers on two doctors, a husband and wife, working together in a small practice struggling with the limitations and the inequities of rural life during the Great Depression, a story that also found resonance with reviewers in the United States and attracted readers there as in Brazil. Encouraged by his editors at Macmillan to develop an epic story of life in southern Brazil, Veríssimo began working on a long novel (eventually seven volumes in the Portuguese-language edition) that traced the fate of a family in rural Rio Grande do Sul from 1745 to 1945. With the publication of the first section, *O Continente* ("The Continent"), in English in 1951, with the title *Time and the Wind*, Herschel Brickell, writing in the *Saturday Review of Literature*, hailed Veríssimo as the most important writer working in Latin America and the new book as being as "fine a novel as Latin America has yet produced at anytime."[46]

The translator of *Crossroads*, a postal clerk from Chicago who taught himself Portuguese by locating new novels that seemed interesting to him and then translating them into English, did not attempt to Americanize the settings or the language. He repeated the Portuguese forms of address that Veríssimo had used, such as *senhor, dona,* and *seu,* each with a distinct set of social registers meaningful to Brazilians addressing each other, but without slowing down the narrative to explain the nuances of each usage. Attentive readers over time might intuit how specific terms function in a society with a somewhat more openly defined social hierarchy than the United States, but readers who did not see that element would still be reminded that despite many similarities, there were fundamental differences between the societies of Brazil and the United States. Readers might well have noticed that many of the characters base their actions on standards set in the United States and Europe, with often ridiculous results; the effects are clear but the book did not explain imitation of the North as a feature of middle-class and elite life in Brazil, nor did the translator make any effort to add any further explanation. Another theme in the book that could easily be misunderstood by most U.S. readers was the exercise of patronage in Brazilian society. The plotline of the book revolves around two characters who have lost their jobs because their employers owe favors to more powerful people with "protégés" in need of positions. To maintain good relations with people whose assistance could be important in the future, the employers invent reasons to fire employees who lack protective patrons. Brazilian readers understood well how systemic *clientelismo* functioned in their country, and Veríssimo's treatment underscored the human costs without needing to explain further. Readers in the United States understood that employers in their country on occasion were known to fire employees to give preferential treatment to friends of friends. U.S. readers, however, would not understand from reading the book that the problem in Brazil was a question of deeply rooted social structures, not simply of personal moral choices, nor would they know that the lack of a patron could make finding a new job difficult to impossible.[47]

Such information would have had to be added into the book, as would more information about the political situation lying behind the occasional discussions in the book about influence and public policy. The price of greater sociological precision might have been a narrative that flowed less fluidly, and the translator chose to focus on the story. This was not the choice of Samuel Putnam, a noted Latin American scholar, when he translated Jorge Amado's novel of labor strife in the cocoa-plantation region of Bahia, *The Violent Land* (original title: *Terras do sem fim*), published by Knopf in 1945 to generally poor reviews. Amado's book in translation could instruct its readers on the complexities of the political and social movements in Brazil in the 1930s and 1940s, potentially valuable information given how important Brazil was as an ally in the war. Veríssimo's book in translation echoed ideas in the United States that politicians are a corrupt and insincere lot, without establishing that different countries have distinctive forms of political corruption. Given the respective political stands that the two authors took—Amado was a militant in the Communist Party, and Veríssimo believed in "a marvelous day when the efforts of men of good will will level all social differences, without violence or extremes"[48]—the strategies adapted by the two translators may well have conveyed what mattered most to their authors.

Chapter 8

On the Road for the Good Neighbor Policy

Gato Preto em Campo de Neve was one of dozens of books published shortly before or during the war describing a Latin American's visit to the United States. Few are memorable, but they document the urge liberals in particular felt to determine whether the United States was up to the challenge of defeating Hitler. The answer always was affirmative. The reasons presented went beyond wealth and industrial power to focus on the idealism of the Americans authors had met. The country's wealth in fact, visitors asserted, was due to the highly developed spiritual qualities of U.S. culture. The answer fit into a long debate within Latin American countries. Conservatives described the United States as materialist, utilitarian, and spiritually empty, lost in a world of machines and, due to excessive levels of immigration, no longer in contact with the country's roots. Liberals responded that only a nation with a highly developed intellectual and cultural life could produce the prodigious wealth that shamed everyone else. Because no previous country had liberated the energy of the average citizen, aristocratic conceptions of culture were no longer valid. The culture emerging in the United States pointed to the future state of humanity when other countries had found their own paths to democracy. In either case, what writers saw was what they came wanting to see, and whether liberal or conservative, they had century-old rhetorical traditions to draw upon. In 1887, a newspaper reporter in Cincinnati interviewed Salvador Camacho Roldán, a prominent Colombian intellectual and political leader touring the United States, about his impressions. Camacho Roldán expressed great admiration for everything he saw except for racial segregation, which he took great pains to single out as a great waste of national resources. His account of what made the United States an admirable model for the rest of the world summarized a classic nineteenth-century liberal view of a moral society that was also inevitably enjoying the fruits of material progress: "the prosperity of the United States is due to its liberal institutions; to the subdivision of wilderness into small easily affordable lots; to foreign demand for its products; to immigration; to public schools; to the absence of a standing army; to an efficient transportation system with low shipping costs making possible a large internal market; to the peace that the country has enjoyed."[1]

The United States, Camacho Roldán wrote, proved that political rights brought prosperity to all and that there were universal values that the entire human race would embrace if given the opportunity. The southern states retained "pride of race" as one of its constituting elements, but to the north and west, the desire to form self-sufficient families by working the land had become the basis of a general culture that remained unique in the world, but whose results were so successful in improving the quality of life that it would be hard to imagine the U.S. model not spreading.[2] After stating that the formation of the United States was the single most important historical event since the fall of the Roman Empire, Camacho Roldán warned that the greatest danger facing the nation was likely that of " exaggerating the grandeur of its destiny."[3] Its solid political, economic, and social foundations could seduce its leaders to overextend the power of the country, a phenomenon he had already observed in a limited form when he served as governor of Panama.

The greatest failing of the United States as a society was the system of racial separation dividing whites and blacks, along with persistent violence against Chinese and Japanese immigrants in the west. Camacho Roldán had worked for the cause of abolition of slavery in his own country, and he hoped that in Colombia, each individual was treated according to his personal abilities without respect to race. The U.S. determination to humiliate people of African descent made no sense to him because it created a resentful enemy in the heart of the nation, separated from the majority and eventually prompted to strike back. The Colombian attitude seemed to him more sensible—recognize individuals for the contributions they make, encourage everyone to do better. Colombia did not have the resources that the United States enjoyed. Too many people with the potential to contribute to the nation's progress were stuck in isolation. His country's future would be hopeless if it wrote off the majority of the population. The U.S. obsession with race puzzled him because it was so at odds, he thought, with the liberal values driving the country's prosperity.

Camacho Roldán was one of thousands of Latin American and European liberals in the nineteenth century who traveled to the United States to see the wonders of the future and to be reassured that U.S. society if not perfect was mostly successful. There were others who saw only disaster, a future that they did not want, even if they were not sure it could be held back. Seven years later, Paul Groussac, one of the leaders of Argentina's literary elite and director of the National Library, wrote in his account of traveling through the United States that North Americans were "impermeable" to everything that was truly civilized.

Newspapers, theater, conversation, clothing, jewelry, parades, food—all were "mammoth" and all were in bad taste. Granting the many innovations he saw everywhere he went, Groussac nonetheless had to conclude that Yankee imagination led to bigger and uglier monstrosities surrounding him at every step he took. Chicago might have its own type of beauty, which at least was more authentic than the aping of European fashion in New York and Boston, but the most genuine expressions of U.S. culture revolved around material accumulation and grandiose size that dwarfed any conceivable human scale. The famous elevated trains blocked out the light of the sun and were so loud that no conversation whatsoever could ever take place on the streets of downtown Chicago. But then Chicagoans had no need for either quiet or reflection. Busy schedules devoured any time for thought. Activity and movement replaced assessing one's thoughts and feelings. As he moved from city to city, from monument to monument, all Groussac could report was physical and emotional distress.[4] Groussac was a man of letters, but also a spokesman for the landowning class that dominated Argentinean society. The chief horror in his account of the United States was workingmen having a say in government because of voting rights and political organization, in the economy because landownership was widespread, or in culture because their tastes shaped commercial media. It was a world turned upside down, though in fact Groussac's imagery used language virtually identical to Julián Martel's description of modernizing, commercializing Buenos Aires of the 1880s in *La Bolsa* ("The Stock Exchange"), his famous novel from 1891.[5]

Whether praising or damning, most treatments have a deeply schematic quality. Nineteenth-century books recounting trips to the United States have much in common with the many later books summarizing trips to the Soviet Union, China, or Cuba. Only a handful of authors lived long enough within the United States to see its complexities. Some, like Ernesto Montenegro in *Puritania* (1934) or Martín García Mérou in *Estudios Americanos* (1900), had a jaundiced view, but one that saw a mixture of power and powerlessness, of grandeur and pathos. The country was capable of great things, including great threats to its neighbors, but it was a place so difficult to organize or focus that worries about what it could do, while not unwarranted, usually overestimated the capacity of the nation to act coherently or strategically. A reasonable message for the leaders of the larger nations prior to the expansion of U.S. military power during World War II and the Cold War, but one that ignored the sufferings of Haitians, Dominicans, or Nicaraguans, the most persistent victims of U.S. gunboat diplomacy between 1910 and 1940.

A message emphasizing the complexity and confusion of life in the United States was not one many wanted to hear in 1941 or 1942, nor did they want to hear about the continuing danger the country posed to smaller, weaker nations, a message that had been taken up by the most vocal pro-Nazi, protofascist forces in Latin America.[6] Instead, liberal visitors writing about their visit to the United States found commitment to antifascism everywhere they went. In addition to Veríssimo's book, two others stand out for the arguments and information that the authors presented. Manuel Seoane had been a Peruvian revolutionary who had spent the 1930s fighting for his country and its neighbors to escape what he called in the title of a book he published in 1930 "la garra yanqui," describing Latin American countries increasingly caught in the iron grip of the Yankee eagle's talons. In 1940, following the publication of Hermann Rauschning's *Hitler Speaks*, a detailed description of Hitler's war aims, Seoane reluctantly came to the conclusion that nationalists had to accept that alliance with the United States had become essential for Latin Americans because German victory meant enslavement. Rauschning reported Hitler promising to take over the "Affenländer" ("monkey lands"), appointing viceroys to govern them, and sending Nordic colonists who would occupy all positions of power and be the only ones in the colonial world allowed to own property. In the book, Hitler singled out Latin America as a part of the world that had never realized its potential for producing wealth because the Spanish, the Portuguese, the British, and the North Americans had shown too much consideration for the people living there, inferior races who would finally learn how to work once they had German masters or disappear from the face of the earth.[7]

The State Department invited Seoane to travel in the United States, and the visit changed his mind about a country he had previously described with scorn. He came to the conclusion that the mining companies that plagued Peru and other Andean countries acted in a manner profoundly untypical of the Americans he met during his visit. Government officials freely admitted that U.S. companies abroad acted in ways that could not be defended and that were ultimately injurious to U.S. interests. Seoane confessed that the culture of everyday Americans impressed him in ways that he had never expected: "I arrived in the United States thinking that everybody would be hostile and cold. Americans were rude to each other, and if you needed help, nobody gave it to you." Instead he found people to be exceptionally friendly and ever ready to go out of their way to help. Nor were they any more obsessed with their work than people in Latin America. On one occasion while he was working late in his hotel room typing up an article he had drafted, he reported that three young airmen in the next room knocked on his door "to suggest that he take a break and drink a whiskey with them instead of working." The number of people who could speak Spanish surprised him, and he discovered that when he could not think of how to say something in English, there was usually somebody around to help who had taken Spanish in high school or university. He returned to his home enthusiastic about the future relations between Latin America and the United States because he was certain that whatever ups and downs there were likely to be, the culture of everyday life in the United States would lead sooner or later to problems getting fixed.[8]

María Rosa Oliver's two books on her life in the United States as a specialist working for the Office of Inter-American Affairs during the war are the works of an especially talented writer who was one of the founders of the journal *Sur* and a frequent contributor to its pages.[9] She left Argentina to work in the United States in 1943 "for the duration," as she put it, because, as a communist, she needed to contribute directly to the defeat of Germany. She understood that there was no material basis for a relationship between Argentina and the United States to be equal. Nor did she doubt the exploitative nature of U.S. domination. Nonetheless, the future of her country, where pro-Nazis were found in the highest levels of government, had come to depend solely on U.S. power. She noted, reflecting on what *Hitler Speaks* suggested could happen were the Germans to prevail, that if she had to choose between masters, she preferred a power that, however materialistic and arrogant, hated spending money on the military to a power that dealt with people it did not like by building gas chambers.[10]

Her job at the OIAA involved three main duties. She and another Argentinean reviewed all proposed publications and films to be distributed in the United States that included material about Argentina. They corrected inaccuracies, but they were also to flag anything that they thought might offend the Argentinean public or create an impression in the United States that could damage efforts to strengthen people-to-people relationships. She noted that in one newsreel reporting on Brazilian soldiers leaving to join the front in Italy, images of friendly, laughing Brazilian soldiers boarding their troop ships were followed by a shot of Argentinean soldiers marching in a style reminiscent of the German goose step. Oliver protested that the shot gave the impression that Argentina was already a German ally, when in fact Argentineans were deeply divided and the aim of U.S. policy was to assist those resisting the fascist sympathizers. The OIAA agreed with her and insisted the newsreel producers remove the shot before the report was sent out to theaters.

Coming from a wealthy landowning family, she was a close friend of the Argentinean ambassador to the United States as well as several of his adjuncts, all sharing her elite social background. Her second duty was to visit with them frequently on an informal basis and gather information, including gossip, about the attitudes of the country's leaders toward the war. Her third responsibility was to give talks across the United States, often on a moment's notice, to help U.S. citizens better understand the importance of their relation to Latin America and how Latin American countries supported the war effort. Fluent in English and cosmopolitan, Oliver was a particularly valuable speaker for women's clubs, religious groups, and college classes.[11] Most of the Latin Americans she met during her stay in the United States were also going out on the road as speakers whose talks served to put human faces on pan-Americanism and the Good Neighbor Policy. As with Seoane, encounters with a broader range of Americans impressed Oliver, whose social life in Washington involved dinners with Nelson Rockefeller, Vice President Henry Wallace, or some other person of power. She noted that, during her four years in the United States, she never once heard a North American insist that the "American way of life" was the path that other countries must follow. Instead, she continually heard both citizens and leaders say that progress came only when each country found its own best way for satisfying the needs and aspirations of the people.[12]

In early 1943, as Érico Veríssimo's *Crossroads* was about to appear in the United States, Richard Pattee from the Division of Cultural Relations in the State Department contacted Veríssimo with an invitation to spend one or two years in the United States, lecturing on Brazilian literature at an American university. Veríssimo was unsure if he should accept the offer, given that he had not even graduated from high school and he had no experience as a teacher in Brazil. Nonetheless, the idea of spending a longer period of time in the United States appealed to him. He hoped he would be able to follow trends in the U.S. publishing business more closely and make better use of the contacts he had developed in the United States to land the Portuguese-language rights for a wider range of U.S. best-sellers. Despite that goal, he and his wife decided they wanted to live in California rather than on the East Coast, opting for a part of the country that had struck Veríssimo as culturally more comfortable for him and his family.[13]

The State Department arranged an appointment at the University of California, Berkeley. Veríssimo was one of 157 visiting professors whose teaching appointments at U.S. colleges and universities the federal government subsidized.[14] Veríssimo joined Colombian historian and essayist Germán Arciniegas as a visiting scholar in the Department of Spanish and Portuguese at Berkeley. Arciniegas, formerly minister of education in Colombia, was at the time the editor of *Revista de América*, a monthly publication of the newspaper *El Tiempo* in Bogotá. He and his journal were ardent defenders of pan-Americanism, advocating the idea that the American nations shared a common history of conquest, slavery, and immigration. Above all, they all struggled to overcome the legacies of economies built for the purpose of exporting primary resources. The United States, as the first American nation to become an industrial power, was, for the time being, the natural leader of the continent, but only to the degree that it aided the other American nations to become self-sufficient. Arciniegas understood the political and economic forces within the United States seeking to put the rest of the continent into a state of subservience. Yet he was convinced that they would ultimately fail because, like his Colombian predecessor Camacho Roldán, Arciniegas was convinced that the forces for greed were in opposition to the basic values that had made the United States prosperous. To the degree they succeeded in their schemes, they weakened the country in ways that would make imperial policies unsustainable. The struggle to achieve the potential of the American continent might go on for generations. His role was to contribute to the ultimate success of liberal values globally by continuing to talk to North Americans as much as to his own compatriots. During his stay at Berkeley, Arciniegas took advantage of government programs to subsidize books by Latin Americans to edit *The Green Continent*, an anthology of contemporary Latin American writing that expressed the distinctive values of the "New World" in an age of global war. Knopf published the book in 1944 to superb reviews and good sales; the book remained in print until the 1970s, going through dozens of new printings.[15] Veríssimo was the sole Brazilian represented in the collection, a reflection of the still limited interaction between intellectuals in Spanish-speaking America and Brazil independent of the Pan American Union.

Veríssimo taught an undergraduate course on Brazilian literature in English three days a week. His class was so successful that the room had to be changed to accommodate the number of students who wanted to enroll. He missed home, he reported, at times wanting to make arrangements to return to all the friends and places he knew so well. But living in the United States offered new opportunities for him. He wrote home to his friends at Editora Globo, "It seems incredible, but even in the middle of a dreadful war, the country remains orderly. There's the same enthusiasm, the same smiling concern for other people." That no one challenged his credentials as a teacher was enlightening and provided insight into an aspect of life in the United States that he thought explained the flexibility of the society: "In the midst of all these wonders, one melancholy thought haunts me. If I were to say that in my hometown I could not be a professor for the simple reasons that I don't have a doctor's degree and I am not a practicing Catholic, they would be floored with surprise."[16]

He wanted to stay long enough to get past the superficial impressions a traveler makes and reach a point where he could understand why this country functioned so well even in the midst of chaos. This question was to be the theme of his second book on the United States, *A Volta do Gato Preto* ("Return of the Black Cat"), but the answers eluded him and important parts of his experience were omitted. Veríssimo may have discovered the truth of Lewis Hanke's warning to another Brazilian writer on his arrival to the United States, "If you are going to write a book about a country, three months is the right period. Either that, or you have to live in it for ten years." The "shock of novelty" generates an initial reaction that, Hanke thought, is lost in a struggle to understand the contradictions deeply embedded in the patterns of everyday life.[17]

As he stayed, Veríssimo grew increasingly ambivalent about the people and the culture surrounding him. He wrote a friend at Editora Globo, "This country is a land of marvels, even with all its defects and problems. But we don't need to copy how they live. We have our own ways, which are better, wiser, kinder. What we need is better health care, better schools, a higher standard of living. Everything else we already have."[18] It is important not to overread this statement as an expression of disillusionment. Since the 1920s, Brazilian modernists had identified cultural imitation as a block to the emergence of a truly national culture, organically flowing from the land and its peoples. Alliance with the United States ought not to lead to finding a new foreign model to imitate. Instead, it offered, as Veríssimo put it, as did many other writers on their travels north, an opportunity to observe the ways of life another American people had developed. The goal remained developing a national culture grounded entirely in the conditions of Brazilian life. Veríssimo's disillusionment with the United States and its place in the world would come, but later with the extension of the Cold War into Latin America and especially with the Vietnam War.

Veríssimo's objectives in his second book on the United States seemed to be to challenge mental habits that reinforced Brazilian dependency, among which were the many anti-American stereotypes that most of his readers took for granted. His description of Mills College, a women's liberal arts school in Oakland, where he taught during the summer session, carefully examines how buildings, the grounds, the furnishings have created a series of environments invoking the ideas of the French symbolists, the Spanish Renaissance, and classical China. For all the fanciful references, the school's design was basically unpretentious and practical. He noted that because U.S. society was so focused on action and results, the country's spiritual life was typically externalized into the places and things Americans built. Religion was not a place to meditate on and accept the limitations of the human condition, but a well-organized institution for accomplishing "good deeds."[19] A widespread inability to confront limitations, either their own or of the external situation, often resulted in many Americans having not very interesting personalities. Americans felt that they should be optimistic, and inner conflict was to be avoided. As a result, conversations in the United States were more likely to be about facts and things, not about ideas or feelings. Americans are always looking for something to do, rather than to dig deeper into their souls. They escaped spiritual predicaments by surrounding themselves with things they could buy. But these deeply rooted cultural predispositions did not mean that North Americans lacked a rich cultural life. The way they lived and their willingness to help people in need proved otherwise, but a Latin American had to discover that rich spiritual life in what surrounded North Americans. What was inside them was usually slow to emerge, but could be pried out if one were patient and sympathetic.[20]

Veríssimo spent six weeks living with his family on the Mills College campus while he taught Brazilian literature in English as well as an advanced course in Portuguese conversation in a summer session organized for intensive study of French, Spanish, Portuguese, and Chinese, along with intensive courses in English for teachers from Mexico. He noted that unlike in his own country or most of the other countries he knew, schools in the United States were as concerned with organizing social activities as with course work. For the summer language programs, students and professors lived together in a separate house with its own guest lecturers, discussion groups, and parties, all orchestrated to help students learn about the cultures of the countries whose languages they were learning.[21]

Veríssimo noted that many of the Latin Americans participating in the summer session arrived with strong anti-American prejudices, and they dismissed efforts to introduce them to U.S. culture as mere propaganda. One of the visiting lecturers, a poet from Ecuador, insisted that Veríssimo's affection for American people and their culture was the result of misplaced generosity. There was no intellectual or cultural life in the United States; nor could there be, with a people entirely mechanical, utilitarian, vulgar, and rude. Veríssimo argued that the Ecuadorian's attitudes had nothing to do with progressive anti-imperialism, but reflected a style of deeply neocolonial thinking widespread among Latin American intellectuals. They could not abide a society organized around the principle of serving the common good and that did not put much importance on satisfying the personal pleasures of the privileged. In the poet's case, Veríssimo thought that since the United States was not like the bohemian and literary Paris where the poet had lived happily as a young man, it must be a miserable place. Equally neocolonial in Veríssimo's estimation was the poet's fashionable embrace of Marxism. The poet touted his love for the masses and popular culture, but Veríssimo observed that this love was theoretical and vague. The poet complained frequently that one of the things he most disliked about life in the United States was the lack of servants for middle-class people like him. "But my dear poet," Veríssimo objected, "didn't you tell me that you are a socialist?" "Yes, of course, my friend, but that's different. There will always be masters and slaves."[22]

Neocolonialism was the theme that Veríssimo stressed to a forum of social scientists at Berkeley that the OIAA assembled to analyze why dictatorships were so common in Latin America. Veríssimo devoted eight pages in his book to the forum and his contribution to the discussion. He noted that the academics who participated were eminent scholars with a tremendous grasp of social theory but were for the most part ignorant of the practical choices Latin Americans had to make to survive. Veríssimo stressed the importance of a psychology of dependence that had developed throughout Latin America. The poor knew they had to have a "protector": "The owner of a sugar mill, the man in the big house is a clan chieftain and a political leader who eventually turns into a military officer. The peon in peacetime is in wartime the common soldier." Intellectuals were indifferent to this situation if not complicit in the ways in which they served leaders while speaking in the abstract of their love of the people. A few rebels rot in prison, but the majority of intellectuals "support and prolong a political regime that provides them with advantages, profits, favors, and positions." Because national governments were constantly in debt to foreign creditors, national elites looked to the governments of the United States and Britain to adopt the traditional role of a "patron." Veríssimo ended his summary of the situation in Brazil with his perspective on the dictatorship of Getúlio Vargas, overthrown the year before his book appeared in Brazil.[23]

Most of what he said about Brazil in *A Volta do Gato Preto* could not have been published during the Vargas dictatorship. The country's plunge into full democracy at the end of 1945 opened up a period of debate about the country's future. The Brazilian Communist Party, operating openly for the first time since 1935, was growing, a good sign, Veríssimo told his readers. Conservative forces were in retreat, but still controlled the government. Liberals were divided into a dozen political parties, and they typically spoke as if Brazil were already an industrialized power, not a poor nation with over half the population illiterate and living in poverty. The solutions, he insisted, would come only from tapping into the "qualities" Brazilians valued in their everyday lives: "their essential goodness, their horror of violence. The mysterious force that has held together a vast, underpopulated land lacking good communication or transportation systems is an indescribable force." Veríssimo stopped short at this point and confessed, "Well, since it's indescribable, I'd better not try to describe it."[24] In reality, Veríssimo was unclear about what aspects of his country's culture would push Brazil to become the democratic, progressive society he wanted, but he could identify ingrained habits of elites that he knew blocked progressive change.

As the arguments of the book about Brazilian society intensified, Veríssimo turned the full force of his at times malicious sense of humor on the figure of Brazilian composer Heitor Villa-Lobos, who visited California in 1944 for a weeklong festival celebrating his music. Veríssimo honored his compatriot for having arrived into the top rank of living composers, a celebrity not only in Brazil but also in the United States and Europe. The thirteen pages dedicated to Villa-Lobos, whose music the Vargas government embraced as one of the most authentic expressions of national culture, serves as a humorous if bitter exposition on his country's inability to tackle a deeply embedded culture of inequality. Villa-Lobos's hosts asked Veríssimo to serve as the composer's interpreter while he was in California. Veríssimo's initial response was a curt, "You know that the maestro is a difficult man, explosive and irritable, don't you?" Reluctantly, Veríssimo agreed as a patriotic sacrifice.[25]

When Villa-Lobos arrived, the composer could not remember Veríssimo's name and decided to call him "Luís," ignoring every reminder of Veríssimo's actual given name. Annoyed by the personal slight and by the composer's many affectations, Veríssimo claims that he added editorial commentary onto his translations of Villa-Lobos's public statements. "It was in the forests of Brazil that I learned the song of liberty!" Villa-Lobos declared to his audience following the performance of one of his string quartets. Veríssimo translated, but observed in English (or so he reported in *A Volta do Gato Preto*), "And I can believe it, because nowadays, liberty in Brazil . . . [is] only in the woods."[26] In a book ostensibly about everyday life in the United States, a scathing portrait of a rude, self-centered genius contributed to the portrait Veríssimo developed of how dictatorship and a history of neocolonial dependence deformed Brazilian spiritual life. The juxtaposition of Villa-Lobos's egoism with Veríssimo's continuing insistence on the openness and generosity of U.S. society must have been meant to challenge his readers. That his letters written at the same time present a more critical reaction to life in the United States underscores Veríssimo's intentions in *A Volta do Gato Preto*. The objective was not to imitate North American practices, which was patently impossible, and not desirable, but to puncture habits that too easily took the place of critical examination of Brazilian life. Veríssimo offered his observations of the United States at war to indicate what his compatriots might learn from how a democratic culture worked, even in a time of crisis. The United States had many faults, but Brazilians nonetheless needed to consider how Americans had organized the relationship of government, intellectuals, and the people.

When he and his family arrived in Miami and prepared to go through immigration and customs, Veríssimo confessed that the prospect made him jittery. He explained to his Brazilian readers, who he assumed would have a similar reaction, "I come from a country in which we learn to fear, or hate, anything connected to the bureaucracy. Law for us is a frightening word. Whenever I was a boy out at night in the dark streets of my hometown, whenever I encountered a municipal police officer, I started trembling in terror because of the evil look of these men and their long knives dangling from their uniforms. They were thugs, symbols of an arbitrary and violent political tradition. I grew up with that fear in my soul, and with the idea that the civil service is designed to make things difficult and that when all is said and done, government is nothing more than a tool of oppression."[27] Veríssimo described in detail but without commentary his relaxed exchange with the officials admitting him into the United States. The contrast itself stressed his conclusion for Brazilians: Americans took for granted that government served the people; Brazilians still needed to make their government accountable to them. Seeing young, well-fed Americans laughing and talking on the streets of Miami reminded Veríssimo of the impoverished children he saw when he passed through Recife on his way to the United States. He expressed a sensation of guilt: what could he as a writer, particularly one about to be living in the United States, do to improve the lives of his impoverished countrymen? Was there anything he could do? And with whom? A question alluding to the alliances he needed to make if he were to become an activist for change in Brazil. The communists were the best organized and most outspoken advocates for the poor, and with the overthrow of Vargas, the Communist Party was growing by speaking out against the privileged and their U.S. backers. Veríssimo had no interest in dictatorships, which whether right or left justified unchecked powers with claims that only they could solve the country's problems. Veríssimo had allied himself with pan-Americanism because the United States, even with its many deficiencies, gave priority to the well-being of the average citizen and could solve problems once the people set their minds to it. Young Brazilians had the same energy and joy as young Americans, but they could not enjoy the same faith in the future because the selfishness of those with power made a mockery of all ideals of the common good. It might be that continued association with the United States, if Brazilians insisted on making decisions for themselves, could teach the young there were no insuperable obstacles to self-improvement.[28]

Veríssimo joined the small army of foreign visitors talking to the U.S. public about their countries and their role in the war effort. The Office of War Information arranged speaking tours and radio appearances that capitalized on his relative fame as a successful novelist. Between 1943 and 1945, I estimate, based on Veríssimo's archives and records from the Division of Cultural Relations, that he spoke to no less than two hundred groups, traveling to all parts of the country to address civic clubs, women's clubs, university groups, businessmen's associations, and religious institutions. His audiences at any given event could be as small as twenty. More often, they were in the lower hundreds, and at one event six thousand people showed up to hear him speak. In addition, Veríssimo regularly recorded broadcasts that the U.S. government beamed to Europe, and he was invited to christen the destroyer named after the Brazilian diplomat Baron Rio-Branco.

Interviewed on a radio program in Sacramento, California, Veríssimo spoke of how much everything in California reminded him of his own home: "the sunlight—the woods smell in the air—the plane and magnolia trees and even the faces of people. Another thing, they don't rush—that's a Brazilian trait.... People on the East Coast and New England are a bit different [from Brazil], but not in California. You have so many foreign influences and a similarity of climate and landscaping makes Brazilians and Californians rather alike. You know, I believe that geography and environment has a lot of influence on the soul of a people." As always, the interviewer asked him to talk about race relations in Brazil. He spoke of the continuing amalgamation of humanity in Brazil, but even with racial differences, the "psychology" of Brazilians was shared across races, and there were no noticeable differences in how blacks and whites spoke Portuguese. With a bit of humor, he added that the special situation of Brazil was evidence that God was a Brazilian. "Now, what am I going to answer to that!" the interviewer exclaimed. "Don't answer it—just believe!" Veríssimo insisted, and the interviewer responded, "They say we Californians claim everything is bigger and better here, but we don't make quite such amazing statements as you do."[29]

The subject shifted to Brazil's contribution to the war effort. Veríssimo spoke of his long history of writing against the Nazis, and the threats he had received from Brazilian fascists. Since Brazil had joined the war, its navy patrolled the South Atlantic taking out German submarines and destroyers, its soldiers were fighting in the Italian campaign, and Brazilian "G-men" had rounded up German saboteurs and their Brazilian agents. Brazil was performing its duties in the war, he assured his listeners, but warned them of the moral saboteurs who were actively trying to break up the U.S.-Brazilian alliance: "Axis sympathizers try to tell Brazilians that you Americans are just an imperialist country and that you are not interested in pure friendship. You just want markets for your products. I think we must at all costs try to promote a better understanding between North and South America." When asked how to achieve "better understanding," Veríssimo advised, "Through the work of honest, clever, and good willing writers who are more interested in serving inter-American relations than to make sensational statements or just best sellers. By sending down to Brazil students and women and not only big shots.... [W]hen [women] like a place they will talk and talk and talk in a very effective way about that place. And they generally are not so much interested in business, but in human relations."[30] Veríssimo's talks were humorous, a point that he himself underscored: a nation in which average citizens have a well-developed sense of humor will not turn toward fascism or communism. The people of the United States and Brazil did not take themselves too seriously, so neither country was truly in danger of being taken over by a radical movement. Still, he insisted to his U.S. audiences that, in both countries, there were leaders in business and politics who did take themselves too seriously. If there were ever problems in the relationship of the two nations, the self-serious men at the top would be the instigators.[31] Veríssimo warned his audiences that how U.S. motion pictures represented life in the United States and how Americans traveling in Brazil behaved were important for the future relationship of the two countries, as ordinary Brazilians judged a person by what they saw rather than by the gossip they heard. He urged his listeners to give more thought about how others viewed their country. If they did not end the system of racial segregation, the United States would alienate Brazilians and the citizens of most of the countries who had banded together to fight the Nazis.[32]

In 1941, when race hatred was motivating the murder of millions around the globe, the Brazilian psychiatrist Arthur Ramos, author of several psychoanalytic studies of race, coined the term "racial democracy" to distinguish Brazil's special contribution to the international struggle against fascism.[33] "Negroes and mulattoes are integral elements of the national life," Ramos declared in an article written to summarize his major arguments to readers in the United States. He continued, "Their opportunities are the same as the other racial groups in the participation in social and cultural activities. This tradition in the treatment of races is a matter of pride in Brazil. . . . The social status of the Negro in Portuguese America appears, therefore, to be the best in all America. The Negro in Brazil does not, in fact, constitute a minority group, but is merely an element participating fully in the melting pot of the Brazilian people." Ramos challenged his readers to consider whether the British, given a long history of colonialism and vicious treatment of non-Europeans, could honestly be said to be fighting for any principle beyond preservation of their empire. Brazilians would have no stake in the war between Britain and Germany were it not that the Nazis had taken imperialism to a new level by fighting to impose the rule of a "master race" on the rest of the world. Racial prejudice diminished the practice of democracy in the United States as well, Ramos added, but as long as the United States remained committed to pan-Americanism and the equality of all nations, the country had taken the path to becoming a "racial democracy."[34]

Ramos was one of several Brazilian writers who during the interwar years developed the proposition that *brasilianidade* ("Brazilianness") had taken shape in the peaceful interaction of the country's native peoples with Portuguese settlers and African slaves. The cultures of "the three races" belonged equally to all Brazilians, regardless of race, national origins, or social class. Gilberto Freyre, a scholar of Brazilian history and culture who had studied at Columbia University with Franz Boas and Ulrich B. Phillips, stated simply in his 1933 study of the interaction of slaves and their masters in Brazil, "Every Brazilian, even the light-skinned fair one, carries about with him on his soul, when not on soul and body alike . . . the shadow, or at least the birthmark of the native or the Black."[35]

Ramos's term "racial democracy" spread widely in the United States, in part thanks to Stefan Zweig's best-selling book, *Brazil, Land of the Future*, published in 1942. Zweig proclaimed that Brazil had carried out a successful social experiment that resulted in a "complete and conscious negation of all color and racial distinctions." Zweig, a popular Austrian novelist who had fled his home after the annexation of Austria into Nazi Germany, pointed to his adopted country as a place that deserved the "admiration of the whole world" for having shown that modern societies could eliminate racial hatred.[36] Brazil's reputation for "harmonious" race relations was a topic that appealed to many Americans. Érico Veríssimo quickly learned that his audiences expected him to talk about the subject and that they expected blunt comparisons of U.S. and Brazilian racial practices.

Even though "racial democracy" poorly described the complexity of social relations in Brazil, the myth served the interests of both the Brazilian and the U.S. governments, and after the conclusion of World War II, race relations in Brazil gained international significance as the new United Nations Educational, Scientific, and Cultural Organization embraced the proposition that the Brazilian model provided the rest of the world with alternatives to racial and ethnic hatred.[37] UNESCO funded a long-term project involving social scientists from the United States, Brazil, France, Italy, India, and Japan studying race and social mobility, internal migrations within Brazil, and Afro-Brazilian participation in political and economic life. The UNESCO-sponsored project started from an assumption that Brazil, as a land of racial harmony could inform other countries with deeper racial and ethnic divides about institutions and practices that promoted more positive intergroup relations.[38] For supporters of civil rights in the United States, the exaggerated image of Brazil was useful in providing detailed evidence that race relations were a product of national history rather than biology. The brutality of race relations within the United States was abnormal and should be shocking to anybody with an open mind and goodwill. But because race relations had no biological foundations, they could change as a result of new cultural priorities.

Perhaps the most insistent message coming from researchers of race relations in Brazil and other countries with large populations descended from slaves brought from Africa was that what people in the United States saw as racial differences, most people in Latin America understood as the result of widespread poverty and lack of access to education. U.S. poet Elizabeth Bishop wrote for *Life* magazine, that, after living in Brazil for a dozen years, she knew that blacks in Brazil were "rarely found in important positions or even good jobs and [were] almost always poor." That did not mean that they were "second-class citizens," she added; "since most of the population is in exactly the same situation and suffers the same deprivations, the Negro's sufferings do not mark him out as being very different from anyone else."[39] North Americans did not understand widespread poverty and were at a loss when confronted by much of what they saw in Brazil: "Anything a foreigner questions in Brazil—from inefficiency to dirt, from unpainted public buildings to rude bus drivers, from bad transportation to the water shortage—he is likely to blame on 'the national character,' or on the government's lack of concern for the people's welfare. But before he does so, he should first ask himself, Can this be explained simply by poverty? Nine times out of 10 it can."[40] If the wartime alliance truly fought for the principles of democracy and equality, the rich northern countries like the United States would have to address their systematic discrimination against people of color and the poorer countries of the South would have to tackle the income inequalities that left the majority of their citizens deeply impoverished. The ability of blacks and whites to live and work together, even to the degree of sharing poverty, was an example for what the United States might become if the right policies were developed based on the lessons to be learned in Brazil. The southern segregation system conflicted with the U.S. position as the leader of a global coalition fighting racism, and the problem was not confined to the South. As the war progressed, race riots broke out in more than a dozen U.S. cities, including Chicago, Detroit, New York, and Los Angeles. Several dozen people died and millions of dollars of property were destroyed as white mobs rampaged through the streets attacking blacks and Mexicans while the police watched passively. In every part of the country, the government faced defiant resistance to the Equal Opportunity Employment Commission and efforts to use federal military contracts to promote integration of workplaces and unions.

The actual state of race relations in the country posed the most serious challenge to the U.S. ability to exercise global leadership, a challenge that government officials working with allies in the Pan American Union could not evade. Spruille Braden, while ambassador to Cuba in 1943, acknowledged that neither the United States nor the United Kingdom had good records on racial matters. "On the contrary," he continued, "we have many things to be ashamed of and to regret; but, at least, it is something that we are ashamed and do regret, for that proves we are progressing. It would be to no avail now to enumerate the injustices and tragedies of the past. The point is to make sure that these errors will not be repeated."[41] In Cuba, as in Brazil, a large black population needed to be courted lest its suspicion of the United States weaken the support its national government gave to the war alliance. Moving beyond white elites to speak to leaders of black social and cultural organizations represented a new development for U.S. diplomats abroad, but they remained timid about what they said. And for very good countervailing political reasons. The administration needed the support of southern Democrats in Congress for a variety of domestic and international initiatives, and white voters in the North and West who typically voted Democratic might well shift their allegiances if the government pursued serious civil rights and equal opportunity programs. Global leadership required a clean break with racial inequality, but domestic politics limited government action to tepid symbolic statements affirming national principles of equality and democracy, and ensuring that cultural exchange programs included African American intellectuals and artists and funded social science research on the international dimensions of race relations. Even those limited activities were too much for some in Congress. Before the war came to an end, an alliance of southern Democrats and midwestern Republicans took shape to replace programs based on the principle of mutual exchange with new programs focused entirely on providing information about the United States to foreigners. Government coordination of cultural exchange could not easily be reconciled with the ideal of real exchange promoting critical self-evaluation and generating reforms needed for the United States to be an effective world leader.

Chapter 9

Postwar Transitions:
From "Exchange" to "Information"

The Brazilian Foreign Ministry's postwar assessment of cultural exchange programs with the United States was largely positive. A report prepared in 1948 stressed the growing availability of accurate information about Brazil in the United States thanks to a decade of sustained effort by the U.S. government. The document noted the publication of books that summarized Brazilian business and labor law, as well as works that explained the principles guiding the Brazilian legal system. Americans had access to more accurate information about Brazilian history, geography, society, and economy. Portuguese classes were available at most American universities and colleges, and the authors were pleased that U.S. students learned Brazilian vocabulary and grammar instead of usages preferred in Portugal. Brazilian artists, musicians, and writers were better known; a few like Heitor Villa-Lobos, with a successful Broadway musical in production and frequent performances of his symphonic works, were broadly known to the concertgoing public. The survey concluded that cultural exchange had improved understanding of Brazil within the United States and that cooperation with these programs should continue.[1]

Despite the enthusiasm of the report's authors, the program that they lauded had ended along with World War II. Cold War priorities inevitably reshaped cultural exchange, as did the need to placate adversaries of the New Deal incorporated into the coalition supporting President Harry Truman's efforts to "contain" the Soviet Union. Conservatives had long complained that the Roosevelt administration's approach to cultural exchange was hostile to the customs and beliefs of the majority of U.S. citizens.[2] In 1944, attempting to deflect congressional critics, the State Department restructured its cultural program. The Division of Cultural Relations was split into a Division of Science, Education, and Art, responsible for cultural and intellectual exchange programs, and a Division of Motion Pictures

Figure 22. Cândido Portinari, *Retirantes*, 1944 ("Migrant Workers"). Oil on canvas 78.8×70.85 in. (190×180 cm). Courtesy Projeto Portinari, right to reproduce kindly provided by João Candido Portinari.

and Radio, charged with producing material about the United States for foreign audiences. Both units were placed within a newly created Office of Public Information, which had a twofold responsibility: to inform the U.S. public about foreign policy activities and to inform the public of other nations about the United States.[3] On the surface, conservatives had prevailed, though in practice, most programs continued as before. One State Department official prominent for his forceful advocacy of global interventionist policies complained that foolish idealism persisted because both the Division of Cultural Relations in the State Department and the Office of Inter-American Affairs had been staffed by "do-gooders and one-worlders like so many in federal agencies at the time."[4] Many in Congress shared his view as the war ended, and legislative efforts to kill cultural exchange programs continued despite the administrative reform.

The shift to "public information" accompanied the appointment of William Benton as assistant secretary of state for public affairs in 1945, succeeding

Archibald MacLeish. Benton had been a legendary advertising executive whose agency pioneered corporate sponsorship of radio programs.[5] At the State Department, Benton's accomplishments included building the Voice of America radio broadcasts into a major program able to attract large numbers of listeners in many countries. He strengthened the State Department's relations with U.S. newspapers and magazines so that their international reporting more reliably conformed to administration priorities and interpretations.[6] Benton's successes reflected his deep knowledge of how mass media worked as well as strong personal connections built over many years in advertising. An internal memorandum produced in 1945 linked a "public information" focus to commitment to "freedom of information," meaning that the U.S. government should actively combat limitations to the free flow of ideas between countries. International cultural agreements should prohibit the jamming of radio broadcasts such as those that the Voice of America prepared for the Soviet Union and communist-controlled eastern Europe. "Freedom of information" also meant working to end quotas limiting the import of books, magazines, or films, or requirements that many governments around the world had, including most close allies of the United States, for a specific percentage of national content or a minimal percentage of national ownership of companies involved in journalism or the media. In an ideal world, there would be no limits on U.S. media entering other countries, or foreign media entering the United States. In every country, the public would decide what it wanted to read or watch, what it found entertaining, what it trusted as a reliable source of information. Advocacy of "free information" developed into a cornerstone of postwar cultural policy, but the primary target was the Soviet Union only for rhetorical purposes. Communist censorship made for effective talking points on the negative consequences of barriers, but practical action focused on laws in Canada, Europe, and Latin America.[7]

Within the United States, veterans of cultural exchange programs were unhappy with the "public information" direction the White House and State Department adopted as the war came to an end. They were convinced that the new approach would alienate close allies. Ben Cherrington, founding director of the Division of Cultural Relations, complained when the State Department announced the creation of the Office of Public Information that "public information is a one-way undertaking; it is the Government informing the people. . . . As viewed by the skeptical recipient, news emanating from any government Office of Public Information is tinged with propaganda. . . . Surely this is the last unit in the Government in which to place responsibility for international cultural relations."[8] Cherrington had left government service to return to the University of Denver as chancellor. From his position as a university executive, Cherrington tried to build a coalition of educational institutions and philanthropies, the two groups most heavily invested in the philosophy of cultural exchange that the division had promoted, to nudge the government back to its original position as a facilitator of two-way exchange handled primarily by nonprofit institutions. The vision for cultural exchange developed in the United States prior to World War II imagined universities, museums, libraries, public education systems, publishers, philanthropies, and other private-sector institutions taking the lead in developing a transnational public sphere, where interested and educated citizens could debate government policies in forums that no government controlled. Advocates of cultural exchange argued that cultural exchange was better able to achieve the goal of reducing barriers to U.S. books and media in foreign markets, particularly if the government continued offering practical and financial assistance to foreign writers, artists, and filmmakers to enter the lucrative U.S. market. The success of Heitor Villa-Lobos and Érico Veríssimo showed that "cultural exchange" could work and should be scaled up rather than replaced by "public information."

As criticism from both liberals and conservatives intensified, the Truman administration looked to a new international agency, the United Nations Educational, Scientific and Cultural Organization, to assume many of the tasks associated with "cultural exchange." President Truman appointed Archibald MacLeish ambassador to UNESCO, putting him in charge of the U.S. delegation as UNESCO developed its initial priorities. In his public statements, MacLeish stressed that the purpose of the new international organization was first and foremost to help the citizens of the United Nations member states to develop a shared vocabulary that they could use to speak to each other directly about the problems their governments were debating. International relations, he added, "are only possible if there is a common agreement as to the meaning of words. And there can only be a common agreement as to the meaning of words if there is a common acceptance of the values to which words refer."[9] The National Commission for UNESCO prepared a platform that repeated the many platitudes surrounding pan-American cultural exchange but applied them to the entire globe.

The founding of UNESCO occurred as U.S. international strategy was restructured around anticommunism, and U.S. policies toward UNESCO marked the shift. An organization initially imagined as transcending immediate political and ideological divisions became a location where the U.S. government pressured other nations to prove they opposed Soviet dictatorship by embracing the concept of "freedom of information." European and Latin American delegations to UNESCO responded by rejecting the candidate the United States nominated to serve as the founding director-general of UNESCO. The Truman administration was deeply unhappy with the alternative candidate the European delegations put forward, Julian Huxley, a British biologist with a history of socialist and pacifist sympathies.[10] Delegations divided as well over initial projects. During the war, the working group preparing for the formation of UNESCO proposed that the new organization create international panels that would review textbooks used around the world and identify nationalist biases that should be eliminated. UNESCO was ultimately to propose standards for a range of subject areas in order to assure that students in every country shared a common understanding of topics with sufficient scientific and scholarly consensus.

Any project subjecting public education to international review would inevitably be controversial in any country. It is difficult to imagine how proposals might ever have passed congressional review or been implemented in schools across the United States, even if limited to scientific and engineering subjects. As UNESCO began its work, it quickly became clear that a shared understanding of humanity's historical experience was unlikely to take shape in any foreseeable future. The proposal for textbook review collapsed when the Mexican delegation to UNESCO's first international conference entered a motion requiring that the review assess how schoolbooks used in Europe, the United States, and the British Commonwealth presented the history of colonialism. The motion failed, but debate over the proposed textbook review program turned ugly and acrimonious. Archibald MacLeish and Henri Bonnet offered a substitute proposal that UNESCO establish an International Commission for a History of the Scientific and Cultural Development of Mankind, a long-term collaborative project in which panels of historians were to prepare a multivolume history of the world written from an international perspective. The completed project was to provide a reference source of global scholarly opinion on major historical topics that educational authorities around the world could use in developing new curricular materials. Fifteen years later in 1963, the first volume finally appeared, produced by scholars from twelve countries.[11] Few reviewers anywhere in the world had anything positive to say about the volumes as they were published. The reviewer for the *American Historical Review* stated in his review of the sixth and final volume, focused on the twentieth century:

> This massive work is a political product, and, as such, is the very opposite of what these UNESCO volumes were originally intended to be. What has emerged from the crosscurrents of collaborative authorship is not the refined gold of historical truth, shining in magnificent purity and purged of error and bias through the devoted efforts of keen and critical experts who were appointed by their governments for the task. Instead we have an unwieldy, uneven book in which the authors resolutely straddled or avoided every important issue and still provoked an

unremitting drumfire of dissent from the official experts who read and, particularly in the Russian case, disapproved of what had been written.[12]

At the beginning of the Cold War, divisions between liberals and communists made consensus an impossible goal, and as Mexico's determined effort to focus attention on the injustices inherent to the formation of the modern world revealed, colonialism was one of many topics that had to be addressed if there were to be a shared language available for global publics to discuss issues of common concern. At a deeper level, consensus is inconsistent with rough and ready debate over tough policy choices, even in times when ideological convictions are not as sharply defined as they were after 1945. Exchange, if it has any value beyond creating the "goodwill" that many foreign-policy-makers dismissed in the 1940s, creates the conditions for people from different nations to argue through the issues that most divide them.

With the outbreak of the war in Korea in 1950, the U.S. delegation pushed for UNESCO to develop public information programs explaining why the United Nations had authorized military action in Korea against the communists. European and Latin American delegations again united to oppose U.S. efforts to align UNESCO more closely with U.S. foreign policy. The American proposals were controversial because they would nullify previous agreements that UNESCO remain neutral in all international disputes. The U.S. delegation argued that when the United Nations itself was party to a conflict, UNESCO had an obligation to support United Nations objectives by developing their intellectual rationale. The organization's second director, Jaime Torres Bodet, a renowned poet who had previously served as foreign minister of Mexico, offered an alternative proposal that UNESCO undertake responsibility for reconstruction of schools and other cultural institutions in Korea destroyed during the fighting. Even that proposal was controversial, but it passed.

As UNESCO struggled to develop a workable set of priorities, the U.S. government's cultural policies took a unilateral and instrumentalist turn. Assistant Secretary of State William Benton declared in 1945 that cultural exchange should not be "a miscellany of goodwill activities" but "support United States foreign policy in its long range sense and serve as an arm of that policy."[13] In 1950, the advisory committee that Congress established to examine the country's rapidly growing educational exchange programs identified four major goals for any cultural program receiving federal funding. In order of importance, the goals were:

- instruct citizens of other nations in American methods and techniques
- educate citizens of other nations about American artistic, scientific, and scholarly accomplishments

- help other nations improve their schools by learning more about the U.S. educational system
- explain U.S. foreign policy initiatives to citizens of other nations[14]

The State Department expanded funding for U.S. cultural figures to tour abroad, even as public controversy over these programs continued. In 1947, the State Department's *Advancing American Art* exhibition featuring modernist U.S. art, much of it abstract, caused a public firestorm when congressional critics lambasted the selection as contrary to the tastes of most Americans and thus unrepresentative of national culture. President Truman contributed to the controversy by stating that the work selected to highlight the sophistication of U.S. art had been done by people who were too "lazy" to learn how to draw or paint properly.[15] The State Department responded to congressional complaints by pressuring artists on government-funded foreign tours to exclude controversial material from their programs, not always successfully. In 1948, new controversy arose when Katherine Dunham (1909–2006, Figure 23), who was touring South

Figure 23. Katherine Dunham (left) rehearsing with Silvana Mangano for a scene in the film *Mambo* (director, Robert Rossen), 1954. Courtesy Morris Library, Southern Illinois University.

America, angrily refused to remove a dance from her program that represented a lynching in the South.[16] From the State Department perspective, Dunham's protest against racial violence was counterproductive given the eagle eye congressional critics of cultural exchange were giving to any programming they considered derogatory to the United States. The State Department also wanted to assure foreign audiences that a dramatic change in race relations was under way with President Truman's executive actions to integrate the military and federal civil service. The Dunham controversy turned into a debate over government efforts to limit free speech, an argument that the State Department lost no matter whether a critic supported or opposed Dunham.

Despite continuing controversies, the federal government expanded funding for tours of U.S. authors, visual artists, and performing arts groups, largely because they were popular with foreign audiences and succeeded in countering claims that the United States was a place without culture.[17] Perhaps because openly funded government programs continued to provoke such intense conservative reaction, the CIA took on the responsibility of providing secret funds for new cultural organizations that were formally independent but voiced arguments that aligned well with basic U.S. policy goals, most prominently the Congress for Cultural Freedom, which at its height had offices in thirty-five countries, had dozens of paid employees, and published over twenty magazines, three of them in Latin America.[18]

As programs went global, goals shifted away from popular participation. Often postwar programs were "exchange" in name only, the term carrying over from a period when mutuality had been one of the "goodwill activities" most closely associated with cultural programs. The evisceration of citizen involvement is remarkably clear in educational programs, all of which exploded after the end of World War II. During the war, opportunities for Latin American students to spend time in the United States grew quickly. By 1945, two thousand Latin Americans were coming to the United States annually to study at U.S. universities, while a thousand secondary-level students from Pan American Union member states spent a year living with U.S. families and attending high school. Planners of the student-exchange program had expected that with the war's end, the program would start sending equal numbers of U.S. students to study in Latin American high schools and universities for a year abroad as part of their general education.

The Fulbright program (Public Law 584), passed in 1946, extended the educational exchange programs developed between the United States and Latin America to all parts of the world. Expansion, however, led to asymmetry in participation, reflecting the new goal that exchange serve to educate foreigners about what the United States had to offer them and their countries. With Public Law 584, the number of Latin American students coming to the United States increased by a factor of ten at both the university and secondary levels, while exchange programs were extended to Europe and Asia. Reciprocal programs within the western hemisphere shifted toward favoring U.S. specialists in Latin American studies or specific topics related to U.S. aid, with priority given to participants assisting in the improvement of elementary and secondary education, as well as scholars and experts working in health and vocational education or the teaching of English.[19] The Fulbright program replaced the goal of encouraging U.S. citizens to know more about the world with the objective of exporting U.S. expertise. Congressional critics in any event remained adamantly opposed to promoting "global citizenship" skills within the United States. Collaboration between educators across the hemisphere to develop curricular materials that could be used in schools across the Pan American Union slowed down when Congress eliminated federal funding for the effort. Plans to expand instruction of Spanish and Portuguese in U.S. elementary schools also lapsed, when Congress cut all funding supporting these programs from the budget of the Office of Education in 1947.[20]

In the cultural sphere, a pivotal point in the shift to a Cold War posture was the passage of the Smith-Mundt Act in 1948 over stiff opposition from conservative members of Congress led by Senator Joseph McCarthy of Wisconsin, who wanted to terminate all exchange programs without exception. During the year preceding passage of the act, fearful that its passage would enshrine "public information" in national law, Ben Cherrington organized a small group of liberal opponents to the bill. Reiterating a position he had long argued, Cherrington wrote Senator Arthur Vandenberg, the chair of the Senate committee reviewing the legislation, to lobby for cultural cooperation and public information to be separated and authorized independently of each other.[21] Vandenberg replied with a tentative concession that the two efforts could be treated independently if public opinion demanded.

Cherrington gained the support of several university leaders for his cause, most notably James Conant, president of Harvard University, and Harold Dodds, president of Princeton University. The American Council on Education and the YMCA also endorsed his position. Overall, however, few educators or philanthropists joined his campaign. Cherrington recognized that among the groups most concerned with the implementation of cultural exchange programs, most leaders did not share his conviction that cultural exchange had to remain separate from Cold War priorities, nor were they interested in allying with Senator McCarthy. One response from "a leader of a national educational, scientific and cultural organization" stated bluntly, "I wonder whether you fully appreciate the situation. If these efforts fail, the program of information is done for. It will be close. The opponents seek every possible opportunity to discredit it. If we insist on a divorce of information and cultural affairs, at this particular moment, we have to take responsibility for injecting an issue that is quite likely to defeat the appropriation, silence the overseas broadcasts, close our overseas libraries, and deny the Department of State the things *it needs to conduct our foreign policy.*"[22]

With the passage of the Smith-Mundt Act in 1948, along with deep cuts to the budget Congress provided the U.S. National Commission for UNESCO, a definitive turn occurred. Government programs for all practical purposes could no longer entertain the question of what would help U.S. citizens become more responsible global citizens. UNESCO provided funding for international research projects, but a variety of divisions between the governments involved meant the organization was unlikely to serve as a vehicle for a broad-based cultural exchange program independent of government interference. With the fading of the prewar vision of what cultural exchange should do, the people who had been most involved in developing a broader, even if instrumental approach to cultural and intellectual ties between the United States and Latin America retreated from the public stage. Frequently attacked in Congress for his presumed leftist connections, Archibald MacLeish resigned from his position at the State Department to go to Harvard University as professor of rhetoric and oratory. His departure from government service was a clear marker that new people were in charge and they had new ideas. The generation that pioneered inter-American cultural exchange between the two world wars, whether through public service like MacLeish and Cherrington or by writing and publishing like Carleton Beals or Waldo Frank, was increasingly isolated. Beals and Frank were politically suspect at the beginning of the Cold War, but even staunch liberals like MacLeish or Cherrington were apparently insufficiently "tough-minded" to help their country gear up for a long-term ideological conflict with the Soviet Union. MacLeish in particular was subject to bitter personal attacks in Congress for his "leftist," New Deal political sympathies. In all U.S. cultural programs, both covert and transparent, both government-funded and privately supported, antagonism to Marxism-Leninism became an absolute requirement. If, as in Czechoslovakia in 1948, communists won national elections, the mere fact of success in the democratic process could not be permitted to allow communists to take control of any additional countries. U.S. politicians saw communists at work wherever there was labor unrest or political instability, while they simultaneously infiltrated governments and waited for the moment when they could seize power from naïve liberals and social democrats. It could only be communists who were orchestrating displays of anti-American populism, growing rapidly throughout Latin America in the aftermath of World

War II, not historically rooted internal divisions heightened by postwar economic difficulties.

The warning bell for the coming half century of war in the western hemisphere came in May 1948 when a popular uprising in Bogotá, Colombia, led to the deaths of thousands and the destruction of millions of dollars of property. Two weeks before scheduled elections, Ernesto Gaitán, the Liberal Party's populist candidate for president, was gunned down as he campaigned. His supporters, the impoverished and already enraged working people of the nation, rose up to protest what they perceived as a direct attack on democracy. El Bogatazo remains a defining event of post–World War II American life, but it was only the prelude for much worse. Over the next ten years, at least two hundred thousand Colombians died in a bitter civil war between the Conservative Party on the one hand and an alliance of the Liberal and Communist Parties, with all three political parties fielding their own paramilitary forces in the countryside. The military alliance between communist and liberal guerrilla forces worried Washington, as did communist-led strikes in Chile in 1947, centered in public transportation and copper mines. The strikes in Chile ended with a presidential decree that outlawed the Communist Party and suspended the voting rights of twenty thousand suspected communists. In Brazil, after the military coup of October 1945 that removed Getúlio Vargas from the position of president, the new government released political prisoners, both left and right, and legalized all political parties. The Brazilian Communist Party did well in the elections of 1945 and 1946, particularly in urban centers like São Paulo and Rio de Janeiro, where they provided a voice for workers bearing the brunt of postwar economic difficulties. Communists formed a sizable bloc in both houses of Congress. The growing strength of the communists and the legitimacy they had gained through an opening up of the political process led the government of President Eurico Gaspar Dutra, the general who won the 1945 presidential election, to outlaw the Communist Party in 1947 and arrest many of its prominent leaders, while allowing others to escape into exile.[23]

Policymakers in Washington worried that communists might "exploit" popular unrest and turn Latin America into a national security threat. The question might have been equally well posed as whether U.S. global priorities were a security threat to the interests of most Latin American citizens, including the middle class that U.S. officials looked to as their natural allies. Throughout Latin America, foreign and national investment increased through the 1940s, but instead of greater productivity leading to higher living standards, there was a deepening of poverty in most countries. Governments faced publics angry over increases in the cost of basic necessities that far outstripped increases in wages. The cost of living in Brazil jumped 83 percent between 1939 and 1945; in Mexico, 109 percent; in Chile 125 percent; in Bolivia, 200 percent. By contrast, in Argentina, where the government had resisted U.S. wartime policies and pressures, the cost of living increased only 30 percent. With the important exceptions of Mexico and Argentina, the people of Latin American nations had a lower standard of living in 1950 than they had during the Depression. In 1940, for example, the average Colombian worker spent 30 percent of his or her income on food; by 1947, the same diet required 80 percent of an average working person's income. Given across-the-board increases in the cost of housing, clothing, medical care, and other basic necessities, many Colombians, like their counterparts across the continent, had to choose which essentials they would do without. With a rapidly growing urban industrial sector, Mexico was an exception, but much of the countryside remained impoverished.[24]

Brazilian historian Eduardo José Affonso has examined how U.S. advisers stationed in Brazil assessed the causes of worker unrest. He found that they were divided over what would be the most effective solutions and sent contradictory assessments to Washington. Attachés in the U.S. Embassy specializing in labor relations emphasized the legitimacy of worker complaints, given increases in the cost of living. The most effective and the most just solution would be to increase Brazilian salaries and to legalize independent trade unions. The latter reform would promote more formal procedures for addressing worker complaints. Attachés specializing in security and intelligence matters emphasized the role of communist activists in protests. In the mid-1940s, independent trade unions were illegal, and few workers bothered to join the unions that the government had organized during the Vargas dictatorship. Communists had filled the leadership void. Affonso has shown that the U.S. government developed a two-track response to avert a crisis for U.S. interests in Brazil. First, the government recruited labor activists from the American Federation of Labor and the Congress of Industrial Unions to spend time in Brazil helping to organize new trade unions based on the U.S. model. Second, the United States increased support for expanding and modernizing the police, who would be the front line of defense against communists operating within the workers' movement. Let us bracket for the moment the appropriateness of U.S. policymakers engaging in internal debates over how best to manage Brazil's domestic divisions. Affonso shows that Brazilian political forces played the decisive role in how U.S. policies were implemented. Given that many in the Brazilian government opposed wage increases and independent unions, as did many Brazilian and foreign employers, addressing the structural issues behind worker discontent occurred only to a small degree, and in any event it would take years for Brazilians to develop trade unions and other economic institutions grounded in their own history and cultural values. On the other hand, Brazilian authorities enthusiastically accepted increased police funding, which they themselves were eager to use against communists, while expanding and upgrading their already formidable internal security organizations.[25] U.S. labor advisers were consistently frustrated in their projects, while security advisers enjoyed amicable relations with their Brazilian partners.

Brazil was a country reasonably well situated, both politically and economically, to address popular demands. That integration into a U.S.-defined world order increased instability and internal repression boded poorly for U.S. global ambitions after 1945. To the degree that U.S. citizens could grasp the complex factors promoting violence in the western hemisphere, they might, were a liberal conception of responsible government accountable to the citizenry to prevail, bring pressure to modify government policies. Had "cultural exchange," the direction taken between 1938 and 1945 continued, particularly efforts to increase access to U.S. media, Latin American voices would have been heard with greater frequency within the United States. The next logical step would have been greater visibility for debates within different countries over how their governments should handle postwar adjustment. This happened only sporadically. With excellent connections to the U.S. publishing world, Érico Veríssimo contributed three opinion pieces on the situation in Brazil to U.S. periodicals. He himself was trying to understand what was going on in his country, but he had no political or economic expertise that could enlighten readers. He knew that in the simplest terms, Brazilians were "tired of never fulfilled promises [and] fed up with high sounding meaningless words from politicians, whereas they live underfed in the real sense of the word."[26]

In 1947, as the U.S. Congress debated reauthorization of the bracero program bringing hundreds of thousands of Mexican farmers into the United States every year on a short-term basis to work for U.S. farmers, Mexican historian and economist Daniel Cosío Villegas, one of the most distinguished intellectuals in his country, published a short essay dissecting the contradiction between urban and rural life in Mexico. "La Crisis de México" ("The Crisis of Mexico") looked behind the glowing economic statistics documenting rapid growth to ask why then so many farmers needed to work in the United States as field hands. Cosío Villegas argued that Mexican development was impressive but deeply distorted by the corrupt practices of national leaders and by proximity to the United States. Instead of addressing the continuing poverty of the Mexican countryside thirty years after the end of the Mexican revolution, leaders invested in showcase projects that benefited them, their friends, and foreign investors, while relying on the bracero program to provide funds to farmers that they should by rights expect to get from their own government. Increased access to U.S. capital exacerbated divisions within Mexico and, as it had during the years of growth preceding the 1910 revolution, promoted social and political unrest.[27]

In another piece, Cosío Villegas warned that postwar U.S. policy was erasing the goodwill that the United States had earned after 1938. He reported that, during a recent tour of Latin American countries for his Mexican publishing company, he found a high level of distrust of the United States everywhere he went. The connections between the United States and other American countries remained vital for everybody. "Without Latin America," he noted, "the United States will not have even the minimum that it needs for its own happiness. As for us, it is hardly necessary to say that good relations with the United States are a problem simply of life or death, of being or not being." He did not think the new position of the United States as the wealthiest and most powerful country in the world explained the reaction, because Britain had never generated the same level of distrust when it had dominated the world. He heard over and over again that U.S. power was "unmerited"; he heard complaints that U.S. policymakers lacked a sense of "delicacy" when dealing with their counterparts in Colombia, Brazil, or Chile. They showed no second thoughts about the right of their country to make decisions about the future of the world. Cosío Villegas reported consensus that individual Americans in their own country were remarkably courteous and generous. When they traveled abroad, especially on official business, however, they came to give instructions. Leaders across the American countries were returning to old stereotypes that North Americans had more interest in things than people. Cosío Villegas worried that progress in changing U.S. stereotypes about Latin Americans was also being reversed, which, if that was the case, would lead to U.S. officials becoming even more imperious and perhaps reckless in the policies they adopted.[28]

The contradictions of the U.S. postwar position were particularly clear in Brazil, where the closest Latin American ally had been a dictatorship. The Roosevelt administration admired and trusted Getúlio Vargas, and the president expected that Vargas would lead his country's transition to democracy. Vargas had scheduled elections for the end of 1945, but instead of promoting debate, the government heightened scrutiny of publishing and enforced censorship laws with greater rigor. Brazilian intellectuals suspected that Vargas had no intention of letting go of power and would proclaim himself a democrat only when he was certain he would triumph at the polls. In January 1945, the first national congress of Brazilian writers convened in Rio de Janeiro to discuss two topics: improving the economic position of writers in the country and ending censorship. The meeting brought together liberals, Catholics, communists, and independent socialists.[29] While there were many debates within the conference, two resolutions passed with overwhelming support. A resolution to end all forms of censorship in Brazil passed by acclamation without a dissenting voice, or any abstentions. The measure called for unceasing opposition to any regime anywhere in the world that limited freedom of opinion, and called for writers to contribute to the struggle by publicizing the crimes of these regimes to the fullest extent possible. The measure also called for the fullest expansion of international cultural exchange programs, so writers from around the world would be able to meet publics in other nations.

A second resolution that passed with an 80 percent majority upheld "America" as a continent developing through the pursuit of "liberty" and asserted that the freedom of the people of the United States to debate all ideas provided a model for a democratic Brazil. Communists did not oppose the motion, which at the time was consistent with their support for the U.S.-USSR alliance. Opposition came instead from conservative Catholics. Discussion of the motion revealed a broad range of opinions about what "liberty" meant, but all participants agreed that liberty required a right to debate different ideas about how societies might be organized without fear of violence. Brazil was a country where violence was used generously to punish those who disagreed with the government and it policies. The coming victory over fascism gave hope that fear might be banished as a factor in public debates. The participants at the Congress looked to the United States to use its global leadership to make "freedom from fear" a universal right.[30]

Chapter 10

Taking Sides in the Cold War

The postwar economic crisis stopped the robust growth of the publishing business in Brazil that had started in the 1930s. Once the war started, higher prices for paper and ink were ominous signs of problems to come, though publishers continued to prosper through the war. In 1945, however, the government adopted a wage squeeze policy, maintained for two decades, a policy that sought to increase Brazilian international competitiveness by keeping the costs of labor low. The government purposefully pursued inflationary policies to keep the prices of domestically produced goods well below those of foreign imports. The middle class experienced a sharp drop in disposable income.[1] Book sales plummeted, though readers still looked forward to new books from established authors like Érico Veríssimo and Jorge Amado.

Editora Globo had grown before World War II by introducing the small but expanding urban middle class to contemporary literature in Europe and North America. Globo responded to the postwar crisis by essentially eliminating foreign literature from its lists.[2] Globo's new business strategy relied on the publication of textbooks, technical books, and reference books such as dictionaries. Book buyers were less likely to be individual readers. The expanding educational system, along with government agencies and private corporations, became the primary buyers of books in the country. In additional to technical books, Globo, like most other Brazilian publishers, increased translation of world classics, books of historic importance in the public domain and needing only a one-time fee for the translator. These books served the academic market, as well as a growing readership with somewhat limited discretionary spending but desirous of becoming more familiar with the classics of Western civilization.[3]

Érico Veríssimo's responsibilities at Globo as foreign acquisitions editor were considerably reduced. He had more time to write, and he threw himself into *O Tempo e o Vento* ("Time and the Wind"), a seven-volume saga of over 2,200 pages, the first three volumes of which appeared in 1949. All his previous books had been under 250 pages, and most under 200 pages. His books continued to sell well, but royalty income declined as his publisher's difficulties grew. Royalties received from Macmillan for U.S. and other foreign sales took on increasing importance, even if not involving enormous sums, in maintaining a modest but comfortable middle-class standard of living for him and his family. In addition to releasing more of his novels, Macmillan published his book *Brazilian Literature*, based on lectures he prepared for his classes at Berkeley. Sales were surprisingly high for what might be considered a scholarly book, but reviews in U.S. papers stressed the humor and humanity with which Veríssimo presented his topic. He gave U.S. readers a basic context for understanding writing from his country, a task he augmented by writing occasional reviews of Brazilian books translated into English.[4] Underlying his work for U.S. editors was an assumption that the alliance between Brazil and the United States was permanent and would grow closer in the postwar years as the two countries collaborated on both hemispheric security and economic development issues.

As the Cold War took hold, Brazilian communists began attacking Veríssimo as an agent of U.S. imperialism. He in turn was increasingly outspoken in his condemnations of Stalin, the world communist movement, and positions that the Brazilian Communist Party took on national and foreign matters. He chastised Brazilian communists for their lack of respect for legal process and democratic procedure: "I think affirming that Russia is a democracy is a colossal bluff," he argued, "and it upsets me when the Brazilian communists talk about the Stalinist dictatorship as if it were a model for the rest of the world."[5] Veríssimo asked why, if the United States was determined to provoke another world war, as Brazilian communists insisted, Truman had not responded to the Soviet blockade of Berlin in 1947 and 1948 or threats against Turkey in 1949 by launching the attack communists had been predicting. As a writer, he was convinced that Soviet dictates on the duties of writers to support the class struggle destroyed the function that artists played as the conscience of their countries. Were the communists to take over Brazil, censorship would dwarf what occurred during the Estado Novo. If what happened in the Soviet Union was to be the model, anyone arrested for publishing something the state did not like would be executed or sent to a slave labor camp deep in the Amazon region.[6]

Veríssimo insisted that moral principles that transcended immediate political conflicts shaped his perspectives, not allegiance to any ideology, and certainly not to the United States. "I am," he declared, "a man who in this battle between two imperialisms prefers to stay equidistant from the White House and the Kremlin."[7] Yet when he had to take positions on specific questions, he usually found himself closer to the U.S. position. In 1948, he resigned from the executive committee of the Comissão Coordenadora Pro-Anistia dos Presos e Exilados Políticos de Espanha e Portugal (Coordinating Commission for

Amnesty of Prisoners and Political Exiles of Spain and Portugal) when the organization's international council rejected a motion to offer aid to political prisoners held in Poland, Czechoslavakia, Hungary, Romania, and Yugoslavia. Veríssimo had helped found the Brazilian branch of the organization during the Spanish Civil War. Friendships he had formed in the group and stories he had heard inspired *Saga*, his novel on the Spanish Civil War, published in 1940. Leaving was painful for him, but unavoidable if the group found suppression of civil and political liberties acceptable in countries where communists governed because Soviet domination of eastern Europe was necessary for what the organization called "the legitimate subjective defense" of peace.[8]

Veríssimo spoke out against President Dutra's decree in 1947 banning the Brazilian Communist Party, one of the few times when he and the communists were in agreement. He reasoned that with the 1930 revolution, when Getúlio Vargas overthrew a republic dominated by large landowners, Vargas promised that he as president would protect the people from the capricious whims of employers, merchants, and landowners. The people remained in a state of dependency, Veríssimo argued in his public protest against the ban on the communists, but on Vargas personally to promulgate and enforce protective legislation. With his removal in 1945, the people felt they had nobody in the federal government concerned with their needs, and they turned to others who promised protection as well. Outlawing the Communist Party because it had been successful in elections deepened the problem of popular demoralization. As long as average Brazilians believed that they had no stake in the decisions the country's leaders made, political life would be unstable and would remain so, he predicted, until democratic processes had a chance to mature.[9]

In 1951, Getúlio Vargas returned to power as president of Brazil, winning the election in a landslide. He suspected the U.S. ambassador of having engineered the coup against him in 1945, and his policies when he resumed governing the nation worked toward greater economic and cultural independence from the United States. In areas where Brazilian entrepreneurs were unable to compete with foreign firms, Vargas decided to create nationally owned enterprises. He nationalized petroleum exploration and production, creating Petrobras, the state-owned oil company. Steel, electricity, and pharmaceuticals were also nationalized. In 1950, the issue of whether growing U.S. investments in Brazil threatened the supposedly "harmonious" nature of Brazilian race relations became a matter of public controversy and debate in the national Congress. African American dancer and choreographer Katherine Dunham (Figure 23) had been touring Brazil with her dance troupe. When she arrived in São Paulo, the hotel her hosts had reserved for her refused to give her a room. They explained that they did not accept Negro guests. The incident was widely reported in Brazilian newspapers. When reporters discovered that a Texas investor owned the hotel, the incident prompted renewed debate over growing North American cultural influence. Would Brazil, in its effort to imitate the success of the United States, adopt attitudes on race fundamentally at odds with its own history? The press reported similar incidents in Cuba, where U.S.-owned hotels and restaurants routinely violated Cuban laws by refusing to serve blacks. Several Brazilians came forward with additional examples of businesses refusing to serve them because of their skin color, and in the majority of these cases Brazilian owners were clearly responsible, not foreign investors, evidence for the power of the U.S. example to cause great harm.[10]

Veríssimo had no clear political home within Brazil. He hated Getúlio Vargas and his allies with intensity, perhaps with more intensity than merited. There was a personal edge behind his animosity to Vargas since many members of Veríssimo's family, his father included, had joined the political machine Vargas created. Veríssimo distrusted President Dutra and his conservative but democratically elected government filled with the men responsible for police repression during the Vargas dictatorship. Veríssimo could not support the communists, and there was no social democratic party in Brazil capable of mounting a credible campaign. Writing a history of Brazil through the two-hundred-year story of a family in Rio Grande do Sul allowed Veríssimo to retreat from the political and economic frustrations of postwar transition and refocus his thoughts on how the political culture of his home state had emerged and developed. He wrote that what he learned in school about the history of Brazil as a land where people had learned the value of compromise made no sense in terms of what he knew about gaúcho society and its development out of military garrisons built to protect Brazil's southern frontier from Spanish invasion.

Time and the Wind starts with the conquest of the Jesuit missions in the Paraguay River valley. Veríssimo presented the missions as an Arcadian society that successfully synthesized Christian and indigenous culture into a politically and economically just order. Ongoing competition of Spain and Portugal for control of the Paraguay River basin led to a political decision to replace a productive agrarian society with a frontier ranching economy. Settlers from Brazil occupied the land, with land grants provided to men able and willing to organize the military force needed for Brazil's first line of defense against Spanish invasion. With war an ever-present reality, intensive agriculture was not economically feasible. The new owners relied on cattle, allowed to roam across vast unfenced grasslands. Gauchos (analogous to cowboys) kept track of the cattle, capturing those needed for consumption or for sale. The leaders of Rio Grande do Sul were always ready to go to war against external enemies, but also needed to keep a rough-and-ready population under control. As a result, the state had an unusually violent history, including a string of civil wars, in which leaders competed for power by massacring their enemies' men.

The pivotal point of the novel is the 1930 revolution that erupted to protest a fraudulent national election. The revolution led to Getúlio Vargas, governor of Rio Grande do Sul, assuming the presidency of the republic. The descent of the nation as a whole into dictatorship could be explained by understanding the unique development of Rio Grande do Sul along lines that gave its leaders a disproportionate role in the armed forces and a political mind-set that allowed them to trump the many advantages that urban elites of Rio de Janeiro and São Paulo enjoyed, or the economic superiority of rural elites in other states whose power had been based in patriarchal authority but who had not developed the deeply entrenched military traditions of the far south. Veríssimo also showed the roots of the Brazilian Communist Party in a revolt of junior officers in the southern states in 1924, protesting the pervasive corruption of Brazil's liberal republic. The national army quickly suppressed the revolt, but insurgents from Rio Grande do Sul, under the leadership of Lieutenant Luiz Carlos Prestes, escaped encirclement by retreating deep into the interior of the country. For three years, the rebel armies evaded pursuit, marching to the far north and then south again, and in 1927, they crossed the border to safety in Bolivia. Prestes became a communist while in exile and subsequently served as president of the Brazilian Communist Party from 1943 to 1970.[11]

For Veríssimo, left and right in Brazil were equally products of a militaristic tradition resting on the personal authority of a protective leader. As a result, avenues to democratic and law-bound institutions were unusually restricted for a country with a sizable middle class. That class had to understand the specifics of Brazilian history if it were to exercise its leadership, which with the overthrow of Vargas in 1945 seemed to be a possibility if political parties could develop that were not merely extensions of individual leaders. The contradictions of a new urban middle class during the Vargas dictatorship and the difficulty it had in building a competing political center provided the focus for the concluding three volumes, published in 1961.

Time and the Wind found tens of thousands of attentive readers in Brazil. Veríssimo once again broke all previous records for book sales in his country. Communist critics fiercely attacked the book's interpretations of recent Brazilian history and claimed that Veríssimo had attempted to demoralize his readers by imitating the lowest standards of North American popular culture.[12] Debates over Veríssimo's novel led to the Brazilian Writers Association splitting into two opposing organizations. The writers association with liberal leadership insisted that universal humanist values were attainable only in liberal, democratic societies, however imperfect they might be. The communist-run writers association argued that universal human values would only be realized after a socialist society had created the conditions for the emergence of a "new man," whose development class domination no longer distorted.

In large part as an answer to *Time and the Wind*, in 1954 Jorge Amado published a three-volume novel, *Os subterrâneos de liberdade* ("Liberty's Underground Army"), narrating a story of Brazilian communist resistance to fascism and U.S. imperialism from 1930 to 1950. The novel, Amado's most overtly Stalinist work, revolved around the difference between intellectuals reformed by accepting communist discipline and demoralized "petty bourgeois" intellectuals who build careers by protesting the powerlessness of the people while seeking out and enjoying North American patronage. It is the weakest of Amado's novels, and its frequent praise of Joseph Stalin proved an embarrassment after Nikita Khrushchev's 1956 speech exposing the extent of Stalin's crimes. Communist parties throughout the world moved quickly to distance themselves from a leader that they, like Amado in his novel, had described as near infallible. Amado left the Brazilian Communist Party in 1957, following the Khrushchev revelations, and his first novel written as an independent socialist, *Gabriela, Cravo e Canela* ("Gabriela, Clove and Cinnamon") was the first of many international best-sellers he published over the last four decades of his life.[13]

Despite growing disenchantment with the U.S. vision of the world found in the Brazilian government, relations with the republic to the north remained of primary importance to national leaders. In 1952, when the Department of Cultural Affairs of the Pan American Union needed a new director, the Brazilian government was determined to have the post filled with one its citizens. Érico Veríssimo's name quickly surfaced as the government's preferred candidate, given his familiarity with the United States and his prestige as an internationally admired novelist. Above all, his reputation as a fierce anticommunist made him an acceptable, even desirable candidate to the U.S. government. The minister of foreign affairs contacted Veríssimo personally to ask him to consider the position. Even if he preferred not to take the job, the minister told him, he should accept because his country needed him in Washington.[14]

Veríssimo accepted. The Pan American Union concurred with the Brazilian nomination. In 1953, Veríssimo and his family returned to the United States to live and work in Washington, D.C., where he directed a large, complex program for hemispheric cultural exchange. He supervised a staff spread across the western hemisphere engaged in a variety of cultural and educational programs, as well as more than eighty employees in the Washington headquarters. His department was responsible for archaeological excavations, preservation of cultural monuments, a publication program, organization of art exhibits, theater performances, concerts and recitals, regular conferences and workshops on subjects ranging from astrophysics to poetry, the preparation of curricular materials, the creation of rural libraries and educational centers, and programs for helping nations end adult illiteracy. In his speech opening a conference on children's needs, he emphasized that his goals as director of a cultural and educational organization could not be separated from his responsibilities as a citizen of America: "Many millions in our America live—and that is stretching the use of the word—at a level more suited to an animal than a human. I do not know of any crusade more noble or glorious for men of letters and of government than to eradicate illness, illiteracy, and poverty among the large number of people who live from day to day. Our mission is to secure for them a better, more beautiful world, in which each person can think about spiritual as well as bodily needs, each person enjoys the right to happiness and an equal share in the benefits the human community provides."[15] He placed the struggle against poverty in the context of an uncompromising, universal struggle against dictatorship by noting that there are two ways modern society destroys the individual. The first was totalitarian government with forced labor and concentration camps. The other way was the indifference of modern Western societies to the poor, "an absolute, cruel neglect of entire populations, without medical care, without hospitals, without schools, lacking everything a person needs." He concluded, "I do not see much difference between one and the other form of *disrespect* for human life."[16]

Once again, his days passed in a flurry of speaking engagements that took him to all parts of the United States and to most of Latin America. In addition to giving talks and meeting with community groups and business leaders in the United States, he appeared regularly on television and radio. His topics usually focused on cultural matters, but he also wanted to educate U.S. citizens to the deficiencies of their nation's global leadership. He wrote friends:

The cities I visited—Albuquerque, Tucson, Los Angeles, San Francisco, Berkeley, Oakland, Eugene, Seattle, Denver, Colorado Springs, Kansas City, St. Louis—are growing very fast. They are very comfortable, but generally they lack grace, anything unpredictable, anything scenic or charming. I was very well treated, much fêted. Many, many questions. My lectures were almost "theatrically" successful. And I improved my "act" as I went from city to city. I spoke with considerable frankness, sweetening the pill, that is to say, by mixing jokes into the information I gave them; and, by making it funny, I succeeded in saying what I wanted. Speaking to businessmen, Babbitts, at the Foreign Affairs Institute of Albuquerque, I wound up getting into arguments with the Republicans in the audience. The question and answer period lasted almost an hour and was very agitated. I said inconvenient things throughout my trip, things that I "am not supposed" to say as a functionary of the Pan American Union. But I said them.[17]

He participated as well in frequent international conferences, which provided him the opportunity to work on developing a network of Latin American intellectuals eager to take charge of the social and cultural programs of the Pan American Union. He felt most strongly about the Pan American Union's campaigns to end illiteracy across the continent.[18] The diplomatic framework of the Pan American Union, however, discouraged him. "A lot of bullshit," he reported wearily, "a lot of empty talk. I've lost all respect for the ambassadors and the delegates." Whenever diplomatic teams could not come to agreement on any matter concerning culture or education, the issue went to a working group that Veríssimo chaired. He had to write up documents that he hoped would be the basis for practical policy, including the Cultural Declaration of Caracas.[19] The month-long conference in Caracas in March 1954, in planning for years, was organized to shift cultural exchange programs from national governments to the Organization of American States. Governments would continue providing information about their countries and policies, but the Pan American Union, designated as the division within the OAS dedicated to nonpolitical activities, was to take over responsibility for most exchange programs. Veríssimo's final draft drew on his experience with U.S. programs during World War II for the model he wanted the OAS to emulate.[20] Making exchange increasingly multilateral was a top priority. The first article of the convention specified that each member nation of the OAS was to send at least one professor and one student annually to teach or study in each of the other member states. More could be sent, but the numbers exchanged between any two countries were to be the same. By 1954, it was clear, given the U.S. focus on sending experts to Latin America, or students developing expertise, while inviting literally tens of thousands of students to study in the United States, that the U.S. government program had become one of instruction rather than exchange. The Caracas convention attempted to address the imbalance caused by expertise coming almost exclusively from the United States by authorizing the Pan American Union's Department of Cultural Affairs to coordinate exchange of specialist advisers between all the member states. The division also was to increase its program for arranging multicountry tours for writers, artists, musicians, and performers. Given that the U.S. delegation enthusiastically endorsed the draft Caracas convention and given that the United States provided the lion's share of funding for Pan American Union cultural programs, there is no reason to believe that efforts to diversify cultural exchange programs developed in opposition to U.S. priorities. It is more likely that the White House and the State Department decided to off-load programs that remained politically controversial in Congress onto an international agency that was formally independent.

Pan-Americanism in the United States relied on committees operating in urban centers across the country. The Chicago Pan America Assembly, for example, helped to organize an alliance of industrialists in Chicago and São Paulo, one of thirty-two "partnerships" that were to promote "friendship and understanding" between businessmen "on a people-to-people" basis. The Pan America Assembly also served as a coalition of the many Latin American community groups that had formed in Chicago's immigrant enclaves. The most important priority for the Chicago group was to raise money to provide medical care to impoverished communities in Latin America. The group solicited donations from U.S. companies doing business in one of the thirty-two cities or rural areas where the Chicago Pan America Assembly had arranged a partnership. The assembly used the donations to build medical clinics, but also brought patients to Chicago for care they could not receive at home. The group built a medical mission in the Tapajos River valley in the Amazon Basin in Brazil, using funds provided by the Squibb Corporation, one of world's largest pharmaceutical companies. The American Hospital Supply Corporation donated equipment and drugs, while the Chicago branch of the American Medical Association arranged for Chicago doctors and nurses to staff the facility. In addition to the medical projects, the Chicago Pan America Assembly funded the construction of a child-care center in Guadalajara, Mexico. General Motors, McGraw-Hill, Clark International, and Insley Manufacturing provided funding to the Chicago group to open technical training centers in Costa Rica, Brazil, and Peru, where teenagers could learn how to operate road-building equipment. The assembly also had an active cultural exchange program, bringing musicians and theater groups from Latin American countries. Most of the programming was in Spanish, considered valuable for students of Spanish and their teachers. The group sponsored a television show on a local station featuring discussions about a range of cultural, political, and economic issues. It also organized tours of Chicago for visiting delegations, including in 1956, a group of women's social action groups who wanted to visit Hull House and discuss Jane Addams's legacy.[21] Veríssimo admired these local committees and their ability to throw themselves into activities that governments avoided. He hoped his office could promote the formation of similar local committees in other OAS member states, important if people-to-people contact were to become a force in inter-American relations. He was not surprised that the brutal dictatorships in Cuba, the Dominican Republic, Venezuela, and Nicaragua opposed what he wanted to do, but even the governments of Mexico, Chile, and Brazil, relatively open societies with democratically elected governments, discouraged the initiative.[22]

In his memoirs, Veríssimo referred to his time at the Pan American Union as years spent in a "marble mausoleum."[23] He came to the conclusion that he would not be able to improve the cultural state of "nuestra madre América," but if he did not take himself too seriously, he could play a positive, if small role.[24] However modest his ambitions as director, at least as reported retrospectively, at the time he was writing letters home stating that he was so busy that he had little time to work on his books. The subsequent modesty may well reflect realism that there was little he could have done to affect either U.S. policy or the power of the dictators who ruled most of Latin America in the 1950s with U.S. acquiescence if not blessing. He maintained good relations with many in the U.S. government and business world. He claimed that he spoke frankly wherever he went, but seldom encountered an angry response. People in the United States, both private citizens and government officials, wanted to hear what he had to say, but he no longer believed that his opinion had any influence on what the U.S. government did.[25]

He felt so strongly about the damage that Latin American dictators did to their countries that when he arrived in Caracas, he refused to shake the hand of the country's president, Marcos Pérez Jiménez, a military officer who had seized power in 1952 and would be overthrown in 1958 as popular demonstrations demanded democratic government. Every document that Veríssimo prepared for official approval at the Caracas conference stressed that OAS programs had two primary goals: strengthening democratic institutions and improving the living conditions of the millions of Americans who lived in poverty. That OAS delegates approved the resolutions he drafted without debate or modification convinced him that change would be difficult, probably violent. His speeches as director increasingly focused on a handful of what he called "commonplaces," truths that he personally needed to repeat wherever he went: dictatorship was the primary cause of poverty; international organizations had to focus on defending the principle of democratic government and the unmet social needs of working people; the security objectives of the Organization of American States were best met by eliminating poverty, ending illiteracy, and suspending the membership of any nation ruled by a dictator.[26]

While he found largely positive public response to his positions in the United States, official policy shifted toward supporting dictators when there was suspicion of communist influence on popular movements. In June 1954, the Eisenhower administration overthrew the elected government of Guatemala, using a proxy army of exiled military officers and property owners opposed to new land reform laws. Veríssimo concluded that the Pan American Union needed fundamental reform because the Eisenhower administration had ignored the overwhelming opinion of the American nations with its intervention. He wrote home,

> As you know, as you must imagine, the issue of Guatemala has caused an uproar in the OAS and the Pan American Union. Round the clock meetings. Exhausted delegates napping on couches in every corner. It's a very serious business, a very melancholy time. I disagree with the State Department's policy. These people will never learn. They lack diplomatic tact, savoir faire, experience. I sympathize with the cause of this small nation that's trying to get out of the middle ages. It's dangerous to make alliances with the communists, but the biggest danger is not from them, but from the formation of one more right-wing dictatorship in the Americas with Washington's approval. *Disgusting!*[27]

He still believed in the mission of the Pan American Union, despite its organizational defects and its reliance on pompous platitudes. Pan-Americanism was a positive force, he thought, to the degree that it kept the United States open to public opinion in other countries.[28] What he saw in the United States in the 1950s did not encourage optimism, nor did the uncompromising attitude of Latin American intellectuals who were communists. When Veríssimo invited Chilean poet Pablo Neruda, a high-profile member of the Chilean Communist Party, to participate in an anthology of Latin American poetry Veríssimo wanted the Department of Cultural Affairs to publish, Neruda sent an angry reply that Veríssimo represented an instrument of the U.S. State Department. How could he explain to his people why he was collaborating with those who "coldly steal our wealth, plan repression, destroy liberty on the continent, and enslave Puerto Rico"?[29] Veríssimo published Neruda's letter and his response in newspapers across the hemisphere and summarized his own position: "It's just too much, don't you think? I don't defend the United States from the *crimes* that the poet imputes (with pardon for the bad word) to this country. But a communist who adores Soviet Russia does not have the right to speak about either freedom of expression or about justice."[30]

Jorge Amado, always a good friend of Veríssimo, declined more graciously.[31] In any event, both the United States and its communist opponents were determined to narrow the options for anyone who tried to create a space for dialogue or questioning. In September 1956, Veríssimo participated in the Congress for Cultural Freedom's meeting in Mexico City to discuss the "future of liberty" in the Americas. The secret funding that the CIA provided the congress has been well documented, but even in 1956, when the details were unknown, the position of the organization as an adjunct to U.S. foreign policy was obvious. Veríssimo joined Alfonso Reyes, Victoria Ocampo, Germán Arciniegas, and other Latin American speakers in condemning the U.S.-organized coup in Guatemala. The U.S. participants, some close personal friends like John Dos Passos, sat stone-faced, responding neither to defend their government's policy, necessary for debate and discussion, nor to join the condemnation, which would have presented a unified voice that the U.S. government might have found more difficult to ignore.[32]

Veríssimo's disenchantment was typical of that of other veterans of pan-Americanism. Victoria Ocampo simply turned her attention away from the United States and focused on deepening literary relations between Europe and Latin America, in particular helping authors she admired get translated into French, German, or Italian. She refused to support any organization she considered a front for Soviet political actions, but she attended meetings of the Congress for Cultural Freedom, both in Europe as well as the organizing meeting for a Latin American chapter in Mexico City. In part, this reflected her liberal sympathies, but she had personal reasons for deciding who were her friends and who she should count as among her enemies. In 1953 the Argentinean police arrested her on suspicion that she had prior knowledge of a plot to assassinate President Juan Perón. The evidence was flimsy, and in her account of what happened, the police seemed intent on connecting as many liberal opponents of Perón to the failed plan as they could. An international campaign in Europe and the United States led to her release after six weeks in prison. The Congress for Cultural Freedom took a particularly active role in protesting what had happened to her, while communists remained notably silent. It was a curious stance for Cold War–era communists, who viewed the Perón dictatorship as a fascist holdover from the war era that needed to be eliminated. But if Ocampo were known as an ally of the United States, then she deserved whatever the fascists did to her.[33] Life in Perón's Argentina had become, Ocampo wrote, a jail without bars:

> Our sleep was infested with foreboding nightmares, because life itself was a bad dream. A bad dream in which we couldn't mail a letter, however innocent it might be, without fearing that it would be read. Nor could we say a word on the phone without suspecting that it was being listened to and perhaps recorded. We writers didn't even have the right to speak our intimate thoughts in newspapers, journals, books or lectures—which, moreover, we were not allowed to give—because everything was censorship and prohibited zones. . . . One could say without exaggeration that we lived in a state of perpetual violation. Everything was violated: correspondence, the law, freedom of thought, even the human person.[34]

She was certain that life in eastern Europe was similar. Just as the Stalinists had replaced the fascists there, Argentinean communists looked forward to replacing the Peronists and perfecting the instruments of dictatorship. In their correspondence, Ocampo and Gabriela Mistral spoke of the appeal "totalitarianism" had for many in their countries, but, after the overthrow of the Árbenz government in Guatemala, neither trusted the U.S. government to defend democratic principles. The U.S. government embraced dictatorship as the most convenient solution to the problem of popular unrest, even though its officials continued to call publicly for democratic governments across the continent. For Ocampo, the way out of the dilemmas inherent to the postwar alliance with the United States remained what she had learned as an intelligent young woman living in a conservative, patriarchal society: develop her independent, critical faculties and express her ideas only to those who were interested.[35]

Unlike many other Latin American liberals, Germán Arciniegas threw himself into the anticommunist campaign with fervor. He was the sole Latin American to attend the organizing conference of the Congress for Cultural Freedom held in Berlin in 1950. He agitated for a Latin American branch, to be headquartered in Mexico City, and his campaign led to the conference in Mexico City. The result was not what he wanted because debate over U.S. intervention in Guatemala two years earlier overshadowed discussion of the then ongoing struggle of Hungary to distance itself from the Soviet Union. Nonetheless, Arciniegas joined other Latin American speakers in denouncing what the United States had done to Guatemala. Arciniegas took over the editorship of *Cuadernos Americanos*, the Congress for Cultural Freedom magazine published for Latin America, also secretly funded by the CIA. He used every platform he found to argue that pan-Americanism remained a movement of global importance because it would bring about the reunification of Catholic and Protestant humanist traditions divided since the sixteenth century, a development of far greater significance than the emergence of a global Marxist movement, which he was convinced would collapse from its own contradictions in his lifetime. He died in 1999, and over the last ten years of his life, he believed that his assessment that communism possessed only superficial strength had proven correct. He had no doubt that pan-Americanism was a movement of lasting importance because it and the formation of the European Union were revitalizing a civilization whose division in the sixteenth century had led to the materialism of the capitalists and the nihilism of the communists. While he recognized the importance of the European Union, he remained dedicated to the idea that the Old World was inherently a place of constraints, most vividly expressed in the twentieth century by both fascism and communism. The New World, because of its violent history and its isolation, had emerged as a place where liberty replaced order as the only viable organizing idea for the nations that had emerged at the beginning of the nineteenth century.[36]

Viewing military dictatorships as the most destabilizing force in Latin America, Arciniegas tried to persuade U.S. officials that they needed to take firmer action against all antidemocratic forces in the western hemisphere, the authoritarian right as well as communists. He argued that there needed to be more revolutions like the one José Figueres had led in Costa Rica in 1948 in the aftermath of a fraudulent election. After his movement took power, Figueres abolished his country's military, pursued a land-reform policy that clipped the power of the largest landowners, and compelled United Fruit Company, the largest foreign investor, to pay higher taxes and fees. Figueres for many Latin American liberals provided the best model for successful social change, particularly because he eschewed personal power and worked to develop stronger governing institutions. After serving as president of the revolutionary government for two years, overseeing the drafting of a new constitution, he declined to run for president in the elections his government organized. He ran for president a few years later and won handily, but stepped aside at the end of his term. Arciniegas initially saw Fidel Castro as a revolutionary in the Figueres mold and succeeded in convincing his many friends in the U.S. government that they should withhold support from the Batista dictatorship in Cuba in its battle against Castro's revolutionary movement. Arciniegas's hopes for the Cuban revolution collapsed when Castro adopted a pro-Soviet policy. By this time, he was Colombia's ambassador to Italy, an elderly scholar in early modern literature and philosophy whose ideas of what would lead to a just society were increasingly at odds with what most younger intellectuals across the western hemisphere thought.

The difference in generational attitudes can be summarized briefly by comparing Germán Arciniegas's review for the *Saturday Review of Literature* of William Benton's 1961 book *The Voice of Latin America* with the review that Claudio Véliz published in *New Left Review*.[37] Benton had traveled across Latin America with his close friend Adlai Stevenson. It was his first trip beyond Mexico, and he returned committed to rebuilding the frayed U.S.–Latin American alliance. Benton proposed radical changes to revitalize the Organization of American States. He wanted the headquarters to be moved outside the United States, preferably to Panama. He recommended that the United States transfer management of the Panama Canal to the OAS. The bulk of his arguments involved providing funding for programs that could substantively increase the living standards of Latin Americans. Benton also argued that these programs needed to be run by Latin Americans through the Pan American Union rather than by U.S. experts working for U.S. government agencies.

Arciniegas approved Benton's proposals, but critiqued Benton's perspective that the United States should "help" Latin America as part of the global fight against communism. Arciniegas argued that all consideration of "help" avoided the basic fact that the people of Latin American countries wanted the same things that the citizens of the United States did. They wanted democratic governments, they wanted jobs, they wanted schools for their children, they wanted to feel that they were safe from both criminals and corrupt police forces, and they wanted opportunity to discover what they could do for themselves. The primary obstacles to their aspirations had not been communism, which he asserted had little appeal to most people, but dictatorships that ran their countries for the private benefit of a few families. Castro's revolution triumphed because the Batista dictatorship lost the support of the people and because dollars donated by supporters in the United States had ensured that Castro's forces received the constant flow of arms they needed to keep fighting. The solution to the international problems of 1961 remained what it had been in 1941: to create a "single America which would be the continent of democracy . . . to make of the American continent, from Alaska to Patagonia, a house of free men who are sufficiently well nourished to be able to enjoy the benefits of justice and progress." In other words, keep working for the utopia of pan-Americanism as the realization of liberal, democratic principles.

Claudio Véliz, a younger Chilean historian and sociologist, who had studied at the University of Florida before doing his Ph.D. work at the London School of Economics, criticized Benton's proposals for similar reasons. Benton wants to end poverty, not because poverty is bad but because poverty gives an opportunity to communists. Benton wants to end illiteracy because illiterate peasants might become communists. Hunger is not an evil in itself, but a breeding ground for communism. The line of argument showed that U.S. policymakers had become intellectually bankrupt, Véliz concluded. Neither the U.S. government nor U.S. businesses cared in the slightest about either democracy or popular well-being. The bold initiatives that President John F. Kennedy launched with the Alliance for Progress would go nowhere because the United States no longer believed in the most basic principles of self-government. If modest social reforms failed to stop popular discontent, the United States would quickly turn to the military to restore order and if that meant dictatorships across the continent, so be it. Though publishing his review in an independent socialist journal, Véliz was one of the continent's strongest advocates of market-based economic policies, a historian whose research examined why the English-speaking settler societies had prospered economically after they became self-governing when former Spanish colonies had not. He was a young liberal whose support the United States needed if the Pan American Union were to offer an intellectual alternative to Castro's revolutionary movement. Instead, Véliz had decided that pan-Americanism was a dead letter, and that Latin American development could come only through global engagement. If the Europeans in particular became involved, they would cut through the dilemmas U.S.-Soviet rivalry posed for Latin American countries. The Europeans would bring new sources of capital, as well as a political perspective more strongly committed to democratic government.

His forecast that the U.S. government would turn to dictatorship proved accurate. In 1964, the U.S. Embassy signaled to the Brazilian military that the U.S. government would not object if the military overthrew the government of João Goulart, a populist veering toward neutralism. The Johnson administration sent a naval force to the coast of Brazil to provide additional support. With widespread support from most political parties and the country's middle class, the Brazilian military easily removed Goulart from office and sent him into exile. Then the military surprised everyone inside Brazil, as well as in Washington, by deciding that it would continue running the country instead of returning power to civil authority. The military dictatorship lasted twenty-one years, until 1985. It became the model for what occurred over the next decade in many countries. With political processes stalemated and revolutionary popular forces on the move, the armed forces in country after country seized power, even in countries like Uruguay that had had democratic government for many decades. As the U.S. government and the Latin American right formed an ever-closer alliance, "counterterrorism" replaced development as the centerpiece of U.S. policy, and with the new emphasis came a rush of additional resources for the military and police.

Chapter 11

The New Latin American Novel
in the United States

Shortly after Alejo Carpentier's *Los pasos perdidos* ("The Lost Steps") had been published in 1953 in Mexico, Harriet de Onís wrote to Knopf suggesting she prepare an English translation. Critics throughout Spanish-speaking America hailed Carpentier's third novel as one of the most important books ever written in their region. Sales were strong even though the book business was depressed across Latin America. The narrator of the book is a composer living in New York City who travels deep into the interior highlands of a South American country to find an indigenous group whose music had been recorded during a previous expedition. He is to bring back examples of the group's musical instruments that may well be similar to those the earliest humans made. Given that his mission is to go back to the dawn of human society, the novel proceeds, section by section, as a series of steps back into time: from the spiritually empty but comfortable modernity of Manhattan to the urban chaos of the modernizing capital city in a country modeled after Venezuela, where the narrator arrives in the midst of a bloody uprising against the local dictator. He escapes the capital city for the nearby farmlands and ranches, where people still live much as they did in the nineteenth century. As he travels up the country's major river into the barely populated interior, he enters an America continuing in the throes of the European conquest, a world that he likens to that of the Homeric epics. Then the narrator plunges into the Stone Age of the continent's indigenous peoples, who live in a world of pure, purposeless freedom. The hero discovers an imaginative universe promising psychological wholeness to anyone prepared to scrape away everything unessential and return to the purity of origins.

Herbert Weinstock, Knopf's foreign acquisitions editor, decided to reject the work, explaining that the book was not original and was "an assemblage of highly recondite references to philosophy, music, religion." He thought that it was impossible for the book to pay back the expense involved in translating, publishing, and marketing it.[1] In defending the book against the initial decision to reject, de Onís compared Carpentier to James Joyce and William Faulkner in terms of potential importance.[2] Weinstock promised to reconsider if a planned French edition did well.[3] The French translation appeared in 1955, and the edition won the Best Foreign Book Prize for the year, auspicious for it suggested that Carpentier was becoming a likely contender for the Nobel Prize in Literature.[4] Weinstock contacted Carpentier's agent in France and de Onís to inform them that Knopf wished to move forward with an English version. He confessed, "My often-expressed despair over interesting American readers in Latin-American novels led me to be overcautious in my first reactions to *Los Pasos Perdidos*."[5]

Weinstock's initial fears that Carpentier's book would fail proved correct. The reviewer in the *New York Times* disliked the book, as did several other reviewers. However, overall critical response was positive, and often strongly so. *Time* magazine's reviewer was the most enthusiastic, and he lauded the book as one of the finest fictional accounts he had yet read of the desire "to shake off the hold of modern life" by returning "to a life more innocent and less complicated."[6] Knopf had many good quotes to excerpt for promotion, but *The Lost Steps* sold less than three thousand copies. Knopf continued with the firm's plans to produce an English-language edition of Carpentier's earlier novel *El reino de este mundo* ("The Kingdom of This World"), a historical novel set during the Haitian revolution. The book appeared in 1957 to positive reviews but sales were once again tepid. Planning for a Hollywood adaptation of *The Lost Steps* starring Tyrone Power and Gina Lollobrigida came to an abrupt end with Power's sudden death in 1958 shortly before filming was scheduled to start. With two failures in a row, Knopf decided not to publish Carpentier's *El acoso* ("Harassment"), and in 1962 declined Carpentier's newest novel, *El siglo de las luces* (released in English translation in 1963 by Little, Brown with the title *Explosion in the Cathedral*).

Successful publication in France had been a factor in Knopf's initial decision to translate Carpentier's book. At the end of World War II, Roger Caillois (1913–1978) returned to France after having spent the war years in Argentina, where he worked with Victoria Ocampo and *Sur* magazine. During his exile, Caillois read work from around the continent and met many authors, all unknown in Europe before the war.[7] Trained as a sociologist, Caillois had written on the collective dimensions of unconscious life expressed in rituals, foodways, games, folktales, and myths. He became interested in Latin American popular culture as a form of resistance to liberal modernity. Communitarian values had kept utilitarian culture at bay. The result was a people who did not need, nor were they interested in, the gadgets that the rich countries of the North wanted to sell them. Latin America was in the throes of a fundamentally moral revolution growing out of the region's unique historic experience. Eventually, societies would emerge that could offer an alternative to both the industrial consumerism of the United States and the bureaucratic socialism of the Soviet Union. The heroes who emerged from the deep roots of popular consciousness would not be "organization men" of either left or right, but brave individuals whose courage and sacrifice had the power to destroy the superficial, rotting edifices that Europeanized elites had created. Revolutionary heroes would bring forth new forms of government consistent with the rich interior lives of the people.

The Latin American revolution was well positioned, Caillois believed, to have global influence because much of everyday Latin American popular culture had roots going back to the ancient cultures of the Latin Mediterranean, but then had been enriched through synthesis with the values and practices of African slaves and the indigenous nations, some of which were never conquered and kept alive an understanding of freedom that the peoples of the North had forgotten.[8] The parallels to Waldo Frank's imagination of Iberian cultures as a source of redemption for the citizens of industrial countries are obvious, but there were important differences. Frank always foregrounded his personal impressions and frankly idiosyncratic interpretations of what he saw. Caillois subsumed romantic identification into a rigorous sociological apparatus that required detailed description and analysis of cultural forms. When he returned to Europe, Caillois founded and edited *Diogenes*, an interdisciplinary journal for the study of culture that UNESCO published. While working for UNESCO, Caillois edited a series translating "representative" older Latin American work into French and English. In 1951, with funding from the Centre National du Livre (National Center for the Book) to subsidize the costs of translation, Caillois launched La Croix du Sud (The Southern Cross), a series published by Gallimard, one of the country's most important presses, presenting Latin American literature in French translation. Jorge Luis Borges's *Ficciones* was the first book to appear, in 1952, and over the next nineteen years, Caillois published forty-one more books, including, almost immediately after its publication in Spanish, Carpentier's *Los pasos perdidos*. In announcing the series at Gallimard, Caillois declared, "In the Southern Cross collection, there will be a place for the most diverse works . . . that provide insight into the formation and development of communities and their values in a still new continent, barely tamed, where the struggle with space and nature remains severe, which possesses a unique lifestyle, and whose rich resources permit a first-rank role in the near future."[9]

A more effusive description of what Caillois hoped the series could communicate was available in a short book of prose poetry that he had previously published in 1949, *Espace américain* ("American Space"). The book's evocation of what America had to offer overcivilized Europeans suggests some of the reasons motivating him to introduce Latin American writing to French readers. His themes were not original; indeed, the book repeated well-known stereotypes. The book opens with a reiteration of the promise the discovery of a "new land" had meant for the "world": "Isolated by an immense expanse of water that humanity did not quickly learn to cross, for a long time this continent remained unknown to the rest of the world. And the day arrived, not long ago, when the existence of a new land beyond the Ocean was revealed to the world, aged and exhausted, ensnared in difficulties that had accumulated over the centuries."[10] Out of an Old World expiring in the poison of ideas came a trickle of refugees peopling America because they craved space and freedom. "Here is what marks this country from others," Caillois continued, "those who became Americans were, by their own will, not by birth, the beginning of a lineage. Men who had abruptly broken with their heritage had formed a new race . . . staking everything on the gamble that they could defy the future and rely only on their own abilities."[11] Leaving lands that more often than not resembled gardens so long had they been worked and reworked to serve human desires, the people who created America found themselves in hostile terrains that humans (presumably, he was referring to the indigenous peoples of the hemisphere) had previously browsed but never tamed. A new question arose: how could humans carve out a place for themselves within a universe that was already complete, that did not fear or hate the newcomers because its grandeur left it indifferent to creatures whose ambitions were infinite but whose capabilities could not overcome the long forgotten obstacles rediscovered in an untended land. From the conflict arose new peoples undefeated by nature's brutality but acutely aware of their limitations. The product of Old World illusions confronting New World realities was a new race unlike any that had preceded them: "Thicker blood runs more energetically in the veins of the children, as if they held onto something, not the failures or the fears of the fathers, but the audacity of their self-confident decision; the expansiveness of an instant continues to define them . . . [even unto] the seventh and the seventeenth generation of the new line. . . . Humanity has won a primary nobility and a strange enlargement of being."[12]

The itinerary in *Espace américain*, abstract yet poetic, previews what Caillois may have seen four years later when he read Carpentier's *Los pasos perdidos*, a book that echoed his own response to America in more vivid and dramatic terms, while deploying rich poetic abstractions that welded an intellectual synopsis of Western history with a deeply emotional hope that returning to a constant struggle with wilderness could be an alternative source of disciplined freedom.[13]

In addition to the deeply personal and existential questions of how imagination could redeem a "world" governed by accumulated illusions and artifices, the

books Caillois published in La Croix du Sud made a critical contribution to ongoing debates among postwar French intellectuals over how to position themselves and their country in what appeared to be a bipolar struggle between U.S.
capitalism and Soviet communism, a struggle that for many had no connection
whatsoever with their own dreams of a just future, yet threatened the entire
world with the fearsome specter of nuclear annihilation. The dilemmas of Latin
American revolution offered a moral alternative that, at least in the mythic contexts that Caillois and others invoked, restored efficacy to individual action while
simultaneously proposing that an alternative international movement was forming with the potential for challenging superpower tyranny. It was a heady, inspi-
rational myth that influenced as well how many intellectuals around the world
responded to the unexpected triumph of the Cuban revolution at the beginning
of 1959. "The world is not absurd," declared Uruguayan philosopher Washington
Lockhart in an essay that linked developments in Cuba to a global existential
movement that French writers like Caillois had initiated in the aftermath of the
Second World War. Lockhart connected contemporary French writers to Cuban
revolutionaries in order to demonstrate that the only legitimate intellectual response to the crisis engulfing the world since 1945 was to be discovered in the
course of action. Fidel Castro and his handful of followers had demonstrated that
heroes with "luminous conscience" vindicated the dream that a "new man" and
"universal harmony" would arise from the ashes of corrupt societies.[14]

Knopf's presentation of The Lost Steps to the U.S. reading public avoided any
of the philosophical, moral, and mythic questions that had been central to discussion of the work in both Latin America and France. The Knopf correspondence files present no evidence that the publisher and his editors ever considered
these questions relevant to what they needed to do. They ignored every plea to
place the book within the context that had made the book successful abroad.
As the U.S. publisher of André Gide, Thomas Mann, and Albert Camus, among
many other writers with global reputations, Knopf had an impressive track record selling foreign literature in translation. They were acutely aware of the
factors limiting what U.S. firms could learn from publishing in other countries.
The Latin American book market was small. Publishers there seldom printed
more than three thousand copies of a book, and success in Latin America usually meant only that the editorial house had decided to do a second, equally
small print run. The French book market was of impressive size, producing a
broad range of titles, but also with print runs smaller than typical for commercial publishing in the United States. The success that Carpentier and most of
the Latin American authors published in the Croix du Sud series achieved was
more of critical esteem, which could lead to a respectable level of sales for
France, but even by French standards, only a handful of the titles that Caillois

chose for the series were "best-sellers." After the failure of *The Lost Steps*, Alfred Knopf and his editors maintained a critical attitude to proposals they received to translate Latin American literature. They looked at how well a book
had done in France or elsewhere in Europe, but for the most part, reports of
critical success abroad did not overcome their doubts because they saw their
own market as fundamentally different.

The commercial success of Jorge Amado's novel *Gabriela, Cravo e Canel* in
Brazil and France, however, did catch the attention of Knopf editors, who thought
that the book might well have the ingredients to attract readers in the United
States. Knopf's earlier experience publishing Amado in 1945 had been a dismal
failure, and the firm had not pursued a second project with him. His new book,
however, broke with his previous socialist realist emphasis on the struggles of the
working class for justice. In the aftermath of the revelations of Stalin's crimes,
Amado left the Brazilian Communist Party, and he began work on the first of
several comic novels rooted in the popular culture of Bahia. In *Gabriela, Clove
and Cinnamon*, foodways and sexual customs combined in a ribald story that
used humor to examine the politics of masculine honor in the cocoa-growing region of Brazil. The book, set in the small coastal city of Ilhéus during the cocoa
boom of the 1920s, begins with a jury acquitting a wealthy landowner of murder.
He has killed his wife and her lover when he discovers them together in their romantic hideaway. The verdict has never been in doubt, since the social order rested
on the expectation that men protected their possessions. The book then tells the
tale of a Syrian immigrant, the owner of the most popular tavern in town, who
divorces his wife instead of killing her when he discovers she has a lover. The most
conservative men in the community condemn his weakness, but the tavern owner
has an unexpected ally. An ambitious young newcomer from Rio de Janeiro has
come to Ilhéus with the idea of modernizing the town's port and, in so doing,
carve out his share of the wealth to be made from selling cocoa beans to the world.
The so-called colonels, wealthy planters with private armies, do not want to raise
their taxes to pay for civic improvements, and the project languishs even with the
support of many of the businessmen in the town. The tavern keeper's case opens
up a political opportunity to challenge the authority of the cocoa growers. In
Amado's weaving together of the diverse elements in his story, the progressive
handling of a common domestic problem goes hand in hand with developing a
modern industrial economy. Rule of law proves to be a prerequisite for the commercial growth and technological progress the town leaders desire, but along with
"progress and order" come new, modern conceptions of honor.[15] The political
story in the novel ends with a jury convicting a landowner who has killed his wife
to protect his honor, while the personal story concludes with the tavern keeper
and his divorced wife rediscovering their attraction to each other.

Amado surrounded the political story with fulsome descriptions of the female body and of sexual pleasures, which while far from explicit were daring
for the time. Amado celebrated as well the myth of Brazil's racial harmony,
symbolized in the title character Gabriela, whose mixed-race background
makes her an embodiment of the Brazilian nation. Like thousands of others,
she has left the impoverished interior in search of a better life in the cities. She
arrives in town caked in mud and wearing only rags, but once cleaned off and
properly dressed, she is revealed to be the most physically attractive woman that
any of the men in the town could ever remember encountering. In addition to
her stunning beauty, she has extraordinary abilities as a cook, and the tavern
keeper offers her a job. Much of the book's attraction is its detailed descriptions
of Bahian specialties that synthesized the culinary cultures of the native peoples,
West Africa, and Portugal. Men find Gabriela irresistible and flirt with her hoping that they can spend the night in her bed. Gabriela has a matter-of-fact attitude
toward sex, following her heart's desire when she encounters a man she finds
attractive. Her boss falls in love with her and proposes marriage, an offer that
she foolishly accepts. The marriage, with its requirement that she adhere to the
puritanical moral standards constraining the lives of urban middle-class women,
comes close to destroying Gabriela's soul. In the happy resolution following the
divorce, Gabriela regains her freedom, she returns to the tavern's kitchen to
work as a cook, and she and her former husband rediscover the sexual desires
they felt for each other when they first met. Their lives remained linked, but as
partners rather than as master and wife. Gabriela in regaining her personal
freedom helps the hero find his as well, for he has learned that the prerogatives
of the "master" made him deeply miserable.

The book appeared in Brazil in 1958 to acclaim; it was the first book to sell
more than one hundred thousand copies in the country. A French translation
appeared in 1960, coinciding with the craze for bossa nova and a French film
shot in Rio de Janeiro during the Carnival celebrations, *Orfeu Negro* ("Black
Orpheus"), featuring music by Tom Jobim and Luiz Bonfá.[16] The French version
of Amado's book sold hundreds of thousands of copies. The craze for bossa nova
had taken hold in the United States as well, while *Black Orpheus* won the Oscar
for Best Foreign Film in 1960, and was one of the biggest successes on the then
rapidly growing art-house circuit. Several U.S. singers, including Frank Sina-
tra, recorded songs from the film in versions that went to the top of the pop
charts. Alfred Knopf exercised his option to do a second book by Amado and
negotiated the English-language rights for *Gabriela*. Released in 1962, *Gabriela, Clove and Cinnamon* leaped onto the *New York Times* best-seller list and
stayed there for weeks. The Book-of-the-Month Club picked up the novel, as
well. Knopf wrote Amado with glee that "these earnings of yours are probably

greater than any Latin American novelist has ever received from a North American publisher." He noted that he had taken "substantial financial losses" trying to promote Brazilian literature, and the success of *Gabriela, Clove and Cinnamon* gave him the satisfaction that his years of interest and investment had finally turned profitable.[17] As a sign of the special place in his list of authors, Knopf arranged for Amado and his family to stay at the Knopfs' Paris apartment whenever they traveled to France. He tried, initially without success due to Amado's well-known history as a communist activist, to secure a visa for Amado so that he would be able to visit the United States and promote his books. Knopf hastened to put out another comic Amado novel, *Home Is the Sailor*, a picaresque story built around the fabricated adventures of a retired janitor in the city of Salvador who pretends to have been a world-traveling ship captain. The book appeared in 1964 to strong reviews and good sales. Between 1962 and 1975, Knopf put eight Amado novels on the market, all of which sold well, though only one of the titles, *Dona Flor and Her Two Husbands*, released in 1969, came close to equaling the particularly strong performance of *Gabriela, Clove and Cinnamon*.

Other publishers added Latin American writers to their lists, hoping to capture a bit of the Amado magic. Macmillan had high hopes for Veríssimo's next book, *His Excellency, the Ambassador*, which the editors there told him had the best chance ever of breaking into the best-seller list, and then being adapted into a successful Broadway play and big budget Hollywood film.[18] In Veríssimo's case, neither sexual romps nor comic situations were the selling point. Instead, the book offered an "insider" view of Washington intrigue applied to the topical subject of Latin American revolution. Allen Drury's *Advise and Consent*, a story of the battle within the Senate over the confirmation of the president's nominee for secretary of state, had become the surprise blockbuster of 1959, pushing presses to look for more books that could fit what seemed to be, at least through the first half of the 1960s, an insatiable reader demand. Macmillan publicity and reviews in the popular press stressed Veríssimo's former position at the Pan American Union as the basis for his knowledge of how Washington actually worked; they also noted his continuing associations with Washington and his status as a part-time resident. (Every year, Veríssimo and his wife visited with their daughter, son-in-law, and three grandchildren in McLean, Virginia, a suburb of Washington.) Hollywood did take an early interest in the story; even before the book was released, Macmillan optioned film rights to Veríssimo's Washington novel to a producer who intended to cast Paul Newman in the lead role.[19]

Knopf claimed the distinction of being the most important publisher of Latin American literature in the United States, but the firm also continued to lament the losses it had suffered from an investment that at times must have struck many at the company as more of a public service than a viable business venture. In 1969, at the time Knopf released *Dona Flor and Her Two Husbands*, the publishing house took out a full-page advertisement in the Book Review of the Sunday *New York Times* that celebrated the publisher's long-standing commitment to Latin American literature. A short statement from Alfred Knopf recalls when Knopf's wife, Blanche, first toured Latin America in 1942 looking for interesting writers. He summoned up the ghost of the Good Neighbor Policy with a quote from Sumner Welles, in 1942 the undersecretary of state for Latin American affairs, who in responding to Knopf's decision to publish books from Latin America, declared: "there could be no more practical method of increasing understanding between all of the American peoples than for all of them to become familiar with the literature [of] every nation in the Western hemisphere." The bulk of the advertisement consists of a list of thirty-six books by sixteen authors that the publishing house had in print, and Knopf assured his readers that "the list on this page is by no means complete."[20] From the list, only Amado's six novels and a short story anthology edited by Germán Arciniegas had been financially successful. The invocation of the Good Neighbor years was out of touch with the times, particularly given that U.S.-Latin American relationships had grown increasingly antagonistic since the Cuban revolution, while the Vietnam War, raging at the time of the advertisement, had turned the United States into a lonely superpower whose leaders were at odds with international public opinion. The authors list highlighted in another way the anachronism of Knopf's approach, for only four related to the latest trends in Latin American literature, and of those only José Donoso's two novels that Knopf had published in English translation, *Coronation* (1965) and *This Sunday* (1967), reflected the new and increasingly popular generation of writers who constituted the so-called boom in Spanish-language writing in the Americas during the 1960s. Donoso (1924–1996) was a central figure in the "boom." Knopf's writers for the most part came from an earlier generation, detached from changes well under way in both Brazil and Spanish-speaking America, and they were not writing works that contemporary readers in the United States were excited to read.

Other U.S. publishers handled those newer writers. Farrar, Straus published the Mexican novelists Carlos Fuentes and Gustavo Sáinz. Hill and Wang had published Miguel Ángel Asturias's most famous novel, *El Señor Presidente*, and Delacorte had become the Guatemalan novelist's U.S. publisher when he won the Nobel Prize for Literature in 1967. Pantheon published Julio Cortázar's difficult experimental novels in English. Harper and Row published Mario Vargas Llosa, Gabriel García Márquez, Mario Benedetti, Guillermo Cabrera Infante, and Reinaldo Arenas, a group of superb storytellers whose books arguably made the publisher the single most important source of Latin American writing in the

United States. Dutton picked up Manuel Puig, whose gay-themed novels exploring the mythic role of Hollywood movies and romance novels in everyday life did particularly well in the 1970s. Frequent advertising for these writers suggest higher sales than Knopf's books from the region, as does a much quicker move to paperback editions.[21] In 1964, the second book by a Latin American writer, Carlos Fuentes's novel *The Death of Artemio Cruz*, broke into best-seller lists. Unlike Jorge Amado's *Gabriela, Clove and Cinnamon*, Fuentes's novel could not be presented as light entertainment. The publisher's publicity summarized the story: "The novel opens with Artemio Cruz in a dying coma, with the voices of his wife Catalina, his daughter Teresa, and his close associates in his ears. He is a very rich man, a great power in Mexico, owner of much land, proprietor of a powerful newspaper. At 71, returning from a meeting with some government officials he has bribed and coerced, he collapses with a fatal illness. Lying on his death-bed, he begins to remember. What Artemio Cruz remembers—his whole life—is also in essence the story of the tragedy of Mexico."[22]

Cruz's memory jumps between seven critical events in his life, stretching from 1910 to 1959. Each moment presents a choice between the ideals Cruz espoused as a young man and practical opportunities to increase his personal power and wealth. The method required patience from the reader, who had to build each of the substories out of scattered fragments and then connect them into a coherent life story. The approach allowed Fuentes to juxtapose historical elements thematically to reveal an underlying, in large part mythic, tension between ideals and ego. The ironic mosaic prevented seeing each moment independently, subverting the instinct to explain what occurred as a result of immediate historical circumstances. The author traces the roots of political corruption in Mexico back to the revolution and the male egos the struggle unleashed. The novel uses the title character's life story to examine the contradictions at the heart of the revolution and why promises made were never kept and could never have been kept. The facts were historical, but the processes as portrayed in the novel operated on a mythic and existential plane. Fuentes spoke of Orson Welles's famous film *Citizen Kane* as a model for his book, and in both works, a lost moment of innocence reemerges as the story nears its conclusion, a moment that suggests what the character might have been had he somehow overcome the pressures turning him into a monster. Despite the violence and mendacity of Cruz's life, a kernel of his idealism survives, sentimentalized through association with a lost romance, but still the basis for a reader discovering the title character's sympathetic side. And readers apparently liked the book, which sold well despite reviews that questioned choices that Fuentes had made in crafting the story.

To help promote the book, Farrar, Straus publicized the difficulties it had bringing Fuentes to the United States for his book launch. In 1962, two years before the release of the English-language translation of *Artemio Cruz*, Fuentes had received an invitation to appear on a national U.S. television news program to debate U.S. policy in Latin America with the undersecretary of state for Latin American affairs. The U.S. Embassy in Mexico City, however, denied him an entry visa. Fuentes learned that his name had been added to a list of foreign figures barred from entering the country because they were communists or engaged in activities hostile to the United States. Consular officials in Mexico City refused to explain how or why this had occurred.[23] Deborah Cohn's research suggests that Thomas Mann, the U.S. ambassador to Mexico in 1961, had personally added Fuentes to the list, likely as a result of the writer's vocal support for Fidel Castro and the Cuban revolution and his public advocacy for Mexico's adopting a more independent foreign policy. Mann's antagonism to Fuentes is well documented, and efforts by Farrar, Straus and others in the United States to secure waivers to the exclusion order failed whenever Mann was needed to sign off on the request. However, journalists who secured Fuentes's FBI files under the Freedom of Information Act determined that the FBI had initiated the hold on Fuentes's visa after one of the bureau's paid informers in Mexico reported that Fuentes was an active if secret member of the Mexican Communist Party.[24]

When Farrar, Straus petitioned for a waiver to allow Fuentes to do a tour across the United States promoting *The Death of Artemio Cruz*, the State Department initially refused but relented after Roger Straus organized a well-publicized campaign that included appealing to personal friends of the publisher who were working in the White House, the State Department, and the Department of Justice. Fuentes received a restricted visa that allowed him to be in the country for five days only. He could not leave the island of Manhattan except to return directly to the airport for a flight out of the country. The restrictions then became part of further discussion of the book. State Department officials concluded that the controversy was generating only negative publicity for the department, and it began waiving his exclusion more regularly, despite agitated FBI protests. Each visit, however, required a separate interview in the U.S. Embassy in Mexico City. Fuentes reported that in each meeting, consular officials advised him that his case would be considerably simpler if he made an occasional anticommunist statement. Coming to the United States, where Fuentes had some of his most important business connections, had become a difficult and humiliating process. Pressure on the White House and State Department continued from publishers, universities, and philanthropies that wanted Fuentes to have unlimited entry privilege because for them he had become one of the most important figures linking North American and Latin American culture. Fuentes's backers finally secured their goal in 1970.[25]

Fuentes was a prolific writer with seemingly unlimited energy. Between 1954, when his first volume of short stories appeared in Mexico, and 1970, he had published seven novels, two volumes of short stories, and three volumes of collected essays. Fondo de Cultura Económica published his first books. Fuentes was convinced that he needed a good U.S. publisher if he were to escape the limitations inherent to Mexican publishing with its limited print runs and uncertain distribution. He secured the services of one of the top literary agents in New York, Carl Brandt, who placed the author with Farrar, Straus. Fuentes's first novel appeared in English in 1960, only two years after its publication in Spanish. Farrar, Straus continued releasing Fuentes's books in translation within a year or two of their original publication. While valuing his U.S. agent and publisher, Fuentes did not want the relationship to limit his ability to move globally. His active support for the Cuban revolution brought him to Havana, where he lived while writing most of *La muerte de Artemio Cruz*. In Cuba, he was actively involved with Casa de las Américas, a new cultural center and publishing house that the revolutionary government of Cuba founded in 1959. Its publishing program aimed to promote writing from across the continent internationally without authors having to rely on either U.S. or European connections. While he lived in Havana, Fuentes met Carlos Barral, a Spanish socialist with a press in Barcelona, Seix Barral. The firm had begun printing young Latin American writers, and Barral signed Fuentes and took over distribution of Fuentes's novels in Spanish-language markets around the world. Fuentes's new connections in Barcelona led to Carmen Balcells becoming his agent for the Spanish-language market. Balcells, Brandt, Farrar Straus, and Seix Barral worked together on European and global rights. The arrangement gave Fuentes more control over his work because he was less dependent on any one publisher or on a single agent.[26]

Fuentes was an avid proponent of the new Latin American literature that his generation was producing. He wanted his own work to be seen as part of a broader movement that was "internationalizing" the writing of Spanish-speaking America. He wanted to break the isolation that limited most writers to their small, often minuscule, national literary situations, with a lucky handful securing recognition in the United States or France. Fuentes argued that even the most serious writers of the interwar years had been too verbose, and their books lacked structure. Serious writers used as few words as possible but conveyed a richer range of feelings, as Borges had done. Serious writers delved into the ugly, sweaty side of life like Pablo Neruda did in poems in which people made love, got drunk, fought each other. Serious writers pushed the Spanish language as César Vallejo had to reveal the pain of conquest and servitude. Serious writers read William Faulkner, Ernest Hemingway, F. Scott Fitzgerald,

William Carlos Williams, and many other modern writers from the United States, including detective novelists like Raymond Chandler and James Cain, because they offered models for how to dig into the ugliness of America and create beauty that would also be true to the world in which Americans lived. For any ambitious modern writer, Latin American writing of the first half of the twentieth century was, with a handful of significant exceptions, insufferable and deservedly provincial.[27]

Internationalization had begun with Roger Caillois's Southern Cross series. Caillois sought out authors who understood American reality but wrote in universal terms based on an understanding of myth, history, and psychology. Nonetheless, Caillois was from an older generation and did not know the authors Fuentes admired as his "compañeros." Fuentes knew many of the writers, critics, and editors on both sides of the Atlantic who might be interested in good, experimental literature, and he made it his business to connect them. In one of the defining moments of what would become the boom, Fuentes sent Emir Rodríguez Monegal a sample chapter from the novel that Gabriel García Márquez was still in the midst of writing, the novel that would appear in 1967 as *Cien años de soledad* (*One Hundred Years of Solitude*). García Márquez, surviving through writing for the Mexican film and television industry, had a book of short stories and a short novel in print, but he was still largely unknown in the Spanish-language book market. The sample chapter astonished Rodríguez Monegal, a prominent Uruguayan critic who was on the faculty of Yale University. He published the first two chapters of *Cien años de soledad* in his new journal, *Mundo Nuevo*, which he had started publishing in Paris in 1966, and offered García Márquez a stipend of $400 per month to write articles for the journal. Ironically, given Gabriel García Márquez's unstinting support for Fidel Castro and the Cuban revolution, the first publication of *Cien años de soledad* occurred in a journal that the CIA had helped launch and covertly funded in order to convince progressive opinion in Latin America that intellectuals' priorities were more in line with thinking in the United States than in communist Cuba. The prepublication was an important element in the stunning sales that the book had when it appeared in Spanish in 1967. Public appetite had been whetted, and readers in every country wanted more. Rodríguez Monegal promoted the new novel wherever he went, and his active support helped convince Harper and Row to take on García Márquez.

The existing international language for understanding contemporary Latin American literature came from Roger Caillois. The approach had worked well in Europe, but in the U.S. context, Caillois's assessments had many overlaps with the romantic rhetoric of the interwar period that, as we have seen, poorly represented the complexity of what was occurring in Latin American countries and failed to sell books at the level that commercial publishers expected. Critical languages had to be developed for the U.S. market that would allow the reading public of the 1960s to understand why works were important. An important step toward the goal of helping see the importance of literature that was both narratively difficult and politically engaged came in 1967, when the Rockefeller Brothers Fund provided money to the Center for Inter-American Relations (CIAR), a nonprofit group based in New York City, for a new translation program focused on commercial publishers with proven ability to produce and market best-sellers.[28] The program required publishers to provide at least half of the translation cost, but CIAR, also led by members of the Rockefeller family, committed resources for promoting books and their authors.

For major publishers, the truly important benefit from the CIAR program was the commitment of CIAR staff to make sure that reviews of works they had funded appeared in the *New York Times,* the *New Yorker, Time* magazine, and a dozen other magazines that CIAR had determined most important for publicizing a new book. The program staff at CIAR recruited reviewers for specific titles and recommended them to journal editors. Whenever possible, they wanted well-known U.S. writers to review a book and in effect introduce a Latin American writer they liked to their U.S. readers. As part of the program to publicize the program's authors, CIAR provided support to a number of journals, including *Books Abroad*, the *Hudson Review,* and *Tri-Quarterly*, to produce special issues on contemporary Latin American literature. With CIAR help, Knopf and Harper and Row each published a book of interviews with contemporary Latin American writers, in both cases translations of books that had originally appeared in Latin America.[29] The program staff focused on works by authors who had sold well in Latin America and Europe but were still unknown in the United States. Writers like Carlos Fuentes, Jorge Amado, or Érico Veríssimo were not eligible for CIAR programs, but the reasoning was that all authors, including those already established in the U.S. market, benefited from a more deeply developed context for their work.[30]

The triumph of the program was having funded the translation of *One Hundred Years of Solitude*, released by Harper and Row, a powerhouse in the U.S. publishing business, in 1970, to stunning reviews and sales. Harper and Row had released García Márquez's first book in English, *No One Writes to the Colonel*, two years earlier, but the book had not done well. CIAR understood that persistence was needed to overcome editorial reluctance to take unknown authors seriously. CIAR developed a long-term strategy that involved a continued partnership with publishers and agents to promote work long after an author's first book had come and gone. CIAR funded four books by Chilean novelist José Donoso, four books by Argentinean writer Manuel Puig, three titles by Julio

Cortázar, and two books by Miguel Ángel Asturias. Of this group of work, Puig's books gained the most attention in the United States, partly due to a successful stage adaptation of *The Kiss of the Spider Woman* that was then made into a film starring William Hurt and Raúl Julia. Stellar sales for any author were rare, but persistence in promoting the field of Latin American writing elevated sales for many authors to levels closer to what publishers expected for a typical novel. As a result, taking on a Latin American writer need not be seen as a contribution to the national interest, but a business venture that would readily pay off the firm's investment in a book, and, in some cases, a title could turn into a winner with significant sales.

CIAR also provided funds that assisted the move of Ernesto Sábato, Jorge Luis Borges, Pablo Neruda, and Octavio Paz from New Directions, the most prestigious publisher of avant-garde literature in the country, to bigger commercial publishing houses. In Sábato's case, CIAR guaranteed the full translation costs of *Sobre héroes y tumbas* ("On Heroes and Tombs") and assured the publisher against losses if sales failed to cover production costs.[31] The moves do not appear to have led to increased sales for these authors, not surprising given that New Directions specialized in experimental poetry and fiction and had long experience in marketing work considered difficult. The move, however, led to more prominently placed advertising and more reviews in major periodicals, supporting the goal of a higher commercial profile within the United States for Latin American authors generally and for CIAR-funded authors specifically.

The central position of the U.S. publishing industry in the international circuit of translations was an important, additional element in program goals. Publishers in most countries looked first to the U.S. and U.K. markets in making decisions about which foreign-language books to translate. A publisher in the Netherlands, for example, waited for an English-language translation to have appeared and established itself before moving forward with a translation into Dutch, even if a book had already appeared in French or German translation.[32] Given that 70 percent of books published in the Netherlands were, and continue to be, translations, choosing which foreign books to present in Dutch is critical for a publisher's ability to survive as a business. Simultaneously, royalties from ancillary language markets had become a major factor for U.S. publishers, who typically insisted, as they did with Veríssimo, that they handle an author's international sales, but were becoming more open, as with Fuentes, to share foreign rights, provided that the author and the author's agent were prepared to work aggressively to place the book internationally. For Latin American authors, even those who had translations into French or German, a U.S. edition was critical for making the transition from being a "prestige" writer to a commercially successful author in the global book market.

The CIAR program was successful in stimulating commercial presses to adopt more titles, and the authors presses picked up tended to be those whose work was discussed in a CIAR journal, *Review: Latin American Literature and Arts*, launched in 1967 shortly after the translation program began. The first issue began with an introductory essay from Emir Rodríguez Monegal. He opened "The New Latin American Literature in the USA" with a terse description of the problem: "With exasperating sluggishness, the effects of the boom in new Latin American literature are beginning to be felt even here in the United States." Ignoring a by-then fifty-year history of Latin American authors in the U.S. book market, Rodríguez Monegal claimed that "the best critics had systematically refused to take any Latin American book seriously." He then identified the major authors who needed to be known in the United States, providing a preview of the program that CIAR followed for the next decade.[33] The point was not historical accuracy but to capture attention and stimulate interest, particularly among the agents, editors, and critics to whom CIAR sent the inaugural issue of *Review*. The term "boom" helped brand a new generation of writers with the expectation that what they were doing was explosively unexpected. Whatever had come before was insignificant in comparison, a record of local customs perhaps, but provincial isolation had limited earlier writers, who therefore had not been able to seize a place for Latin America on the stage of world literature.

The issue followed with reprints of recent reviews of translated books by poets César Vallejo, Pablo Neruda, and Nicanor Parra, and fiction by Jorge Luis Borges, Miguel Ángel Asturias, João Guimarães Rosa, Juan Carlos Onetti, Gabriel García Márquez, Mario Vargas Llosa, Carlos Fuentes, and Gustavo Sáinz. The eighty-page issue provided a concise introduction to CIAR's objectives, along with a sampling of strongly positive critical response from a broad cross section of U.S. newspapers and magazines that were most important in setting cultural trends inside the country. Several of the books reviewed in the issue had received CIAR financial backing, but most had not. Subsequent issues of *Review* explored individual writers in detail, providing editors, agents, and critics with a representative sample of work and critical articles that contextualized the author, offering a language for discussing any book a U.S. publisher were to release from the featured author. In 1970, *Review* produced a special issue celebrating *One Hundred Years of Solitude*, which brought together Latin American and U.S. writers to comment on a book that was already breaking sales records in every country where it had been published. Publicity for *One Hundred Years of Solitude* began a full year before the English translation appeared. Cass Canfield, Jr., García Márquez's editor at Harper and Row, told the *New York Times* in April 1969 that the publishing house was "certain" that the new book would "cause the same sensation as some of the postwar French and

German writers brought to the American literary scene." Canfield described the forthcoming book, chapters of which were being previewed in several journals, as a "witty fantasy about a mythical rural community" told "in the style of the Arabian Nights." In the same article, José Guillermo Castillo, the director of CIAR's literature program, affirmed that Latin American writers were excited about the prospect of publication in the United States, and he told the reporter that the writers his program supported were good storytellers who would help readers in the United States understand the "contemporary scene" on the continent, leaving open, as frequently happened in publicity statements, whether he was referring to new cultural movements or to the political events pushing their way into the daily newspapers.[34]

Publishers rushed to find the next unexpected best-seller that might come out of Latin America, and a flurry of translations appeared in English. Attention was selective. While CIAR promoted authors whose distinction critics in Latin America had recognized, publishers and reviewers in the United States were looking for work that might explain continental social upheaval. The reviewer at *Time* magazine of Borges's *Ficciones* opined that Argentina had such fragile national institutions that "the *only* thing an intelligent, sensitive person could do was to rise up and say NO."[35] In an article on *Ficciones* in the *New York Times*, the poet John Ashbery claimed that "across this largely unknown continent, a radical spiritual revolution was underway."[36] These were two reviews of Borges, a complex writer whose work resists ideological classification, but who was introduced to U.S. readers with rhetorical flourishes linking him to the challenge Cuba had made to U.S. hegemony—an ironic use of an author who as a liberal had little sympathy for Cuban socialism, or for that matter, for populist movements in general, which he dismissed as inherently totalitarian.

Latin American writing had attained a definable niche in the U.S. publishing business, but only a few books were truly successful. José Donoso in a book on the boom that he published in 1972 insisted that international recognition had not meant that the best-known writers were earning tons of money. Gabriel García Márquez was the only writer of his generation whose income as a writer was "substantial." Even with the growth of the Spanish-language book market and the success of translations, writers typically needed university positions, diplomatic posts, and journalism assignments to survive, positions that Donoso knew were generally necessary for most North American and European writers as well. The boom for Donoso meant escaping the limitations of being a writer from a "developing" country. There was an economic aspect to the change. He recalled that in 1957, when he published his first novel, his publisher in Chile did a print run of three thousand copies. Donoso was to receive no royalties from sales of the book. The publisher gave him seven hundred copies for him to sell personally. That would be the only income he received for the book until Knopf brought it out in English translation.[37] By the 1970s, the marketing capabilities of Spanish-language publishers had grown. They paid advances and royalties to their authors. Equally important was international recognition that authors were writing about topics that went beyond the immediate concerns of their individual countries or even of the region. The generation that emerged after 1955 rebelled against the dogmas of social realism and nationalism, where they found only "stagnancy and poverty."[38] Some writers—Donoso cited Ciro Alegría, Germán Arciniegas, Miguel Ángel Asturias, Eduardo Mallea—"were able to represent the qualities of their continent with dignity . . . identifying themselves with the most obvious levels of their countries' struggles."[39] They were translated into a few other languages, but the world *as a whole* ignored them, probably had never even heard of them. Success in New York or Paris did not lead to readers in Cairo or Jakarta. The new generation had no choice but to start fresh and find new models for how to be a writer.

Although the ambition Donoso described was global, the writers most important to him were the modernist experimenters of Europe and North America. They helped him forget what the earlier generation had assumed was essential to being "Hispanic" and "American." He and others in his generation became *writers* first and foremost, not well-behaved spokesmen for their countries. Their stories were unruly, impolite, at times chaotic. They enjoyed putting language and narrative into play. They were not limited by the goal of reflecting social reality in their books; they used language to create new realities. As a result, for the first time ever, Spanish-speaking writers broke into the international republic of letters. People from around the world wanted to read them, including readers across Latin America, whose numbers swelled. Donoso's account summarized the language that Carlos Fuentes, Emir Rodríguez Monegal, and others had developed in the 1960s to explain what was new. It was a particularly effective summary because he described what he had learned through his own personal experience. Yet seven years earlier in 1965, Robert Clements writing in *Saturday Review of Literature* had already framed the basic argument used to explain why the literature of the day was not beholden to anything readers might have previously seen from other American countries: the Latin American novel had "reached maturity" because "the experimental narratives of Fuentes in Mexico or Cortázar in Argentina" had replaced "the nationalistic or indigenista works of the recent past," a framing that Rodríguez Monegal cited with emphatic approval in his essay from 1967 introducing CIAR's new journal, *Review: Latin American Literature and Art*.[40]

The new literature unabashedly exemplified a movement for the political, economic, and cultural independence of the writers' countries, but it rested on a liberal conception of society consisting of autonomous zones. Democratic government promoted their differentiation and development along increasingly separate paths, so that literature, for example, moved away from the goal of expressing or reflecting social reality to inventing, as Jorge Luis Borges had pioneered in his early fiction, artificial worlds that offered readers experiments in imaginative thinking that no other social practice could duplicate. The domain of "publicity" served to unite otherwise semiautonomous spheres and allow imaginative exercises to enter into public life. In a liberal culture, advertising one's gifts and attracting attention was paramount for anyone aiming to be a public figure. Self-advertising was a skill for which Carlos Fuentes had a natural gift. He could speak with confidence if superficially about a dazzling range of political, literary, and philosophical matters. By positing that he was part of a broader, transnational movement of contemporary Spanish-language writers working in a tradition of literary invention that he traced back to the *Arabian Nights*, Cervantes, and the Spanish Renaissance, Fuentes offered critics and casual readers a capacious context for talking about his work that transcended the limits of possible social or political interpretations. Most writers lacked Fuentes's talent for promotion, but CIAR's focus allowed a select group of writers to appear to the reading public in the United States as a movement whose novels one needed to read to understand ongoing conflicts spreading across the western hemisphere, while simultaneously thinking about the emergence of Latin American literature as a turning point in global culture. The writers who were promoted, with Gabriel García Márquez at the top of the list, had a more critical understanding of the history of U.S.–Latin American relations. They were strongly committed to the Cuban revolution, which they viewed as the first stage in the liberation of the continent from foreign domination. Their works challenged the facile liberal assumptions underlying pan-Americanism, but no simple political program could be abstracted from their work. Critics hailed the new work as a cultural breakthrough of global importance because the books stood apart from the everyday world to invite open-ended reflection that then changed how a reader experienced his or her own more immediate world.[41]

For their part, the foundations supporting the translation and publication of new Latin American writing, largely associated with the Rockefeller family, wanted to demonstrate to Latin American intellectuals that despite their disagreements with the U.S. government policies, liberal societies cherished and protected the relative autonomy of critical cultural work. The epistemological autonomy of literature that Donoso emphasized in his memoir of the boom proved, as dictatorships spread and the Cold War intensified in the western hemisphere, to be compatible with U.S. conceptions of culture but deeply at odds with those the Cuban revolution developed as its leaders defended their country's national sovereignty. For Érico Veríssimo, whose commitment to a liberal vision of moral order had made him one of the leading midcentury voices of pan-Americanism, the changing political crisis sapped whatever remaining hopes he had for the international order that the United States was building. He still believed that good writing was a socially and morally engaged practice. The principle of literary autonomy was a practical matter: censorship of any kind was an affront to freedom of conscience and to democratic government. The deepening crisis in Brazil and around the world pushed him in the 1960s to intensify his critique of militarism and the ways a romantic embrace of violence had deformed Brazil, the United States, and Cuba alike since the end of World War II. He stood firmly for the principle that a healthy society excluded violence as a means for political change.

Chapter 12

"I Now Believe That American Imperialism Is Real"

On March 31, 1964, with the blessings of the National Congress in Brasilia and the White House in Washington, the Brazilian military removed President João Goulart from office and jailed many of his supporters. The general whom the Congress then selected to serve as president for the remainder of Goulart's term promised that military rule would end in 1966 with national elections. Two years later, however, the Congress agreed to cancel the election and selected another military leader to serve as president. As resistance to continued military rule spread across the political spectrum, the dictatorship responded by banning all existing political parties, exiling political leaders like former president Juscelino Kubitschek, whom most had expected to win the canceled election, and limiting rights to assemble and protest. In 1968, support for the military in the Congress dwindled, while street demonstrations demanding restoration of democratic government drew larger and larger crowds. The military then shut down the National Congress, abandoning all pretense of governing in concert with elected civilian leadership. When several leftist groups began armed resistance, the dictatorship suspended constitutional protections and barred the courts from interfering with security matters. Torture became commonplace, as did extralegal kidnappings. In its 2014 report, the Brazilian National Truth Commission concluded that the military had secretly executed 434 suspected opponents after they had been arrested. Interrogators trained at schools that the U.S. government established to professionalize the police and military of its allies learned about techniques the French had used in Algeria with captured members of the independence movement, the British had used in Kenya and Malaysia when they fought insurgents, and the U.S. military developed in Vietnam. Dilma Rousseff, elected president of Brazil in 2010, reelected in 2014, and then impeached and removed from office by the National Congress in 2016, was one of thousands of prisoners tortured while interrogated. With her wrists and ankles bound, she was suspended hanging upside down for hours in the "parrot's perch" position, periodically subjected to electric shocks to her feet and ears. Nearly 6,500 members of the military were arrested (and some tortured as suspected communist militants) for refusing to participate in the government's campaign to suppress all opposition.[1]

Such practices were the subject of rumor during the dictatorship, but strict censorship provisions prohibited investigative reporting as well as public discussion in the media of government strategies for combating "communist subversion." Military authorities reviewed every publication before it could be printed and distributed to the public. They also reviewed films before they were released, as well as the scripts of television and radio programming. However, the government exempted Jorge Amado and Érico Veríssimo from full application of censorship provisions. Both were open critics of the dictatorship, but as the country's two most prominent writers, their status as aging national treasures protected them in a period when the government arrested many writers, musicians, and filmmakers for producing so-called antisocial work or for suspicion of supporting underground militants.[2]

As Érico Veríssimo looked at the state of Latin America, the world, and his own country, he saw a military ethos crushing democratic values, with both the left and the right embracing violence as the best path to very different visions of a just and stable society. In the last three novels he wrote before his death in 1975, he explored the militarization of politics in dramatically different contexts. He no longer saw the United States as competent to lead a global campaign for justice and freedom. As a person who twenty years earlier had told his fellow citizens that alliance with the United States was not only strategically necessary but would lead to a more just and peaceful world, Veríssimo had to speak bluntly on the failures of U.S. global leadership and what that meant for those like him who did not want to live in a world of perpetual war.

O Senhor Embaixador (translated as *His Excellency, the Ambassador*) appeared in 1965, a period when the military dictatorship was still relatively mild and more or less observing legal due process. The book is set in 1959, and the story revolves around the political travails of an imaginary Caribbean nation with a long history of U.S. occupation and rule by corrupt dictators. It is one of the poorest countries in the western hemisphere, and two large U.S. food corporations own the most productive land. When a newly elected president promulgates a land reform law that will, as in Guatemala before the coup of 1954, distribute unused land to poor peasants, the two corporations, with the assistance of the country's wealthiest landowners, ask the army to overthrow the government on the grounds of communist infiltration. The new military dictatorship suspends civil liberties along with the land reform law. Hundreds of the overthrown government's supporters are arrested, tortured, and murdered. Secret police sneak into the United States to murder exiles. Castro's revolutionary government in Cuba begins training and arming a guerrilla force of exiles who are readying to return home and fight.

The first three-quarters of the book unfolds in Washington, D.C. The military dictatorship's new ambassador, the title character, has arrived needing to negotiate an end to the arms embargo that the U.S. government imposed on the country when the elected government fell. U.S. leaders are concerned only with the challenge that Castro's Cuba poses to U.S. control of the Caribbean. They are dubious that the country is capable of democratic government, but they have decided that the new dictatorship, the brutality of which Veríssimo modeled after what happened in Cuba under Fulgencio Batista, the Dominican Republic under Rafael Trujillo, Nicaragua under Anastasio Somoza, or Venezuela under Marcos Pérez Jiménez, promotes the appeal of communist insurgents. The U.S. characters in any event are secondary, looming in the background, while the narrative focus remains on the interactions of the diplomatic staff, torn between supporters of the dictator and liberals who want to see democracy restored. As U.S. leaders wait with increasing impatience for liberal exiles to create a credible opposition to the dictatorship, Cuban-supported rebels land on the island, the people rally to their support, and after a brief civil war, a new revolutionary government takes power.

As he finished the book, Veríssimo told a friend that writing the book had helped him see things about life in America that he, like most of the people he knew, preferred to ignore. He arrived at a conclusion that he had not anticipated when he began the project: there was no room for effective political action once opponents turned to brute force to settle disagreements instead of debate and persuasion. Above all, he had become pessimistic about any of the options available to countries in America now that the Cold War had arrived in full force. All parties were so attached to a romance of heroic violence that a lengthy period of dictatorship and war would prevail across the western hemisphere.[3] When the book appeared in the United States, reviews as usual were strongly positive. The reviewer at the New York Times stressed Veríssimo's insider Washington status as a veteran of the Pan American Union and his knowledge of the city's "peculiar folkways." In addition to lauding the writing and Veríssimo's storytelling skills, the reviewer praised the novel for providing relevant insight into recent Caribbean history, particularly in Cuba and the Dominican Republic. In 1965 shortly before the book appeared, U.S. troops had once again occupied the latter country to prevent supposed supporters of Fidel Castro from establishing a new government with strong popular support. The reviewer framed the conflict at the center of the novel as one between authoritarian political realists and an upper-class liberal who hopes to see his country develop into a modern, productive nation like the United States, but without giving up its unique and more human culture. The *New York Times* reviewer concluded his discussion of the novel by noting that the book's liberal hero is "kin to those who fought Batista and were crushed by Castro." The reviewer wanted more on why revolutions turn defenders of the poor into dictators, but overall, he strongly recommended Veríssimo's exploration of the contest between liberal idealism and revolutionary will, praising both the skillfully drawn characters from Latin America and Veríssimo's understanding if at times caustic portraits of U.S. officials, journalists, politicians, lobbyists, and pan-American enthusiasts.[4]

As reviewers in the United States consistently noted, the core of the story focuses on the dilemmas revolutionary movements posed for liberals from Latin America who wanted to see their countries progress. The novel's main character, the secretary of his country's embassy in Washington, pursues his interests in haiku poetry while surreptitiously supporting exiles working for restoration of democratic government. The turning point for him comes when secret police from his country kidnap and murder his old professor, an exiled leader of the movement for democracy with a faculty appointment at a U.S. university. The young man throws his lot in with the revolutionaries training in Cuba. He distrusts them, but they have become the only force capable of bringing change to his country. He fights in the civil war, and after victory, the revolutionary junta appoints him minister of propaganda and public information. Instructed to implement new censorship laws more draconian than those of the previous dictatorship, the young liberal refuses. The communist leader who organized the revolution and has taken charge of the new government tells him, "For you bourgeois liberals, freedom is something that exists outside the context of life and the well-being of the people. A jewel to be guarded, a family heirloom that is never worn. A false jewel, in my opinion. Useless. . . . Freedom cannot be an end in and of itself. It is a *means* for providing the majority with a better life. If it doesn't serve that objective, it has no value whatsoever."[5]

The battle between communist and liberal ideals escalates when the young liberal publicly opposes the show trials and televised executions of members of the former government, an account modeled on the public trials and executions of over five hundred police and military officials in Cuba after the revolutionary government took charge in 1959. He volunteers to serve as the attorney defending the ambassador for whom he worked in Washington. The deposed ambassador, on trial for his life for his role in the fallen dictatorship, has no illusions about what will happen to him. Had his side prevailed, he would have made sure that the leaders of the rebellion were summarily executed. Not out of love for violence, he says, but because in poor countries, power rests on frequent use of unforgiving brutal force. At the televised trial, the young liberal offers a stirring defense of due process and legal norms as necessary if the country is ever to become peaceful and prosperous. The defense offered gives the communist leader, acting in the role of prosecutor, an opportunity to put liberal values on trial as the cause of the nation's prolonged misery. Veríssimo narrates much of the final section of the book from the viewpoint of a retired U.S. journalist, who had spent most of his career covering revolutionary movements across Latin America. Modeled loosely on that of Carleton Beals, the fictional journalist's career took off in the 1920s when he was able to interview a guerrilla leader leading a ragtag army fighting a U.S. occupation army. He had spent a lifetime trying to report what he observed as simply and truthfully as he could. The journalist comes out of retirement to report on the new revolution, allowing Veríssimo to use him for an ongoing commentary on the ultimate failure of pan-Americanism.

Veríssimo crafted the concluding section to stress that what was new about the socialist revolutionaries emulating the Cuban path to national liberation was neither their reliance on violence nor their cynicism. That they shared with every successful political leader. Nor did he doubt their commitment to improving the welfare of the people, but, as Veríssimo narrated the story, communists see themselves as the defenders of a population that has been corrupted and demoralized by centuries of oppression. They cannot trust the citizens they have freed to make the sacrifices necessary for the nation to progress. Several generations must pass before a new nation emerges where the citizens understand what sovereignty and self-sufficiency require from them. Until then, the leaders will use the media to create a simulacrum of popular participation, while creating a secret police force that seeks out discontent before it can become a threat to the regime. According to Veríssimo's description of how a communist government takes hold, the revolution creates a nation based on pervasive suspicion, a nation where real feelings are hidden under passionate-looking but ultimately pretend displays of revolutionary enthusiasm.

The book's view is bleak, for all the alternatives are horrendous. U.S. political leaders remain in the background, but when they are glimpsed, they too are producing positive-looking media images to camouflage their cynical use of force. The difference as Veríssimo presents it is that with abundant resources and a deeper history, U.S. leaders are more refined than their communist opponents, they are better positioned to be generous if generosity makes for good politics, and they are generally more skilled at the use of naked power. At the book's end, a U.S. invasion force is assembling, and occupation looms as the likely outcome of a revolution that, at least as the novel presents the situation, the people no longer supported. Veríssimo's position in the novel is unclear as to whether he thought U.S. occupation was preferable to communist dictator-ship, or simply one more disaster in the long tragic history of his fictional coun-try. In the final pages, the novel shifts from geopolitics to the existential realities of leadership. The closing scene presents the televised execution of the former ambassador, who is determined to deny his captors the spectacle they desire by facing his death with bravery and honor. Men like him, whether of the right or the left, who have staked their lives on action and brute force understand that gambling for power always involves the risk of failure and paying the penalty fate sends them. Liberals in the book who take their principles seriously, whether North American, Latin American, European, or Japanese, cannot comprehend that imposing their principles on the world requires risking everything, their lives certainly, but even the very values that they hold most deeply. Unable to compromise on their principles, they wield at best symbolic power. The hard-ness of the book lies in its refusal of romantic escape. For the foreseeable future, the initiative belongs to those ready to use force, not to those who believe in the transcendent power of ideas. The will to power will bring change, but anyone who believes that either the Pax Americana or the Cuban revolution will make the world more just or, at the least, more prosperous will inevitably discover the emp-tiness of their hopes.

In 1965, when the book appeared, not one of the Spanish-language authors associated with the boom would have published even the most minor criticism of the Cuban revolution or the many movements it had inspired across the hemisphere. The overwhelming majority of writers in Brazil sympathized with the Cuban cause, as did many prominent writers in the United States. For most on the left, Cuba under Castro was the only place in the Americas where U.S. economic and military power no longer dictated what a country could do. The Cuban people had said no to corrupt dictators and to imperialism. This accom-plishment alone required putting aside any misgivings about any specific poli-cies revolutionary leaders had taken. In addition, through the 1960s, the rapid pace of social projects—land and housing reform, universal education, univer-sal access to health care, the elimination of racial discrimination—provided convincing evidence that revolutionary Cuba was addressing the basic problems of the Cuban people in ways that surpassed every other country in the Ameri-cas, perhaps including the United States. So universal was the sympathy for Cuba among Latin American intellectuals that Emir Rodríguez Monegal did not allow criticisms of Cuba to appear in *Mundo Nuevo*, and the Center for Inter-American Relations was equally insistent that its publications maintain a neutral tone whenever the Cuban revolution was discussed.

Veríssimo had long taken a firm stand against communism. He had argued that communists relied on manufactured images that supporters bought because sentimental ideas made them feel good. When potential contradictions appeared like the show trials in Moscow or the Soviet pact with the Nazis, supporters denied facts that were obvious to everybody else. Veríssimo concluded that communists preferred to live in a world of romantic fantasies only tenuously connected to reality. He had been the target of public vitriol within Brazil as a result. He was not inclined to temper his criticisms of the left when communism came to power in an American country. He recognized the appeal that the communist message had for many, but he was dubious that the reforms that inspired so many of his closest friends would actually improve the lives of the Cuban people. Everyone judged Cuba by its ideals, while they were fed up with the actual conditions of their own countries. Toward the end of *O Senhor Embaixador*, a Brazilian diplomat in Washington, a young friend of the main character, like him from a prominent family and deeply committed to liberal values, explodes with an angry diatribe about the continuous looting, found at all levels of society, that shaped every aspect of life in his country. Bribes and payoffs had become a necessary, expected part of life, he complains. The communists were brutal, but their methods if carried to their logical conclusion would eliminate evils that everyone knew kept the country in a disastrous state. Communists did not value money, so the compulsion to take part in the looting had no appeal to them. Could humanists formed in debates over principles ever discover the power necessary to counter the communist appeal? If they could not, the military would seize power to lead the resistance to communism, as it had already in Brazil, when Veríssimo's novel appeared. The tragic conclusion: revolutionary existential demands that intellectuals transform themselves into "new men" through heroic action led only to dictatorship, either of the right or of the left.[6]

This was a message that few other intellectuals wanted to hear in 1965. Over the next few years, the Latin American intellectual left divided over how to respond to new developments in Cuba that were more consistent with Veríssimo's analysis than with their initial enthusiasm. The first glimmer of dissension came in 1966 when Alejo Carpentier, joined by a distinguished group of Cuban writers, published an open letter in the Cuban journal *Casa de las Américas* and the Uruguayan journal *Marcha* condemning Pablo Neruda for having participated in an international writers conference in New York City and then doing a circuit of spectacularly successful poetry readings during a brief visit to the United States. The letter singled out Carlos Fuentes as well, criticizing him for helping writers find U.S. publishers. Carpentier and his colleagues declared that solidarity with the global revolutionary movement required them to reject any future requests to publish their books in the United States and to boycott cultural activities organized by U.S. institutions, whether run by the government or private institutions. The personal attack incensed

Fuentes, but he decided not to respond lest he get embroiled in a fruitless dispute with the Cuban novelist.[7]

A criticism of Neruda, a prominent international figure who was also a leading member of a fraternal communist party and a prominent voice defending the Cuban revolution, was unlikely to have occurred without Fidel Castro's personal approval. The attack put a chill in the relation between intellectuals and the revolutionary government, but like Carlos Fuentes, no one wanted to get into an open quarrel. Things worsened in 1968, when Fidel Castro strongly supported the Soviet invasion of Czechoslovakia. Castro's stand was incomprehensible to writers like Carlos Fuentes, Mario Vargas Llosa, and José Donoso, who had traveled to Prague during the short-lived experiment in democratic socialism. Fuentes had thought that the Czech attempt to claim independence from the Soviet Union was potentially as important as what Cuba had done, pointing, he claimed, to a possible end to the Cold War through the refusal of the world's small countries to participate. But even if one had qualms about what the Czechs were doing, did not the principle of national sovereignty, so important to Latin America, demand principled opposition to Soviet intervention?[8]

For many intellectuals, the definitive break came in 1971, when several Cuban writers went on trial on charges of counterrevolutionary activity. Heberto Padilla, young but already gaining international recognition for his poetry, made a televised confession that his writings that criticized aspects of life in revolutionary Cuba were the result of his having become friends with exiled antisocialist eastern European writers he had met while working in the Cuban Embassy in London. The confession had all the earmarks of a show trial from the Stalin era.[9] Writers from around the world, including many of the writers most closely associated with the boom, signed a letter condemning the treatment Padilla had received. The Cuban government responded by equating any criticism of the revolutionary government with counterrevolutionary support for the United States. Fidel personally dismissed several writers, including Carlos Fuentes and José Donoso, as bourgeois opportunists whose support for the revolution had been a platform for promoting their own work in the United States. The writers who had achieved success split over how to respond to Cuba: Julio Cortázar and Gabriel García Márquez maintained their loyalty to Cuba, explaining the actions of the Cuban government as necessary to protect their country from continuous imperialist attack. García Márquez had little sympathy for Padilla, but the Soviet occupation of Czechoslovakia had shaken him. He told a friend, "My world collapsed but now I think maybe it's better like this: to demonstrate, without nuances, that we stand between two imperialisms, equally cruel and voracious, is in a certain sense a liberation for one's conscience." The moral example that the Cuban revolution continued to provide to Latin America and Africa outweighed inevitable political and economic shortcomings. If Castro's endorsement of Soviet policies had been a tragic error, to make public pronouncements that effectively put one in alliance with the United States was an even greater mistake. "It's our dirty washing and we'll do it at home," García Márquez said, adding with realistic frankness that politics required a different ethics than literature or everyday morals. "But the truth is I don't think it will be washed very easily."[10]

Only a minority of the authors associated with the boom shared his position. For José Donoso, for example, the autonomy of literature in the revolutionary process was an existential question that no writer could compromise. As he explained in his "personal history" of the boom, the job of the writer was not to set forth facts and arguments, which others (social scientists, journalists, lawyers, polemicists) could do more accurately. Writers have a unique skill—the exploration of metaphor, which allows many questions to be experienced in a new way, allows for unexpected connections to emerge, which is a perception of the world in new ways because less hemmed in by starting assumptions. Indeed, for Donoso, the task of writing requires abandoning all starting points so that following the inner logic of the material leads to conclusions impossible to imagine before writing began. Cuba like other revolutionary socialist societies had decided that writing had to serve the government's political priorities. In the capitalist United States, writers faced another form of oppression: the market determined that most books were read and sold as "entertainment." Fortunately, universities provided a viable space where reading was not done for "entertainment" but for "pleasure."[11] Given that space—which in the United States was well developed and well funded, indeed a source of pride for national culture, if also of irritation—the university provided serious writing with a home that justified the work of small publishers and university presses, and at times influenced the decisions that commercial publishers made. As relations with Cuba soured, Donoso realized that U.S. society, despite the viciousness of its foreign policy, remained open to what he most valued. Finding a warm welcome and intelligent exploration of the questions that good writing posed in the U.S. university, he taught in the creative writing program at the University of Iowa.[12]

Disillusionment with the Cuban revolution was the central theme of Jorge Edwards's book *Persona non grata*.[13] Edwards, a Chilean novelist who worked in the Chilean Foreign Service from 1957 to 1973, arrived in Havana at the end of 1970, sent by the newly elected Allende government to prepare for reopening the Chilean Embassy. Four months later, Fidel Castro personally ordered the expulsion of Edwards for activities Castro deemed hostile to the revolution. Heberto Padilla's frequent association with Edwards during the Chilean's short time in Cuba was the catalyst leading to Padilla's arrest, trial, and public confession. In the introduction to the 1993 edition of his account, Edwards described his work as the first book "by a left-wing Latin American intellectual . . . that was openly critical of the Cuban regime."[14] The book challenged leftist writers in Europe and Latin America to rethink the association of the Cuban revolution with a uniquely moral and humanist revolution. If his story was accurate, Cuba had become another socialist dictatorship unable to satisfy either its people's material needs or their moral aspirations.

Edwards put himself forward as a socialist intellectual forced to confront bitter and disappointing realities. He arrived in Cuba shortly before Christmas 1970 to assume his duties as the first Chilean diplomatic representative in the country since 1964, when the Organization of American States voted to expel Cuba, and all the members, save Mexico, severed diplomatic relations. He had visited Cuba only once before, in 1968, to participate in a writers workshop. It had been a short trip, spent entirely among writers. Despite intimations from most of the Cuban writers participating in the event that much was wrong in Cuba, Edwards left in 1968 convinced that the political and cultural revolutions in Cuba were moving forward. When he returned in 1970, the country no longer seemed hopeful. The sugar harvest had failed, food supplies were being rationed, and Havana was a city in an advanced state of decay. People's lives were miserable, and a police state had formed even though the Cuban people still seemed to support Fidel. But after twelve years of revolution, their lives were getting worse, not better, and the revolutionary government was determined to suppress any expression of popular discontent. As a result, the Cubans Edwards met, regular working people as well as writers and intellectuals, seemed to move about in a constant state of fear, always careful about what they said, for someone might inform on them, or there might be a hidden microphone allowing the police to listen in on otherwise private conversations.

At his last meeting with Fidel Castro, when Edwards received his expulsion orders, he told Castro, "I must explain to you what happens to a Chilean of good faith, a person who has never skimped on his friendship for the Cuban Revolution, who arrives in Cuba today. . . . A Chilean reads in the situation of Cuba today one of the possibilities of his own country's future. To speak with complete frankness, I think it is only natural that this Chilean not particularly enjoy contemplating that future as it may be seen in the situation of Cuba today. Nor would the people of Cuba have much enjoyed contemplating that future if they had been able to anticipate in 1959 what Cuba would be like in 1971."[15] Fidel responded, Edwards reported, that the history of Cuba had not produced a people who were good at building things, but they were great fighters who preferred to go down fighting rather than compromise. Edwards gloomily predicted that the failures of the revolution would lead to military adventures.

Fidel had wanted to send his army to Chile. Allende had refused, but Edwards was convinced that Castro would find other countries for military adventures that might compensate for the revolution's failures.

The final section of *Persona non grata* focuses on his work at the Chilean Embassy in Paris, as personal assistant to Pablo Neruda, charged as ambassador to France with negotiating a settlement that could end the economic embargo strangling Chile's economy after Allende's inauguration as president in 1970. The United States proved an implacable enemy, clear about what it wanted and was prepared to do. The Allende government had equally implacable enemies within Chile. Nor could it count on the support of western European governments, which, despite considerable verbal support for Allende's peaceful and democratic transition to socialism, were unwilling to compromise in the slightest on the issues of greatest concern to the Chilean government. Frustrated with the failure of diplomacy to find solutions to Chile's problems, Edwards resigned his position in the diplomatic service to dedicate his time to writing. He was living in Spain when the news of the military coup in Chile came on September 11, 1973. He published his book on his Cuban experiences shortly after Allende's fall, with the final chapters dealing with the buildup to the coup. The juxtaposition was clear: the convergence of left and right on the continent in the form of military-based dictatorships. Were U.S. leftists prepared to recognize Edwards's bravery in criticizing the Castro regime? No reviews appeared in the left press. A Cuban-American academic reviewing *Persona non grata* in 1994 admitted that the book had been a difficult challenge for her when it first appeared and it remained hard to read in the 1990s even though she could acknowledge that historical developments largely vindicated Edwards's arguments. She asked herself, if Edwards's descriptions were indeed accurate, had it nonetheless been imperative to support the Cuban revolution even if it were a police state? A review from 1974 published in an academic journal dedicated to Latin American literature noted that Edwards dealt with a fundamental theme, "the struggle of the thinking man to reconcile ideals with realities," but concluded that the Cuban government had been correct to eject a foreign diplomat who was more concerned about the status of writers in Cuba than the threat to the revolution that U.S. imperialism posed.[16] After the 1973 coup in Chile, Edwards affirmed his commitment to democratic socialism and maintained a distance from the United States, but he had joined a coalition that was successfully equating freedom of expression with a global movement against dictatorship of any ideological stripe. Indeed, he was an active leader in the movement. He returned to Chile in 1978, where he participated in the founding of a national committee to defend freedom of expression in Chile. The ability of the organization to continue working in a particularly repressive environment was due to the support it received from international groups, including philanthropies and advocacy groups in the United States.

Well before the end of the Cold War, the space for the relative autonomy of civil society and of literature within the United States incorporated the writers of the boom into a liberal social order, even as the revolutionary policies that Cuba pursued insisted on subordination of cultural work to the objectives that the revolutionary government determined. U.S. civil society, even in its relatively conservative forms like CIAR, could contest with rigid cold warriors over how best to combat communism in Latin America. At times, groups like CIAR succeeded in putting limits to what government policymakers were free to do. They whittled away at the exclusion of writers from the United States who had been supportive of Castro, and they contributed to making human rights an increasingly salient issue. In 1974, publicity about the disappearances, the widespread use of torture in interrogations, and the extent of summary executions led Congress to suspend training and financial assistance programs for Vietnamese and most Latin American police.[17] Simultaneously, the Organization of American States strengthened its Commission on Human Rights to give OAS investigators greater powers to document human rights abuses in the member states. Civil society operating on liberal values moved very slowly, but the liberal premise that debate must remain open for there to be responsible governance led to shifts in policy that on occasion had major effects.

In the last decade of his life, however, Veríssimo's trajectory went in a direction dramatically different from those of Donoso and Edwards. His next novel, *O Prisoneiro* ("The Prisoner"), published in 1967, took on the Vietnam War. He developed a story of American soldiers stationed in Vietnam—the country in the novel is unnamed, but is described as a former French colony in Southeast Asia where U.S. soldiers are fighting communist insurgents. They have captured a young guerrilla soldier who their commanders believe has precise information about planned attacks within a city modeled after Hué. When it appeared, the book might have played the role that Elihu Root had proposed for writers like Veríssimo: as the United States fought through deep internal divisions over Vietnam and the larger foreign policy directions the war indicated, sympathetic neighbors could contribute to the debate with independent perspectives needed as a reality check. Veríssimo was asking had the militarization of U.S. society undermined norms that encouraged decency and respect for law? Why, after World War II, had the United States failed so dramatically "to bring the world to a more decent and just place"?[18] Veríssimo's connections to the United States had grown much closer than ever before after he returned home to Brazil in 1958, but not at an official level. His daughter married a North American, a young physicist she had met at a community theater group while the family lived in Washington, D.C. For the remaining seventeen years of his life, the novelist had a North American branch of his family that quickly grew to include three Yankee grandchildren, living in Virginia, on the outskirts of Washington. Veríssimo and his wife made regular yearly visits, often staying for months at a time. When staying with his daughter and her family, he resumed the routine of traveling around the United States to give talks.[19]

The militarization of the United States increasingly worried him, not only for what it portended for his country and for the continent but, with the Vietnam War, Veríssimo worried that his three grandsons would be drafted as soon as they turned eighteen to fight in an endless series of colonial wars somewhere in Asia, Africa, or Latin America. The United States he admired under Franklin Delano Roosevelt had turned into something ugly under Harry Truman and Dwight D. Eisenhower. When President Kennedy replaced Eisenhower, Veríssimo briefly hoped that the United States would no longer turn itself against the rest of the world. The Vietnam War destroyed those hopes permanently.

The "prisoner" indicated in the title has multiple connotations as the story unfolds. At the center of the story is the captured communist soldier. Because he is labeled a "terrorist," the U.S. soldiers need not treat him according to the laws of war. When he refuses to cooperate, they turn to torture. At an allegorical level, Veríssimo presents the war as a defense of neocolonial relations, a campaign launched to enforce a global hierarchy. Nations like Vietnam, or Brazil, have become prisoners of a U.S. foreign policy that cannot acknowledge nations of color as equals and will destroy them if popular movements emerge to challenge their subordinate position within the international community. The novel articulates a grim indictment: the United States has failed to use its global leadership to create a better world, the good soldier of the Second World War has been turned into a monster, brutal violence defines the U.S. position in the world. Veríssimo identifies the source of the problem as the failure of the United States to eradicate its domestic racial hierarchy and continue the country's development into a fuller democracy. The third prisoner in the story is the lieutenant in charge of the interrogation. He is a light-skinned African American, who has passed for white whenever it was in his interest. The interrogation intensifies a message that the lieutenant has been receiving since he arrived in Vietnam. The subordination of Asians internationally reinforces his own subordination within the United States. The character's mixed-race status dramatizes the deadly choice he must make: does he identify with those who oppress him and only pretend that he is one with them, or does he embrace the links he feels with the young Vietnamese prisoner who never breaks or surrenders his inherent dignity even as the soldiers torture him? Ultimately, the title highlights the status of anyone trapped in a racialized, neocolonial relationship with U.S.

power. The Vietnam War had revealed with brutal clarity that the world that the United States wanted to lead was doomed to be unequal, that U.S. leadership required the continuing humiliation of the majority of the world's peoples. Anticommunism served as a rationale for U.S. supremacy, which in practice was inseparable from white supremacy. The United States had proven itself no different from its communist opponents, or the European empires that preceded it. All talk of improving how people lived, whether it came from U.S. liberals, from Soviet communists, or from Cuban revolutionary nationalists masked the system of terror each needed. While Veríssimo wanted this book to reach his readers in the United States, he wrote the book primarily for Brazilians at a time when the Brazilian military dictatorship had entered into a particularly close alliance with the United States based on anticommunism.

Veríssimo could explain the United States to Brazilians, what he had been doing since 1941, but he could no longer be part of a project to develop a conversation between the nations, a conversation that, were utopia realizable, might contribute to responsible world governance. In the United States, the questions raised in O Prisoneiro were never considered, even in the superficial format of book reviews and brief interviews with the media, because the book was not translated. Given the ferocity of 1967 and 1968 in the United States, it may not be surprising that the book's argument was not heard. Veríssimo's long history as an anticommunist and apologist for the United States meant that he did not fit well into the categories dividing "radicals" from the "establishment." With intelligent marketing, O Prisoneiro might have been seen as a companion to Graham Greene's The Quiet American, first published in 1955 as U.S. advisers appeared in Vietnam. However, Veríssimo's inability to contribute to the din reflected economic rather than political pressures within the U.S. publishing business. In 1960, Crowell-Collier Publishing Company, a giant in the magazine business, took over Macmillan. The company diversified with the purchase of a major bookstore chain, language schools, a large manufacturer of musical instruments, and a chain of specialty clothing stores. In addition, the company acquired several companies involved with data processing, as management made expanding the firm's position in technology its highest priority. Books were increasingly a smaller and less profitable part of the corporate portfolio, although book profits provided a steady source of cash underwriting the costs of diversification. In 1966, the new owners shook up the Macmillan editorial staff and implemented new policies intended to decrease the number of titles published while looking for books that could meet higher minimum sales goals. By 1970, over half the authors that Macmillan had published had been dropped, Veríssimo included.[20]

His New York agent, Lucille Sullivan from the prestigious and very old Maurice Crain agency, started searching for a new U.S. press to take on Veríssimo's work. She tried placing him with Knopf, Jorge Amado's publisher, but her take was that, despite the many supportive things Alfred Knopf said to Veríssimo and to her personally, he remained deeply offended that Veríssimo had had success with Macmillan and was happy that the major Brazilian competitor to Jorge Amado in the English-language market was in trouble.[21] Having failed with Knopf, Sullivan negotiated a contract with Greenwood Press, a commercial publisher that had done well in the social science and legal markets and wanted to expand into fiction. Greenwood agreed to reprint all of Veríssimo's translations, in both paper and hardback, along with translations of *O Prisioneiro*, a new travel book he had written about a stay in Israel, and any future work he produced. But as the Vietnam War began to weaken the national economy, Greenwood found itself overextended with its new venture in fiction publishing. The owners were forced to sell the firm to Williamhouse-Regency, a paper and stationery manufacturing company with no prior experience in publishing. The new owners reorganized the company, eliminating the fiction division entirely. Sullivan then decided to retire, and the Maurice Crain agency closed, another victim of a difficult economic climate. The agency that took over Veríssimo in 1971 had no personal connections with him. The generation of agents, editors, and publishers he had worked with was gone or going. His new agents handled opportunities as they developed, but they had no incentive to save the career of a writer whose heyday, at least in the United States, had passed, and whose books expressed cultural perspectives of an earlier, disappearing generation.[22]

   At the end of his life, Veríssimo was thrown back onto the Brazilian book market, which was growing rapidly once again. While the dictatorship increased supervision of all publishers, it provided incentives to publishers that would promote growth. The 1967 constitution exempted publishers from most taxes. Government credits assisted publishers who wanted to purchase new equipment. With lower costs for materials and improved technology, publishers could do larger print runs, which allowed for lower unit costs per book. With literacy increasing and a growing middle class in the cities, earning more money in the 1960s, the number of books printed grew from 43 million copies in 1966 to 245 million in 1980.[23] By the beginning of the 1970s, Brazilian publishers and bookstores began to operate at volumes more comparable to North America and Europe. Best-sellers could sell hundreds of thousands of copies. Growth provided more stable income for an older generation of well-established Brazilian writers. For many of them, the biggest change was that they no longer were writing exclusively for other intellectuals, but now had to consider the ideas and tastes of a broader urban middle class. If we go by sales figures, Brazilian readers continued to prefer translated books by foreign writers, but also wanted to read national authors. Given limitations on what the government allowed to be printed, public desires for something daring, perhaps slightly oppositional, took unusual turns. Erotic novels from Europe and the United States were popular, but so were U.S. poets associated with the Beat movement, particularly Allen Ginsberg, Lawrence Ferlinghetti, and Charles Bukowski. Several U.S. modernist poets including William Carlos Williams and Ezra Pound sold very well. Irene Hirsch and John Milton, analyzing the impact of U.S. involvement in Brazilian publishing during the dictatorship, point out its contradictory nature: ideologically conservative but culturally innovative.[24] Brazilian writers, however, remained constrained by censorship laws and the government's propensity to arrest, often torture, writers and editors identified as threats.

Veríssimo's next novel was directed to Brazilians above all for he decided to write about Brazil's current military dictatorship. *Incidente em Antares* ("Incident in Antares," not translated into English), published in 1971, is set in a small fictional town in Rio Grande do Sul. The everyday use of torture by security forces forms a central thread in the story. Even though the book appeared during a particularly brutal phase of the dictatorship, the government chose not to suppress it. Partly because of its subject matter and the absence of anything comparable speaking as daringly about current actualities, *Incidente em Antares* quickly became the biggest selling book in Brazilian history up to that point. The liberal Veríssimo, tainted for many on the left because of his close connections to the United States, produced a book that stood out for its critical analysis of the social origins of the military dictatorship and the reasons behind its reliance on torture.

The book has two contrasting sections: first, a history of the fictional town of Antares, located on the eastern bank of the Uruguay River on the border with Argentina, from its foundation in 1830 to the eve of the military dictatorship in 1964. The history is presented as a university report examining the social, economic, and political conditions of the small city. The report emphasizes that as Antares modernized, it became an increasingly stratified community, with two wealthy families owning most of the wealth and making all decisions. Dictatorship proved convenient and comfortable for the town's leaders, who approved wholeheartedly of the military remaining indefinitely in charge of government. They did not want public debate about how to improve the community, nor did they like research done at the university showing that racism was rampant or that the lives of the working classes had deteriorated as the city increased its production for foreign markets. They did not want to hear that the very poor living on the outskirts of the city lacked basic sanitation. Or that tuberculosis was rampant among the poor, along with other diseases indicating widespread malnourishment. The wealthy condemned the university report as a pack of lies intended to stir up trouble, and the controversy becomes a factor in the novel explaining their enthusiasm in 1964 for the military coup. Veríssimo's social science credentials were limited, and the novel's university report has little in common with what Brazilian academics were producing at the time. His limitations as an economic and political theorist notwithstanding, he succeeded in forcing public discussion of social phenemona that censorship prohibited from appearing in the news media.[25]

The "incident" at the heart of the novel forms the second, more clearly novelistic section of the book. Workers in the city have called a general strike demanding wage increases to keep up with inflation. Because funeral workers have joined the strike, the bodies of those who died in the town over the weekend remain unburied. One was the matriarch of the town's wealthiest family, another a militant who died while the police tortured him. The rest present a typical Veríssimo cross section of the community: a music teacher, an anarcho-syndicalist shoemaker, an alcoholic, a prostitute, and a lawyer. The noise of fighting between workers and the police outside on the street awakens the matriarch as she lies in her coffin. Used to governing others, she demands the other six corpses awaken and assist her in forcing the living to bury them. The dead march into the center of town to demand the respect due them. For four days, the temporarily awakened corpses terrorize the city with their peaceful protests, marked by their continuing decomposition and the mordant satire of their observations, for as the lawyer warns, "Given that we are dead and are no longer players in the human comedy, I can be absolutely frank."[26] The dead visit the places where each of them had lived to demand that relatives and neighbors do something. Each stage in the pilgrimage reveals another feature of the city's devastating social and political corruption. Only in one of the stories did Veríssimo allow for hope for those who remain in the "human comedy": the murdered militant visits his pregnant wife and helps her to escape to Argentina, foiling a police conspiracy to kill her. The most disturbing revelation for the dead is that police violence is systematic and appears necessary for how the government believes it should manage society.

Even if the book was written for Brazilians, Veríssimo wanted the work translated internationally. The United States bore partial responsibility for the dictatorship, and its citizens ought to have better understanding of the societies swallowed into the U.S. imperium. His agent submitted the book to Knopf, but reader reports were negative. The editors concluded that they could not successfully introduce it to a U.S. audience. Alfred Knopf personally wrote to Veríssimo that his press was declining the work. He added that if he were younger, he would override his editors' judgment. "But now," he concluded, "the dice are loaded against any such arbitrary action on my part. I am nearing eighty and cannot hope to continue to have any active voice at all in the day-by-day running of the business. It would be cruel for both of us if I were to insist on publishing a book by you or anyone which my younger colleagues had no heart for."[27] The decision at Knopf no doubt reflected the generally poor sales of the books on its Latin American list, outside the novels of Jorge Amado. After the publication of *O Tempo e o Vento*, Veríssimo had become a contender for the Nobel Prize for Literature, but that possibility faded in the mid-1960s, when international anger over the Vietnam War made it extremely unlikely that authors like Veríssimo or Borges who had close associations with the United States would be chosen.

Veríssimo's success in the United States had always been likely to be temporary because few authors continue to be read generally by succeeding generations. The rapid decline of his reputation in the United States parallels that of authors he knew personally and admired like Thornton Wilder, John Dos Passos, Hendrik Van Loon, or even Aldous Huxley and John Steinbeck. While Veríssimo was committed to the autonomy of literature, his last set of books had overt social and political functions, albeit in the service of liberal, democratic values. His stories, even with the fantasy element of the dead demonstrating to be allowed to depart in peace, focused on contemporary social dilemmas without engaging in the anthropologically inflected narrative experiments that characterized the generation of writers around the world who emerged in the 1960s. In a period when U.S. strategic objectives in the Cold War included emphasizing the professional autonomy of cultural and intellectual work, Veríssimo's insistence on addressing contemporary political questions harked back to the expectations of the 1930s that important literature spoke clearly and directly to difficult social realities. He strove to communicate in easily understandable terms, avoiding the narrative and linguistic exploration defining the new Latin American literature on the international stage. Veríssimo's social realism may well have naively repeated universalist values without digging into their limitations, but, since he had begun writing in the 1930s, the author's belief in democracy as a necessary foundation for economic and social progress pushed him to write a series of books that spoke directly to the immediate political challenges of the moment in terms that a broad range of readers found meaningful even if the subject matter was disturbing. Veríssimo's books offered an opportunity for readers to insist, in the aftermath of *Incidente em Antares*, on public discussion of whether torture was an instrument of state policy in Brazil. Few books achieve comparable effects, which require readers disengaging from reading as a form of entertainment—or of enchantment in the case of profoundly important and powerful writers like Gabriel García Márquez—and deciding that they must talk about a book and listen to others talking about it.

Veríssimo's ability to transform readers into a potential public was an important factor in his continuing success from the mid-1930s to his death. His conviction that writing could not be autonomous from everyday realities was central to what allowed him, from the mid-1930s to the 1970s, to provoke public discussion of topics that a succession of governments preferred be left ignored. With *Incidente em Antares,* Veríssimo's fame within Brazil, already significant, became nearly unassailable, even if uncomfortable for some on the left or for critics who preferred more creative experimentation and ideological decoding. In the United States, Veríssimo disappeared from the public stage. With a new emphasis on literature as the invention of alternative realities, Jorge Luis Borges joined Gabriel García Márquez as the preeminent Latin American writers, the almost obligatory reads. Borges's liberal politics could be shunted aside for they were irrelevant to understanding what his work proposed about the relationship of imagination, free will, and obsession. Veríssimo explored the damage, personal as well as collective, accompanying the twentieth-century romance of violence and force. His liberal politics could not be ignored, nor could his condemnation of the left as equally culpable. His anticommunism had no marketable value in the United States even if his perspectives might have much to say about the failures of U.S. global leadership. Veríssimo's books posed a puzzle for marketing departments that the publishing industry in the 1960s and 1970s did not know how to solve. By purging him from the U.S. book market, they effectively ignored a complicating perspective that would have been valuable simply for understanding the complexity of thought in another country. The decisions at Macmillan, Knopf, and Greenwood reflected each company's assessment of the publishing market and how a given author fit into a firm's business priorities. The result was not ideologically driven but reinforced an ideological divide that had proved profitable over many years.

At the beginning of the Cold War, Richard Pattee looked back on the eight years he had spent at the State Department working to facilitate exchange between the United States and its allies in the Pan American Union. He concluded that "actual knowledge" of Latin America remained thin in the United States.[28] Even good books continued to present a partial, distorted view of thought and values in Latin America, with too much emphasis on the sources of social chaos and not enough on the depth of the resources for holding things together. The most serious failing was that the variety of opinions actually present in every country was missing, particularly the strong levels of support that conservatives enjoyed among the poor. The result was that the outcome of political and social disputes in Latin American countries generally appeared mysterious to North Americans, for the information U.S. readers received suggested that radicals were always on the verge of taking power, even if experts with more detailed information understood that revolutionaries had limited, albeit vocal support. Twenty-five years later, little had changed. U.S. readers, given the writers presented to them after 1960, still primarily saw the more politically and aesthetically radical aspects of cultural thought in Spanish- and Portuguese-speaking America. Through a sequence of no doubt reasonable publishing decisions, the shape of a continent emerged for U.S. readers that had considerably greater literary depth but lacked political complexity or ambiguity. As translation increased in the 1960s, a puzzling phenomenon became clearer: even when cultural products crossed borders in larger quantities, the earlier expectation that shared cultural markets would lead to shared public spaces, shared expectations, and accountable systems for making decisions together did not materialize, was in fact perversely further away. It was an unexpected outcome given the rapid growth of international media markets increasingly producing work for sale in every part of the globe.

Chapter 13

Exiting Pan-Americanism

The shift in the visual arts after World War II from figurative to abstract painting dramatically changed the reception in the United States of artists from Latin America as museums and galleries showing contemporary art turned their attention to the forward movement of visual expression toward pure expression freed from any connections to nonart realities. While Diego Rivera and Cândido Portinari, the two most prominent star artists from Latin America before the Second World War, could in theory have fit into a story linking French modernism to contemporary art in the western hemisphere, their work continued to interpret social reality instead of turning toward the intersection of psychological response and formal experimentation. Nor did either painter fit well into a narrative celebrating the emergence of New York City as the world's most important center for the production of art. Their disjunction from the art historical narratives curators and critics wanted to tell after 1945 was the chief factor in their fading from attention, rather than their communist sympathies, which never disqualified Pablo Picasso from being lauded as the premier modern artist. The Mexican painter Rufino Tamayo (1899–1991) and Roberto Matta Echaurren (1911–2002), a Chilean painter, took over as the most broadly exhibited and collected Latin American artists in the decade following the end of the Second World War (see Table 7 in the Appendix). Tamayo's fanciful figurative paintings attracted gallerygoers,[1] but Matta's more austere abstractions fit changing curatorial and critical tastes. He had studied architecture and design at the Pontifical Catholic University in Santiago. Graduating in 1935, he went to Paris, where he associated with André Breton and the surrealists. During this period, he developed the distinctive biomorphic forms immersed in imaginary three-dimensional spaces that quickly made Matta internationally famous. In 1938, Matta moved to New York, where he lived and worked until 1948. He returned to Europe at that point, settling eventually in Italy, but he maintained close personal connections with other painters, writers, and curators in the United States, as well as with the family he left behind, most prominently his son Gordon Matta-Clark (1943–1978), among the most important of the artists who pioneered conceptualism in the United States.

Reviews and museum catalogues almost always mentioned that Roberto Matta was Chilean, but his personal background was no more important than Jackson Pollock's origins in Arizona and California.[2] Unlike in critical assessment of Gabriela Mistral, critics did not discuss Matta's work as growing from the unique relationship to the ocean and mountains that Chileans were supposed to have developed over the centuries. Instead, both Pollock and Matta illustrated how prewar experiments in surrealism prepared the ground for the postwar leap into a pure form of expression based in abstraction, with the critical step in both careers having been the move to New York City in the late 1930s. The intense creative maelstrom they entered pushed them to their most important breakthroughs. Many artists from all parts of the world participated in the 1940s turn toward abstraction, but institutions in the United States were most interested in artists who had worked in Paris and New York, with secondary, but considerably less attention given to parallel developments in Britain and Italy. Important artists whose careers exemplified the truly international character of contemporary art received minimal attention in the United States even if they were well known elsewhere. The most internationally influential abstract painter from Brazil was Iberê Camargo (1914–1994), who came from Porto Alegre, in the far south of Brazil. He studied art at the local university and then at the Escola Nacional de Belas Artes (National School of the Fine Arts) in Rio de Janeiro, but then returned home where he lived and worked for the rest of his life. Like those of most artists whose careers began before the war, his early paintings were figurative, with the people and places of his home state providing him with subject matter that might have appeared derivative of late nineteenth-century academic painting styles were it not for his adventurous approach to color and texture. There was little surrealist influence on his early work, nor was there a discernible response to cubism, the fauves, or other pre–World War II European modernist movements. In 1948, the Brazilian government awarded him a fellowship to study abroad. He chose to go to Italy to study with Giorgio Di Chirico and France to study with André Lhote. Given the absence of general art museums in Brazil at the time, the trip exposed Camargo to a range of work very different from what most of his contemporaries in Brazil were doing. He returned home in 1950 deeply influenced by the physical manipulation of the canvas found in the work of the tâchistes, as well as by Giorgio Morandi's eerily monumental still lifes. His work in the early 1950s remained figurative, continuing to interpret the people and landscapes he saw around him in southern Brazil, but with images rendered using techniques borrowed from abstract painting. By the end of the 1950s, he increasingly painted pure abstractions.[3]

The figurative and the abstract work were equally powerful, and Camargo captured the attention of critics and museum curators at home and abroad. His work first showed in the United States in a group show on contemporary painting in Latin America that the Guggenheim Museum in New York organized in 1956. He had his first one-artist show in 1959 at the art gallery of the Pan American Union in Washington, D.C., an exhibition that Érico Veríssimo had personally arranged. In 1962, Camargo was one of eighteen Brazilian artists included in a show, *Selection of New Art from Brazil*, that the Walker Art Center in Minneapolis organized with a grant from the Brazilian government. The Guggenheim Museum subsequently included him in an exhibition organized in 1965, *The Emergent Decade: Latin American Painters and Paintings*. In 1969, the Center for Inter-American Relations showed his work in the gallery the organization opened in New York City for its ongoing series of contemporary art exhibitions. His next exhibition in the United States occurred in 1993. Not having a gallery in New York City representing him may well have been the most important practical factor for his relative invisibility in the United States. With offers for shows, commissions, and honors coming to him continuously from around the world, he had little time and felt no need to seek out U.S. dealers or agents. Tellingly, no U.S. dealer courted him despite his formidable international reputation. The circumstances of his first shows in the United States labeled him as "Latin American artist," suggesting that he and others shown in special exhibitions to introduce new work from the region were not full, much less equal participants in global culture. Hilton Kramer, reviewing the second Guggenheim exhibition, asserted that the show made no distinction between the "talented" and the "untalented," both presented on equal footing. "Far from inviting any critical generalization on the state of art in Latin America," he concluded, "the exhibition simply leaves one thoroughly uninterested in the whole subject." Group shows are often uneven because one of their purposes has been to see which artists stand out from the crowd. However, Kramer refused to name even one work or one artist that captured his fancy. He saw examples of skillful technique, but the problems that the artists posed left him cold.[4]

Because he lived in New York City, Kramer did not have an opportunity to see a broad range of contemporary work from Latin America on a daily basis. For the first two decades following World War II, the Pan American Union's Division of Visual Arts, directed by José Gómez Sicre (1916–1991) from 1946 to 1976, offered the most consistent exhibition program within the United States for promoting Latin American art. Originally from Cuba and trained as a lawyer, Gómez Sicre had an enthusiasm for contemporary art that led the Museum of Modern Art to hire him as an adjunct curator preparing an exhibition in 1944 of Cuban modernist painting. He had strong, independent opinions, which he had no hesitation arguing even when they contradicted the preferences of his employers at MoMA. He decided not to include the work of Wilfredo Lam in the MoMA show of modern Cuban art, even though MoMA owned a number of important Lam paintings and U.S. critics unanimously talked of Lam as the single most important painter of twentieth-century Cuba.[5] Gómez Sicre, however, viewed Lam's work as untypical and overly influenced by Lam's many years working in Paris. American artists had for too long been dependent on European models, Gómez Sicre thought. Those who needed the most exposure were artists whose ideas were truly independent. In 1946, Gómez Sicre landed a job at the Pan American Union, where he founded the visual arts unit.[6] He was among a small handful of curators working in the United States who were genuinely knowledgeable about Latin American art, and initially, he was the only curator in the country whose sole focus was contemporary art in the western hemisphere. He single-handedly built an art collection that formed the basis for the Art Museum of the Americas, which opened in Washington, D.C., in 1976, with Gómez Sicre serving as the founding director. During his three decades at the Pan American Union, he mounted nine to eleven exhibitions a year in a small gallery space at the headquarters of the Organization of American States in Washington. He edited the Pan American Union's *Boletín de Artes Visuales* ("Bulletin of Visual Arts"), which served as a record of the shows the Pan American Union presented while providing its readers with an ongoing survey of exhibitions and controversies across the western hemisphere, including Canada, as well as the British, French, and Dutch West Indies. He built a large library of slides and other visual aids documenting the history of art in the western hemisphere that schools and libraries were able to duplicate to build up their reference collections in a subject that previously had almost no visual sources readily available for study.

An uncompromising cold warrior, Gómez Sicre criticized the Mexican muralists for their aesthetic conservatism, which he asserted was an inevitable consequence of communist politics untempered by genuine aesthetic imagination. He viewed the continuing popularity of Diego Rivera within the United States as a disaster that contributed to the postwar marginalization of contemporary Latin American art. Rivera and those he had influenced provided North Americans, and Europeans as well, with a "carnival-type, descriptive, and superficial pictorial chronicle" that satisfied desires in wealthy countries for vicarious tourism in countries that were poor and perhaps too dangerous to visit. He argued that the continuing prominence of the muralists obscured the fact that, as in the United States, "in the last twenty years there has evolved a magnificent art movement of very high quality and extreme importance, so in Latin America there are many artists—with more or less the same intentions and the same ambitions as the modern United States painter—who have been working in a progressive manner and with deep intellectual feeling."[7] Intellectually and creatively, he continued, artists from other American countries were fully the equals of their U.S. peers. What they lacked was adequate support. In an editorial from 1962, Gómez Sicre complained that artists throughout Latin America were overly dependent on state support, which while not generous was in most countries the only source of funding for cultural work. There were few individual collectors, which meant that there could be only a handful of galleries representing artists. Neither the wealthy nor the biggest companies supported art, as did their counterparts in the United States. Exhibitions and commissions were politically rather than aesthetically motivated, leading to exhibition of too many artists who were inferior and not enough shows for the artists with genuine talent. To take their place on the world stage, Latin American artists needed to work in an environment much more like the United States. In 1970, he stated with evident pride that he had developed a cadre of art collectors in every country of the western hemisphere without exception and that he had convinced major businesses in most countries to build sizable corporate collections.[8]

The *Boletín de Artes Visuales* appeared in Spanish only, suggesting that its primary purpose was to develop a network within Spanish-speaking America for the support of the visual arts. With many illustrations, the *Boletín* allowed curators and artists to see work from other countries, while funding from the Organization of American States helped support traveling exhibitions. Gómez Sicre's work depended on OAS funding, yet by his own logic, to establish that artists in Latin America were fully equivalent in quality and intellectual depth to anybody working in the United States, he had to counter any implication that political rationales were the primary motivator for the exhibition of work from Latin American countries. On an intellectual level, he strove to present artists and their work from different countries on a fully equal basis. On a practical level, given the disparity in needs and limitations in funding, the Division of Visual Arts seldom showed U.S. and Latin American work together in thematically defined shows. Exhibitions in Washington served the purpose of introducing artists from countries that were allies in the Cold War to influential people in the United States, many of whom, like First Lady Jacqueline Bouvier Kennedy, an important supporter of Gómez Sicre's activities, had a mix of motivations driving the causes they endorsed, but political considerations always were in the forefront even when it was a question of learning about international developments in contemporary art (Figure 24). The quantity of work Gómez Sicre introduced into the United States remains impressive. He showed more than any other curator working in the United States at the time, and in most

Figure 24. Jacqueline Bouvier Kennedy touring the First Biennale of Latin American Art at the Organization of American States, Washington, D.C., 1962. Courtesy Organization of American States Visual Arts Unit, Museum of the Americas, Washington, D.C.

respects he outdid the activities of the Office of Inter-American Affairs between 1940 and 1945 despite the OIAA's considerably greater levels of funding. The quality of the work Gómez Sicre presented varied, as one would expect if a curator aims to help the public assess artists and art movements in more than twenty countries across a thirty-year period.

His hostility to communism and the revolution in Cuba became an important factor in choices that he made after 1959. He provided considerable exposure to Cuban artists who left the country, and he documented in detail difficulties confronting artists who stayed. However, he did not exclude artists simply because they were communists. Gómez Sicre viewed Cândido Portinari as the single most important modernist painter from any country in Latin America. Whenever he could, he exhibited and promoted Portinari's work, comfortable in the knowledge that his opinion coincided with those of the most important art critics in the United States. Gómez Sicre was unable to adjust to the radical changes in the visual arts that occurred during the 1960s. He hated pop art when it emerged, dismissing it as a movement particular to New York City and totally divorced from the circumstances motivating artists around the western hemisphere.[9] He refused to show any of the artists in Mexico City, Rio de Janeiro, or Buenos Aires in the active pop art scenes in those cities. That the work of Latin American pop artists was often much more politically pointed than the work of Latin American modernists was a factor in his condemnation, for he saw superficial political enthusiasms diminishing the intellectual integrity that the modern movements' integration of form and content had put at the center of art practice.[10] He also dismissed conceptual work as fundamentally hostile to humanistic values and therefore not really art. His conservative views, both political and aesthetic, made him increasingly out of touch with what younger artists were doing, and by the 1970s, he shifted his focus to consolidating a comprehensive collection of modern art from the western hemisphere, leaving the presentation of contemporary work to younger curators.

Given the quality of the work Gómez Sicre presented, it is difficult to explain why newspapers and magazines seldom reviewed his exhibitions at the Pan American Union gallery.[11] Museums and cultural centers in the United States continued to organize exhibitions of work from Latin America after 1945, but by persistent isolation into geographically defined shows, the artists selected remained representatives of their countries educating the U.S. public about their southern neighbors rather than participants in an international project pushing the boundaries of what the plastic arts could say and do. To participate in public debate in the United States about its transformation from arsenal of democracy into provisioner of torturers required breaking out of the limits placed on inter-American exchange while taking advantage of the standpoint artists held as citizens of countries suffering the effects of U.S. policies (Figure 25). Given that Luis Camnitzer (born 1937) was deeply involved in the shift to conceptual art, it is not surprising that his name appeared only once in the *Boletín de Artes Visuales*, when he participated in an exhibition of engravings from his native country, Uruguay. At the age of twenty-seven, Camnitzer moved to New York City in 1964, where he partnered with four other artists—two from the United States, one from Argentina, and one from Venezuela—to form the New York Graphic Workshop. When the U.S. members left the group, the workshop began to speak more clearly as a voice of Latin American artists living in the New York region. The three remaining members developed their ideas on interventions artists could make into the rapidly escalating political crises of the period, while pondering their position as artists from poor, semicolonized countries working in the wealthiest country in the world. They had trained in printmaking, a relatively inexpensive and accessible art form, but with low prestige in the United States. They were convinced that reproducible art forms like

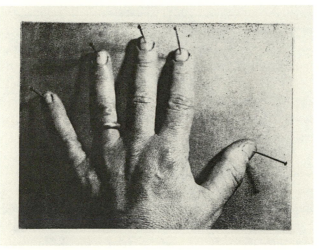

Figure 25. Luis Camnitzer, *He Practiced Every Day,* from the *Uruguayan Torture Series,* color photoetching, 1983–1984. Courtesy Alexander Gray Associates, New York, © 2016 Luis Camnitzer, Artists Rights Society (ARS), New York.

prints, engravings, and posters were particularly well suited to the conditions of contemporary life in both poor and wealthy countries, but the medium lacked the traditions of theoretical reflection that had accompanied the development of modern painting and sculpture. The workshop's manifestos proposed remedying the theoretical poverty of printmaking so that artists working in print media, able to reach a much wider audience than most painters or sculptors, could help their viewers think about the political and cultural turmoil of the period in new ways. The new group began organizing exhibitions and publications, most of which initially were thematically focused and thoroughly international in terms of the participating artists.

As the workshop developed through the 1960s, its statements increasingly directly attacked the centrality that critics and museums had given abstraction after 1945. The art object as the champions of modern art had defined it was "a superreality" whose importance was evaluated by its separation from and superiority to the facts of human existence. The public looked to art for an absolute value that transcended the messiness of everyday life. Mired in the necessities of everyday survival, they needed the "context provided by museums, galleries, collecting (museum individual), and books" to tell them what art said and why it was important, which always had to do with its uselessness for people's practical concerns. Modern art's alienation from everyday life remained a defining feature of new, postmodern forms like the happening, which also needed verbal interpretation to convey what direct experience of an event could not because connection with lived experience threatened the autonomy of art as a professionalized institution. The workshop's leaders began working in a more clearly conceptual framework that they claimed and hoped could communicate directly with their audiences.[12] Liliana Porter (born 1941) made a series of works of wrinkled paper that she then photographed and printed as photoetchings. Camnitzer began substituting words for images in prints he was making (Figure 26). Galleries and museums in New York and surrounding communities did not respond to either artist's work, which was shown in the United States only in informal artist co-op galleries, but circulated more widely in the workshop's print publications.

Museums in Venezuela, Argentina, and Chile, after receiving the workshop's mailings, invited Camnitzer and Porter to expand their ideas into gallery installations. In Caracas, Porter encased a room at the Museo de Bellas Artes with wrinkled paper. In the middle of the room, she placed a large paper figure she had made, also wrinkled. Camnitzer went to Chile, where he decided to use his method of replacing images with printed words to make a pointed comment on a recent political event that had become an issue in the approaching presidential elections. He restaged the massacre in Puerto Montt, Chile, of protesting agricultural workers associated with Salvador Allende's Socialist Party, filling his exhibition space at the national museum in Santiago with verbal prompts that guided the public through a process of reconstructing the events leading up to soldiers shooting live ammunition into the protests. Where the record of events was unclear, he provided his viewers with options for them to choose as the most likely sequence of events. The goal of the exercise was to prompt his viewers to ask if there could be any justification for a political protest to end with a dozen people dead.

In the United States, curators and critics expected work by artists from Latin America to look recognizably Latin American. Neither Porter's nor Camnitzer's work had a distinctive ethnically identifiable visual feel. Their work explored the political and social contradictions of their countries using conceptual approaches that younger artists in every part of the world were using to transform the relationship of artists, viewers, and art objects (Figure 27). *Massacre at Puerto Montt* dealt with a specific event in Chile that was tragically common throughout Latin American countries, but also around the world, including the United States before World War II. The event itself did not spring from Latin American culture, but out of the political rules modern countries developed to govern the relations of labor and capital. To define the work as protest art that was distinctively Latin American was to miss the point, but that was how many, including sympathizers on the left, understood Camnitzer's piece. His goal was not to inform people about a massacre, which in Chile was not necessary, for

250 METERS OF THICK CHAIN ACCUMULATED IN A CUBE OF HEAVY GLASS, IN ORDER THAT HALF OF THE SPACE IS FILLED.	A PRISMATIC BEAM OF BLUE LIGHT, WITH A SECTION OF 10 METERS SQUARE, THAT GOES FROM ONE HOUSE FRONT TO THE ONE ACROSS THE STREET.	A PERFECT CIRCULAR HORIZON.
A STRAIGHT THICK LINE THAT RUNS FROM HERE THROUGH YOU TO THE END OF THE ROOM.	A SURROUNDED SPACE THAT EXPANDS IN THE DIRECTION YOU WALK.	A ROOM WITH THE CENTER POINT OF THE CEILING TOUCHING THE FLOOR.
THIS IS A MIRROR. YOU ARE A WRITTEN SENTENCE.	FOUR BRIDGES, 1 KILOMETER LONG, FORMING A SQUARE WITHOUT EXIT, OVER POPULATED AREA.	A TEN STORY BUILDING WITH STYROFOAM FLOWING OUT OF THE WINDOWS.

MAIL EXHIBITION #1
NEW YORK GRAPHIC
WORKSHOP

LUIS CAMNITZER

Figure 26. Luis Camnitzer, *Sentences*, from the series First Class Mail Exhibition #1 of the New York Graphic Workshop, 1967, offset with rubber stamping. Courtesy Alexander Gray Associates, New York, © 2016 Luis Camnitzer, Artists Rights Society (ARS), New York.

Figure 27. Liliana Porter, *Untitled (Liliana Porter and Luis Camnitzer with Drawing)*, 1973. © 2016 Liliana Porter, image courtesy of Barbara Krakow Gallery, Boston.

the news media had already done that and Chilean popular singer Víctor Jara had written a song on the events. Camnitzer's goal was to get the public to confront the events in new, he hoped uncomfortable, ways that would push them to rethink what a growing tendency toward violence might portend for Chilean politics.

Twenty years later, he described art projects as "the meeting ground of two radically opposed dynamics. With the created object or situation the artist is trying to work his or her way out of a known ground and push the audience into the unknown. The manipulation by the artist is orchestrated to achieve the crossing of the border. The audience, on the other hand, tries desperately to push the disconcerting feeling of the unknown back into the context of everyday cultural commonplaces."[13] The conceptual processes that Camnitzer explored made his work part of an international conversation that included the United States. He thought his work was different from those of his North American colleagues in that he applied the methods developed by conceptual artists to specific contemporary events. The determination in U.S. arts institutions that protest art and conceptual art must remain in separate compartments distorted a potentially limitless and utopian dialogue that crisscrossed both genre and national boundaries. With conceptual art defined as dealing with basic epistemological issues, its themes were, by definition, "eternal" and hence superior in

every way to otherwise laudable work that Latin American artists might produce protesting intolerable situations in their native countries. The barrier between "real" art and political art was one of many ways in which Latin American
artists found themselves always occupying a marginal position in U.S. art exhibitions and publications, but it was only one of many distinctions that made
their position in the United States untenable.[14] In analyzing the collection at the
Guggenheim Museum, the institution in the 1960s most open to Latin American art in New York City, Camnitzer saw a haphazard assortment of colonial
and twentieth-century work, collected without any consideration of the traditions important for the artists or the relationship of their work to what was
going on simultaneously in Europe and the United States. He asked why work
from Latin America always appeared in separate shows, why were no Latin
American works included in the Guggenheim's *Sculpture of the Modern Era* exhibit or *Painting of the Modern Masters*?[15]

In his challenge to the separation based on national origins, he nonetheless
noted that his identification as a "Latin American" was central to how he saw
himself, particularly after he moved to the United States. Whatever he produced
expressed aspects of his youth growing up in a Jewish community in Uruguay
along with his formation in a Spanish-language intellectual world that did not
automatically share presuppositions that English-speaking intellectuals took for
granted. When he spoke of art as a problem-solving activity, his North American
listeners assumed that John Dewey's thought had influenced his approach to art.
Instead, Camnitzer was referring to the work of Simón Rodríguez, a Venezuelan
philosopher and educator from the early nineteenth century. Rodríguez and
Dewey's ideas were not inherently opposed, but it was Rodríguez that Camnitzer
had read and discussed with fellow students in Uruguay, not Dewey. Spanish-
speaking American perspectives on the relation of art and society were not derivative from U.S. pragmatism, as Camnitzer's U.S. friends assumed. They had
developed across nearly two centuries in an autonomous tradition that confronted distinct practical realities, culminating, Camnitzer thought, in the revolutionary teaching theories of Paulo Freire, whose book *Pedagogy of the Oppressed*
should be obligatory reading for every artist.[16] For him, this persistent misunderstanding proved that pan-Americanism had failed in its most basic goals. The
unity of the American nations should have led to a particularly creative and productive dialogue of students from distinct educational traditions, encouraging
everyone to rethink and broaden their conceptions of art in society.

The concerns that Camnitzer and the New York Graphic Workshop articulated in particularly clear ways were circulating among Latin American artists
living and working in New York as the Center for Inter-American Relations developed a new program to support increased exhibition in the United States of

work by contemporary Latin American artists. As with CIAR's literature program, funding went to publicity as much as to the organization of exhibits. Given the relative lack of interest in contemporary Latin American art in major galleries and museums and given Gómez Sicre's well-known antipathy to current international art trends, CIAR opened a gallery in New York City for regular exhibitions of work from Latin America, both historical and contemporary. The founding director of the gallery, Stanton Loomis Catlin, had been a protégé of Alfred Barr and learned the museum craft by working at the Museum of Modern Art in its formative first decade. During World War II, Catlin joined the staff of the Office of Inter-American Affairs, serving in the Santiago, Chile, and Tegucigalpa, Honduras, offices. When he returned home from the war, he entered the master's program in art history at New York University, where he wrote a thesis on Diego Rivera's use of pre-Columbian motifs. He then worked as a curator at the Walker Art Center and Yale University's Art Gallery as a specialist in Latin American art. His inaugural exhibition for CIAR's gallery space, scheduled for the fall of 1967, was a historical show, "Artists of the Western Hemisphere: Precursors of Modernism, 1860–1930." Responding to Latin American artists who disliked their art always being relegated to segregated shows, Catlin combined seven classic U.S. artists, including Winslow Homer, Thomas Eakins, and Stuart Chase, with thirteen artists of comparable stature from Canada, Argentina, Uruguay, Brazil, and Mexico. Catlin wanted the work to express what he called "grass roots" explorations of modern painting in each country. The show neither assumed nor implied connections among the artists included other than that each, in developing his own personal vision, moved away from the models that French painting, both academic and avant-garde, had provided artists around the world from the 1840s to the 1940s.

Unlike the literary program, which received strong support from most writers and critics, CIAR's art program came under instant attack from Latin American artists in New York City as soon as the first show opened. The New York Graphic Workshop called for a boycott of CIAR. Thirty-seven other artists added their names to the workshop's petitition.[17] In explaining the boycott, Camnitzer remained adamant that Catlin, despite all the self-evident "goodwill" of his effort, really did not understand why Latin American artists were angry about their treatment in the United States. What they wanted was simple: recognition as full participants in an ongoing dialogue about modern art that had always been international. The opening show's focus on artists who rebelled against French influence set up all American artists as recalcitrant provincials rather than as a creative people who had made independent and indeed often idiosyncratic contributions to what became modern art. For the purposes of Catlin's exhibition, the only thing that made a work shown interesting was difference from the school of Paris. The show had nothing to reveal about the quality of the paintings or their relation to intellectual and cultural traditions in each of the countries. Those traditions, decisive for understanding many of the artists, disappeared because of the single-minded focus on rebellion against Paris. The show's proposition that the most original art of American countries emerged in opposition to developments in France was factually incorrect, as much for the U.S. artists Catlin included in the show as for the Latin Americans. In addition to challenging the pan-American and "New World" assumptions underlying the show, the organizers of the boycott had another point that became equally important for the protests. The CIAR board of trustees included three men—Dean Rusk, Lincoln Gordon, and Thomas Mann—directly responsible for U.S. efforts to overthrow the revolutionary government in Cuba. They had also conspired with reactionaries in Brazil and the Dominican Republic to overthrow democratically elected governments and install dictatorships. Latin American artists could not in good conscience collaborate with CIAR until the board removed its members who had been guilty of intervening in the internal affairs of other countries. The artists demanded that CIAR programming expand to include Cuban participation, while the gallery was to be dedicated to art addressing the realities of military coups, torture, disappearances, and genocidal massacres in the western hemisphere.

Alejo Carpentier had made similar arguments in 1966, when he demanded that prominent Latin American authors boycott meetings in the United States and suspend their association with U.S. publishers. Most authors, including Pablo Neruda, decided that engagement with the United States and participation in its cultural life had practical benefits that overrode Carpentier's objections.[18] Many artists living outside the United States found similar compelling reasons to work with CIAR, despite the distaste that many must have felt for some of the organization's trustees. CIAR gallery shows were never simply intended to offer a brief spotlight on younger and midcareer artists. The gallery adopted the strategies of persistence and publicity that had been so successful in the literary program. In 1969, for example, CIAR organized the first one-artist show in New York City of Colombian painter Fernando Botero (born 1932). Local critics panned the work, but CIAR continued its commitment to Botero. CIAR connections facilitated the artist having a second show at the Marlborough Gallery. This time critics responded more positively. The prestigious international dealer scheduled regular exhibitions of Botero's work in both the United States and Europe. CIAR also built up international connections for artists they championed by arranging for them to exhibit at Documenta in Germany and other European art fairs. Successful reception in Europe with a publication record available that critics could turn to for language about what an artist was doing led to more frequent exhibition in the United States. As with its literature program, CIAR expected that most of the artists it worked with were critical of the U.S. role in the world, many strongly so, and that participation in CIAR programs was not likely to mute their criticism.[19] In 1987, on the twentieth anniversary of the CIAR programs, Botero showed his gratitude to CIAR for its help at a critical moment in his career by donating a major work that the organization auctioned off, raising several hundred thousand dollars for its education program.[20]

Younger artists living and working in New York in the early 1970s, however, remained critical of CIAR activities and did not stop their protests. In 1971, Catlin proposed a Latin American Art Week with fifteen major galleries in New York City agreeing to feature a locally based Latin American artist during the opening week of a new group show Catlin had planned for the CIAR space. Camnitzer circulated a protest, arguing that the week was a promotional gimmick for CIAR that reinforced the impression that the work of artists from Latin America was simply not up to the quality required for being included in the regular schedules of major commercial galleries. The artists included would have to dedicate considerable amounts of time for casual shows unlikely to be reviewed because the work would be gone in a matter of days. CIAR would reinforce its role as the ultimate arbiter of which Latin American artists should receive public attention. Camnitzer circulated a protest petition among Latin American and Latino artists in the city that culminated in a public meeting where the protestors formed a new group, El Museo Latinoamericano, invoking the yet-to-exist institution that Latin Americans and U.S. Latinos needed to run themselves if they were to have genuine self-determination in the U.S. art world.[21] The group promised to picket the events CIAR had planned. Twelve galleries chose to withdraw from the event, which CIAR then canceled.[22] The new group, enjoying even greater participation after the success of its campaign against the Latin American Art Week, issued a new call for artists to boycott the upcoming São Paulo Biennial in solidarity with Brazilian resistance to the military dictatorship. CIAR again was a major target for this campaign, at least in New York City, as Catlin had decided to build future programming around the work of artists featured in the Biennial. El Museo Latinoamericano organized a counterbiennial, taking the form of a publication for which artists created work documenting the violence of the Brazilian military rulers.[23] The protestors found allies outside the relatively small local Latin American artist community, including art critic Grace Glueck at the *New York Times*, who wrote a column endorsing their position.[24]

Forty years later, Camnitzer thought that the protests against CIAR and the São Paulo Biennial had succeeded in forcing many Latin American artists in

New York to think about how their identities as artists and as Latin Americans intersected. He concluded, however, that the movement had failed to provide artists a new way of thinking about their relationship to society grounded in ongoing activities that could be self-sustaining. The members' professional ambitions prevented the group developing into a strong political force.[25] Like many ad hoc groups that younger artists form, the Museo Latinoamericano broke apart after a brief period of intense activity. In its case, an apparently unbridgeable disagreement over a political issue provided the catalyst. As with Latin American writers, how to respond to new developments in Cuba, in particular the prosecution of poet Heberto Padilla, sparked deep divisions. In 1971, in the midst of planning activities for the counterbiennial, the Museo's members began debating the Padilla affair and its implications for artists and cultural workers in other Latin American countries. A majority of the members of the Museo Latinoamericano voted to condemn the Cuban government for its treatment of the poet, insisting that a genuine revolution guarantees the right of free artistic expression. Six of the group's members, including Luis Camnitzer and Liliana Porter, seceded to form a more militant group, El Movimiento por la Independencia Cultural de Latino América (Movement for the Cultural Independence of Latin America). They argued that Padilla's "individualism" in the face of continuing U.S. attacks on Cuba and hemispheric war merited condemnation. They identified the defense of free speech as an essential part of the neocolonial structures that the United States had developed to dominate other societies. The artists of the militant group defined themselves as "politically engaged," focused on producing art and events unconditionally supporting the Cuban revolution and insurgent movements in other countries. The two groups were able to work together to complete the São Paulo counterbiennial project while continuing to criticize each other's respective positions. Less than a year later, both groups had disappeared.

Younger artists had struggled for a decade to create a public for their work. Many had turned to print media and new forms like mail art or happenings to see if they could establish a direct relationship with people in the community, many of whom might know nothing about contemporary art but who might be interested in work if they actually saw its relevance to their own lives. That effort produced significant work, but the goal of artists expanding access to their work beyond already existing arts institutions and communities had limited results. As Camnitzer's and Porter's experience underscored, museums with sympathetic curators, usually far from New York, were the most consistent venues for their work. Mail art proved, in practice, to be a form of alternative publicity capable of circumventing the control galleries generally had over what appeared in major art journals. The publicity gained from several years of protest activity, much of it accompanied by important artistic production, led to invitations from museums and cultural centers across the United States, as well as in other countries, to exhibit art that the protest movements had generated.

CIAR adapted to the criticism, but without substantially changing its priorities. Given that José Guillermo Castillo (1938–1999), founding director of the CIAR literature program, had also been a founder of the New York Graphic Workshop, CIAR might have anticipated the problems its approach to art would have with locally based Latin American artists. CIAR responded to the artists' challenge by changing directors of the art program, replacing Stanton Catlin with a specialist in contemporary art who promised to work more closely with the local community in planning future shows and projects.[26] The new director asked the artists to come up with ideas for future exhibits and to suggest curators who could organize the projects. The regular community meetings he hosted to gather artist input generated more controversy and argument, much of it centering on the Padilla affair and the fundamental disagreements artists had over what "social responsibility" meant for an artist. The new director resigned after less than a year in the post, and Castillo, while continuing as director of the literature program, took over as interim director of the gallery. He continued to meet with artists but made recruiting more Latin American curators his chief priority. They introduced a broader range of shows often with starkly contrasting perspectives. The CIAR gallery became one of the major sites internationally for debating the degree to which Latin American modernists had participated in the international movements that fomented the development of modern and contemporary art. Younger curators and critics advanced a new position that Latin Americans had been so peripheral and isolated from developments in Europe and the United States that modernism in the region developed independently with minimal influence from imperial centers and thus represented a genuinely new form of visual thought with roots in indigenous and popular culture.[27] The exhibition schedule continued unabated by either continuing controversy or the turnover in directors. In this case, controversy did not make for positive publicity, but did stimulate CIAR leadership to think creatively about how to respond without losing sight of the organization's primary objectives. In 1977, CIAR expanded its utility for the Latin American artist community with annual auctions that aimed to introduce wealthy collectors to CIAR's favored artists.[28] The CIAR model lacked poetry, but it spoke to the post–Cuban revolution generation who saw not even a remnant of utopian aspiration in pan-Americanism. The space for "autonomy" that liberal civil society appeared to offer for literature and art incorporated professionals with careers to maintain into a liberal social order whose utopian dimensions might be up for dispute but which could be experienced as steady, secure, and at times even protective in its practicality. The pan-American emphasis on "goodwill" based on supposedly shared values had given way to more fluid relationships with frequently strong philosophical and political disagreements that an emphasis on shared practical goals could at times transcend.

The end of the Cold War in 1989 seemed to ratify the CIAR strategy of protecting the autonomy of cultural practice, as well as early twentieth-century ideas about how governance of international affairs might be organized. The end of the contest between two opposed revolutionary societies, the United States and the Soviet Union,[29] had valorized, though perhaps not truly validated, the liberal utopian ideals that U.S. leaders like Elihu Root had put forward at the beginning of the twentieth century. The simultaneous return of democratically elected governments throughout the western hemisphere was further evidence that liberalism had proven stronger than either its conservative or its revolutionary antagonists. At the end of the 1980s, the Argentinean scholar of contemporary global culture Néstor García Canclini observed, in terms that many but certainly not all on the left might have used, that the social transformations under way in many of the countries had been "produced in a different way from what we expected in earlier decades." From the 1920s on, vanguard intellectuals had believed that they could literally create nations by mobilizing popular discontent against "oligarchs, conservatives, and foreign dominators." The nation, defined as the people united, would throw forward a popular state speaking for and protecting its citizens. Certainly no power was stronger than the "people united."[30] What Canclini had never expected was how much more effective private enterprise, and its auxiliary partner civil society, had been than government in bringing change, political as well as economic. Inequalities permeated cultural and social life, "but that inequality no longer takes the simple and polarized form we thought we would encounter when we were dividing every country into dominant or dominated, or the world turned into empires and dependent nations."[31]

The success of liberal institutions grew from their ability to recognize and work with the many differences within society, while the left typically saw difference as a threat to popular unity. Canclini advanced the term "hybridity" to describe the improvised nature of cultural life at the end of the twentieth century. The hybridity characterizing the late twentieth century grew from the interplay of difference inherent to market processes. Sellers respond to differences in disposable income by proposing different types of products for different categories of consumers. In democracies, however, citizens are formally equal. Each citizen's vote has equal weight, no matter what other differences there might be. Each person had an equal claim on due process of law. To the degree that decision making shifted increasingly to market situations, differences, inherently unequal, replaced equality as the basis of social life at the end of the twentieth century and reproduced inequalities that had long plagued most countries. The discontents market-based inequality generated magnified because when the state weakened, so did the potentiality for a public consensus to form demanding equal enforcement of rights. Many found the weakening of government acceptable only because the state in many countries had been an institution both murderous and incompetent. The state failed to bring peace or prosperity, but it could kill, torture, kidnap, and imprison people in the thousands, while blithely pursuing policies that often pushed their countries toward insolvency.

At the same time, the rise of feminism, the emergence of gay and lesbian claims for justice and equal treatment, and the reemergence of indigenous movements challenging European conceptions of the nation, as well as movements for defense of the environment, had all been unexpected, shattering a world built around the contests of "right" and "left." New social movements transformed every aspect of political life after 1970. The new movements challenged conservatives, liberals, and revolutionaries alike, but liberal states had been better able to adapt to broader conceptions of social rights than had either authoritarian military dictatorships or the socialist states. The socialist conception of democracy aimed to eradicate existing differences in order to arrive at a society without inequality. The new social movements required difference as a permanent aspect of social life allowing citizens to disclose attachments that both left and right had previously ignored and often disparaged or persecuted. Indeed, midcentury revolutionary movements treated sexual difference as a taboo topic, treatment that left them unprepared for the growing power of the feminist and queer perspectives they had excluded, while socialist societies had turned out to be environmental nightmares.

When Canclini's book *Culturas híbridas* ("Hybrid Cultures") appeared in Spanish, the Berlin Wall had just fallen. By 1995, when the English translation appeared, personal computers and the Internet were recreating the world economy, centering it firmly around U.S. corporations—an outcome that ten years earlier seemed dubious amid suddenly quaint prophecies that the industrial superiority of Japanese and western European capitalism would overturn North American hegemony. President Bill Clinton promised that the globalizing economy could "lift billions of people around the world into the global middle class."[32] Canclini thought that those who had fought for national sovereignty and improving the lives of the people should not resist private initiative out of a romantic attachment to older revolutionary ideals. Some private initiatives accentuated and exploited differences, but others stimulated popular creativity and promoted greater equality between nations and peoples. Given that private initiative had demonstrated its transformative power, Canclini argued, cultural and social critics in the post–Cold War era maintained the revolutionary struggle for democracy most effectively by reinserting the question of social justice into public discussion.

Even if pan-Americanism had become a bankrupt ideal, the Organization of American States continued to function as an important international organization. Its purposes have been reduced to practical and procedural matters, and as such, remain useful to the member states. The balance of power within the OAS started to change in 1972, when Canada began participating in OAS activities, finally becoming a full member in 1990. Former British and Dutch colonies in the West Indies also joined the OAS after gaining their independence. As a more diverse body more fully representing the western hemisphere, the organization expanded its activities in many areas that were by definition controversial. In 1979, for example, the OAS created the Inter-American Court for Human Rights. The new body, consisting of judges nominated by the member states, including the United States, provided a forum for formal review of claims that human rights protected in both the OAS and UN charters had been violated. Decisions determined when abuses had occurred and whether governments were cooperating with or obstructing remediation efforts. The court's powers to sanction violators have been weak, but publicity can have powerful consequences. The U.S. government, which on the one hand encouraged forceful repression of revolutionaries, on the other hand insisted, along with other countries, on the importance of due process and respect for legal rights.[33]

The dictatorships in both Chile and Brazil hastened to demonstrate that they did govern with popular assent, despite abundant evidence to the contrary. In 1979, Brazil began a process toward restoration of elected government and liberalization of public debate with an amnesty law that allowed exiled activists to return home. The same law also shielded police and military personnel from prosecution for any instances of torture, kidnapping, or summary execution they might have committed. In Brazil's case, the basic laws of the land flatly prohibited these acts, and to the degree that anyone in the government had authorized their use, they acted contrary to law. In 1985 the Brazilian Congress elected the first civilian president in two decades. In 1990, for the first time in thirty years, the citizenry went to the polls to choose their national leader. The country's first elected president was subsequently impeached for corruption, a crisis that the still nascent democratic institutions handled without loss of civilian authority through formal constitutional procedures. More recently, in 2010, the Inter-American Court for Human Rights ruled that Brazil's 1979 amnesty law violated OAS conventions that Brazil had signed and ratified. Brazilian prosecutors increased their inquiries into crimes committed during the dictatorship, while the country's National Truth Commission speeded up efforts to complete a report on torture and summary executions during the dictatorship, finally released in December 2014.[34]

In Chile, the military junta faced broad international condemnation including in the United States, where the regime's closest allies had lost their influence in the government. In 1978, the U.S. Congress passed a measure cutting off military aid, in part in response to covert Chilean security operations within the United States that had targeted exiled Chileans, including the dramatic assassination of Orlando Letelier by placing a bomb in his car when parked on a Washington, D.C., street. The Pinochet dictatorship responded to international condemnation by organizing a plebiscite asking Chilean voters to approve the powers that the military had seized by force. The plebiscite also provided a blanket amnesty to police and military officials for any possibly criminal actions committed during or since the coup. Two years later, a referendum held on the seventh anniversary of the coup asked voters to approve a new constitution that consolidated military authority over all security issues but established a timetable for a very slow transition to civilian-led government. If voters approved the measure, and the official tally showed 67 percent voting yes, Augusto Pinochet was to run unopposed for an eight-year term as president, a position he held as a civilian rather than as an active-duty military officer. The referendum measure officially vested the military forces with all legislative power, but it also provided for voters to return to the polls in 1988 to determine whether the military-led government would continue for an additional eight years. Opponents of the dictatorship questioned the integrity of the vote, and given the brutality of the government and limitations on public debate, how free voters felt to express their opinions will remain an open question. The concession to international public opinion, however, established formal procedures that culminated in the unexpected outcome in the 1988 plebiscite, with a majority of voters saying no to eight more years of dictatorship. The military under international pressure accepted the result, and a democratically elected government replaced the dictatorship in 1990.[35]

The OAS court had minimal impact on Argentina, Guatemala, and El Salvador, all in states of war at the beginning of the 1980s, but publicity given to the widespread abuses in those countries led to a series of conventions that the OAS adopted banning torture (1985), banning kidnappings for political purposes (1994), and protecting the right to free expression (2000). The Inter-American Court also assumed jurisdiction to investigate violence against women (1994) and discrimination against people with disabilities (1999). Often the United States has stood to the sidelines on the expansion of the OAS's human rights regime, at times signing onto initiatives that came from other countries, at times refusing to support conventions that would be politically untenable within the United States, such as an OAS prohibition of capital punishment, subscribed to by every other member. The OAS gained in losing its idealistic and ideological edge, for the hopes it inspired were what most made the organization an appendage of U.S. foreign policy. Instead, the OAS has become a place for practical activities that provide a greater degree of predictability to many aspects of inter-American relations. It was in effect a model for liberal governance as flowing from codified rules and procedures that allow routine to prevail over passion. It is a truism that liberal governance, designed to balance competing interests, acts slowly. Due process, particularly when dealing with issues where consensus is unlikely, can delay accountability and reconciliation until the day comes when a majority of the population was born after those who were most actively engaged in past political turmoil have died or are very old.

In an era marked by a return of liberal utopia, remembering alternative utopias that once captured the imaginations of millions strengthens an ability to recognize how current shibboleths fail, as *any* set of ideals must, to address desires and needs that other ideas handled with greater ease. Alternative utopias, even if defeated, provide distinct imaginations of justice, democracy, and individuation, aspects of which may speak to needs unmet in today's America. To understand the strengths and weaknesses of the current liberal utopia, counter-universalisms need to be understood and respected, even when one disagrees, for what they still have to say about the diversity of dreams people have. Rethinking the conflicts of the mid-twentieth century has been an important task performed in the cultural sphere as those of the twenty-first century struggle with what democracy means in the international sphere. Is it possible to have accountability and public debate involving citizens of different nations instead of the more powerful political leaders dictating what must happen? This has been one of the themes that inter-American cultural exchange has explored in the new century in an effort to understand a legacy of revolution and dictatorship without normalizing or romanticizing either.

Chapter 14

A Twenty-First-Century American Epiphany

In his travel journal, Ernesto "Che" Guevara jotted down a speech he had made at a birthday party given for him in 1952 at a leper colony deep in the Peruvian Amazon. Guevara thanked his hosts by telling them that after six months on the road, overcoming the many obstacles to travel between his home in Argentina and other American countries, "We believe, after this trip more strongly than before, that the division of America into baseless, illusory nationalities is completely fictitious. We are a single mixed-blood race that from Mexico down to the Magellan Straits presents remarkable ethnographic similarities. With this in mind and wishing to be free of even the slightest charge of provincialism, I raise a toast to Peru and to a United America."[1]

As presented in the climactic scenes of Walter Salles's film *The Motorcycle Diaries* (2004), Guevara's toast transforms from a polite restatement of clichés into a symbol of a young man's moral awakening. The film retells the story of Guevara's eight-thousand-mile trek across the South American continent in 1951 and 1952 as a parable of a sensitive but somewhat callow youth coming into moral consciousness, who can say at the film's end: "That aimless roaming through our enormous America has changed me more than I thought. I am not myself anymore. At least, I'm not the same inside." Leaving the relative privilege of his family home, he confronted the misery surrounding the grandeur of the continent. In the process, he became an American. As the movie's Guevara struggles to articulate the strong feelings his experiences have inspired, the simple words the screenwriter incorporated from Guevara's posthumously published diaries transform into a call for intellectuals to find their vocation by dedicating their lives to improving the lives of their fellow citizens. Alberto Granado, Guevara's traveling companion, presented in the film as a self-indulgent, roguish playboy, wipes away a tear. The message has been heard by another young intellectual who will straighten out and dedicate his skills as a pharmaceutical chemist toward improving the health of his people, understood at last as the working people of the entire continent. Immediately following the short speech, the filmmakers dramatize the theme of a unity that transcends class, race, and national citizenship by having Guevara leap into the Amazon River and swim across to the opposite bank to the compound where the patients live separated from the doctors and nurses. He literally bridges the chasm dividing the professional staff of the hospital and the lepers with his own fragile body.[2] Guevara has become a man with a purpose prepared to assume his responsibilities as a leader of his people.

Many viewers of the film likely knew that a few years after the events dramatized in *The Motorcycle Diaries*, Guevara joined Fidel Castro's armed rebellion against the Batista dictatorship in Cuba. He became a leader of the new government, perhaps the single most visible symbol of the new revolutionary consciousness it claimed to promote. His specific charge was to develop a new industrial policy for Cuba. His policies were effective at first in boosting productivity, but then faltered. After the 1962 Cuban missile crisis, Guevara resigned his position and left Cuba to expand the revolution, fighting with a revolutionary movement in the Congo before going to Bolivia to lead an insurrection he hoped would spread from the Andes across the continent. In 1967 the Bolivian army captured and summarily executed him. In the aftermath of his martyrdom, Che's visual image became and remains the symbol without equal of the twentieth-century American revolution.

Others, perhaps the majority of the younger viewers who saw the film when it played in theaters, knew little of the history beyond what the film told them about Guevara. That story is one of an American youth coming to self-awareness through embrace of an ideal. What makes young Guevara a hero is his growing commitment to treat the people at the base of society with dignity, an outcome overlapping with but nonetheless distinct from a revolutionary commitment to tear down an economic system that requires privilege and inequality. Guevara's growth in the film is marked by a series of small acts of charity as he encounters representatives of his continent's poor: he gives his asthma medicine to an old woman dying from emphysema and too poor to buy what she needs to alleviate her suffering; he gives the U.S. dollars his girlfriend entrusted to him to buy her a bathing suit when he reached Miami to a mine worker and his wife, two communist activists in Chile who have fled death squads and need the money to continue their work organizing a workers movement; he convinces a young girl suffering from leprosy who has sunk into despondency to undergo the operation that might save her arm from amputation. None of these acts are found in either his diary of the journey or Granado's two published accounts. In those sources, there is no need for them to dramatize Guevara's growth because he is a committed communist from beginning to end. There is no leap of political consciousness. Granado described the trip across South America as "practical ratification of theoretical knowledge."[3] The immediate impetus for the trip was Granado's losing his job in a government biochemistry laboratory after he refused to become a member of the ruling Peronist Justicialist Party. Leaving the country was a way of avoiding further scrutiny into his activities, and traveling provided an opportunity to compare the situation in Argentina, with a sizable middle class and a population that was overwhelmingly white due to European immigration, to the poorer, less developed, more racially mixed countries of the Andes.

In Guevara's diaries and Granado's two books, the two men set off already convinced that, everywhere in the world, the capitalist system had created the class and racial hierarchies they would encounter. They saw the division between bosses and workers as the primary cause of the many problems facing the American nations. As a medical student, as an intellectual, Guevara had to choose whether he would serve the bosses or the workers. Social reality is like the two sides of a coin, Granado reports Guevara telling him during their trip. The wealth of a country is inseparable from the poverty of those who labor. Heads or tails, everything is one or the other. Each person must choose a side.[4] Even though the image reappears in the books on which the film was based, it was removed from the film, along with the political dogmas that divided everything in the modern world into a simple dichotomy: if not revolutionary, then reactionary.

The filmmakers curtailed the explicitly Marxist convictions that the young Guevara already had formed and in effect placed his ideas into an older, liberal conception of American unity that receded as racial and class divisions within America grew stronger. In Spanish-speaking America, these older liberal conceptions are often called *arielism*, after the title of the book by the Uruguayan essayist and philosopher José Enrique Rodó published in 1900, *Ariel, a la juventud de América* ("Ariel, to the Youth of America"), discussed in Chapter 1. Rodó galvanized his contemporaries with the idea of an inherent but hidden American unity based on a common Iberian heritage. The quest for union would be realized if every generation of young people turned their societies toward the ideals already embedded in the humanist tradition of their ancestral Latin culture. The division of the continent into nation-states had fostered a political culture in which self-interest and passion trumped principle. The challenge was to establish stable civil societies organized around the exchange of ideas and political structures that adhered to and respected the rule of law. Individual growth, not commercial development, was the core of modernity, Rodó argued, but the egoism that had flourished during the revolutions and the first century of American independence had to give way to the more difficult task of institution building.

Ariel became a classic of American literature, read in schools everywhere throughout Spanish-speaking America. Certainly both Guevara and Granado had read him and probably dismissed him, as most mid-twentieth-century Marxists did, as an old-fashioned liberal unable to see the deep inequalities at the heart of American society. Nonetheless, Guevara's toast to his hosts in the leper colony, as he reported it in his travel diary, is drawn from the Rodonian repertoire. The liberal faith in social progress and individual growth that Rodó propagated served to invisibilize Guevara's far harsher vision of a world that required heroes to give up their lives to the movement for liberation.

In 1956, as he prepared to join Castro's revolution in Cuba, Guevara wrote his mother that she must never expect moderation from him or even humility. "Every great work requires," he told her, "passion and audacity in large doses."[5] To act was already to win, he insisted, even if to act meant death. This was a radical humanism that Guevara summed up at the end of the diary of his first journey across America with the words of a humble, anonymous working man he met in Caracas, Venezuela: "The future belongs to the people. Little by little or all in one blow they will conquer power here and in every part of the world. What will be bad is that the people will have to become civilized, and this is not possible to do before taking power, only after. The people will become civilized only through learning the costs of their mistakes, which will be very serious." Everyone alive in today's corrupt world deserves to die for their very being has been infected with corruption. Indeed they must die before a future generation of new men and women can emerge endowed with a new psychology that assumes living in utopia is their natural right. The revolution will, and it must, consume everyone, both those who resist and those who join it. In the end, a new world arises where idea, action, and result are in harmony. Guevara concluded his own account of his trip by reconfirming that since humanity is divided "just into two opposing groups, I will be with the people." He saw himself falling gun in hand "sacrificed to the authentic revolution, origin of all our purposes."[6]

The makers of *The Motorcycle Diaries* structured their narrative around a fictional epiphany that recuperated Guevara for the post–Cold War world by eliminating the radical, existential politics that were at the core of his personal motivations and to the violent conflicts that gripped Latin America from 1948 to 1989. The film shifts Guevara to the liberal humanist tradition that Rodó epitomized—a tradition that regained pertinence as the organization of civil society and rule of law grew in importance as practical alternatives to revolutionary action. Additionally, the understanding of social difference shifted from a hard-edged Marxist understanding of class and race as products of an economic structure to a more moral foundation. One of the key images of *The Motorcycle Diaries* occurs as Ernesto and Alberto travel down the Amazon to the leper colony on a river cruiser. The spacious and comfortable cruiser, where foreigners and middle-class professionals like Alberto and Ernesto find many diversions, tows a crammed little vessel with a makeshift roof where the poor have been segregated. They are completely apart, completely helpless were a problem to develop. "So much injustice," Ernesto says as he studies the towline separating him, a young man of good education and a respectable family, from the common masses. The film emphasizes that Ernesto and Alberto were broke, but their backgrounds gave them a presumption to security and comfort that most of their fellow Americans were forbidden to enjoy.

W. E. B. Du Bois stated at the beginning of the twentieth century that the color line defined the modern world, a position that Marxists for much of the century found an irritant to their representation of the world as structured by class and economic power. We should be clear that the division of the world Du Bois described was not simply a question of difference, whether cultural or biological, nor was it simply a question of hierarchy and stratification. The question facing the world in the form of the color line was one of a system based on active separation of people. The color line meant a forcible division of the world into the *sano* and the *enfermo*, to use Ernesto's language in the leper colony as he responded to what struck him as arbitrary and demeaning treatment of the patients the doctors were in theory there to serve. The *well* and the *ill*, which is another way of saying the *pure* and the *impure*, or in the peculiar twist that contemporary U.S. politics has provided, the *legal* and the *illegal*.[7]

As a result, even if the *Motorcycle Diaries* liberalized Che by refocusing the political message from revolutionary challenges to an economic system to the moral dilemmas of a society ideologically dedicated to personal growth, there nonetheless remains in the film's presentation of social difference glimmers of who he already was. In a scene adapted from Granado's travel diary, the filmmakers have Alberto announcing his fantastical plans to dedicate himself to an American revolution based on interracial sex that would created a united mestizo American people through the power of love and desire. Ernesto dismisses the idea curtly, "A revolution with no guns? No way."[8]

That revolutionary change requires violence was a conviction that Granado insisted Guevara already had as a middle-school student. In 1943 Granado asked Guevara to organize a student strike at his school to demand the release of Granado and other political prisoners. "You're going out to march without guns so that they can beat us with clubs?," the fifteen-year-old Guevara asked his friend before rejecting the idea. "That's crazy. I'm not going without a revolver."[9] The necessity for violence to achieve liberation hovers around the film as a kind of excess that will not go away despite all the good feelings that the filmmakers worked hard to produce. The question of violence must be put in the shadows, a puzzling remainder to the problem of how to achieve both justice and unity in the Americas. Over the closing credits, a voice-over narrator gives due homage to the aspiration for liberation that the *image* of Che Guevara had come to symbolize around the world, an image that said that the division and separation of the world into the privileged and the despised be ended once and for all. The voice-over then asks, "Was our vision to narrow, too partial, too rushed? Were our conclusions too rigid? Maybe." The answer implied is yes, and indeed one of Guevara's more recent biographers has noted that despite Che's romantic, idealistic image, to plunge into his life and environment is to return to the failed and static political mind-set of the post–World War II decades where contradictions between communist theory and actual practice and everyday life were explained away as "petty-bourgeois deviations."[10]

Even so the ideal was neither false nor disingenuous. The trap was in being seduced into believing that sheer willpower could achieve the goal of social transformation. Whoever questioned either goals or methods became a demoralizing element "objectively" serving foreign capital and domestic privilege. Romantic identification with the impoverished seemed to require an insistent dismissal of intellectuals as a perpetual threat to revolutionary action. Granado recalls that while traveling through Peru they witnessed a small group of fellow passengers clear off a blocked road in short order. Ernesto remarked that the episode was a demonstration that the people can easily work miracles, but they are usually held back by the hesitations of intellectuals: "It's true that there is strength in unity, but it must be the strength of people who work. If anyone had said that they weren't going to up a pick and shovel, the unity would have broken. This is surely what would have happened if instead of a busload of truck drivers, peasants, and some loose canons like us, there had appeared a couple of professionals like we knew back home."[11]

But are not voluntarism and a belief in the power of the will to break through long-standing barriers inherent features of the liberal vision? Is not the hero the purest expression of individuality uncompromised by collective demands? Is not the vocation of the hero to illuminate the consciousness of others so that they see the world in new, previously unimaginable ways and suddenly see new ways of acting within it? The combination of willpower, vision, and discipline was at the core of José Enrique Rodó's vision of Americans slowly uniting into a political union after they had built a whole set of shared cultural institutions that would allow for regular exchange of ideas and perspectives.

Developing America into a single community that could discuss matters of mind and beauty required transnational institutions, particularly markets for books and periodicals, that did not yet exist in 1900 when Rodó's *Ariel* was published, nor in 1915 when the Second Pan-American Scientific Congress convened in Washington, D.C. Cooperation between governments, universities, and other not-for-profit public institutions over the following decades facilitated more regular interchange between intellectuals and artists from different countries. In the 1930s in particular, mass media markets began to appear across the western hemisphere, and whether the product was books, magazines, motion pictures, radio programs, or phonograph records, exchange between producers in different countries helped establish a cultural market where profits were reliable only if cultural goods crossed national boundaries.

Pan-Americanism contributed to each nation separating from Europe as the indispensable cultural homeland, a belief that for centuries had rendered the Americas as inherently savage or barbarian, a series of "wild wests" where fortunes could be made but no stable, civilized order could take root. Imaginary connection to other nations in the western hemisphere facilitated new forces within each country working to develop robust national cultures to proceed without simultaneously falling into isolation. In principle, pan-Americanism celebrated symmetric difference as the foundation for a utopian vision of the world. In practice, it hardened asymmetric differences and shaped the process by which media markets developed to favor particular results, those most consistent with U.S. practices. These could be imagined by its proponents, who could be Mexican or Brazilian as well as from the United States, as the time-tested, most efficient way of distributing national culture. Critics saw the direct hand of cultural imperialism. In general, cultural producers in most countries needed international sales to cover basic production costs. Given a large national market and citizens with relatively large levels of disposable income, U.S. firms entered international cultural markets with basic costs already covered. Any income they earned in other countries was additional profit, which gave U.S. firms considerable flexibility in the arrangements they could make with local distributors of their work. Over time, the structures of cultural markets converged, but in the process asymmetries provided opportunities for the unscrupulous and an orientation that reinforced stereotypes on all sides rather than insight and learning. Jürgen Habermas, replying to critics of his arguments about the democratic potential of the public sphere, has noted that "it's not the notion that makes the difficulties; it's the implementation."[12] The asymmetrical relationships within the Pan American Union were never hidden. Always in plain sight, they demanded response, and some responses involved acting to correct evident problems, which had been Elihu Root's starting point for how to achieve effective and lasting social transformation. Pan-Americanism promoted the development of regional markets in publishing, film, phonograph records, and radio, but an essential feature of a media market sharing both content and methods across borders has been national segmentation. A transnational market appeared to consumers to be national in nature, because each market privileged national ways of looking as an essential element in the packaging of similar content.

The irony was that the construction of a continental cultural market linking the different nations of the Americas was achieved first by Hollywood, followed by mass media industries largely based on a North American model, even in those cases where national capital took the lead. Given their divisions and the orientation of their economies toward export to the more industrially developed North, the countries of Latin America did not initially have the resources to do it themselves. Spanish firms, though long organized to reach the book market across the continent, were too small to expand beyond the role they had secured of providing books and journals for educated élites. Their model of a global market was one that need reach only a tiny fraction of the population, a group that took its privileges for granted and its cultural distinction very seriously. Enterprises based in the United States had the capital and the organizational ability to produce and distribute cultural products on a truly hemispheric *and* mass basis. Often, U.S. companies marketed the same products they made for domestic distribution. With increasing frequency, U.S. firms invested in developing a continental market that applied the same principles and procedures used at home for products developed specifically for Spanish-speaking or Portuguese-speaking America relying on local talent to provide the content. The cultural market that emerged through the twentieth century supported a Latin American identity but one that has been difficult to separate from Anglo American cultural hegemony.[13]

In the late 1960s, U.S. investment in Latin American media markets declined, and in the larger countries, local entrepreneurs took over as the primary producers of programming. *Telenovelas* developed as the signature genre for television programming produced in Latin America, quickly dominating prime-time hours. The system shaping the broadcast industry and the production of telenovelas was North American in its origins, developing from adaptation of the radio soap opera genre to Latin American social situations. In the process, dramatic conventions incorporated many elements from Iberian and Latin American narrative traditions. Given lower advertising rates, production budgets initially were considerably smaller than those of equivalent North American productions. The genre could be inexpensive but still attractive to viewers because shows spoke to their own life situations and values in a manner that mirrored their own limited personal resources. Even with costs considerably below those found in U.S. television production, program sales had to be continental given the anemic state of national television markets in a period when television programming could be very popular but television sets were not a product most households could afford. Television producers like book publishers before them had to appeal to regional identity instead of national loyalties if they were to survive. Class differences and social inequalities proved a popular topic for many telenovelas, as did the continuing relevance of Catholic mores in emerging consumer societies. Questions that had less relevance in North America but were vital across Latin America shaped the emergence of national media companies that grew in importance as consumer markets grew.

By the 1980s, Globo in Brazil and Televisa in Mexico were among the five largest media companies in the world. Both began investing in North American and European media companies, in some cases acquiring control. In the 1980s, export of Latin American television programs outside Latin America became increasingly important. Production budgets increased, and editorial controls reshaped stories and other production elements to appeal more to international viewers. In the United States, programs generally played only on Spanish-language television, which was a rapidly growing market. Telenovelas were particularly popular in southern Europe, where cultural roots and social-political questions were similar. In the 1990s, Latin American programming was popular in postcommunist eastern Europe. Telenovelas found markets in northern Europe, Britain, and Australia as well. For a brief period, the share of U.S. television programs in major markets around the world declined. By the beginning of the twenty-first century, U.S. series, generally developed for cable networks like HBO or Showtime, resecured North American dominance of international television markets. *The Sopranos*, *Mad Men*, or *Breaking Bad* broke the older U.S. broadcasting model of an open-ended series by developing a more novelistic form with an ongoing story across multiple episodes. The Latin American share of international television markets declined, but producers responded to the U.S. development with comparable series, many coproduced with U.S. cable networks and presented in the United States. *Epitafios* (2004, 2009), produced in Argentina with HBO participation, featured an emotionally disturbed rogue cop in Buenos Aires working with a psychiatrist to track down serial killers. *City of Men* (2002–2005, Globo TV, released in the United States on the Sundance Channel and then on DVD) was derived from Paulo Lins's novel *City of God* and the internationally successful film adaptation that Fernando Meirelles had made. Starring two young boys who had secondary roles in the film, the television series explored life in Rio's favelas through the lives of two high school students trying to get by without joining one of the gangs. The show and its actors won Emmy Awards in the United States, a triumph that was made a central event in the series' finale. In 2009, Meirelles created a second successful television series for Globo TV, *Som e Fúria* ("Sound and Fury"). The second series had equally good actors, scripts, and production values, but has not yet been released in United States on cable or DVD. Set in a struggling theater company in São Paulo, the series focused on the lives of middle-class Brazilian professionals. Their problems would be recognizable to North Americans, but middle-class Brazilians have been fated to remain invisible in the North except as victims in crime shows. Since 2000, U.S. cable networks have been very successful in Latin America, recapturing ground lost by U.S. television programming the last four decades of the twentieth century. To some degree, resurgence may reflect significantly improved quality, but it could as likely have been a by-product of U.S. dominance of digital technology in all formats and media. The extent of U.S. control over media programming in Latin America and other parts of the world remains a major topic for debate among communications industry scholars, as does the question of whether Brazilian and Mexican television producers have changed the programs they make to reflect global rather than national culture.[14]

One point needs to be stressed: television viewers in Latin America watch programs produced in a range of countries, including news programming. U.S. television on the other hand remains restricted to nationally produced shows plus a few British programs that typically appear on public television. The U.S. public has only occasional exposure to information and ideas that are commonplace in Europe, Latin America, or Asia. The integration of television and computer services will make it feasible for more people to access much more than was possible at the beginning of the twenty-first century. The question remains, though, that Elihu Root posed a century ago: can a country be a responsible global leader if its citizens know nothing about other places, and have no interest in hearing what people in other countries find important and compelling? That the question remains as pertinent a century after Root posed it would not have surprised him, given how many generations he believed significant changes need to overcome deeply entrenched habits—and organized resistance.

What then is the nationality of *The Motorcycle Diaries*? The director Walter Salles is Brazilian, and the screenwriter José Rivera a U.S. playwright from New York, the son of a Puerto Rican family that had migrated to the mainland. The idea for the film originated with Robert Redford, a Hollywood movie star turned producer with a well-known track record of promoting independent films and a reputation as a social progressive. He assembled the funding, hired the writer and director, and remained engaged in the shaping of the film throughout its production. Gaël García Bernal, a young Mexican movie actor with international star appeal, played the role of Ernesto Guevara. *The Motorcycle Diaries* is a Hollywood film produced by a U.S. company and distributed by Universal Pictures. It is safe to say that it is an "American" film, in more than one sense of that contentious word.

As a collaborative artistic statement, it is an American film in the sense that Americans from different nation-states came together to express the sentiment of "nuestra América," the America that is not the United States (or Canada). The film allowed several Latin American intellectuals to speak about the relationship of intellectuals to the working poor of their countries. But Redford's role was not incidental, nor was that of Universal Pictures. As a commercial product, it is a U.S. film, and its form and content rely on many tried and true Hollywood conventions that audiences around the world have demonstrated they like. *The Motorcycle Diaries* was designed to be compelling to American audiences, whether they speak English, Spanish, or Portuguese. The film, whatever else it may be, is a stepping-stone in the synthesis of the Americas, not excluding the United States, into a shared cultural market that involves more than blockbusters. Walter Salles and José Rivera working with other producers continued their collaboration with a film adaptation of Jack Kerouac's *On the Road* (2012), tackling a very different icon of post–World War II American rebellion against the status quo.

Robert Redford's Sundance Institute, critical for developing a market niche for U.S. "independent" films that did not fit into the Hollywood big-budget machine, has made a priority of developing "independent" film production in other American countries. It is one of several U.S.-based organizations that have become involved in helping develop an "alternative" Latin American cinema and then providing a distribution outlet within the United States that has increasingly shifted from theatrical release to availability on cable and digital streaming services like Netflix, Amazon, or Hulu. Latin American films of a broad variety of types have become increasingly available to U.S. consumers in the digital and DVD markets. No film from a Latin American filmmaker, however, has matched the phenomenal success of Ang Lee's Chinese-language U.S. film *Crouching Tiger, Hidden Dragon*. Lee adamantly refused to release his film, a philosophically inflected martial arts spectacle set in imperial China, with an English-dubbed track. The film still found the mass audience he was confident was there for the genre. Despite Redford's stature in the film business, *The Motorcycle Diaries* played exclusively in the art house circuit.

At the same time, Hollywood began recruiting the best talent developing in the Latin American film and television industries. Alfonso Cuarón, the director of *Y tu Mamá también*, one of the most commercially successful films ever made in Mexico, went on to make one of the Harry Potter films, an adaptation of P. D. James's novel *Children of Men*, and *Gravity*, a science fiction film. The creative team behind *Amores perros*, another commercial success from Mexico, then made *24 Grams*, an English-language film set in the United States using Hollywood stars, followed by *Babel*, weaving together actors from and situations in the United States, Mexico, Morocco, and Japan to construct a parable of "globalization" and its linking of the personal and local crises of people from different parts of the world. Alejandro González Iñárritu, the director, has since made *Biutiful*, a Spanish coproduction starring Javier Bardem as a petty crook dying of cancer in Barcelona; *Birdman*, a U.S. coproduction set in New York City filmed entirely in English with a cast of prominent U.S. actors led by Michael Keaton in the title role; and *The Revenant*, another English-language film starring Leonardo DiCaprio set in the Rocky Mountains during the 1820s with a visceral story conveying the physical and psychological terror inherent to creating a "new world." The ability of Iñárritu and his largely Spanish-speaking creative team to move between countries and languages, cobbling together financing from a variety of sources, points to an embryonic "global culture" that escapes national situations to explore different aspects of the "human condition" (meaning reality as understood by a global middle class?) without ever letting go of the specifics of being criminals in Spain; theater performers in Manhattan; or Yankees, French Canadians, and Native peoples fighting over control of the fur trade. In Spanish-speaking Latin America, Spanish television has played a central role in building a regional film industry, expanding the opportunities to work for actors, writers, and directors, while encouraging them to think of their films and television programs as set in particular countries but being produced for international audiences who take market economies and democratically elected governments as signs of normal societies. Some Brazilian filmmakers like Walter Salles and Fernando Meirelles work in the United States and Europe, and then are able to leverage their more commercially oriented projects to find funding for smaller budgeted films. In 2008, Meirelles directed the film *Blindness*, from a novel by the Portuguese Nobel Prize winner José Saramago. The film was shot in English, with an international cast including Gaël García Bernal, Julianne Moore, Mark Ruffalo, Danny Glover, Alice Braga, and Yoshino Kimura. The film, an allegorical drama of society collapsing into Hobbesian chaos as an epidemic sweeps the world leaving the survivors blind, was unlikely ever to be a major theatrical success. That it could be made reflects the emergence of a group of creative people emerging around the world whose careers are as much transnational as rooted in the cultural industries of their native countries. Their ability to work rests on being able to think about their audiences as global and diverse, united by education and an ability to participate relatively freely in consumer society. At the end of 2016, Gaël García Bernal and Chilean film director Pablo Larraín responded to the election of Donald Trump as president of the United States with a determination to use their filmmaking skills to speak to audiences in the United States and around the world about divisive issues that have made the future seem so unpredictable. As Latin Americans from countries with violent political histories, they asserted that their films can help the public understand what is at stake in the temptation to seek radical solutions to difficult problems.[15] Given the work García Bernal and Larraín have done directly for U.S. films and television programs, the U.S. public may well turn to them for perspectives that only a foreign observer can provide.

Which returns us to the question of why contemporary liberals who have done so well in the commercial mass media might reserve a place for Ernesto Guevara in their pantheon of heroes. Liberalism need not be synonymous with the dominance of the market, which can be understood as a mechanism that serves human purposes, but only one mechanism of many that we need. *The Motorcycle Diaries* might then be seen as part of an effort to recover liberalism as a moral philosophy fostering individual growth, freedom of choice, and responsible self-government of formal equals, whose differences may, but need not, result in actual inequalities. Despite two hundred years of polemics from opponents left and right, liberalism remains a living ideology, contradictory, multiple, diverse, hybrid. Its tradition includes a long debate on the relation of legal rights, private property, and moral development. It is a debate that Redford as a well-known progressive entered with a vengeance. The saga of young Ernesto Guevara helped convey to early twenty-first-century audiences that individual moral stance and a sense of responsibility to others in the community might well be the most important and defining characteristics of liberal philosophy. The continuity between the heroes of the revolutionary wars and the present is maintained, for if the film's somewhat awkward coda acknowledges the limitations of the *actual* Guevara's politics, it recuperates the ideals as fundamental for a developing global civilization, which may well have a robust market-based economy but need not be defined or governed solely by market mechanisms.

Appendix

Table 1. Latin American Books Translated into English in the United States by Genre and by Type of Press, 1916–1940

	1916–1920	1921–1925	1926–1930	1931–1935	1936–1940
Total	**15**	**14**	**18**	**21**	**18**
Poetry	4	4	4	7	3
Fiction/drama	6	7	10	12	3
Nonfiction	5	3	4	2	12
Commercial presses	14	13	18	17	10
University presses	0	0	0	2	6
Independent organizations	1	1	0	2	1
U.S. government	0	0	0	0	1

Sources: Charles J. Fleener and Ron L. Seckinger, *The Guide to Latin American Paperback Literature* (Gainesville: Center for Latin American Studies, University of Florida, 1966); Claude L. Hulet, *Latin American Prose in English Translation: A Bibliography* (Washington, D.C.: Pan American Union, 1964); Suzanne Jill Levine, *Latin America: Fiction and Poetry in Translation* (New York: Center for Inter-American Relations, 1970); Remigio U. Pane, "Two Hundred Latin American Books in English Translation: A Bibliography," *Modern Language Journal* 27 (1943), 593–694; Bradley A. Shaw, *Latin American Literature in English Translation: An Annotated Bibliography* (New York: New York University Press, 1976); Bradley A. Shaw, *Latin American Literature in English, 1975–1978* (New York: Center for Inter-American Relations, 1979); Nancy Saporta Sternbach, "Latin American Women Writers in Translation: An Annotated Bibliography," *Feminist Teacher* 2 (1986), 14–17.

Table 2. Latin American Books Translated into English in the United States by Genre and by Type of Press, 1941–1980

	1941–1945	1946–1950	1951–1955	1956–1960	1961–1965	1966–1970	1971–1975	1976–1980
Total	**47**	**38**	**30**	**44**	**95**	**107**	**118**	**69**
Poetry	8	8	1	11	12	27	49	24
Fiction/drama	21	12	20	26	47	65	53	32
Nonfiction	15	16	9	6	34	7	14	11
General anthologies	3	2	0	1	2	8	2	2
Commercial presses	32	30	25	30	59	80	96	54
University presses	9	5	3	8	33	27	19	12
Independent organizations	3	0	0	0	0	0	3	3
Pan American Union	3	3	2	6	3	0	0	0

Sources: Fleener and Seckinger, *The Guide to Latin American Paperback Literature*; Hulet, *Latin American Prose in English Translation*; Levine, *Latin America*; Pane, "Two Hundred Latin American Books in English Translation"; Shaw, *Latin American Literature in English Translation*; Shaw, *Latin American Literature in English, 1975–1978*; Sternbach, "Latin American Women Writers in Translation."

Note: For purposes of comparison: in 2013, U.S. publishers issued 525 translations, of which 59 were by authors from other American countries, which also included Puerto Rico and Quebec; in 2014, a total of 443 translations appeared, of which 55 were by authors from other American countries; in 2015, the total was 550 translations, of which 74 were by authors from other American countries (source: Three Percent, a translation database at the University of Rochester, http://www.rochester.edu/College/translation/threepercent/index.php?s=database).

Table 3. Latin American Authors with Seven or More U.S. Publications, 1941–1989

	1941–1945	1946–1950	1951–1955	1956–1960	1961–1965	1966–1970	1971–1975	1976–1980	1981–1985	1986–1989	Total
Jorge Amado	1				3	2	2	1	4	2	15
Miguel Ángel Asturias					1	2	5	1			9
Adolfo Bioy Casares					1		3	2	1	1	8
Jorge Luis Borges					4	3	5	3	8		23
Ernesto Cardenal							4	2	4	1	11
Alejo Carpentier				2	1	1		1		2	7
Julio Cortázar					1	3	2	2	2	2	12
José Donoso					1	1	2	4	1	1	10
Paulo Freire						1	1	1	1	3	7
Carlos Fuentes				1	2	2	2	3	3	2	15
Gabriel García Márquez						2	1	3	2	3	11
Machado de Assis			3		3	1	1	2	1		11
José Martí			1				1	2	2	1	7
Pablo Neruda	2	3			4	6	9	4	7	6	41
Octavio Paz				1	3	1	7				12
Manuel Puig							2	1	3	1	7
César Vallejo						3	4	4	2	2	15
Mario Vargas Llosa						2	1	2	2	4	11
Érico Veríssimo	1	4	1	1	1	1					9

Sources: Fleener and Seckinger, *The Guide to Latin American Paperback Literature*; Hulet, *Latin American Prose in English Translation*; Levine, *Latin America*; Pane, "Two Hundred Latin American Books in English Translation"; Shaw, *Latin American Literature in English Translation*; Shaw, *Latin American Literature in English, 1975–1978.*

Table 4. The Ten U.S. Publishers with the Largest Lists of Latin American Authors, 1911–1980

	1910s	1920s	1930s	1940s	1950s	1960s	1970s	Total
Dutton	1	2				4	14	**21**
Farrar and Rinehart[a]		2	3	8				**13**
Farrar, Straus, Giroux				2	5	7	11	**25**
Grove Press					1	6	3	**10**
Harper and Row[b]	2				1	4	12	**19**
Knopf	1	2		13	8	21	10	**55**
Macmillan				12	3	4	1	**20**
New Directions				2		3	8	**13**
University of California Press			1		1	11	4	**17**
University of Texas Press				1	2	22	8	**33**

[a] Farrar and Rinehart closed in 1948, two years after John C. Farrar left the firm to partner with Roger Straus in the new publishing house that became Farrar, Straus, Giroux.
[b] Harper before 1962.

Sources: Fleener and Seckinger, *The Guide to Latin American Paperback Literature*; Hulet, *Latin American Prose in English Translation*; Levine, *Latin America*; Pane, "Two Hundred Latin American Books in English Translation"; Shaw, *Latin American Literature in English Translation*; Shaw, *Latin American Literature in English, 1975–1978*; Sternbach, "Latin American Women Writers in Translation."

Table 5. Museum Survey and Single-Artist Exhibitions of Latin American Art in the United States, with a Printed Publication, by Region, 1926–1975

	1926–1930	1931–1935	1936–1940	1941–1945	1946–1950	1951–1955	1956–1960	1961–1965	1966–1970	1971–1975
New York City	3	3	8	24	4	2	5	6	15	4
East Coast	1	1	1	6	5	1	3	13	8	1
Midwest	0	3	0	6	3	4	5	4	2	1
Texas/Gulf Coast	0	0	0	0	1	2	5	4	7	1
Pacific Coast	3	3	8	18	6	4	1	7	7	3
Total	**7**	**10**	**17**	**54**	**19**	**13**	**19**	**34**	**39**	**10**

Source: Library of Congress catalog *Art in America*, 1920–1989.

Table 6. Museum Survey and Single-Artist Exhibitions of Latin American Art in the United States, with a Printed Publication, by Type of Show, 1926–1975

	1926–1930	1931–1935	1936–1940	1941–1945	1946–1950	1951–1955	1956–1960	1961–1965	1966–1970	1971–1975
Historical survey	1	2	4	4	5	1	6	5	10	3
Contemporary survey	0	2	7	24	4	2	6	8	14	4
Single-artist shows	6	6	6	26	10	10	7	21	15	3
Total	**7**	**10**	**17**	**54**	**19**	**13**	**19**	**34**	**39**	**10**

Source: Library of Congress catalog *Art in America*, 1920–1989.

Table 7. Latin American Artists with Five or More Solo Exhibitions in U.S. Museums and Galleries, 1920–1989

	1920s	1930s	1940s	1950s	1960s	1970s	1980s	*Total*
Antonio Berni					5			**5**
Fernando Botero					3	2	3	**8**
Mario Carreño			5	2				**7**
Rafael Ferrer					1	6		**7**
Lucio Fontana					4	3		**7**
Antonio Frasconi			2	1	2			**5**
Pedro Friedeberg					5			**5**
Leonel Góngora				1	10			**11**
Wilfredo Lam				5				**5**
Mauricio Lasansky			3	1	5	2		**11**
Julio LeParc					3	2		**5**
Marisol				1	5	2		**8**
Maria Martins			5					**5**
Roberto Matta Echaurren			12	3	1		2	**18**
Carlos Mérida	1	6	2		2		2	**13**
José Clemente Orozco	1	5	2	1	2		1	**12**
Emilio Pettoruti			7					**7**
Cândido Portinari			14	1				**15**
Omar Rayo					7	1		**8**
Diego Rivera	2	10	6	1		2	3	**24**
David Alfaro Siqueiros		2	2		3	1		**8**
Rufino Tamayo	2	4	16	9	3	9	5	**48**
Joaquín Torres-García					3	3		**6**

Source: Library of Congress catalog *Art in America*, 1920–1989.

Notes

Except in the few cases where I quote directly from a published translation and cite the source in the notes, I am responsible for all the translations into English found in this book. The original text of material I have translated can be found in the notes.

Introduction

1. Veríssimo wrote in detail about this particular speaking tour in two letters to Henrique Bertaso, his publisher in Brazil. See Érico Veríssimo to Henrique Bertaso, 14 February 1945, 17 April 1945, Acervo de Érico Veríssimo, Instituto Moreira Salles, Rio de Janeiro (hereafter Acervo de EV, IMS).

2. The title of Veríssimo's talk alludes to lines in the Brazilian national anthem, and ideas widespread in Brazilian patriotic rhetoric of Brazil as a potentially powerful, but inherently peaceful country: Gigante pela própria natureza, / És belo, és forte, impávido colosso, / E o teu futuro espelha essa grandeza. [Giant by thine own nature, / thou art beautiful, thou art strong, an intrepid colossus, / and thy future mirrors thy greatness.] / . . . / Dos filhos deste solo / És mãe gentil, / Pátria amada, / Brasil! [To the children of this land / thou art a gentle mother, / beloved homeland, / Brazil!].

3. Veríssimo, *A Volta do Gato Preto* (Rio de Janeiro: Editora Globo, 1987), 141. Original Portuguese text: num *melting pot* como é o Brasil (e diga-se de passagem, também os Estados Unidos) a gente nunca sabe ao certo que espécie de sangue traz nas veias. . . . Sou um ser humano.

4. The study does not provide a comprehensive review of Latin American creative people who worked in the United States between 1915 and 1975. I decided not to include cultural figures who emigrated to the United States and then established their careers. This was a large group, including many who became prominent. As successful members of U.S. society they reflect a different aspect of how international connections enriched national life. Nor, aside from a few comments in passing, does the study discuss musicians and actors. Some had stellar careers in the United States, while continuing to work, usually under very different conditions, in their home countries. My decision to exclude them from the study was based on their having entered U.S. cultural life primarily as entertainers, not as public intellectuals, admittedly a thin, perhaps arbitrary distinction, but appropriate in this case because the public did not look to actors like Ramón Navarro or singers like Astrud Gilberto for insight into inter-American relations. Finally, work discussed in this book was not produced for "specialists" but for a general public that editors and curators presumed to be middle class and educated. Pan-Americanism promoted an ongoing relationship between U.S. and Latin American scholars in a broad variety of fields. Examining how cultural and educational exchange affected the practice of sociology, anthropology, or economics, to name only three of the many disciplines where exchange has been important, if at times contentious, requires analyzing how national scholarly traditions intersected with epistemological debates over theory and method. A synoptic study of exchange across the many disciplines involved would of necessity require a superficial treatment of the intellectual questions that exchange raised in each field.

5. See, for an exemplary discussion of the place of pan-Americanism in the overall goals of U.S. foreign policy, Walter LaFeber, *The New Empire: An Interpretation of American Expansion, 1860–1898* (Ithaca, N.Y.: Cornell University Press, 1963), 202–218. On Latin American motivations for pursuing pan-Americanism, see Tulio Halperín Donghi, *Historia contemporánea de América latina* (Madrid: Alianza Editorial, 1998), 213, 225–228, 285–289; and Javier Corrales and Richard E. Feinberg, "Regimes of Cooperation in the Western Hemisphere: Power, Interests, and Intellectual Traditions," *International Studies Quarterly* 43 (1999), 1–36. The 1890 conference ended with the creation of the International Bureau of the American Republics, with permanent offices in Washington. In 1910, the organizational name was changed to the Pan American Union. In 1947, the member states renamed the group the Organization of American States. The name Pan American Union continued to be used to cover a variety of cultural, educational, health, and other activities that fostered citizen-to-citizen engagement rather than formal relations between the member states. The formation of the Pan American Union was, in part, a defensive reaction against British domination of trade in the western hemisphere and the division of Africa, Asia, and the Pacific after 1880 by competing colonial powers. If the Pan American Union provided an effective bulwark against resurgent European imperialism, it also provided a cover for U.S. expansion by demarcating the western hemisphere as a sphere of influence that the United States dominated. For work exploring the topic of imperialism at the end of the nineteenth century, including the relation of the U.S. informal empire to the formal imperialism of the European powers and Japan, see, Jane Burbank and Frederick Cooper, *Empires in World History: Power and the Politics of Difference* (Princeton, N.J.: Princeton University Press, 2011); P. J. Cain and A. G. Hopkins, *British Imperialism: 1688–2000* (London: Routledge, 2001); Dipesh Chakrabarty, *Provincializing Europe: Postcolonial Thought and Historical Difference* (Princeton, N.J.: Princeton University Press, 2007); Frederick Cooper and Ann Laura Stoler, *Tensions of Empire: Colonial Cultures in a Bourgeois World* (Berkeley: University of California Press, 1997); Marilyn Lake and Henry Reynolds, *Drawing the Global Colour Line: White Men's Countries and the International Challenge of Racial Equality* (Cambridge: Cambridge University Press, 2008); Anne McClintock, *Imperial Leather: Race, Gender, and Sexuality in the Colonial Contest* (New York: Routledge, 1995); David Northrup, *Indentured Labor in the Age of Imperialism, 1834–1922* (Cambridge: Cambridge University Press, 1995); Jürgen Osterhammel, *The Transformation of the World: A Global History of the Nineteenth Century*, trans. Patrick Camiller (Princeton, N.J.: Princeton University Press, 2014).

6. See Philippe Sands, *Lawless World: America and the Making and Breaking of Global Rules from FDR's Atlantic Charter to George W. Bush's Illegal War* (New York: Viking, 2006), for a summary of how long-standing U.S. concerns with establishing a stable international legal system took shape during and after World War II.

7. Fredrick B. Pike, *The United States and Latin America: Myths and Stereotypes of Civilization and Nature* (Austin: University of Texas Press, 1992), seems to be the only book in English organized around a comparative examination of U.S. and Latin American ideas. Pike focuses on ideas of nature and U.S. projections of "nature" onto a "raw" Latin America. It is more a study of stereotypes than of ideas about nature and the environment. It contains an interesting discussion of the influence of arielism, one of the most important Latin American intellectual movements of the early twentieth century, on U.S. cultural figures. *Do the Americas Have a Common Literature?*, edited by Gustavo Pérez Firmat and published by the Modern Language Association (Durham, N.C.: Duke University Press, 1990), is a collection of essays examining how to teach foundational texts in the literatures of the Americas. It works primarily as comparisons of individual texts rather than in any way being a systematic retelling of the literary history of the Americas or the social and intellectual contexts shaping the development of literature in different American nations. The most important comparative intellectual histories of Latin America are Eduardo Devés Valdés, *El pensamiento latinoamericano en el siglo XX* (Buenos Aires: Editorial Biblos, 3 vols., 2000–2004); Dina V. Picotti, ed., *Pensar desde América: Vigencia y desafíos actuales* (Buenos Aires: Catálogos Editora, 1995); Clara Alicia Jalif de Bertranou et al., *Pensamiento latinoamericano* (Mendoza: Editorial de la Universidad Nacional de Cuyo, 1991). José Antonio Aguilar Rivera's *La sombra de Ulises: Ensayos sobre intelec-*

tuales mexicanos y norteamericanos (Mexico City: CIDE, 1998) is an excellent historical study of the linkages between U.S. and Mexican intellectuals through the twentieth century. There are numerous intellectual and cultural histories of individual countries, all in the language of the country. Important works on the diplomatic history of U.S.-Latin American relations include Marano Baptista Gumucio, *Latinoamericanos y norteamericanos: Cinco siglos de dos culturas* (La Paz: CELA, 1986); Samuel Flagg Bemis, *The Latin American Policy of the United States* (New York: Harcourt, Brace, 1943), a presentation of standard mid-twentieth-century arguments used to justify U.S. dominance of the western hemisphere; Jules Benjamin, "The Framework of U.S. Relations with Latin America in the Twentieth Century: An Interpretive Essay," *Diplomatic History* 11 (1987), 91–112; Donald Dozer, *Are We Good Neighbors? Three Decades of Inter-American Relations, 1930–1960* (Gainesville: University of Florida Press, 1959), a critical but largely positive assessment of U.S. policies; Laurence Duggan, *The Americas: The Search for Hemisphere Security* (New York: Henry Holt, 1949), a highly critical discussion from a veteran of U.S. cultural exchange programs; Irwin F. Gellman, *Good Neighbor Diplomacy: United States Policies in Latin America, 1933–1945* (Baltimore: Johns Hopkins University Press, 1979); David Green, *The Containment of Latin America: A History of the Myths and Realities of the Good Neighbor Policy* (Chicago: Quadrangle Books, 1971); Samuel G. Inman, *Inter-American Conferences, 1826–1954* (Washington: U.S. Department of State, 1965), another justification of U.S. policy from the position of a liberal defending Cold War toughness; Lester D. Langley, *MexAmerica: Two Countries, One Future* (New York: Crown, 1988); Lester D. Langley, *America and the Americas: The United States in the Western Hemisphere* (Athens: University of Georgia Press, 1989); Carlos Rangel, *Del buen salvaje al buen revolucionario* (Caracas: Monte Avila, 1976); Samuel Shapiro, ed., *Cultural Factors in Inter-American Relations* (Notre Dame, Ind.: Notre Dame University Press, 1968); Dick Steward, *Trade and Hemisphere: The Good Neighbor Policy and Reciprocal Trade* (Columbia: University of Missouri Press, 1975); Arthur P. Whitaker, *The Western Hemisphere Idea: Its Rise and Decline* (Ithaca, N.Y.: Cornell University Press, 1954); Bryce Wood, *The Making of the Good Neighbor Policy* (New York: Columbia University Press, 1961).

8. Halperín Donghi, *Historia contemporánea de América latina*, 285–286.

9. See Serge Guilbaut's *How New York Stole the Idea of Modern Art*, trans. Arthur Goldhammer (Chicago: University of Chicago Press, 1985), for an assessment of how State Department–led efforts to promote abstract expressionism reduced the complex work painters in New York had produced in the 1940s to simplistic examples of the "freedom" and individual initiative supposedly definitive of U.S. society. See also Taylor D. Littleton and Maltby Sykes, eds., *Advancing American Art: Painting, Politics, and Cultural Confrontation at Mid-Century* (Tuscaloosa: University of Alabama Press, 2005), for an in-depth examination of a touring exhibition of contemporary U.S. painting that the State Department organized in 1946.

10. Penny Von Eschen, *Satchmo Blows Up the World: Jazz Ambassadors Play the Cold War* (Cambridge, Mass.: Harvard University Press, 2004).

11. For connections between jazz, beat poetry, method acting, abstract expressionism, and other artistic forms that had become increasingly physicalized in the 1940s and 1950s, see Daniel Belgrad, *The Culture of Spontaneity: Improvisation and the Arts in Postwar America* (Chicago: University of Chicago Press, 1998).

12. Akira Iriye's *Cultural Internationalism and World Order* (Baltimore: Johns Hopkins University Press, 1997) remains the classic account of the rise of "cultural diplomacy" and the belief that intellectuals and artists had important contributions to make to international relations. The most definitive histories of the emergence and implementation of cultural exchange programs in the United States are Frank A. Ninkovich, *The Diplomacy of Ideas: U.S. Foreign Policy and Cultural Relations, 1938–1950* (Cambridge: Cambridge University Press, 1981); and Richard T. Arndt, *The First Resort of Kings: American Cultural Diplomacy in the Twentieth Century* (Washington, D.C.: Potomac Books, 2005). On the growth of cosmopolitan thinking among U.S. elites, see Frank A. Ninkovich, *Global Dawn: The Cultural Foundation of American Internationalism, 1865–1890* (Cambridge, Mass.: Harvard University Press, 2009); and Frank A. Ninkovich, *The Global Republic: America's Inadvertent Rise to World Power* (Chicago: University of Chicago Press, 2014). Ninkovich

and Arndt agree that U.S. cultural and educational policies frequently stumbled because U.S. strategists assumed the universality of their own values. U.S. leaders recognized and, at least those who were cosmopolitans, valued cultural differences. They believed that, ultimately, differences could be transcended through dialogue and interaction revealing common interests deeply rooted in the "human condition." The persistence of misunderstanding, instead of being understood as coming from a conflict of interests that needed to be discussed and negotiated, became evidence that force might be necessary to override resistance. Several historians have assessed cultural exchange programs the United States developed after 1938 to convince Latin Americans to support U.S. efforts to oppose Nazi Germany, with particular attention given to the ambitious activities of the Office of the Coordinator for Inter-American Affairs, established in August 1940 with Nelson Rockefeller as its charismatic and politically astute leader. See Darlene J. Sadlier, *Americans All: Good Neighbor Cultural Diplomacy in World War II* (Austin: University of Texas Press, 2012); Gisela Cramer and Ursula Prutsch, "Nelson A. Rockefeller's Office of Inter-American Affairs (1940–1946) and Record Group 229," *Hispanic American Historical Review* 86 (2006), 785–806; Claude C. Erb, "Prelude to Point Four: The Institute of Inter-American Affairs," *Diplomatic History* 9 (1985), 249–269; Seth Fein, "Transnationalization and Cultural Collaboration: Mexican Film Propaganda During World War II," *Studies in Latin American Popular Culture* 17 (1998), 105–128. These authors largely concur that the efforts failed to develop understanding of, much less sympathy for, life in the United States in Latin America. In any event, with the end of the war, U.S. strategic priorities shifted from Latin America to building a global anticommunist alliance centered on western Europe and the western Pacific, and World War II cultural exchange programs had little impact on U.S.–Latin American relations during the Cold War. Frances Stonor Saunders's work on the Congress for Cultural Freedom, *The Cultural Cold War: The CIA and the World of Arts and Letters* (New York: New Press, 2000), used careful archival research to trace how the CIA funded and surreptitiously directed a supposedly autonomous cultural organization of international intellectuals dedicated to defending freedom of expression during the Cold War. Other historical studies of the Congress of Cultural Freedom are Christopher Lasch, "The Cultural Cold War: A Short History of the Congress for Cultural Freedom," in *Towards a New Past: Dissenting Essays in American History*, ed. Barton J. Bernstein (New York: Pantheon, 1968), 322–359; Peter Coleman, *The Liberal Conspiracy: The Congress for Cultural Freedom and the Struggle for the Mind of Postwar Europe* (New York: Free Press, 1989); Pierre Grémion, *Intelligence de l'anticommunisme: Le Congrès pour la Liberté de la Culture, 1950–1975* (Paris: Fayard, 1995); Giles Scott Smith, *The Politics of Apolitical Culture: The Congress for Cultural Freedom and Postwar American Hegemony* (New York: Routledge, 2002); Andrew N. Rubin, *Archives of Authority: Empire, Culture, and the Cold War* (Princeton, N.J.: Princeton University Press, 2012). Patrick J. Iber's *Neither Peace nor Freedom: The Cultural Cold War in Latin America* (Cambridge, Mass.: Harvard University Press, 2015) demonstrates the critical and political independence of the intellectuals Iber covers from both the United States and the Soviet Union despite decisions to ally with one side or the other during the Cold War. Antônio Pedro Tota's *The Seduction of Brazil: The Americanization of Brazil During World War II*, trans. Lorena B. Ellis (Austin: University of Texas Press, 2010), presents a case study of how, even in Latin America, where U.S. policy increasingly supported dictatorships, the liberatory appeal of U.S. culture nonetheless was also surprisingly strong. The transgressive appeal of U.S. culture forms the core of Reinhold Wagnleitner's study of U.S. cultural exchange programs in Austria, *Coca-colonization and the Cold War: The Cultural Mission of the United States in Austria after the Second World War* (Chapel Hill: University of North Carolina Press, 1994), and is an important theme in Victoria De Grazia's *Irresistible Empire: America's Advance Through Twentieth-Century Europe* (Cambridge, Mass.: Belknap Press of Harvard University Press, 2005). Penny Von Eschen's *Race Against Empire: Black Americans and Anticolonialism, 1937–1957* (Ithaca, N.Y.: Cornell University Press, 1997), provided me with an indispensable model for the study of how cultural exchange could spark important change within the United States. Von Eschen traces the activity of the African American press in reporting to its readers about anticolonial movements around the world and familiarizing them with the ideas of activists and theorists. African American newspapers were seeking to inspire their readers and give them a sense of connection with a world of people of color rising up to become full citizens and masters of their destiny.

13. Reinhart Koselleck, "'Space of Experience' and 'Horizon of Expectation,'" in Reinhart Koselleck, *Futures Past: On the Semantics of Historical Time*, trans. Keith Tribe (New York: Columbia University Press, 1983), 255–275; on the relation of experience and expectation, see 257–258, quoted phrase on 258.

14. See Greg Grandin, "The Liberal Traditions in the Americas: Rights, Sovereignty, and the Origins of Liberal Multilateralism," *American Historical Review* 117 (2012), 68–91, for an excellent quick survey of liberal traditions in the western hemisphere. See also Greg Grandin, "Your Americanism and Mine: Americanism and Anti-Americanism in the Americas," *American Historical Review* 111 (2006), 1042–1066.

15. The term "public" is one of many vexed terms that must, for want of alternative comprehensible terms, circulate in this book. I do not use the term in relation to ongoing debates about the "public sphere" derived from Jürgen Habermas's work. I rely on a pragmatic understanding of the term that professionals in the mass media use. Every author has a public, as does every genre, meaning a set of consumers available to consider a work for purchase. The public, in that sense, is simply whomever a marketing campaign targets. As a term constructed for use by professionals in the media, the specific audiences that the term indicated shifted during the period covered by this book. Within any given period, different entities and their publicists had their own, at times idiosyncratic, understanding of who or what constituted a public. Overall, I have found Paddy Scannell's essay on a creative figure's relationship with his or her public to be helpful and convincing; see Scannell, "For-Anyone-as-Someone Structures," *Media Culture Society* 22 (2000), 5–24.

16. Frederick Cooper's observations on the methodological questions involved in understanding imperialism and neocolonialism have shaped my approach. See Cooper, *Decolonization and African Society: The Labor Question in French and British Africa* (Cambridge: Cambridge University Press, 1996), especially the discussion of the relation of external restraints to the exercise of domestic political power on 465.

17. Pierre Bourdieu's concepts of *habitus*, a predisposition to particular cultural perspectives based on routine embodied practices, and *hexis*, the totality of the embodied relations that connect individuals within a particular group, offer good starting points for explaining how socially determined, statistically predictable responses can feel individual and innermost. Bourdieu's exposition of his methodology is *Outline of a Theory of Practice*, trans. Richard Nice (Cambridge: Cambridge University Press, 1977). Bourdieu applied his methods to the relationship between class, education, and cultural preferences in *Distinction: A Social Critique of the Judgment of Taste*, trans. Richard Nice (Cambridge, Mass.: Harvard University Press, 1984). However, Bernard Lahire and Tony Bennett have provided necessary qualifications to Bourdieu's conclusions. In separate research projects expanding on Bourdieu's research into the relationship of class and cultural preferences, they collected data indicating that individuals are capable of multiple, contradictory tastes. For every social classification, they discovered statistical variances in individual responses to work greater than what class-, gender-, or race-based *habitus* would predict. Both Lahire and Bennett stress that the volume of material necessary for cultural markets has dramatically increased since Bourdieu did his initial research in the 1960s on how class and education in France intersected with preferences for cultural material. Markets rely on a large volume of material, only a handful of which sell enormously well. The average by definition fills time but has the least hold, that is to say expresses only the schematic bare minimum of consumer interest. See Tony Bennett, "Habitus Clivé: Aesthetics and Politics in the Work of Pierre Bourdieu," *New Literary History* 38 (2007), 201–228; Bernard Lahire, "From the Habitus to an Individual Heritage of Dispositions: Towards a Sociology at the Level of the Individual," *Poetics* 31 (2003), 329–355; Bernard Lahire, "The Individual and the Mixing of Genres: Cultural Dissonance and Self-Distinction," *Poetics* 36 (2008), 166–188.

18. A collective study of life stories that exemplify the choices available to a particular group of people is called prosopography. The approach is not technically biographical since the full life is not covered, only those aspects pertinent to a group portrait. For a clear summary of prosopographical methods, including assessment of their limitations, see Lawrence Stone, "Prosopography," *Daeda-*

lus 100 (1971), 46–79. Santiago Colás's article "Of Creole Symptoms, Cuban Fantasies, and Other Latin American Postcolonial Ideologies," *PMLA* 110 (1995), 382–396, helped me in thinking about application to a history of inter-American cultural production.

19. Hannah Arendt, *The Human Condition* (Chicago: University of Chicago Press, 1958), 26–31, 41, 194–197.

20. Arendt, *The Human Condition*, 236–247.

Chapter 1

1. In 1890, the population of the western hemisphere was slightly under 122 million, with 63 million living in the United States. Only in 1940 did the U.S. population share decline below 50 percent of the total population in the hemisphere, with 132 million U.S. residents out of a total of nearly 273 million. In the fifty years between 1890 and 1940, the balance within the Pan American Union was even more strongly on the U.s. side, with the other member states having a total population of 51 million in 1890 and 123 million in 1940. High population growth rates during this period were due primarily to immigration into the western hemisphere from Europe, Asia, and Africa, with approximately 60 to 65 percent of immigrants coming to the United States, which with its rapid industrial and commercial growth accompanied by persistent labor shortages in many areas of the economy was the most volatile sector of the global labor market at the beginning of the twentieth century. Population figures are online at "Population Statistics: Historical Demography of All Countries, Their Divisions and Towns," http://www.populstat.info/.

2. See for example, *Commercial Directory of the American Republics: Comprising the Manufacturers, Merchants, Shippers, and Banks and Bankers Engaged in Foreign Trade; Together with the Names of Officials, Maps, Commercial Statistics, Industrial Data, and Other Information Concerning the Countries of the International Union of American Republics, the American Colonies, and Hawaii*, 2 vols. (Washington, D.C.: Government Printing Office, 1897).

3. In 1947, when the Pan American Union was renamed the Organization of American States, it became a formal collective security organization.

4. For reports on the 1908 congress, see "International Law at the First Pan-American Scientific Congress," *American Journal of International Law* 3 (April 1909), 429–431; and W. H. Holmes, "The First Pan-American Scientific Congress, Held in Santiago, Chile, December 25, 1908-January 6, 1909," *Science*, new series, 29 (19 March 1909), 441–448.

5. After two years of effort, Wilson's proposal collapsed. For a detailed history of the diplomatic efforts to develop a unified response to the European war from the American nations, see Mark T. Gilderhus, *Pan American Visions: Woodrow Wilson in the Western Hemisphere, 1913–1921* (Tucson: University of Arizona Press, 1986).

6. Jane Addams, "Toward Internationalism," in Mrs. Glen Levin Swiggett, *Report on the Women's Auxiliary Conference Held in the City of Washington, U.S.A. in Connection with the Second Pan American Scientific Congress* (Washington, D.C.: Government Printing Office, 1916), 59.

7. In *Global Dawn: The Cultural Foundation of American Internationalism, 1865–1890* (Cambridge, Mass.: Harvard University Press, 2009), Frank Ninkovich has examined the extent to which post–Civil War liberal intellectuals in the United States developed an international perspective that placed citizen-to-citizen cultural contact as more important to the relation of nations than politics, diplomacy, or war; see in particular 12–13. My thoughts on the relation of cultural production to international "public opinion" have been shaped by my readings of Jürgen Habermas, *Strukturwandel der Öffentlichkeit: Untersuchungen zu einer Kategorie der bürgerlichen Gesellschaft* (Berlin: Luchterhand, 1965); Geoff Eley, "Nations, Publics, and Political Cultures: Placing Habermas in the Nineteenth Century," in *Culture/Power/History: A Reader in Contemporary Social Theory*, ed. Nicholas B. Dirks, Geoff Eley, and Sherry B. Ortner (Princeton, N.J.: Princeton University Press, 1994); Günther Lottes, *Politische Aufklärung und plebejisches Publikum: Zur Theorie und Praxis des englischen Radikalismus im späten 18. Jahrhundert* (Munich: Oldenbourg, 1979).

8. On the development of public opinion in Latin America in the nineteenth and early twentieth centuries, see Hugo Achugar, "Parnasos fundacionales, letra, nación y estado en el siglo XIX," *Revista Iberoamericana* 63 (1997), 13–31; María C. Albin, "De Avellaneda: La esfera pública y la crítica de la modernidad," *Cincinnati Romance Review* 14 (1995), 73–79; Jesús Martín-Barbero, *De los medios a las mediaciones: Comunicación, cultura y hegemonía* (Mexico City: Ediciones G. Gili, 1987), 14–30; Francine Masiello, "Introducción," in *La mujer y el espacio público*, ed. Francine Masiello (Buenos Aires: Feminaria, 1994), 7–19; Juan Poblete, "La construcción social de la lectura y la novela nacional: El caso chileno," *Latin American Research Review* 32, no. 2 (1999), 75–108; Ángel Rama, *La ciudad letrada* (Hanover, N.H.: Ediciones del Norte, 1984); Fernando Unzueta, "The Nineteenth-Century Novel: Toward a Public Sphere or a Mass Media?" in *Latin American Literature and Mass Media*, ed. Edmundo Paz-Soldán and Debra A. Castillo (New York: Garland, 2001), 21–40.

9. Carnegie Endowment for International Peace, *Year Book for 1916* (Washington, D.C.: Carnegie Endowment for International Peace, 1916), 17–18, 28, 31, 57.

10. Manuel Ugarte, "Carta abierta al presidente de Estados Unidos," in Manuel Ugarte, *La patria grande* (Madrid: Editorial Mundo Latino, 1924; originally published in 1913), 11–24, quote on 11. The original Spanish quote: de ratones presididos por un gato.

11. Ernesto Quesada, *El nuevo panamericanismo y el Congreso Científico de Washington* (Buenos Aires: Talleres Gráficos del Ministerio de Agricultura de la Nación, 1916), 134–138.

12. Rubén Darío, "A Roosevelt" (1904), in Rubén Darío, *Poesía: Libros poéticos completos y antología de la obra dispersa* (Mexico City: Fondo de Cultura Económica, 1952), 260–262.

13. Quoted in E. Bradford Burns, *The Unwritten Alliance: Rio-Branco and Brazilian-American Relations* (New York: Columbia University Press, 1966), 112.

14. Rubén Darío, "Salutación al águila" (1906), in Darío, *Poesía*, 312–313. In another poem, published in 1907 in *El canto errante*, Darío confessed about this particular poem and his positive response to the meet in Rio de Janeiro, "Yo pan-americanicé / con un vago temor y con muy poca fe / ... mas encontré también un gran núcleo cordial / de almas llenas de amor, de ensueños, de ideal" ("Epístola: A la señora de Leopoldo Lugones," in Rubén Darío, *Poesías completas I* (Buenos Aires: Claridad, 2005), 99; "I pan Americanized / with some fear and not much faith / ... but I met as well a warm nucleus / of souls filled with love, dreams, and the ideal."

15. Original Spanish for quote: Por esto comprenderéis que el terrible cazador es un varón sensato. Rubén Darío, "Dilucidaciones" (preface to *El canto errante*), in Darío, *Poesías completas I*, 53.

16. Rubén Darío, "La gran cosmópolis" (1915), in Darío, *Poesía*, 476.

17. After leaving the executive branch, Root remained in government, representing the state of New York in the U.S. Senate from 1909 to 1915. After 1915, he continued to be an influential, if at times controversial leader of the Republican Party. Given its twenty endowments, the Carnegie Corporation involved itself in a broad range of activities. The Carnegie Corporation was the single largest funder of public and university libraries in the United States prior to 1940. See Robert M. Lester, *Forty Years of Carnegie Giving* (New York: Scribner's, 1941); George Sylvan Bobinski, "Andrew Carnegie's Role in American Public Library Development," Ph.D. dissertation, University of Michigan, 1966; Barbara Howe, "The Emergence of Scientific Philanthropy, 1900–1920: Origins, Issues, and Outcomes," in *Philanthropy and Cultural Imperialism: The Foundations at Home and Abroad*, ed. Robert F. Arnove (Boston: G. K. Hall, 1980), 25–54; Neil A. Radford, *The Carnegie Corporation and the Development of American College Libraries, 1928–1941* (Chicago: American Library Association, 1984).

18. Carnegie Endowment, *Year Book for 1916*, 17–18, 28, 31, 57, quote on 17.

19. For a discussion of Elihu Root's conceptions of international governance in relation to transatlantic interactions, particularly negotiations to form the League of Nations, see Mark Mazower, *Governing the World: The History of an Idea, 1815 to the Present* (New York: Penguin Books, 2012), 89–93, 116–122.

20. Michel Foucault described the process of including public opinion as a formative element in governance as central to the shift from a *sovereign* to a *normalizing* state in the nineteenth and

twentieth centuries. Civil society and public sphere that shape what is possible to do *and* to feel require exclusion of those who do not fit. *Respectability* defines the "enemy"; either one lacks it and must be controlled or one has it and must therefore be resisted. See Michel Foucault, *Discipline and Punish: The Birth of the Prison*, trans. Alan Sheridan (New York: Vintage, 1995); *History of Sexuality*, trans. Robert Hurley (New York: Pantheon, 1978); *Security, Territory, Population: Lectures at the Collège de France 1977–1978*, trans. Graham Burchell (New York: Picador, 2007); see also Erving Goffman, *Frame Analysis: An Essay on the Organization of Experience* (New York: Harper and Row, 1974); and Aldon Morris and Carol McClurg Mueller, eds., *Frontiers in Social Movement Theory* (New Haven, Conn.: Yale University Press, 1992).

21. Elihu Root, "The Mexican Resolution" (first published 1914), in Elihu Root, *Addresses on International Subjects* (Cambridge, Mass.: Harvard University Press, 1916), 327–335; "The Real Monroe Doctrine" (first published 1914), in Root, *Addresses on International Subjects*, 105–123; "Should International Law Be Codified?" (first published 1915), in Root, *Addresses on International Subjects*, 405–411; "Foreign Affairs" (first published 1916), in Root, *Addresses on International Subjects*, 427–447; Elihu Root, "The Campaign of 1916" (first published 1916), in Elihu Root, *The United States and the War, the Mission to Russia, Political Addresses*, (Cambridge, Mass.: Harvard University Press, 1918), 323–349; Elihu Root, *The Effect of Democracy on International Law* (Washington, D.C.: Carnegie Endowment for International Peace, 1917). On Root's conceptions of the proper relation of civil society and government in the United States, see Elihu Root, *Experiments in Government and the Essentials of the Constitution* (Princeton, N.J.: Princeton University Press, 1913).

22. Elihu Root, "The Need of Popular Understanding of International Law," *American Journal of International Law* 1 (1907), 1–2, reprinted in *Recommendations on International Law and Official Commentary Thereon of the Second Pan American Scientific Congress*, ed. James Brown Scott (New York: Oxford University Press, 1916), 1–3.

23. Elihu Root to Frederick P. Keppel, 1929, quoted in Philip C. Jessup, *Elihu Root* (New York: Dodd, Mead, 1938), 2:492.

24. Elihu Root, "President Root's Letter of Instructions," in Robert Bacon, *For Better Relations with Our Latin American Neighbors: A Journey to South America* (Washington, D.C.: Carnegie Endowment for International Peace, 1915), 3–4.

25. Carnegie Endowment, *Year Book for 1916*, 67–69; Harry Erwin Bard, *Intellectual and Cultural Relations Between the United States and the Other Republics of America* (Washington, D.C.: Carnegie Endowment for International Peace, 1914), 2–5.

26. Bacon, *For Better Relations with Our Latin American Neighbors*, 138.

27. In addition to the references already cited in note 22, see Elihu Root, "The Sanction of International Law," in Root, *Addresses on International Subjects*, 25–32; "The Relations Between International Tribunals of Arbitration and the Jurisdiction of National Courts," in Root, *Addresses on International Subjects*, 33–42; "The Problem of Private Codification in International Law," in Root, *Addresses on International Subjects*, 57–72; "Francis Lieber," in Root, *Addresses on International Subjects*, 89–104; "The Importance of Judicial Settlement," in Root, *Addresses on International Subjects*, 145–152; "Nobel Peace Prize Address," in Root, *Addresses on International Subjects*, 153–174; "The Outlook for International Law," in Root, *Addresses on International Subjects*, 391–404; "Should International Law Be Codified?" in Root, *Addresses on International Subjects*, 405–411.

28. J. Manuel Espinosa, *Inter-American Beginnings of U.S. Cultural Diplomacy, 1936–1948* (Washington, D.C.: Bureau of Educational and Cultural Affairs, U.S. Department of State, 1976), 47–49.

29. William Berrien, "The Study of Portuguese," in *A Handbook on the Teaching of Spanish and Portuguese, with Special Reference to Latin America*, ed. Henry Gratton Doyle (Boston: Heath, 1945), 44–49; Jacob Ornstein, "A Bird's-Eye View of Brazilian-Portuguese Studies in the United States," *Americas* 10 (1954), 463–470.

30. For an account of how the book came to be published, see Instituto de las Españas, "Palabras preliminares," in Gabriela Mistral, *Desolación* (New York: Instituto de las Españas, 1922), n.p. Mistral's first chapbook, *Sonetos de la muerte*, was published in Santiago, Chile, in 1914 in an

edition of four hundred copies. Typical of many books published in Spanish-speaking America at the time, publicity was by word of mouth and distribution relied on the author and others mailing copies to people they hoped might appreciate the work. Some of Mistral's early work was anthologized in U.S. publications. In 1920, Thomas Walsh included her work in his *Hispanic Anthology*, an eight-hundred-plus-page volume presenting Spanish poetry from the medieval *Lay of the Cid* to contemporary poets on both sides of the Atlantic in English translation. Three essays she had written on poetry and education appeared in *Inter-America*, a monthly magazine that the Pan American Union in cooperation with Doubleday, Page launched in 1917 to reprint articles from major Latin American periodicals in English translation.

31. "Gabriela," *Bulletin of the Pan American Union* 58 (July 1924), 652–653. The distinction between "Latin" and "Anglo-Saxon" civilizations was commonplace at the end of the nineteenth century and beginning of the twentieth, though not unchallenged. Edith Wharton in the preface to her 1919 book on France admitted that "use of the two is open to the easy derision of the scholar. Yet they are too convenient as symbols to be abandoned and are safe enough if, for instance, they are used simply as a loose way of drawing a line between . . . those whose social polity dates from the Forum, and those who still feel and legislate in terms of the primaeval forest" (Edith Wharton, *French Ways and Their Meaning* [New York: Appleton, 1919], viii).

32. Gabriela Mistral, "Message to American Youth on Pan American Day," *Bulletin of the Pan American Union* 65 (1931), 354–356.

33. Gabriela Mistral, *Selected Poems of Gabriela Mistral*, trans. Langston Hughes (Bloomington: Indiana University Press, 1957). Doris Dana published a book of her translations of Mistral's poetry in 1971 (*Selected Poems of Gabriela Mistral* [Baltimore: Johns Hopkins University Press, 1971]). Six other books appeared between 1993 and 2008.

34. Jonathan Cohen, "Toward a Common Destiny on the American Continent: The Pan Americanism of Gabriela Mistral," in *Gabriela Mistral: The Audacious Traveler*, ed. Marjorie Agosín (Athens: Ohio University Press, 2003), 1–46.

35. On the activities of the Carnegie Endowment for International Peace during the interwar period, see Merle Curti, *American Philanthropy Abroad* (New Brunswick, N.J.: Transaction, 1988; first published 1963).

36. José Vasconcelos's *Aspects of Mexican Civilization* and Manuel Gamio's *The Indian Basis of Mexican Civilization* appeared in a single volume (Chicago: University of Chicago Press, 1926), with Moisés Sáenz, *Some Mexican Problems* (Chicago: University of Chicago Press, 1926) completing the trilogy of lectures presented at the university. Gamio's books on Mexican migrant laborers are *Mexican Immigration to the United States: A Study of Human Migration and Adjustment* (Chicago: University of Chicago Press, 1930) and *The Mexican Immigrant, His Life-Story: Autobiographic Documents Collected by Manuel Gamio* (Chicago: University of Chicago Press, 1931).

37. Henry E. Armstrong, "Democracy and Science Must Make the New Mexico: Four Students of Her Problems Emphasize Also the Cultural Ability of Her Proletariat," *New York Times* (23 January 1927), Book Review sec., 3.

38. John Tebbel, *A History of Book Publishing in the United States*, vol. 3, *The Golden Age Between Two Wars* (New York: Bowker, 1978), 657–690. The Carnegie Corporation was the single largest funder of libraries in the United States prior to 1940 with policies that transformed both reading and publishing opportunities. See the sources in note 17.

39. Cover flap for Ricardo Güiraldes, *Don Segundo Sombra: Shadow on the Pampas*, trans. Harriet de Onís (New York: Farrar and Rinehart, 1935). In *South American Journey* (New York: Duell, Sloan and Pearce, 1943), Waldo Frank characterized Jorge Luis Borges as the best literary stylist among contemporary Argentinean authors but a writer solely of "fantasy and utter escape" (72). On Frank's efforts to translate Latin American literature in the 1930s, see Irene Rostagno, "Waldo Frank's Crusade for Latin American Literature," *Americas* 46 (July 1989), 41–69.

40. G.R.B.R., review of *Don Segundo Sombra: Shadows on the Pampas*, *Boston Transcript* (30 January 1935), sec. 2, p. 2; F. T. Marsh, untitled review, *New York Times* (6 January 1935), p. 5; Lewis Gannett, untitled review, *New York Herald Tribune* (16 January 1935), p. 17; Anita Brenner, untitled

review, *Nation* 140 (30 January 1935), 333. The famous Argentinean writer Jorge Luis Borges argued that the English translation of *Don Segundo Sombra* was superior to the Spanish original because the translator had replaced the "excesses" of the author's late nineteenth-century style with crisp modern English, making the story and characters more direct. As Borges put it, "English is an imperial language, which is to say a language that can express almost all of human experience and the very different ways in which one can be a man. There are dialects of English that can replace the exhausted Spanish of the cattle drivers of our Ricardo Güiraldes, but still precisely express their sentiments. I speak of the equestrian English of Montana, of Arizona, or of Texas, homes of incomparable horse riders—as Whitman said of the gaucho. . . . The American translator . . . could turn to an English perfect for being on horseback." Original Spanish: El idioma inglés es idioma imperial, vale decir, idioma que corresponde a casi todos los destinos humanos, a las maneras más diversas de ser un hombre. Hay una zona del inglés que puede superponerse con precisión al cansado español de los troperos de nuestro Ricardo Güiraldes. Hablo del inglés ecuestre de Montana, de Arizona o de Texas, madres de incomparables *rider of horses*—como dijo Whitman del gaucho. . . . El traductor americano . . . ha podido recurrir a un inglés que es bien de al caballo (Jorge Luis Borges, "*Don Segundo Sombra* en ingles," in Jorge Luis Borges, *Borges: Obras, reseñas y traducciones inéditas*, 2nd ed. [Buenos Aires: Atlántida, 1999], 205).

41. Waldo Frank, introduction, in Güiraldes, *Don Segundo Sombra: Shadows on the Pampas*, ix–x.

42. "President Taft Helps President Díaz," *Seattle Republican* (10 March 1911), p. 2. The database for Chronicling America: Historic American Newspapers reports that over sixty-seven thousand articles in U.S. newspapers were published on the Mexican revolution between 1910 and 1920. An overview of U.S. writing on the Mexican revolution can be found in John A. Britton, *Revolution and Ideology: Images of the Mexican Revolution in the United States* (Lexington: University Press of Kentucky, 1995).

43. On the translation, see Timothy Murad, "*Los de abajo* vs. *The Underdogs*: The Translation of Mariano Azuela's Masterpiece," *Hispania* 65 (1982), 554–561.

44. J.R.T., "Under Dogs (Book Review)," *Boston Transcript* (11 September 1929), sec. 2, p. 2; L. Gannett, untitled review of *The Underdogs*, *New York Herald Tribune* (25 August 1929), Book Review sec., p. 1; Waldo Frank, "Under Dogs (Book Review)," *New Republic* 60 (23 October 1929), 275.

45. Angel Rama, *The Lettered City* (Durham, N.C.: Duke University Press, 1996), 78–83; Carlos Real de Azúa, *Medio Siglo de Ariel: Su Significación y trascendencia literario-filosófica* (Montevideo: Academia Nacional de Letras, 2001; written in 1950), 50, 52.

46. The context for the publication of *Ulises criollo* and its appeal to readers in Mexico and other Spanish-speaking countries can be found in Sergio Pitol, "Liminar *Ulises criollo*," in José Vasconcelos, *Ulises criollo*, critical edition, ed. Claude Fell (Paris: ALLCA XX, 2000), xix–xxxiv, and Claude Fell, "Introducción del coordinador," in Vasconcelos *Ulises criollo* (2000), xxxv–lxvi. See also Joaquín Cárdenas Noriega, *José Vasconcelos, caudillo cultural: "Por mi raza hablará el espíritu"* (Oaxaca: Universidad José Vasconcelos de Oaxaca, 2002; first published 1982), 196–201.

47. The report was reprinted as "La industria editorial y la cultura," in Daniel Cosio Villegas's collection of essays, *Extremos de América* (Mexico City: Fondo de Cultura Económica, 1949), 235–263; see also Daniel Cosío Villegas, "España contra América en la industrial editorial," *Cuadernos Americanos* 8, no. 1 (January 1949), 74–88.

Chapter 2

1. John Reed, *Insurgent Mexico* (New York: Appleton, 1914). Following the success of his reporting on Mexico, Reed went to Europe to report on World War I and published a book on the eastern front. His star declined as rapidly as it rose in 1917, when he took a vocal stand against U.S. entry into the European war. He traveled to Russia to cover the revolution there. His book *Ten Days That Shook the World* presented the process that led to the Bolsheviks taking over the country. Reed

became a Leninist and helped to found the U.S. Communist Party after he returned home. He died in 1920 from typhus on a visit to Russia. See Robert A. Rosenstone, *Romantic Revolutionary: A Biography of John Reed* (Cambridge, Mass.: Harvard University Press, 1990), 149–169; Christine Stansell, *American Moderns: Bohemian New York and the Creation of a New Century* (New York: Metropolitan Books, 2000), 188–193; Daniel W. Lehman, *John Reed and the Writing of Revolution* (Athens: Ohio University Press, 2002), 94–128.

2. Wallace Thompson, *The Mexican Mind: A Study in National Psychology* (Boston: Little, Brown, 1922), 5.

3. "Thinks Oil Failure Would Aid Mexico: Wallace Thompson Tells City Club That Resultant Poverty Might Spell Progress," *New York Times* (7 February 1922), p. 30.

4. In addition to *The Mexican Mind*, Wallace Thompson wrote *The People of Mexico: Who They Are and How They Live* (New York: Harper's, 1921); *Trading with Mexico* (New York: Dodd, Mead, 1921); *Rainbow Countries of Central America* (New York: E. P. Dutton, 1926); *Greater America: An Interpretation of Latin America in Relation to Anglo-Saxon America* (New York: E. P. Dutton, 1932).

5. "Book Notes," *Political Science Quarterly* 37 (1922), 727.

6. Review of *The Mexican Mind: A Study of National Psychology*, *New York Times* (25 June 1922), p. 11.

7. Carleton Beals, *Mexico: An Interpretation* (New York: Huebsch, 1923); *The Church Problem in Mexico* (New York: Academy Press, 1926); *Brimstone and Chili: A Book of Personal Experiences in the Southwest and in Mexico* (New York: Knopf, 1927); *Mexican Maze* (Philadelphia: J. B. Lippincott, 1931); *Porfirio Díaz, Dictator of Mexico* (Philadelphia: J. B. Lippincott, 1932); *Banana Gold* (Philadelphia: J. B. Lippincott, 1932); *The Crime of Cuba* (Philadelphia: J. B. Lippincott, 1933); *Fire on the Andes* (Philadelphia: J. B. Lippincott, 1934); *Black River* (Philadelphia: J. B. Lippincott, 1934); *The Stones Awake* (Philadelphia: J. B. Lippincott, 1936); *America South* (Philadelphia: J. B. Lippincott, 1937); *The Coming Struggle for Latin America* (Philadelphia: J. B. Lippincott, 1938); *Pan America* (Boston: Houghton Mifflin, 1940); *Rio Grande to Cape Horn* (Boston: Houghton Mifflin, 1943); *Dawn over the Amazon* (New York: Duell, Sloan and Pearce, 1943); *What the South Americans Think of Us* (New York: McBride, 1945); *Lands of the Dawning Morrow: The Awakening from Rio Grande to Cape Horn* (Indianapolis: Bobbs-Merrill, 1948); *The Long Land: Chile* (New York: Coward-McCann, 1949).

8. Carleton Beals, *Glass Houses: Ten Years of Free-Lancing* (Philadelphia: J. B. Lippincott, 1938), 9.

9. Beals, *Mexico: An Interpretation*.

10. John A. Britton, *Carleton Beals: A Radical Journalist in Latin America* (Albuquerque: University of New Mexico Press, 1987), 52–55. For Beals's account of the controversy with Ambassador Wilson, see Beals, *Glass Houses*, 250–256.

11. "The Meaning of the Hearst Documents," *New Republic* 53 (18 January 1928), 243–244; Report of Special Committee to Investigate Propaganda or Money Alleged to Have Been Used by Foreign Governments to Influence United States Senators (Washington, D.C.: Government Printing Office, 1928). See also Beals, *Glass Houses*, 257–265.

12. Intervening in a Nicaraguan civil war, the United States occupied Nicaragua in 1912 and ran the country as a nominally independent protectorate until 1925. The election following the withdrawal of U.S. marines led to renewed civil war between the Liberal and Conservative Parties, each of which had formed a "constitutionalist" government. President Coolidge sent General Frank R. McCoy to Nicaragua to negotiate an end to the civil war. The two parties accepted U.S. proposals to disarm their armies, which would be combined into a new National Guard that the U.S. military was to train and professionalize. McCoy drafted new election laws, modeled on U.S. practices, and he remained in Nicaragua to oversee the elections while supervising the daily functions of the national government, in effect making him the unelected ruler of the country. U.S. marines returned to Nicaragua in 1926 to enforce the agreement. Sandino, who had been a commander in the Liberal army, rejected the agreement, claiming that the United States could not act as a fair broker given its long history of interference in Nicaraguan politics. He and a small army retreated into the northern

mountains to begin a war against foreign occupation that lasted until 1933, when the U.S. government withdrew its forces. Sandino disbanded his army and returned home to manage his coffee farm. In 1934, National Guard officers executed Sandino when he came to Managua, the country's capital, to meet with the president. For an overview of the U.S. war against Sandino, see Neill Macaulay, *The Sandino Affair* (Chicago: Quadrangle Books, 1967).

13. Carleton Beals, "With Sandino in Nicaragua," a series of five articles published in the *Nation* 22 February 1928, 29 February 1928, 7 March 1928, 14 March 1928, and 21 March 1928. On 4 April, Beals published an analysis of the election law that General Frank R. McCoy, President Coolidge's special envoy, had drafted for Nicaragua, and on 11 April, Beals reported on the murder of civilians by U.S. marines in the course of their campaign against Sandino as well as the extensive bombing of civilian homes by U.S. airplanes.

14. Carleton Beals, "This Is War, Gentlemen!" *Nation* (11 April 1928), 375.

15. Harold N. Denny, "Sandino Leads Band Against Americans," *New York Times* (10 February 1928), p. 4; "Yankee Tells of Visit to Sandino's Camp," *Chicago Daily Tribune* (10 February 1928), p. 9; Louis Rosenthal, "Rebels Frolic as Marines Nap 200 Yards Away," *Chicago Daily Tribune* (11 February 1928), p. 8; "New Fights Predicted by Sandino," *Los Angeles Times* (11 February 1928), p. 3; "Fighting in Managua Soon, Sandino Predicts," *Washington Post* (11 February 1928), p. 3.

16. For an example of a public debate between Beals and the State Department over how to interpret the situation in Nicaragua, see "Gives Symposium on Latin America: September Current History Presents Views of 19 Experts on Our Policy to Neighbors," *New York Times* (28 August 1927), sec. E, p. 3.

17. William W. Cumberland to secretary of state, Managua, 10 March 1928, 817.51/1921, General Records of the Department of State Relating to the Internal Affairs of Nicaragua, 1910–1929, rl. 89, M-632, RG 59, U.S. National Archives.

18. Stuart Chase, *Mexico: A Study of Two Americas* (New York: Macmillan, 1931).

19. Chase, *Mexico: A Study of Two Americas*, v.

20. Chase, *Mexico: A Study of Two Americas*, 207.

21. Chase, *Mexico: A Study of Two Americas*, 223.

22. Rexford G. Tugwell, Stuart Chase, and Robert W. Dunn, *Soviet Russia in the Second Decade: A Joint Survey by the Technical Staff of the First American Trade Union Delegation* (New York: John Day, 1928).

23. Waldo Frank, *Memoirs of Waldo Frank*, ed. Alan Trachtenberg (Amherst: University of Massachusetts Press, 1973), 132–133.

24. Waldo Frank, *América Hispana: A Portrait and a Prospect* (New York: Scribner's, 1931), 7, 9.

25. Frank, *América Hispana*, 87.

26. Frank, *América Hispana*, 128.

27. Ferner Nuhn, review of Waldo Frank, *América Hispana*, *Nation* 133 (20 September 1931), 337.

28. Mary Austin, untitled review, *New York Herald Tribune* (20 September 1931), Book Review sec., p. 1.

29. W. C. Abbott, review of Waldo Frank, *América Hispana*, *Yale Review* 21 (1932), 412.

30. José Carlos Mariátegui, untitled article from *Variedades*, reprinted in *Waldo Frank in America Hispana*, ed. M. J. Bernadete (New York: Instituto de las Españas en los Estados Unidos, 1931), 71; Luis Alberto Sánchez, untitled article from *Letras*, reprinted in Bernadete, *Waldo Frank in America Hispana*, 111.

31. Waldo Frank, unpublished typescript, 1 December 1957, Waldo Frank Papers, Department of Special Collections, University of Pennsylvania Libraries.

32. Casey Nelson Blake, *Beloved Community: The Cultural Criticism of Randolph Bourne, Van Wyck Brooks, Waldo Frank, and Lewis Mumford* (Chapel Hill: University of North Carolina Press, 1990), 35.

33. Blake, *Beloved Community*, 143–146.

34. Frank, *América Hispana*, 348–349.

35. Frank, *América Hispana*, 197.

36. The source is Frank, *Memoirs*, 159. See also Michael A. Ogorzaly, *Waldo Frank: Prophet of Hispanic Regeneration* (Lewisburg, Pa.: Bucknell University Press, 1994), 14.

37. Frank, *Memoirs*, 159–160.

38. For an excellent summary of Moisés Sáenz's priorities and the programs he developed to increase the self-sufficiency of Mexican communities, see Ruben Flores, *Backroads Pragmatists: Mexico's Melting Pot and Civil Rights in the United States* (Philadelphia: University of Pennsylvania Press, 2014), 28–35, 42–46, 56–60, 287–289. Sáenz outlined his vision of Mexican economic development in his book for U.S. readers, *Some Mexican Problems* (Chicago: University of Chicago Press, 1926); for his ideas on developing labor skills and improving productivity, see in particular 29–30, 33–53.

39. For a vivid example of Ocampo's disagreements with Frank over the authors he chose for translation into English, see Victoria Ocampo to Waldo Frank, 13 July 1931, Waldo Frank Papers.

40. On *Sur*, see John King, *Sur: A Study of the Argentine Literary Journal and Its Role in the Development of a Culture, 1931–1970* (Cambridge: Cambridge University Press, 1986); María Teresa Gramuglio, "Hacia una antología de *Sur*: Materiales para el debate," in *La cultura de un siglo: América latina en sus revistas* (Madrid: Alianza Editorial, 1999), 249–260; Rosalie Sitman, *Victoria Ocampo y Sur: Entre Europa y América* (Buenos Aires: Lumiere, 2003).

41. Victoria Ocampo, *Autobiografía*, selection, prologue, and notes by Francisco Ayala (Buenos Aires: Alianza Editorial, 1991), 197. Spanish text: Trabajá como si no pasara nada, como si nada te hubieron dicho, insensible a ese tipo de crítica.

Chapter 3

1. William Carlos Williams, *Autobiography* (New York: New Directions, 1951), 178. Williams used the American History Room at the New York Public Library to find the rare books and manuscripts he adapted for his book. On the influence of his parents' Puerto Rican, Caribbean, and Spanish-language backgrounds on Williams's writing, see Julio Marzán, *The Spanish American Roots of William Carlos Williams* (Austin: University of Texas Press, 1994); and Lisa Sánchez González, "Modernism and Boricua Literature: A Reconsideration of Arturo Schomburg and William Carlos Williams," *American Literary History* 13 (2001), 242–264. Literary historians studying Williams have often considered *In the American Grain* as a response to the publication of T. S. Eliot's *The Waste Land* in 1922, with its banishing of the Whitman, demotic tradition in U.S. poetry. Williams viewed this as an effort to subsume U.S. literature into high European literary traditions, and from this perspective, *In the American Grain* was an effort to reclaim the independent character of American writing. For more on this, see James E. B. Breslin, *William Carlos Williams: An American Artist* (Chicago: University of Chicago Press, 1985), 37–38, 61–65; and Paul Mariani, *William Carlos Williams: A New World Naked* (New York: McGraw-Hill, 1981), 290ff.

2. William Carlos Williams, *Yes, Mrs. Williams: A Personal Record of My Mother* (New York: McDowell, Obolensky, 1959), 4.

3. William Carlos Williams, *In the American Grain* (New York: New Directions, 1939; first published 1925), 188–189.

4. Williams, *In the American Grain*, 11.

5. Williams, *In the American Grain*, 27.

6. Williams, *In the American Grain*, 39.

7. Williams, *In the American Grain*, 59.

8. Williams, *In the American Grain*, 109.

9. Williams, *Autobiography*, 361.

10. Williams, *In the American Grain*, 213.

11. Williams, *In the American Grain*, 177. On gender as the organizing principle for *In the American Grain*, see Bryce Conrad, "Engendering History: The Sexual Structure of William Carlos

Williams' *In the American Grain*," *Twentieth Century Literature* 35 (1989), 254–287; and Linda A. Kinnahan, *Poetics of the Feminine: Authority and Literary Tradition in William Carlos Williams, Mina Loy, Denise Levertov, and Kathleen Fraser* (Cambridge: Cambridge University Press, 1994), 75–117.

12. Williams, *Yes, Mrs. Williams*, 30, 35.

13. Williams, *Yes, Mrs. Williams*, 136.

14. Williams, *In the American Grain*, 121. On *mestizaje*, see Olivia Gall, ed., *Racismo, mestizaje y modernidad: Visiones desde latitudes diversas* (Mexico City: Universidad Nacional Autónoma de México, 2007); Tace Hedrick, *Mestizo Modernism: Race, Nation, and Identity in Latin American Culture, 1900–1940* (New Brunswick, N.J.: Rutgers University Press, 2003); Marilyn Grace Miller, *Rise and Fall of the Cosmic Race: The Cult of Mestizaje in Latin America* (Austin: University of Texas Press, 2004); José Vasconcelos, "The Latin-American Basis of Mexican Civilization," and Manuel Gamio, "The Indian Basis of Mexican Civilization," in José Vasconcelos and Manuel Gamio, *Aspects of Mexican Civilization* (Chicago: University of Chicago Press, 1926).

15. Williams, *In the American Grain*, 195.

16. Williams, *In the American Grain*, 136.

17. Williams, *In the American Grain*, 108.

18. William Carlos Williams, "To Elsie," no. 18 of *Spring and All*, in William Carlos Williams, *The Collected Poems of William Carlos Williams*, vol 1, 1909–1939, eds. A. Walton Litz and Christopher MacGowan (New York: New Directions, 1986; originally published 1923), 217.

19. Williams, *In the American Grain*, 197, 196.

20. William Carlos Williams, "A Democratic Party Poem" (ca. 1928), manuscript in the William Carlos Williams Papers, Poetry Collection of the Lockwood Memorial Library, University of Buffalo, reprinted in Mariani, *William Carlos Williams,* 268–269.

21. William Carlos Williams, "The Writers of the American Revolution," in William Carlos Williams, *Selected Essays* (New York: New Directions, 1969; essay originally published in 1925), 39.

22. William Carlos Williams, untitled review, *New York Post* (31 December 1927), p. 10.

23. Waldo Frank to William Carlos Williams, 1 July 1926, in Williams Papers.

24. "American Pot-Pourri," *New York Times* (7 February 1926), p. 21.

25. See in particular the reviews in the *Nation* (14 April 1926, p. 413), the *New Republic* (24 March 1926, p. 148), and the *Saturday Review of Literature* (19 December 1925, p. 425).

26. Summary of plans for second volume in Williams, *Autobiography*, 236. Williams wrote extensively about the Mexican revolution in *The Great American Novel*, published in a limited edition of three hundred copies in 1923.

27. Bram Dijkstra, *Cubism, Stieglitz, and the Early Poetry of William Carlos Williams* (Princeton, N.J.: Princeton University Press, 1969), 9, 80, 134–139; Hugh Kenner, *A Homemade World: The American Modernist Writer* (New York: Morrow, 1975), 58–62.

28. The emphasis on failure within *In the American Grain* is central to the arguments that Alan Holder made in "In the American Grain: Williams Carlos Williams on the American Past," *American Quarterly* 19 (1967), 499–515.

29. On Williams's "proletarian" writing in the 1930s, see Bob Johnson, "'A Whole Synthesis of His Time': Political Ideology and Cultural Politics in the Writings of William Carlos Williams, 1929–1939," *American Quarterly* 54 (2002), 179–215. On Williams's relationship with James Laughlin and New Directions, see Stephen Cushman, "The Differing Impulses of William Carlos Williams," *American Literary History* 3 (1991), 614–622.

30. Williams discussed his reasons for coming to Puerto Rico despite his otherwise busy schedule in an interview for *Alma Latina* (San Juan, Puerto Rico, 22 March 1941), p. 51, clipping in William Carlos Williams Archives, Beinecke Rare Book and Manuscript Library, Yale University.

31. Octavio Paz, "La flor saxífraga: W. C. Williams," in Octavio Paz, *Excursiones e incursiones: Dominio extranjero*, vol. 2 of *Obras completas de Octavio Paz* (Barcelona: Círculo de Lectores, 1994), 311.

32. Paz, "La flor saxífraga," 295. Original Spanish text: América [dijo Williams] no es una realidad dada sino algo que entre todos hacemos con nuestros manos, nuestros ojos, nuestro cerebro

y nuestros labios. La realidad de América es material, mental, visual, y, sobre todo, verbal—hable castellano, ingles, portugués o francés, el hombre americano habla una lengua distinta a la europea original. . . . América es una realidad que decimos.

33. Williams noted this praise later in *Paterson*, his epic history of northern New Jersey.

34. Prior to his trip to Puerto Rico in 1941, Williams went to Mexico briefly while he was an intern training at the French Hospital and Nursery. A wealthy Mexican landowner visiting New York City fell ill and wanted a Spanish-speaking physician to treat him. Williams accompanied his patient back to Mexico. See Williams, *Autobiography*, 73–74, for Williams's comments on this experience.

35. Menotti del Picchia, Plinio Salgado, and Cassiano Ricardo, *O Curupira e o Carão* (São Paulo: Editorial Helios, 1927), 43.

36. Oswald de Andrade, "Manifesto Antropofago," *Revista de Antropofagia* (May 1928), 3, 7. Original Portuguese text: Só a antropofagia nos une. Socialmente. Economicamente. Philosophicamente. Única lei do mundo. . . . Só me interessa o que não é meu. Lei do homem. Lei do antropófago. . . . Só as puras elites conseguiram realizar a antropofagia carnal, que traz em si o mais alto sentido da vida. . . . De carnal, ele se torna eletivo e cria a amizade. Afetivo, o amor. Especulativo, a ciência. Desvia-se e transfere-se.

37. Gilberto Freyre, *Casa Grande e Senzala* (Rio de Janeiro: José Olympio, 1933), 83–84. Original Portuguese text: misturando-se gostosamente com mulheres de cor logo ao primeiro contato e multiplicando-se em filhos mestiços.

38. Freyre, *Casa Grande e Senzala*, 404. Original Portuguese text: Muito menino brasileiro do tempo da escravidão foi criado inteiramente pelas mucamas. Raro o que não foi amamentado por negra. Que não aprendeu a falar mais com a escrava do que com o pai e a mãe. Que não cresceu entre moleques. Brincando com moleques. Aprendendo safadeza com eles e com as negras da copa. E cedo perdendo a virgindade. Virgindade do corpo. Virgindade de espírito.

39. Édouard Glissant, *Le discours antillais* (Paris: Gallimard, 1997).

40. Marzán, *The Spanish American Roots of William Carlos Williams*, xiii–xv.

41. The publication of Valéry Larbaud's famous French translation of Herman Melville's *Moby-Dick* in 1923 alerted North Americans to a book that had been out of print since the 1850s and was important for the rise of Melville's reputation as one of the most important U.S. writers of the nineteenth century. On Larbaud's translations, see Georges May, "Valéry Larbaud: Translator and Scholar," *Yale French Studies* 6 (1950), 83–90; George Steiner, *After Babel: Aspects of Language and Translation*, 2nd ed. (Oxford: Oxford University Press, 1992), 284–289.

42. Williams, *In the American Grain*, 108–109.

43. Williams, no. 1, *Spring and All*, in Williams, *Collected Poems*, vol. 1, 183.

Chapter 4

1. Diego Rivera, with Gladys March, *My Art, My Life: An Autobiography* (New York: Citadel Press, 1960), 174.

2. The Brazilian writer Monteiro Lobato had described Helen Wills Moody as the epitome of the American new woman: "these charming creatures, unique in the world . . . the prettiest beings on Earth, most perfect body, physically slim, solid . . . self-assured . . . these flowers of flesh . . . who trot in the street to their clerical work, where they walk out on men, and who keep a series of boyfriends" (José Bento Monteiro Lobato, *America: Estados Unidos de 1929* [São Paulo: Editora Brasiliense, 1948], 54).

3. Allen C. Harris, "Art to the Rescue of Tired Businessmen," *Arts and Architecture* 37 (December 1931), 32.

4. Rivera, *My Art, My Life*, 178.

5. On muralism in the postrevolutionary period, see Alicia Azuela de la Cueva, *Arte y poder: Renacimiento artístico y revolución social, México, 1910–1945* (Zamora: El Colegio de Michoacán,

2005); and Mary K. Coffey, *How Revolutionary Art Became Official Culture: Murals, Museums, and the Mexican State* (Durham, N.C.: Duke University Press, 2012). Azuela makes a compelling case that most government-sponsored mural art in Mexico was conservative aesthetically and avoided strong political messages. The three most famous Mexican muralists, Rivera, Orozco, and Siqueiros were unusual in their approaches, part of what made them stand out internationally. For other interpretations, see José Clemente Orozco, "Autobiografía de José Clemente Orozco: La mesa puesta," *Excelsior* (13 March 1942), online at http://icaadocs.mfah.org; Jean Charlot, *The Mexican Mural Renaissance, 1920–1925* (New Haven, Conn.: Yale University Press, 1967); Shifra M. Goldman, *Mexican Muralism: Its Social-Educative Roles in Latin America and the United States* (Austin: University of Texas Press, 1980); David Craven, *Diego Rivera as Epic Modernist* (New York: G. K. Hall, 1997); David Craven, "Postcolonial Modernism in the Work of Diego Rivera and José Carlos Mariátegui, or New Light on a Neglected Relationship," *Third Text* 15 (2001), 3–16; Alberto Híjar Serrano, "The Latin American Left and the Contribution of Diego Rivera to National Liberation," *Third Text* 19 (2005), 637–646. MacKinley Helm, in *Modern Mexican Painters* (New York: Harper Brothers, 1941), provided readers in the United States with a breezy introduction to some three dozen Mexican artists American critics, dealers, and curators had recognized as interesting. Helm devoted a chapter each to Rivera, Orozco, and Siqueiros, but most of the painters discussed in the book were not associated with the mural movement.

6. "The Museum's Activities, 1932–1933," *Bulletin of the Museum of Modern Art* 1 (February 1934), 1–2, 4; Elodie Courter, "Circulating Exhibition," *Bulletin of the Museum of Modern Art* 1 (March 1934), 2, 4; "Circulating Exhibitions, 1931–1954," *Bulletin of the Museum of Modern Art* 21 (Summer 1954), 21, 28.

7. Terry Smith, *Making the Modern: Industry, Art, and Design in America* (Chicago: University of Chicago Press, 1993), 236–245.

8. Rudolf Hess, "The Tragedy of Rivera," *Argus* 4 (1928), 1–2.

9. Frances Flynn Paine, *Diego Rivera* (New York: Museum of Modern Art, 1931), 35, 30.

10. Rivera, *My Art, My Life*, 181.

11. The definitive book on the work that Rivera, Orozco, and Siqueiros did in the United States is Laurance P. Hurlburt, *The Mexican Muralists in the United States* (Albuquerque: University of New Mexico Press, 1989).

12. On the Morrow family collection of Mexican art, which was only one of several collecting emphases, see *Casa Mañana: The Morrow Collection of Mexican Popular Arts* (Albuquerque: University of New Mexico Press for Mead Art Museum, Amherst College, 2002). On Dwight Morrow's goals as ambassador to Mexico, see Joaquín Cárdenas, *Morrow, Calles y el PRI: Según los archivos de Washington, D.C.* (Mexico City: Editorial PAC, 1986).

13. Elizabeth Fuentes Rojas, *Diego Rivera en San Francisco: Una historia artística y documental* (Guanajuato: Gobierno del Estado de Guanajuato, 1991), 9–19; Masha Zakheim, *Diego Rivera en San Francisco*, trans. Antonio Saborit (Mexico City: Círculo de Art, 1998), n.p. For a record of Stackpole's efforts to mediate between Rivera and his potential San Francisco patrons and of Rivera's efforts to develop his California contacts, see Ralph Stackpole to Diego Rivera, 26 September 1926; Diego Rivera to Ralph Stackpole, October 1926; Rivera to Stackpole, 13 October 1926; Rivera to Stackpole, 15 December 1926; Rivera to Stackpole, 24 December 1926; Rivera to Stackpole, 8 February 1927; Rivera to Stackpole, 3 May 1930; Ralph Stackpole Papers, Bancroft Library, University of California, Berkeley.

14. On Gerstle, Bender, and Pflueger and their respective roles in the San Francisco arts community, see Anthony W. Lee, *Painting on the Left: Diego Rivera, Radical Politics, and San Francisco's Public Murals* (Berkeley: University of California Press, 1999), 47–56.

15. On Rivera's relations with the U.S. Communist Party, see Lee, *Painting on the Left*, 52–55; Smith, *Making the Modern*, 236; Linda Bank Downs, *Diego Rivera: The Detroit Industry Murals* (New York: Norton, 1999), 53–54. The Mexican Communist Party expelled Rivera in 1929 on the grounds that he had accepted an appointment from the government as director of the San Carlos Academy after the Mexican government had outlawed the Mexican Communist Party. The division between Rivera

and the party rested on his having sided with Leon Trotsky in the schism dividing the Soviet Union and the world communist movement between supporters of Trotsky and supporters of Joseph Stalin.

16. "Fresco Painting Resurrected: Art, Centuries Dormant, Revived by Mexican Genius," *Los Angeles Times* (18 June 1932), sec. 2, p. 2; "California Group Studies Fresco Technique with Siqueiros," *Art Digest* (1 August 1932), 13.

17. "Great Art Work to Be Unveiled: Ceremony for Siqueiros's Fresco Scheduled for Tonight," *Los Angeles Times* (9 October 1932), sec. 1, p. 11; "Siqueiros Plaza Art Dedicated: Fresco of Jungle Scene Hailed by Dean Cornwell as Start of New Movement," *Los Angeles Times* (10 October 1932), sec. 2, p. 2; Arthur Millier, "Power Unadorned Marks Olvera Street Fresco: 'Tropical Mexico' Painting by Siqueiros Is Strong Tragic Conception of His Native Land," *Los Angeles Times* (16 October 1932), sec. 3, pp. 16, 20.

18. Quoted in Shifra M. Goldman, "Siqueiros and Three Early Murals in Los Angeles," *Art Journal* 33 (1974), 325.

19. E. F. P. Coughlin, "Deportation Looms for Noted Mexican Artist on Eve of Greatest Triumph," *Los Angeles Daily News* (8 October 1932), C1, C5; Arthur Millier, "Brush Strokes: Fresco Whitewashed," *Los Angeles Times* (18 March 1934), sec. A, p. 8; Elso Rogo, "David Alfaro Siqueiros," *Parnassus* (1 April 1934), 5–7. In 2012, conservation of *Tropical America* had reached a stage where the painting can once again be viewed. The mural cannot be restored to its original appearance without repainting it, which would require eliminating all of Siqueiros's original work that still remains.

20. Laurance Hurlburt, "The Siqueiros Experimental Workshop: New York, 1936," *Art Journal* 35 (1976), 237–246; Hurlburt, *The Mexican Muralists in the United States*, 220–231.

21. Alfred H. Barr, Jr., foreword, in *The Latin American Collection of the Museum of Modern Art*, ed. Lincoln Kirstein (New York: Museum of Modern Art, 1943), 3.

22. On Valentiner's vision for the Detroit Institute of Arts, see Margaret Sterne, *The Passionate Eye: The Life of William Valentiner* (Detroit: Wayne State University Press, 1980).

23. Grace McCann Morley, "Art, Artists, Museums, and the San Francisco Museum of Art," interview by Suzanne B. Riess, Regional Oral History Office, University of California, Berkeley, 1960, 43.

24. For the exhibit that Morley organized, see Grace McCann Morley, *Emilio Pettoruti of Argentina* (San Francisco: San Francisco Museum of Art, 1943). On the dispute between Barr and Morley, see Alfred H. Barr, Jr., to Grace McCann Morley, 16 November 1942; Grace McCann Morley to René d'Harnoncourt, 23 November 1942; Alfred H. Barr, Jr., to René d'Harnoncourt, 19 January 1943; René d'Harnoncourt Papers, folder II.3, Museum of Modern Art Archives. See also Luisa Fabiana Serviddio, "Intercambios culturales panamericanos durante la Segunda Guerra Mundial: El viaje de Pettoruti en los Estados Unidos," in *Arte argentino y latinoamericano del siglo XX: Sus interrelaciones*, ed. María Amalia García, Luisa Fabiana Serviddio, and María Cristina Rossi (Buenos Aires: Fundación Espigas, 2004), 55–82.

25. Morley, "Art, Artists, Museums, and the San Francisco Museum of Art," 25–26.

26. Rockwell Kent, "Brazilian Report," in Rockwell Kent Papers, reel 5164, frames 186–210, Archives of American Art, Smithsonian Institution. Karin Philippov discusses Kent's relationship with Osvaldo Aranha and how the trip fit into debates at the highest level of the Brazilian government over how best to maintain good relations with the United States in "'Brazil and Vargas': Reflexões sobre o Relatório de Rockwell Kent após sua Viagem ao Rio de Janeiro em 1937," *Revista de História da Arte e Arqueologia* 7 (2007), 99–102.

27. On his feeling that they shared a common cause, see Cândido Portinari to Rockwell Kent, 5 April 1938, Rockwell Kent Papers, reel 5164, frame 160.

28. Rockwell Kent to Cândido Portinari, 22 January 1938, Rockwell Kent Papers, reel 5223, frames 1345–1346; Gustavo Campanema, minister of education, to Rockwell Kent, 23 February 1938, Rockwell Kent Papers, reel 5164, frames 166–167; Cândido Portinari to Rockwell Kent, 7 March 1938, Rockwell Kent Papers, reel 5223, frames 1347–1348; Rockwell Kent to "Exmo. Ministro de Educación" [*sic*], 18 May 1938, Rockwell Kent Papers, reel 5164, frame 175; Rockwell Kent to Cândido Portinari, 18 May 1938, Rockwell Kent Papers, reel 5223, frames 1349–1350.

29. In 1941 and 1942, Kent was still sending photographs of Portinari paintings to the Museum of Modern Art encouraging it to exhibit or purchase the works; Elodie Courter to Rockwell Kent, 21 April 1941; Amy Abraham to Rockwell Kent, 10 August 1942; Rockwell Kent to Amy Abraham, 13 August 1942; Rockwell Kent Papers, reel 5214, frames 317, 323, 324.

30. Cândido Portinari to Rockwell Kent, 7 July 1941, Rockwell Kent Papers, reel 5223, frame 1439.

31. In 1935, Portinari submitted a painting to the Carnegie Institute's International Exposition of Painting, held biennially in Pittsburgh. Portinari's painting won second prize. He was not in a position to follow up on this success, but as people like Kent began working on his behalf, the honor reinforced that he was a painter who had already made an impression, however brief, on American curators.

32. Florence Horn, "Brazil: Paintings by Candido Portinari," *Fortune* 19 (June 1939), 42–43.

33. Florence Horn to Cândido Portinari, April 1939, Acervo de Cândido Portinari, Pontifícia Universidade Católica–Rio de Janeiro, CO-5001; Horn to Portinari, 12 April 1939, Acervo de Cândido Portinari, CO-4965; Florence Horn to Maria Portinari, 14 May 1939, Acervo de Cândido Portinari, CO-5015.

34. Doris Brian, "Portinari Steams into Port," *Art News* 39 (October 1940), 8–9, quote on 8.

35. Milton Brown, "Exhibitions: New York," *Parnassus* 12 (November 1940), 37–39, quote on 37. See also Doris Brian, "Latin American Exhibit: Five Countries at Riverside Museum," *Art News* 38 (August 1940), 9; Robert Chester Smith, "The Art of Candido Portinari," *Carnegie Magazine* 14 (January 1941), 244–246; "Brazilian Artist: Portinari," *Minneapolis Institute of Arts Bulletin* 30 (12 April 1941), 73–75; Webb Rhodes, "Portinari of Brazil at Museum of Modern Art," *Arts and Decoration* 52 (November 1940), 15; "Portinari Exhibition, San Francisco," *California Arts and Architecture* 58 (July 1941), 5.

36. Alonzo J. Aden to Cândido Portinari, 22 November 1940, Acervo de Cândido Portinari, CO-21.

37. "Brazil Artist Is Here for His One-Man Show," *New York Herald Tribune* (18 September 1940), p. 18.

38. Florence Horn, "Portinari of Brazil," *Bulletin of the Museum of Modern Art* 7 (October 1940), 3.

39. "Brazil Artist Is Here for His One-Man Show."

40. Horn, "Portinari of Brazil," 6. The details of Portinari's humble origins and his struggle to overcome poverty were repeated almost every time in U.S. publications about the artist. Manuel Bandeira's introduction to the booklet the Brazilian Ministry of Education published on the completion of the murals for the ministry's new building mentions in passing that Portinari's parents were agricultural laborers in São Paulo's coffee-growing region. Bandeira did not highlight the family's poverty as presumably Brazilians would take the fact as a given. The central element in Bandeira's account is that Portinari returned from his studies in Europe unaffected by the art he encountered there. He had to escape Europe in order to construct his own style, a style that was personal and therefore truly national. Portinari had learned that the European masters offered little that was relevant to the unique characteristics of Brazilian life; see Bandeira's untitled introductory essay to *Portinari* (Rio de Janeiro: Ministério da Educação, 1939), n.p.

41. *Portinari: His Life and Art* (Chicago: University of Chicago Press, 1940); for a discussion of Kent's framing of his introduction to the book on Portinari, see Florence Horn to Rockwell Kent, undated [1939], Rockwell Kent Papers, reel 5223, frame 1362; Rockwell Kent to Florence Horn, 21 September 1939, Rockwell Kent Papers, reel 5223, frame 1363. Josias Leão, vice-consul of the Brazilian Consulate in Chicago and a friend of Portinari, had originally proposed the book and raised money to support the publication among Portinari's friends and collectors in Brazil. Given the high cost of publication in the United States, the funds collected in Brazil were inadequate for producing a book in the United States. Leão then convinced the University of Chicago Press to publish the book (Josias Leão to Rockwell Kent, 25 April 1940, 12 May 1940, and 4 October 1940; Rockwell Kent to Josias Leão, 3 May 1940, 8 October 1940, and 11 October 1940; Rollin D. Hemens, University of Chi-

cago Press, to Rockwell Kent, 10 July 1940 and 4 November 1940; Rockwell Kent to Rollin D. Hemens, 3 November 1940; Rockwell Kent Papers, reel 5223, frames 1397–1402, 1405, 1412, 1416–1417,
1421, 1427).

42. Rockwell Kent, "Portinari—His Art," in *Portinari: His Life and Art*, 8.

43. Kent, "Portinari—His Art," 9, 6.

44. Roosevelt articulated the Four Freedoms in his State of the Union address in January 1941,
online at http://americanrhetoric.com/speeches/fdrthefourfreedoms.htm.

45. Maureen Hart Hennessey and Anne Knutson, "The Four Freedoms," in *Norman Rockwell:
Pictures for the American People* (New York: Harry N. Abrams, 1999), 94–102.

46. Florence Horn described to Portinari an encounter that she had with MacLeish that illustrated the deep personal enthusiasm he had for the painter's work; Florence Horn to Cândido Portinari, November 1941, Acervo de Cândido Portinari, CO-5013.

47. "Art: In Congress' Library," *Time* 39 (5 January 1942), 67; Mario Pedrosa, "Portinari: From
Brodowski to the Library of Congress," *Bulletin of the Pan American Union* 76 (April 1942), 199–
213; Frederic Allen Whiting, Jr., "Portinari's Murals at Washington," *Magazine of Art* 35 (February 1942), 64–66. The Brazilian government reciprocated the invitation Portinari had received by
inviting the American artist George Biddle to paint two murals in the lobby of the National Library
in Rio de Janeiro, unveiled in December 1942. Biddle's murals portrayed the conflict between "Charity" and "Death" under way in the world. In his presentation, Charity's victory came as a result of
the "wisdom" gained from culture.

48. "Art: In Congress' Library," 67.

Chapter 5

1. On the history of U.S. government cultural exchange programs, see Richard T. Arndt, *The
First Resort of Kings: American Cultural Diplomacy in the Twentieth Century* (Washington, D.C.:
Potomac Books, 2005); Frank A. Ninkovich, *The Diplomacy of Ideas: U.S. Foreign Policy and Cultural Relations, 1938–1950* (Cambridge: Cambridge University Press, 1981); J. Manuel Espinosa,
Inter-American Beginnings of U.S. Cultural Diplomacy, 1936–1948 (Washington, D.C.: Bureau of Educational and Cultural Affairs, Department of State, 1976), a semiofficial history written by a staff
member of the Division of Cultural Relations (subsequently renamed the Division of Cultural Affairs before being incorporated into the Bureau of Educational and Cultural Affairs); Ruth Emily
McMurray and Muna Lee, *The Cultural Approach: Another Way in International Relations* (Chapel
Hill: University of North Carolina Press,1947), a comparison of U.S. cultural exchange efforts with
those of several other major world powers written by veterans of the U.S. program.

2. Richard Pattee, "The Role of the Teacher of Spanish in the Promotion of Inter-American Cultural Relations," *Hispania* 22 (1939), 236.

3. Pattee's memo is in the papers of the U.S. Department of State, RG 59, decimal file for 1930–
1939, 841.43/30, National Archives, Washington, D.C.; reproduced in full in Espinosa, *Inter-
American Beginnings of U.S. Cultural Diplomacy*, 167–169. See also Richard Pattee, "Intellectual
Cooperation Between the United States and Latin America," RG 59, 810.42711/492-3/4; Helen R.
Pinkney, "The Division of Cultural Cooperation," unpublished TS, December 1945, in RG 59, War
History Branch Studies, box 10: CU file.

4. Quotes from Richard Pattee, untitled review of Dantès Bellegarde, *La nation haïtienne*, in
Journal of Negro History 23 (1938), 383.

5. For official statements of the Division of Cultural Relations objectives, see Ben M. Cher-
rington, "The Division of Cultural Relations," *Public Opinion Quarterly* 3 (1939), 136–138; "Cultural
Ties That Bind in the Relations of the American Nations," *Hispania* 22 (1939), 243–250; "Editorial:
Education and Cultural Relations," *Phi Delta Kappan* 22 (November 1939), 75–76. See also Rich-
ard T. Arndt, "Welles, MacLeish, and Fulbright as Architect-Exemplars of Early Postwar Cultural
Diplomacy," online at http://streitcouncil.org/uploads/PDF/As%20Architect-Exemplars%20-%20

Arndt.pdf; and Arndt, *The First Resort of Kings*, 75–97. State Department programs built on principles of exchange moving in both directions have been overshadowed in the historical literature by discussion of the Office of Inter-American Affairs (OIAA), housed in the White House, under the direction of Nelson Rockefeller, who reported directly to the president. OIAA cultural programs focused on projecting U.S. positions into Latin America, but also included sending U.S. writers, artists, filmmakers, and photographers to Latin America to develop work for U.S. audiences about their allies in the Pan American Union. OIAA activities included commercial programs, as well as overseeing contractors constructing military bases, launching public health programs, mitigating crises caused by interruptions in prewar trade or credit relations, and in general assuring that U.S. strategic goals in Latin America remained on track. One of its major goals was the removal of pro-Axis employees from U.S. firms operating in Latin America as well as developing a blacklist of Latin American firms and individuals identified as sympathetic to the German, Italian, or Japanese governments. The OIAA had a maximum of fourteen hundred employees, and like the Division of Cultural Relations, the OIAA relied on U.S. and foreign nongovernmental entities, as well as Latin American government agencies, to accomplish its extensive objectives. On the OIAA, see Cary Reich, *The Life of Nelson A. Rockefeller: Worlds to Conquer, 1942–45* (New York: Doubleday, 1996), 189–261; Gisela Cramer and Ursula Prutsch, "Nelson A. Rockefeller's Office of Inter-American Affairs (1940–1946) and Record Group 229," *Hispanic American Historical Review* 86 (2006), 785–806; Claude C. Erb, "Prelude to Point Four: The Institute of Inter-American Affairs," *Diplomatic History* 9 (1985), 249–269. On the conflicts between the Office of Inter-American Affairs and other federal agencies, see Reich, *The Life of Nelson A. Rockefeller*; Office of Inter-American Affairs, *History of the Office of the Coordinator of Inter-American Affairs: Historical Reports on War Administration* (Washington, D.C.: GPO, 1947), 181–220.

6. Harry Domincovich, "Latin American Literature for the English Classroom," *English Journal* 31 (1942), 590–597.

7. See for example in the field of visual art, "Conference on Inter-American Relations in the Field of Art: Analysis and Digest of the Conference Proceedings [11 and 12 October 1939]" (Washington, D.C.: Department of State, January 1940), and "Continuation Committee of the Conference on Inter-American Relations in the Field of Art: Minutes of the Meeting of February 15–16, 1940" (Washington, D.C.: Department of State, February 1940), available at the International Center for the Arts of the Americas at the Fine Arts Museum, Houston, records 837785 and 837946.

8. On U.S. conceptions underlying the organization of the United Nations as a replacement for the League of Nations, see Mark Mazower, *Governing the World: The History of an Idea, 1815 to the Present* (New York: Penguin Books, 2012), 191–213. On hemispheric defense planning, see David G. Haglund, *Latin America and the Transformation of U.S. Strategic Thought, 1936–1940* (Albuquerque: University of New Mexico Press, 1984).

9. Stanley E. Hilton, "Argentine Neutrality, September, 1939–June, 1940: A Re-Examination," *Americas* 22 (1966), 252–256.

10. Jorge Luis Borges, "Notas: Los Libros," *Sur* 70 (July 1940), 62. Original Spanish text: Escribo en julio de 1940; cada mañana la realidad se parece más a una pesadilla. Sólo es posible la lectura de páginas que no aluden siquiera a la realidad [como los] problemas frívolos de Queen.

11. Benjamin Fondane, "En las riberas del Iliso," *Sur* 70 (July 1940), 31, 37–38, quote on 31. Original Spanish text: Estoy *forzado* a aceptarlo. Pero nadie, jamás, me podrá *persuadir* de que ese hecho sea digno del predicado de la verdad.

12. Victoria Ocampo, "Notas: Cinematógrafo, *The Grapes of Wrath*," *Sur* 70 (July 1940), 91–98, quote on 97; originally published in *La Nación* (Buenos Aires, 21 July 1940). Original Spanish text: El que se nos da despierta un respeto conmovido y una estima profunda hacia la nación suficientemente fuerte, libre y segura de sí mismo para permitir esta *muestra* (*mostra!*), esta divulgación en su proprio territorio, y en los ajenos, de tan doloroso y humillante documento social, humillante para sistemas (¿u hombres?) que no han llegado aún a remediar tales injusticias. . . . ¿Qué nación, fuera de una gran nación democrática, permitiría la exhibición de un *mea culpa* como *The Grapes of Wrath*?

13. Archibald MacLeish, "The Art of the Good Neighbor," *Nation* 150 (10 February 1940), 170–172.

14. MacLeish, "The Art of the Good Neighbor," 171. Published in Spanish as Archibald MacLeish, "El Arte de la Buena Vecindad," *Sur* 73 (October 1940), 70.

15. On Latin American appreciation for Langston Hughes, see Richard Jackson, "The Shared Vision of Langston Hughes and Black Hispanic Writers," *Black American Literature Forum* 15 (1981), 89–92; Vera M. Kutzinski, "Yo también soy América: Langston Hughes Translated," *American Literary History* 18 (2006), 550–578; Edward J. Mullen, *Langston Hughes in the Hispanic World and Haiti* (Hamdon, Conn.: Archon Books, 1977).

16. Transcript of the evening published under the title "Debates sobre temas sociológicas: Relaciones interamericanas," *Sur* 72 (September 1940), 100–123.

17. Quote on 108. Original Spanish text quoted: Por primera vez se han oído con toda su intensidad los acentos de los humildes de todas las razas, blanca y de color. A fuller expression of Arciniegas's argument made at this public meeting in Buenos Aires can be found in Germán Arciniegas's address to a conference on intellectual cooperation that the Pan American Union organized in Havana in November 1941, "Discurso," *Proceedings of the Second International Conference on Intellectual Cooperation* (Washington, D.C.: Pan American Union, 1942), n.p.

18. Doris Meyer, *Victoria Ocampo: Against the Wind and the Tide* (New York: George Braziller, 1979), 141.

19. On *Sur*'s editorial policy during World War II, see John King, *Sur: A Study of the Argentine Literary Journal and Its Role in the Development of a Culture, 1931–1970* (Cambridge: Cambridge University Press, 1986), 105–115.

20. Meyer, *Victoria Ocampo*, 141–142.

21. The official history of the Office of Inter-American Affairs discusses the work of coordinating committees it funded in Office of Inter-American Affairs, *History of the Office of the Coordinator of Inter-American Affairs: Historical Reports on War Administration* (Washington, D.C.: GPO, 1947), 127–136, 181–220, 231–243. On activities in Argentina, see Norman Richard Pyle, "A Study of the United States' Propaganda Efforts and Pro-Allied Sentiments in Argentina During World War II," Ph.D. dissertation, Georgetown University, 1968; Gisela Cramer, "Der Krieg im Äther: Radiopropaganda am Rio de la Plata, 1939–1945," in *Argentinien und das Dritte Reich: Mediale und reale Präsenz, Ideologietransfer, Folgewirkungen,* ed. Holder M. Meding and Georg Ismar (Berlin: Wissenschaftlicher, 2008), 151–177; María Inés Tato and Luis Alberto Romero, "La prensa periódica argentina y el régimen nazi," in *Sobre nazis y nazismo en la cultura argentina,* ed. Ignacio Klich (Buenos Aires: Ediciones Hispamérica, 2002), 157–175.

22. Paulo Knauss, "Os Sentidos da Arte Estrangeira no Brasil: Exposições de Pintura no Contexto da Segunda Guerra Mundial," in *Encantos da Imagem: Estâncias para a Prática Historiográfica entre História e Arte,* ed. Maria Bernardete Ramos Flores and Ana Lucia Vilela (Curitiba: Letras Contemporâneas, 2010), 134–136.

23. Helen Appleton Read, "Apresentação," in *Pintura Contemporânea Norte-americana* (Rio de Janeiro: Museu Nacional das Belas Artes, 1941), 9; Darlene J. Sadlier, "Good Neighbor Cultural Diplomacy in World War II: The Art of Making Friends," online at http://www.culturaldiplomacy.org/academy/content/pdf/participant-papers/2012-03-cdp/Good-Neighbor-Cultural-Diplomacy-in-World-War-II-The-Art-of-Making-Friends—Dr-Darlene-J-Sadlier.pdf.

24. Diego Rivera and Dorothy Puccinelli, *Diego Rivera: The Story of His Mural at the 1940 Golden Gate International Exposition* (San Francisco: Golden Gate International Exposition, 1940), n.p. At the time Rivera returned to California, he was in a political limbo. He had broken with Leon Trotsky in 1939, which severed him from any organized communist activity. He had painted no mural projects in Mexico since 1936, and he had had to rely on sale of his paintings to survive. There had been attacks on his life in Mexico, and he continued to feel uncertain about his safety. The unexpected invitation to return to San Francisco in 1940 allowed him to return to the type of artwork that had established his international activity, while allowing him to escape Mexico at a time when he felt particularly unsafe (see Rivera to Timothy Pflueger, 15 April 1940 [Diego Rivera Archive, City

College of San Francisco], for Rivera's insistence that he be able to leave Mexico for California immediately).

25. Rivera and Puccinelli, *Diego Rivera*, n.p.

26. Diego Rivera, "El arte, base del Panamericanismo," *Así* (Mexico City, 14 August 1943), 8.

27. Rivera claimed that he had been expelled from the Mexican Communist Party in 1929 because he had criticized Stalin's "repeated attacks upon the democratic principles of the workers' and peasants' organizations." He considered Stalinism inherently antidemocratic. While he was in San Francisco working on *Pan American Unity*, he published a brief statement about his political beliefs in a community newspaper. See Diego Rivera, "I Am Not a Communist," *Russian Hill Runt* (6 December 1940), 1–2. Rivera told the *San Francisco Chronicle* that communist revolution led to "totalitarian dictatorship." Rivera noted that Mussolini had executed 2,000 people, Hitler 1 million, but Stalin by "his own published figures has killed off 2,700,000, jailed 6,000,000, and records the death of 5,000,000 peasants" (quoted in Alfred Frankenstein, "Another Chapter in Rivera's Kampf," *San Francisco Chronicle*, 8 September 1940, 24).

28. Rivera, "El arte, base del Panamericanismo," quote on 8. Original Spanish: en realidad César Augusto nunca tuvo.

29. Rivera, "El arte, base del Panamericanismo," 54. Original Spanish: Por eso, es un factor de primer orden dentro del esfuerzo necesario e indispensable para la construcción de la Unión Pan-Americana, cuya tarea tenemos que cumplir si no queremos perecer.

30. Annateresa Fabris, *Portinari, Pintor Social* (São Paulo: Editora da Universidade de São Paulo, 1990), 81.

31. Cândido Portinari, "Sentido social del arte," in *Candido Portinari y el sentido social del arte*, ed. Andrea Guinti (Buenos Aires: Siglo XXI, 2005), 310. Text in Spanish: El lado técnico registra el conocimiento y el desarrollo de la sensibilidad del artista. La técnica es el medio con que el artista transmite su sensibilidad.

32. Fabris notes that Portinari remembered poor migrants from the northern states passing through his hometown of Brodósqui when he was a child (Fabris, *Portinari, Pintor Social*, 108–109). See also Antônio Bento, "Candido Portinari," in *Aspectos da Arte Brasileira*, eds. Wladimir Alves de Souza et al. (Rio de Janeiro: Edição Funarte, 1980), 121–122; Lelio Landucci, *Portinari* (Rio de Janeiro: Edições Pinguim, 1947), 12–14.

33. For a contemporary discussion in Brazil of Portinari's humanist social vision, see Mário Dionísio, "Portinari, Pintor de Camponeses," *Vértice* 3 (1946), 150–151.

34. Berenice Cavalcante, "'Las esperanzas que no mueren': Portinari y la utopía comunista," in Guinti, *Candido Portinari y el sentido social del arte*, 93–97; Laura Malosetti Costa, "Tiempo de exilio: Recepción rioplatense," in *Candido Portinari y el sentido social del arte*, 249–252.

35. See articles on Portinari after 1945, "Entrance into the Forest," *Time* (21 April 1947), 40; "Victims of the Drought," *Life* 29 (11 December 1950), 108.

36. Lincoln Kirstein, introduction, in *The Latin-American Collection of the Museum of Modern Art*, ed. Lincoln Kirstein (New York: Museum of Modern Art, 1943), 5–10.

37. A summary of MoMA's Latin American exhibitions in the 1940s is in "Circulating Exhibitions, 1931–1954," *Museum of Modern Art Bulletin* 21 (Summer 1954).

Chapter 6

1. The office underwent several name changes during its short existence. I have decided to use Office for Inter-American Affairs as the most convenient name for the agency.

2. On the U.S. airbase program, see Rebecca Herman Weber, "In Defense of Sovereignty: Labor, Sex, Crime and Nation at U.S. Military Bases in Latin America, 1940–1947," Ph.D. dissertation, University of California, Berkeley, 2014. On U.S. efforts to develop a hemispheric radio network, see Fred Fejes, *Imperialism, Media and the Good Neighbor: New Deal Foreign Policy and United States*

Shortwave Broadcasting to Latin America (New York: Praeger, 1986). Even after Mexico declared war on Germany, Italy, and Japan in May 1942, the government refused U.S requests for airfields and antiaircraft batteries inside Mexico. Instead, the Mexican government requested U.S. funding for military installations to be under the sole control of Mexican armed forces. The Mexicans took over responsibility for air patrols over a sector of the Pacific Ocean, and it sent air units to participate in the recapture of the Philippines from Japan.

3. On the Volta Redonda project, see "Um capítulo do planjamento econômico: A engenharia brasileira no projeto de Volta Redonda," *Revista do Clube de Engenharia* 11 (1944), 190–205; John F. Hennessy, Jr., "Industrial Brazil," *Commercial Pan American* 14 (1945), 20–22; Oliver Dinius, *Brazil's Steel City: Developmentalism, Strategic Power, and Industrial Relations in Volta Redonda, 1941–1964* (Stanford, Calif.: Stanford University Press, 2011).

4. The two credos come from "Philosophy and Objectives of the Office of Inter-American Affairs" (undated), folder 61, box 8, subseries 1: Coordinator of Inter-American Affairs (Office of the Coordinator of Inter-American Affairs), 1940–1944, series O: Washington, D.C., RG 4, NAR Personal, Rockefeller Family Archives, Rockefeller Archive Center, pp. 2–3.

5. See, for example, the summary of OIAA educational program goals offered by the program's last director, Harold E. Davis, "Permanent Bases of Inter-American Education," *English Journal* 34, no. 4 (1945), 211.

6. For a listing of funded cultural projects, see "Approved Projects Under the Cultural Relations Program," folder 35, box 5, subseries 1: Coordinator of Inter-American Affairs (Office of the Coordinator of Inter-American Affairs), 1940–1944, series O: Washington, D.C., RG 4, NAR Personal. On the relationship of the Division of Cultural Affairs in the State Department and the Office of the Coordinator of Inter-American Affairs, see Frank A. Ninkovich, *The Diplomacy of Ideas: U.S. Foreign Policy and Cultural Relations, 1938–1950* (Cambridge: Cambridge University Press, 1981), 35–60; and Richard T. Arndt, *The First Resort of Kings: American Cultural Diplomacy in the Twentieth Century* (Washington, D.C.: Potomac Books, 2005), 75–97. In 1944, all cultural exchange programs were centralized once again, if only temporarily, in the State Department.

7. For an assessment of Brazil's position in U.S. strategic planning in 1941 and 1942, see Office of Strategic Services/State Department Intelligence and Research Reports, "The Relation of Brazil to the Defense of the Northeast" (4 October 1941) and "Preliminary Report on the Elements of Insecurity in Brazil" (13 October 1941); Office of Strategic Services, Research Analysis Branch, "Short Guide to Brazil" (report no. 60, 10 July 1942); all in O.S.S./State Department Intelligence and Research Reports, part 14: Latin America, 1941–1961, reel 6 (Washington, D.C.: University Publications of America, 1980).

8. On the intersection of U.S. and Brazilian policymaking between 1938 and 1945, see Stanley E. Hilton, "Brazilian Diplomacy and the Washington-Rio de Janeiro 'Axis' During the World War II Era," *Hispanic American Historical Review* 59 (1979), 201–231; Gerson Moura, *Autonomia na Dependência: A Política Externa Brasileira de 1935 a 1942* (Rio de Janeiro: Nova Fronteira, 1980); Frank D. McCann, *The Brazilian-American Alliance, 1937–1945* (Princeton, N.J.: Princeton University Press, 1974). For a broader analysis of U.S. and Latin American priorities, see R. A. Humphreys, *Latin America and the Second World War* (London: Athlone, 1981); David Rock, ed., *Latin America in the 1940s: War and Postwar Transitions* (Berkeley: University of California Press, 1994); Gerald K. Haines, "Under the Eagle's Wing: The Franklin Roosevelt Administration Forges an American Hemisphere," *Diplomatic History* 1 (1977), 373–388; Francisco Luiz Corsi, *Estado Novo: Política Externa e Projeto Nacional* (São Paulo: Editora Unesp/Fapesp, 1999).

9. See Carleton Beals, *Pan America* (Boston: Houghton Mifflin, 1940); Carleton Beals, "Future of the Amazon," *Survey Graphic* (March 1941), 149–150, 194–195; John Gunther, *Inside Latin America* (New York: Harper and Brothers, 1941); Vera Kelsey, *Seven Keys to Brazil* (New York: Funk and Wagnalls, 1940); Stefan Zweig, *Brazil, Land of the Future*, trans. Andrew St. James (New York: Viking, 1942).

10. George E. Kidder Smith and Philip Lippincott Goodwin, *Brazil Builds: Architecture New and Old, 1652–1942* (New York: Museum of Modern Art, 1943).

11. Alan Fisher, interview by G. Lewis Schmidt, 27 July 1989, the Association for Diplomatic Studies and Training Foreign Affairs Oral History Project, 1–6 (online at http://www.adst.org /OH%20TOCs/Fisher,%20Alan.toc.pdf). At the end of the war, Fisher became a career State Department employee. His primary responsibilities were supervising distribution of films about the United States made for foreign audiences in Brazil and handling the insertion of U.S. propaganda messages into newsreels, in Brazil, France, and Vietnam.

12. Reznikoff had been one of Naylor's art teachers at the Music Box, an arts school in western Massachusetts. In 1933, they began living together in New York City, where they were part of overlapping radical political and avant-garde cultural circles. Naylor and Reznikoff married after returning to the United States in 1943.

13. Robert M. Levine, *The Brazilian Photographs of Genevieve Naylor, 1940–1942* (Durham, N.C.: Duke University Press, 1998), 37–38.

14. Vinícius de Moraes, "A Última Catedral," *A Manhã* (19 October 1941), p. 5. Original Portuguese text: Genevieve se chama, mulher desse grande Micha que conquistou a nossa pequena cidade artística com a sua simpatia e sua sensibilidade plástica. Genevieve parece ter saído de uma história de Robin-Hood, com seu arzinho de jovem pagem, sua elegância bem colorida, uma pena sempre atrevidamente espetada no chapéu. Nada escapa, no entanto, à maquinazinha dessa enfeitiçada. Perto dela não há momento fotográfico que passe sem cair naquela arapuca bem armada. Genevieve dá um pulinho—e a vida ali ficou batendo asa na sua chapa impressionada.

15. Quoted in Ana Maria Mauad, "Genevieve Naylor, Fotógrafa: Impressões de Viagem (Brasil, 1941–1942)," in Ana Maria Mauad, *Poses e Flagrantes: Ensaios sobre História e Fotografias* (Niterói: EDUFF, 2008), 204. Original Portuguese text for quote from Machado: Mais que a excelência técnica, o que é preciso louvar nos trabalhos de Miss Genevieve é o sentido sociológico com que ela utilizou a objetiva, revelando um espírito corajoso e sincero, e, não raras vezes, comovido diante da realidade brasileira. . . . Os assuntos populares, humildes, os tais elementos essenciais que compõem a fisionomia do nosso povo são captados, pela fotógrafa da Boa Vizinhança. Mas sua maneira de fixar a realidade nada tem de monumental. Nada de cachoeiras, de edifícios monumentais, de paisagens idílicas.

16. H.D. [Howard Devree], "More of Brazil," *New York Times* (27 January 1943), p. 26.

17. This argument is developed in Mauad, "Genevieve Naylor, Fotógrafa," 196–200, 204.

18. See as an example of complaints primarily coming from Republican members of Congress over expenditures in Brazil and other countries U.S., Congress, House, Hearings, Appropriations Committee, National War Agencies Appropriation Bill, 1944 (Washington, D.C., 1945), 250.

19. On the development of social documentation photography in the United States, see Lewis Hine, *Photo Story: Selected Letters and Photographs* (Washington, D.C.: Smithsonian Institution Press, 1992); Daile Kaplan, *Lewis Hine in Europe: The Lost Photographs* (New York: Abbeville Press, 1988); Alison Nordström and Elizabeth McCausland, *Lewis Hine* (New York: Distributed Art Publishers, 2012); Alan Trachtenberg, *Reading American Photographs: Images as History, Mathew Brady to Walker Evans* (New York: Hill and Wang, 1989), 164–230; John Tagg, "The Currency of the Photograph: New Deal Reformism and Documentary Rhetoric," in John Tagg, *The Burden of Representation: Essays on Photographies and Histories* (Minneapolis: University of Minnesota Press, 1993), 153–183. On Dorothea Lange and the Farm Security Administration, see Linda Gordon, *Dorothea Lange: A Life Beyond Limits* (New York: Norton, 2009), 191–290; Anne Whiston Spirn, *Daring to Look: Dorothea Lange's Photographs and Reports from the Field* (Chicago: University of Chicago Press, 2009). For an overview of the Farm Security Administration photography program, see Stu Cohen, *The Likes of Us: Photography in the Eyes of the Farm Security Administration* (Boston: Godine, 2008).

20. On the use of propaganda by the Vargas dictatorship, see Daryle Williams, *Culture Wars in Brazil: The First Vargas Regime, 1930–1945* (Durham, N.C.: Duke University Press, 2001), 83–87; Robert M. Levine, *Father of the Poor: Vargas and His Era* (Cambridge: Cambridge University Press, 1998), 60–65; Luiza Franco Moreira, "Frente conjectural: Escritores brasileños de izquierda y el *Estado Novo*," *Revista de Indias* 249 (2010), 381–408; Maria Helena Capelato, "Propaganda Política e

Controle dos Meios de Comunicação," in *Repensando o Estado Novo*, ed. Dulce Pandolfi (Rio de Janeiro: Editora Fundação Getúlio Vargas, 1999), 167–178.

21. On the emergence of the "working girl" as a symbol of individual freedom in the U.S. mass media of the early twentieth century, see Richard Cándida Smith, *Mallarmé's Children: Symbolism and the Renewal of Experience* (Berkeley: University of California Press, 1999), 175–184. On the development of social documentation conventions for the representation of working women, see Andrea Fisher, *Let Us Now Praise Famous Women: Women Photographers for the U.S. Government, 1935 to 1944* (London: Pandora Press, 1987).

22. Levine, *The Brazilian Photographs of Genevieve Naylor*, 36–38; Mauad, "Genevieve Naylor, fotógrafa," 204–205.

23. Online at http://www.youtube.com/watch?v=t3h0iQEcEGo.

24. Online at http://www.travelfilmarchive.com/item.php?id=12002.

25. Online at the Prelinger Archives, https://archive.org/details/0039_Day_is_New_The_15_00_38_00.

26. In 1956, RKO released a feature-length film based on the story of the bull whose life was spared, *The Brave One*, directed by Irving Rapper and written by Dalton Trumbo.

27. "Four Men on a Raft," *Time* 38 (8 December 1941), 30.

28. For a thorough reconstruction and analysis of the events surrounding Welles's failed pan-American film, see Catherine L. Benamou, *It's All True: Orson Welles's Pan-American Odyssey* (Berkeley: University of California Press, 2007). Restorations of the three segments that Welles filmed are available on the DVD *It's All True, Based on an Unfinished Film by Orson Welles* (Les Films Balenciaga and Paramount Pictures, 1993, ISBN: 1415701997).

29. Ana Maria Mauad, "Foto-ícones, a História por detrás das Imagens," in Mauad, *Poses e Flagrantes*, 42–43.

30. "Brazil, Land of Opportunity for Foreigners," *Life* (22 May 1939), 62–73.

31. "Brazil, Land of Opportunity for Foreigners," 65.

32. "Brazil, the Americans Found It a Very Gay Place," *Life* (30 April 1945), 65.

33. On Miranda's career in the United States, see Shari Roberts, " 'The Lady in the Tutti-Frutti Hat': Carmen Miranda, a Spectacle of Ethnicity," *Cinema Journal* 32 (1993), 3–23; Ana Maria Mauad, "As Três Américas de Carmem Miranda: Cultura Política e Cinema no Contexto da Política da Boa Vizinhança," *Transit Circle: Revista Brasileira de Estudos Americanos* 1, new ser. (2002), 52–77.

34. Quoted in Henry F. Pringle, "Rolling Up from Rio," *Collier's* (12 August 1939), 31.

35. Vinícius de Moraes, "Uma Noite no Rio," *A Manhã* (28 August 1941), p. 5. Original Portuguese text: um gesto simpático de Hollywood, em relação a nós. . . . O filme em si não vale nada.

36. "Speech of Nelson A. Rockefeller, Coordinator of Inter-American affairs, at Macy's Latin American Fair, New York City, January 16, 1942," in *Addresses of Nelson A. Rockefeller, 1940–1944*, Office of the Coordinator of Inter-American Affairs bound volumes, subseries 1: Coordinator of Inter-American Affairs (Office of the Coordinator of Inter-American Affairs), 1940–1944, series O: Washington, D.C., RG 4, NAR Personal.

37. See "Fair to Aid Trade of Latin America," *New York Times* (15 October 1941), p. 16; "Macy's to Conduct Latin American Fair as Aid to Trade with Southern Republics," *Wall Street Journal* (15 October 1941), p. 3; "Fiesta of Fashion, *New York Times* (11 January 1942), sec. R, p. 4; "Preview Tonight of Latin American Exhibit," *New York Times* (16 January 1942), p. 16; "Latin American Fair Ends," *New York Times* (8 February 1942), p. 51.

38. See Allen Woll, *The Latin Image in American Film* (Los Angeles: UCLA Latin American Studies Center, 1980); Gaizka S. de Usabel, *The High Noon of American Films in Latin America* (Ann Arbor, Mich.: UMI, 1982); Clayton R. Koppes and Gregory D. Black, *Hollywood Goes to War: How Politics, Profits, and Propaganda Shaped World War II Movies* (New York: Free Press, 1987). On U.S.-Mexican co-productions during the war, see Seth Fein, "Transnationalization and Cultural Collaboration: Mexican Film Propaganda During World War II," *Studies in Latin American Popular Culture* 17 (1998), 105–128. See Constance Rourke, *American Humor: A Study in American National*

Character (New York: Harcourt, Brace, 1931), for analysis of the centrality of self-deprecating stereotypes in the development of U.S. national identity.

Chapter 7

1. Daniel M. Braddock, U.S. consul, Porto Alegre, to Érico Veríssimo, 29 November 1940, Acervo de Érico Veríssimo, Instituto Moreira Salles (hereafter Acervo de EV, IMS). Veríssimo was the first Brazilian recipient of a "Leader Grant" from the U.S. State Department. Among the several hundred Brazilians brought to the United States between 1941 and 1945 were anthropologist Gilberto Freyre, historian Sérgio Buarque de Holanda, historian and novelist Vianna Moog, and journalist and novelist Orígenes Lessa. Worldwide, the State Department offered approximately one thousand grants a year between 1940 and 1948, money used to fund visits to or extended stays in the United States (Richard T. Arndt, *The First Resort of Kings: American Cultural Diplomacy in the Twentieth Century* [Washington, D.C.: Potomac Books, 2005], 137). Veríssimo described the circumstances of the invitation in his memoirs, *Solo de Clarineta: Memórias*, vol. 1 (Porto Alegre: Editora Globo, 1973), 276–277.

2. Sales figures cited in L. L. Barrett, review of an edited version of *Gato Preto em Campo de Neve* prepared for Portuguese students in the United States, *Hispania* 32 (1949), 265. Veríssimo's papers at the Instituto Moreira Salles suggest that initial sales of *Gato Preto* in 1941 may well have been as high as twenty thousand copies.

3. On the question of growing U.S. influence within Brazilian society, see Antonio Pedro Tota, *O Imperialismo Sedutor: A Americanização do Brasil na Época da Segunda Guerra* (São Paulo: Companhia das Letras, 2000). A revised version prepared by the author for U.S. readers was translated by Lorena B. Ellis into English as *The Seduction of Brazil: The Americanization of Brazil During World War II* (Austin: University of Texas Press, 2009).

4. Veríssimo, *Gato Preto em Campo de Neve* (São Paulo: Companhia das Letras, 2006), 130. Original Portuguese text: mostra-me gráficos e instrumentos com ar um pouco protetor como se estivesse revelando a um selvagem recém-chegado à civilização as maravilhas produzidas pelo cérebro privilegiado do homem branco. Fica entre surpreendido e incrédulo quando lhe digo que no Brasil conhecemos a luz elétrica, o microscópio e a máquina fotográfica.

5. Veríssimo, *Gato Preto em Campo de Neve*, 161. Original Portuguese text: sente a beleza . . . é capaz de poesia.

6. Veríssimo, *Gato Preto em Campo de Neve*, 130–133, 473–477.

7. Veríssimo, *Solo de Clarineta*, 1:113. He also attended a high school in Porto Alegre, Brazil, run by Americans. While a student there, he developed his fluency in English.

8. Veríssimo, *Gato Preto em Campo de Neve*, 206. Original Portuguese text: de certo modo, guardadas as proporções, os nossos problemas são os mesmos com que lutam os editores norte-americanos.

9. The firm also got half of its business from the production and sales of textbooks. Macmillan had been the pioneer in the U.S. book-publishing business of establishing regional warehouses, which allowed the firm to supply a larger volume of inventory across the country than its competitors. On the history of Macmillan, see John Tebbel, *A History of Book Publishing in the United States*, vol. 3, *The Golden Age Between Two Wars, 1920–1940* (New York: Bowker, 1978), 101–103, 535–537; John Tebbel, *A History of Book Publishing in the United States*, vol. 4, *The Great Change, 1940–1980* (New York: Bowker, 1981), 118–130.

10. Veríssimo, *Gato Preto em Campo de Neve*, 364. Original Portuguese text: A casa editora que quiser ter recursos materiais suficientes para se aventurar ao lançamento de livros de autores, como, por exemplo, Thomas Mann . . . terá de ir buscar esses recursos na publicação . . . duma Agatha Christie. . . . O artista que se entrega passivamente ao povo, fazendo-lhe todas as vontades do afã de ser-lhe sempre agradável, corre um risco de destruição irremediável; mas o que despreza esse mesmo público fica sujeito a se tornar inumano, precioso e isolado da vida e das suas verdades simples.

11. Veríssimo, *Gato Preto em Campo de Neve*, 364–366.

12. "Memória Seletiva: O Tempo e os Ventos," *Cadernos de Literatura Brasileira* 16 (2003), 8–10, issue on Érico Veríssimo.

13. The state of Rio Grande do Sul had laws protecting publishers who pirated materials from other countries, or even other parts of Brazil. The principle behind the laws was that providing as much information as possible to the people had higher value than protecting intellectual property rights. With the onset of the Great Depression, foreign books became prohibitively expensive, and imports stopped. Publishing foreign titles in pirated translations allowed Brazilian readers to remain in contact with literary developments in other countries. See Laurence Hallewell, *Books in Brazil: A History of the Publishing Trade* (Metuchen, N.J.: Scarecrow Press, 1982), 228–232.

14. Veríssimo, *Solo de Clarineta*, 1:233–252; "Guia Érico Veríssimo: O Arquipélago," *Cadernos de Literatura Brasileira* 16 (2003), 164–165; Felipe José Lindoso, "A Indústria Editorial no Brasil no Século XX," in *Historia de las empresas editoriales de América Latina, siglo XX*, ed. Juan Gustavo Cobo Borda (Bogotá: Centro Regional para el Fomento del Libro en América Latina y el Caribe, 2000), 122–124; Hallewell, *Books in Brazil*, 227–242.

15. Veríssimo, *Solo de Clarineta*, 1:253.

16. Veríssimo, *Solo de Clarineta*, 1:254. Original Portuguese text: dentro das "aparas" de tempo que me sobravam das outras funções.

17. In 1942, Veríssimo wrote a fellow Brazilian author whose book he had convinced Editora Globo to republish, "Since 1938, my relation with the company has been almost exclusively that of editors and author. I still have an office in the establishment where I work every day. The only job I do directly is choosing foreign works. Aside from that, I devote my time to my own books" (Érico Veríssimo to Oswald de Andrade, 3 August 1942, Acervo de EV, IMS). Original Portuguese: De 1938 para cá minhas relações com a livraria são quasi exclusivamente as de editores e editado. Tenho ainda um escritório no 'estabelecimento,' onde sou encontrado diariamente. E só tenho a ver diretamente com a escolha da obras estrangeiras. Fora disso, entrego-me a meus próprios livros.

18. When Veríssimo began planning a new book, his initial notes were typically written in English ("Manuscritos/Inéditos," *Cadernos de Literatura Brasileira* 16 [2003], 75).

19. Untitled, undated notes, Acervo de EV, IMS. In the 1930s, Veríssimo produced at least one book a year. In the 1940s, he began to spend more time on the books he wrote. The note states he had written six novels, which would date it between 1940 and 1943.

20. Érico Veríssimo to John Leroy Johnston, 14 May 1942, Acervo de EV, IMS.

21. In 1940, Veríssimo was the first Brazilian author to do a public book-signing event, when Livraria Saraiva in São Paulo advertised his appearance and drew hundreds of readers who wanted to meet him (Veríssimo, *Solo de Clarineta*, 1:274).

22. Wayne A. Wiegand, "The American Public Library: Construction of a Community Reading Institution," in *A History of the Book in America*, vol. 4, *Print in Motion: The Expansion of Publishing and Reading in the United States, 1880–1940*, ed, Carl F. Kaestle and Janice A. Radway (Chapel Hill: University of North Carolina Press, 2009), 431–451. See also Tebbel, *A History of Book Publishing in the United States*, 3:657–690. Statistics for titles and copies produced are available, but publishing firms long have been reluctant to release firm information about the sales of individual titles.

23. Angèle Kathleen Gingras to Érico Veríssimo, 10 February 1941, Acervo de EV, IMS. Veríssimo thought Montenegro was wrong in his evaluation of the U.S. book market. Numerous bestsellers, among them *Rebecca*, *Gone with the Wind*, and *How Green Was My Valley*, proved that many U.S. readers liked a story that made them weep (Érico Veríssimo to Angèle Gingras, 31 May 1941, Acervo de EV, IMS). In 1940, *O Diário*, a newspaper in Recife, conducted a survey of its women readers and found that Veríssimo was the favorite Brazilian author among the women who responded (Altamira Cunha, a journalist working for the newspaper in Recife, to Érico Veríssimo, 23 May 1940, Acervo de EV, IMS).

24. J. W. Greenberg, Greenberg publisher, to Érico Veríssimo, 5 February 1941; Frederick Drimmer, dditor, Greenberg Publisher, to Érico Veríssimo, 19 August 1941; both Acervo de EV, IMS.

25. Theodore Purdy, Jr., to Érico Veríssimo, 19 May 1941; Lois Dwight Cole, associate editor, the Macmillan Company, to Érico Veríssimo, 4 June 1941; Doris S. Patee to Érico Veríssimo, 5 June 1941; Purdy to Veríssimo, 13 June 1941; Purdy to Veríssimo, 23 June 1941; all Acervo de EV, IMS.

26. Robert E. Luckey, "Materials for a Course in English on Portuguese and Brazilian Literature and Culture," *Modern Language Journal* 34 (1950), 422.

27. Walter A. Jessup to Érico Veríssimo, 17 August 1941, Acervo de EV, IMS.

28. From dust jacket of Magdalena Petit Marfán, *La Quintrala*, trans. Lulu Vargas Vila (New York: Macmillan, 1942).

29. Doris Patee to Érico Veríssimo, 17 March 1941, Acervo de EV, IMS.

30. Doris Patee to Érico Veríssimo, 12 April 1943, Acervo de EV, IMS.

31. In 1942, Doubleday and Moran published *Maria Rosa: Everyday Fun and Carnival Frolic in Brazil*, a children's book by Vera Kelsey centered on a young Brazilian girl. Cândido Portinari provided twenty-two illustrations. Kelsey was a journalist and novelist whose book *Seven Keys to Brazil* (New York: Funk and Wagnalls, 1940) provided Americans with an overview of Brazilian society.

32. Joaquín Ortega, School of Inter-American Affairs, University of New Mexico, to Érico Veríssimo, 6 December 1941; Providence Raimond, secretary, School of Inter-American Affairs, University of New Mexico, to Érico Veríssimo, 2 April 1942; both Acervo de EV, IMS.

33. Theodore Purdy, Jr., to Érico Veríssimo, 31 July 1941; Purdy to Veríssimo, 25 August 1941; Purdy to Veríssimo, 27 October 1941; Purdy to Veríssimo, 31 December 1941; Mary S. Thompson, Publicity Department, the Macmillan Company, to Érico Veríssimo, 16 September 1942; Purdy to Veríssimo, 20 September 1942; all Acervo de EV, IMS.

34. "Books—Authors," *New York Times* (16 January 1943), 11.

35. Érico Veríssimo to Louis Kaplan, 9 January 1942, Acervo de EV, IMS.

36. Barrett, review of *Gato Preto em Campo de Neve*, 265.

37. For more on this argument about the relation of family and social transformation in Veríssimo's work, see Ligia Chiappini Moraes Leite, *Modernismo no Rio Grande do Sul: Materiais para o seu Estudo* (São Paulo: Instituto de Estudos Brasileiros, 1972); Ligia Chiappini Moraes Leite, *Regionalismo e Modernismo: O Caso Gaúcho* (São Paulo: Editora Ática, 1978); B. A. Richards, *Érico Veríssimo: The Brazilian Novels Assessed in the Context of Modernism and Latin American Fiction* (London: King's College, University of London, 1981); Maria Antonieta Antonacci, *Rio Grande do Sul: As Oposições e a Revolução de 1923* (Porto Alegre: Mercado Aberto, 1981); Luiza H. Schmitz Kleimann, *Rio Grande do Sul, Terra e Poder: História da Questão Agrária* (Porto Alegre: Mercado Aberto, 1986); Sandra Jatahy Pesavento, *A Burguesia Gaúcha: Dominação do Capital e Disciplina do Trabalho, Rio Grande do Sul, 1889–1930* (Porto Alegre: Mercado Aberto, 1988); Carlos Cortez Minchillo, *Erico Verissimo, Escritor do Mundo: Circulação Literária, Cosmopolitismo e Relações Interamericanas* (São Paulo: Editora da Universidade de São Paulo, 2015), 69–135.

38. Annotation for Érico Veríssimo, *Olhae os lyrios do campo* [*sic*, current correct spelling is *Olhai os Lirios do Campo*], *Handbook of Latin American Studies*, vol. 4 (1938), HLAS item#: re394248a. Brazilian writers of the 1920s and 1930s are generally conceived of as rejecting the Francophile culture of the so-called Old Republic (1889–1930) by embracing either modernism, with a focus on exploring the unique characteristics of Brazilian nationality, or regionalism, which also explored Brazilian identity but by returning to the cultural and social roots of each state. Veríssimo can be seen as operating in the intersection of modernism and regionalism. He was familiar with literary trends in Europe and North America, but with a stronger inclination toward work written for a broad middle class, while his subject matter critically explored social relations in Rio Grande do Sul. That said, the framework poorly describes Veríssimo's goals as a writer or his position in national letters. See Wilson Martins, *The Modernist Idea: A Critical Survey of Brazilian Writing in the Twentieth Century* (New York: New York University Press, 1970); Antônio Cândido, *On Literature and Society* (Princeton, N.J.: Princeton University Press, 1995); Roberto Schwarz, *Misplaced Ideas: Essays on Brazilian Culture* (London: Verso, 1992).

39. George P. Brett, Jr., president, Macmillan Company, to Érico Veríssimo, 6 August 1943, Acervo de EV, IMS.

40. In addition to Macmillan's publications, in 1947, Henry Holt released a condensed version of *Black Cat on a Field of Snow* for use in U.S. schools.

41. The language used in these reviews from 1943 and 1944 follow a template for how U.S. reviewers continue to review foreign cultural work. In 2015, the reviewer for *Variety* writing of a Brazilian film recently released in the United States asserted, "Brazilian filmmaker Anna Muylaert spins a culturally specific tale with the universal appeal required for international arthouse success in *The Second Mother*" (Geoff Berkshire, "Regina Casé Shines in Anna Muylaert's Warm Character Study," *Variety* [19 February 2015], online at http://variety.com/2015/film/reviews/film-review-the -second-mother-1201434972/).

42. F.B., "Books: South American Writes a Tense, Dramatic Story," *Chicago Tribune* (17 February 1943), 23.

43. William Du Bois, untitled review, *New York Times* (24 January 1943), Book Review sec., p. 6.

44. *Library Journal* 67 (1 November 1942), 952; *Booklist* 39 (1 March 1943), 275.

45. Granville Hicks, untitled review of *Time and the Wind*, *New York Herald Tribune* (8 November 1951), Book Review sec., p. 7.

46. Herschel Brickell, untitled review of *Time and the Wind*, *Saturday Review of Literature* 34 (22 September 1951), 15.

47. On *clientelismo* in Brazil, see Luiz Henrique Nunes Baía, *O Poder do Clientelismo: Raízes e Fundamentos da Troca Política* (Rio de Janeiro: Editora Renovar, 2003); Edson de Oliveira Nunes, *A Gramática Política do Brasil: Clientelismo e Insulamento Burocrático* (Rio de Janeiro: Jorge Zahar Editora, 2003); Paul Cammack, "Clientelism and Military Government in Brazil," in *Private Patronage and Public Power: Political Clientelism in the Modern State*, ed. Christopher Clapham (London: Frances Pinter, 1982), 53–75; José Murilo de Carvalho, "Barbacena: A Família, a Política e uma Hipótese," *Revista Brasileira de Estudos Políticos* 20 (1966), 153–194; Luis de A. Costa Pinto, *Lutas de Família no Brasil: Introdução ao seu Estudo* (São Paulo: Editora Nacional, 1949); Nestor Duarte, *A Ordem Privada e a Organização Política Nacional* (São Paulo: Editora Nacional, 1939); Linda Lewin, *Política e Parentela na Paraíba: Um Estudo de Caso da Oligarquia de Base Familiar* (Rio de Janeiro: Record, 1993); Sérgio Buarque de Holanda, *Raízes do Brasil* (São Paulo: Companhia das Letras, 1995; originally published, 1936).

48. Érico Veríssimo, *Crossroads* (New York: Macmillan, 1943), 176. Original text: o esforço dos homens de boa vontade, sem violência nem fanatismo, possa igualar as diferencias sociais (Érico Veríssimo, *Caminhos Cruzados* [São Paulo: Companhia das Letras, 2005], 153).

Chapter 8

1. Quoted in Salvador Camacho Roldán, *Notas de viaje: Colombia y Estados Unidos de América* (Bogota: Librería Colombiana, 1898), 598–599. Original Spanish: la prosperidad de los Estados Unidos se debe a sus institucionales liberales; a la división de las tierras baldías en pequeños lotes, al alcance de todo el pueblo; a los productos de la exportación; a la inmigración extranjera; a las escuelas públicas; a la ausencia de ejército permanente; a las vías de comunicación rápidas, que proporcionan transportes baratos y un inmenso comercio interior; a la paz de que ustedes han disfrutado.

2. Camacho Roldán, *Notas de viaje*, 458–460.

3. Camacho Roldán, *Notas de viaje*, 659, 663. Original quote: la exageración de la grandeza de sus destinos.

4. Paul Groussac, *Del Plata al Niágara* (Buenos Aires: Administración de la Biblioteca, 1894).

5. Brazilian literature had a comparable contrast of responses. On the one hand, Eduardo Prado's famous *A Ilusão Americana* ("The American Illusion"), published in 1895, presented a conservative defense of monarchy and rule by large landowners as necessary for Brazil to remain a stable, well-governed society. A classic liberal perspective, on the other hand, can be found in a book that José Bento Monteiro Lobato, a pioneering commercial publisher in Brazil, wrote on his travels

in the United States, *América: Os Estados Unidos de 1929* (São Paulo: Editora Brasiliense, 1948; originally published 1932). In this work, Monteiro Lobato vigorously defended the liberal model that the United States presented to countries like Brazil with enterprising property owners, a large labor force, and rich natural resources. He was convinced that if Brazil developed its steel and petroleum industries, his country could achieve the productivity of the United States and become the dominant power of the southern hemisphere. Veríssimo's two books on the United States differ from those of his most famous predecessors by focusing on his personal impressions and avoiding any simple conclusions about what life in the United States did or did not mean for how Brazilians organized life in their country.

6. In 1940 and 1941, José Vasconcelos edited *El Timón*, the leading pro-Nazi journal in Latin America. The Mexican government closed down the periodical when the U.S. government provided convincing evidence that funding came entirely from the German government. On *El Timón* and its defense of German policies, see Héctor Orestes Águilar, "Ese olvidado nazi mexicano de nombre José Vasconcelos," *Istor* 8 (2007), 148–157; and Mauricio Pilatowsky, "El acercamiento de José Vasconcelos al Nazismo y su dirección de la revista *El Timón*," *Estudios* 110 (2014), 159–175. On pro-Nazi political movements in Mexico, see Alicia Gojman, *Camisas, escudos y desfiles militares: Los dorados y el antisemitismo en México (1934–1940)* (Mexico City: Fondo de Cultura Económica, 2000). On fascist movements in Latin America, see Friedrich Katz, *Hitler sobre América Latina: El fascismo alemán en Latinoamérica, 1933–1943* (Mexico City: Editorial Fondo de Cultura Popular, 1968); Hémlgio Trindade, *O Nazi-fascismo na América Latina: Mito e Realidade* (Porto Alegre: Editora UFRGS, 2004); Franco Savarino Roggero and João Fábio Bertonha, *El fascismo en Brasil y América Latina: Ecos europeos y desarrollos autóctonos* (Mexico City: Instituto Nacional de Antropolía e Historia, 2013); Agustín Cueva, *Autoritarismo y fascismo en América Latina* (Quito: Centro de Pensamiento Crítico, 2013).

7. Herman Rauschning's *Hitler Speaks* was published in France early in 1940. Historians of Nazi Germany had long accepted Rauschning's transcripts of conversations he had with Hitler between 1932 and 1934, when Rauschning was a member of the Nazi Party, as reasonably accurate. In the 1980s, Swiss historian Wolfgang Hänel challenged the authenticity of the account, dismissing the book as fabricated war propaganda for the Allies. Hänel has also questioned standard accounts of the Holocaust, and much of his research has focused on Allied atrocities against Germans during the war. Currently, the authenticity of *Hitler Speaks* is not taken for granted, but a number of historians have critiqued Hänel's argument about Rauschning's book as part of their broader assault on his revisionist interpretations of the war. In the 1940s, the book was read as the best available account for Hitler's strategic plans for reorganizing global relations. The most authoritative study of Hitler's broader war aims remains Norman Rich's two-volume work *Hitler's War Aims* (New York: W. W. Norton, 1973–1974). Rich argues that racial ideology dominated every aspect of German war planning, even though refusal to compromise on questions of race hierarchy made administration of conquered territories chaotic and prevented Germany from benefiting from its alliances with Spain, Italy, and Japan.

8. Manuel Seoane, *El gran vecino: América en la crucijada*, 2nd ed. (Santiago, Chile: Editorial Orbe, 1944), 64–65. Seoane's pro-U.S. position lasted into the Cold War. In the 1960s, he served as an administrator organizing Alliance for Progress programs in the Andean region. Original Spanish text: Yo llegué a Estados Unidos pensando en una población hostil y fría, donde la gente anda a empujones y nadie auxilia a nadie. . . . a proponerme que respetara el descanso y bebiera un whiskey con ellos en lugar de trabajar.

9. María Rosa Oliver, *América vista por una mujer argentina* (Buenos Aires: Salzmann, 1945); and María Rosa Oliver, *Mi fe es el hombre* (Buenos Aires: Ediciones Carlos Lohlé, 1981).

10. Oliver, *Mi fe es el hombre*, 153.

11. Drafts of Oliver's talks during her stay in the United States and press clippings are in the María Oliver Rosa Papers, box 1, folder 22, Manuscripts Division, Department of Rare Books and Special Collections, Library, Princeton University.

12. Oliver, *Mi fe es el hombre*, 122.

13. Érico Veríssimo to Richard Pattee, 13 January 1943 and 21 May 1943, Acervo de Érico Veríssimo, Instituto Moreira Salles (hereafter, Acervo de EV, IMS). In June 1942, he had written a friend in the United States that he hoped to spend one or two years in California after the war (Érico Veríssimo to Angèle Kathleen Gingras, 15 June 1942, Acervo de EV, IMS). For a report from the University of California on the expectations of the Department of Spanish and Portuguese regarding Veríssimo's visiting professorship, see, S. G. Morley, chair of the Department of Spanish and Portuguese, University of California, Berkeley, to Harry H. Pierson, Division of Cultural Relations, U.S. Department of State, 26 May 1944, in folder of correspondence received 1944 pertaining to the United States of America, in archives of Secretaria de Estado das Relações Exteriores, Arquivo Histórico do Itamaraty. For an excellent investigation of Veríssimo's stay in the United States from 1943 to 1945 and a comparison of *Gato Preto em Campo de Neve* and his follow-up book, *A Volta do Gato Preto*, see Carlos Cortez Minchillo, *Erico Verissimo, Escritor do Mundo: Circulação Literária, Cosmopolitismo e Relações Interamericanas* (São Paulo: Editora da Universidade de São Paulo, 2015), 185–205.

14. J. Manuel Espinosa, "Exchange of Professors Between the United States and Other American Republics," *Americas* 3 (1947), 535–543.

15. On Arciniegas, see Juan Gustavo Cobo Borda, *Una visión de América: La obra de Germán Arciniegas desde la perspectiva de sus contemporáneos* (Bogotá: Instituto Caro y Cuervo, 1990); Juan Gustavo Cobo Borda, *Germán Arciniegas* (Bogotá: Procultura, 1992); Roberto Esquenazi-Mayo, "Arciniegas y Havel: Dos generaciones, dos continentes, un pensamiento," *Revista Hispánica Moderna* 49 (1996), 308–316; Eduardo Sáenz Rovner, "Germán Arciniegas, entre la libertad y el establecimiento," *Historia crítica* 21 (2008), 76–83.

16. Érico Veríssimo to Henrique Bertaso, 8 November 1943, Acervo de EV, IMS. Original Portuguese: Parece incrível que com toda esta guerra pavorosa este país anda dentro dos eixos com ordem, entusiasmo pela vida, a mesma sorridente delicadeza de homem para homem. . . . E no meio de todas essas manifestações, eu só fico a pensar nesta coisa melancólica. Se eu dissesse que na minha cidade eu não poderia ser professor pela simples razão de não ter um titulo de doutor e não ser católico praticante, eles cairiam para trás de surpresa.

17. Hanke's remark quoted from an interview with Brazilian historian Sérgio Buarque de Holanda, in which he recalls a conversation with Hanke in 1941 when Buarque de Holanda visited the United States at the invitation of the State Department. See Sérgio Buarque de Holanda and Richard Graham, "An Interview with Sérgio Buarque de Holanda," *Hispanic American Historical Review* 62 (1982), 14.

18. Érico Veríssimo to Manoelito, 10 November 1943, Acervo de EV, IMS. Original Portuguese text: Este país é maravilhoso, seu Manoelito. Mesmo com todos os seus defeitos e problemas. Mas nós não precisamos copiar este tipo de vida. Temos os nosso, que é melhor, mais sábio, mais amável. Precisamos é de melhor saúde, mais a melhor educação, um nível de vida mais alto. O resto nós temos.

19. Érico Veríssimo, *A Volta do Gato Preto* (Rio de Janeiro: Editora Globo, 1987; originally published 1946), 343–349, quote on 365.

20. Veríssimo, *A Volta do Gato Preto*, 474.

21. Veríssimo, *A Volta do Gato Preto*, 260.

22. Veríssimo, *A Volta do Gato Preto*, 271–273, quote on 273. Original text: "Mas, meu caro poeta, você não me disse que era socialista?" "Pues sí, amigo . . . Pero eso es diferente. Siempre habrá señores y esclavos."

23. Veríssimo, *A Volta do Gato Preto*, 280–287, quotes on 283. Original text: O senhor do engenho, o homem da casa-grande é um chefe de clã e um líder político que eventualmente se transforma em general. O peão em tempo de paz é o eleitor e em tempo de guerra o soldado. . . . Tudo fazem por prestigiar, amparar e prolongar um regime político que lhes proporciona vantagens, lucros, favores e posições.

24. Veríssimo, *A Volta do Gato Preto*, 462. Original Portuguese text: na sua bondade essencial, no seu horror à violência, enfim, nessa misteriosa força que tem mantido unido aquele país tão vasto,

tão despovoado, tão pobre de meios de comunicação e transporte. Nessa força indescritível que. . . .
Bom, se é indescritível o melhor mesmo é não tentar descrevê-la.

25. Veríssimo, *A Volta do Gato Preto*, 330–343, quote on 330. Original Portuguese texts: Você sabe que o maestro é um homem difícil, explosivo, irritadiço?

26. Veríssimo, *A Volta do Gato Preto*, 334. Original Portuguese texts: Foi na selva brasileira que aprendi a canção da liberdade! . . . E eu acredito, porque liberdade no Brasil hoje em dia . . . só mesmo na selva.

27. Veríssimo, *A Volta do Gato Preto*, 16–17. Original Portuguese: Venho dum país em que aprendemos a temer ou aborrecer tudo quanto diga respeito à burocracia. Lei para nós chega a ser uma palavra temível. Nos meus tempos de menino, sempre que à noite, nas sombrias ruas de minha cidade natal, eu encontrava um guarda da polícia municipal, estremecia de horror, porque esses homens de má catadura, de uniforme zuarte e espadagões à cinta, era o símbolo do capanguismo político, tinham uma tradição de violência e arbitrariedade. Cresci com esse medo na alma, e com a ideia de que o funcionalismo público é uma organização destinada especialmente a dificultar as coisas e de que no fim de contas o Governo não passa mesmo dum instrumento de opressão.

28. Veríssimo, *A Volta do Gato Preto*, 47–49.

29. Érico Veríssimo, interview by Eloise Keeler on the radio program *At Your Service*, KFBK, 1530 (Sacramento, Calif.), 9:00 AM, Tuesday, 3 July 1944, transcript in Acervo de EV, IMS.

30. Interview with Veríssimo on *At Your Service*.

31. Bess M. Wilson, "Brazilian Views Told by Author," *Los Angeles Times* (6 November 1944), p. A6. In sharp contrast to Veríssimo's assessment, Selden Chapin, a career foreign service officer and assistant chief of the Division of the American Republics in the State Department, had penned a memorandum advising the department that U.S. visitors to Brazil should avoid humor as Brazilians did not take public speakers who used jokes in their talks seriously (Chapin, "Need of Cultural Relations with Brazil," 5 April 1937, Department of State DS/RG59, lot files, entry 209, Office of American Republic Affairs, Its Predecessors, and Its Successors, Memorandums Relating to General Latin American Affairs, country file B24), National Archives, Washington, D.C.

32. "Relations with Brazil Reported Deteriorating: Brazil Cools Toward U.S.," *Los Angeles Times* (14 November 1944), p. A1.

33. Arthur Ramos, "The Scientific Basis of Pan-Americanism," *Inter-American Quarterly* 3 (1941), 1–5.

34. Quote from Ramos, "The Negro in Brazil," 522. Richard Pattee, from the Division of Cultural Relations at the State Department, translated one of Ramos's books into English in 1939, *The Negro in Brazil* (Washington, D.C.: Associated Publishers, 1939). In 1941, following the attention given to Ramos's discussion of Brazil as a "racial democracy" in "The Scientific Basis of Pan-Americanism," three U.S. academic journals associated with the civil rights movement published short articles that they asked him to write summarizing his research into Afro-Brazilian culture; see Arthur Ramos, "Acculturation Among the Brazilian Negroes," *Journal of Negro History* 26 (1941), 244–250; "Contact of Races in Brazil," *Social Forces* 19 (1941), 533–538; "The Negro in Brazil," *Journal of Negro Education* 10 (1941), 515–523.

35. Gilberto Freyre, *The Masters and the Slaves*, trans. from *A Casa Grande e a Senzala* (1933) by Samuel Putnam (New York: Knopf, 1946), 278.

36. Stefan Zweig, *Brazil, Land of the Future* (New York: Viking, 1942), 7, 9.

37. On the myth of Brazil as a racial democracy, see Thomas E. Skidmore, *Black into White: Race and Nationality in Brazilian Thought* (Durham, N.C.: Duke University Press, 1993), 216–217; G. Reginald Daniel, *Race and Multiraciality in Brazil and the United States: Converging Paths?* (University Park: Pennsylvania State University Press, 2006), 40–51; Robert Stam and Ella Shohat, *Race in Translation: Culture Wars Around the Postcolonial Atlantic* (New York: New York University Press, 2012), 175–193.

38. Charles Wagley et al., "Race Relations in Brazil," *Courier* 5 (August–September 1952), 6–15; Charles Wagley, *Race and Class in Rural Brazil* (New York: Columbia University Press, 1952); Roger Bastide and Florestan Fernandes, *Relações Raciais entre Negros e Brancos em São Paulo* (São Paulo:

Editôra Anhembi, 1955); Roger Bastide, "Race Relations in Brazil," *UNESCO International Social Science Bulletin* 9 (1957), 495–512. On UNESCO's role in the study of Brazilian race relations, see Marcos Chor Maio, "UNESCO and the Study of Race Relations in Brazil: Regional or National Issue?" *Latin American Research Review* 36 (2001), 118–136. During the 1960s, social scientists in Brazil, led by Florestan Fernandes, challenged the most basic assumptions of Brazilian racial democracy and asked whether class could explain Brazilian poverty.

39. Elizabeth Bishop's reports formed the basis of her book *Brazil* (New York: Time, 1962), quote on 114.

40. Bishop, *Brazil*, 147.

41. Quoted in Mercer Cook, "U.S. Ambassador Spreads Interracial Flavor in Cuba," *Afro-American* (13 February 1943), 1.

Chapter 9

1. File 6921/914, Indice: Conhecimento sobre o Brasil nos Estados Unidos, 19 November 1948, in archives of Secretária de Estado das Relações Exteriores, Arquivo Histórico do Itamaraty. Villa-Lobos's musical *Magdalena, a Musical Adventure*, set in an Amazonian river town near the border of Brazil and Colombia, premiered at the Los Angeles Civic Light Opera in July 1948, moved to San Francisco in August, and then opened at the Ziegfeld Theatre in New York City in September to enthusiastic reviews. The production closed in December 1948 after 88 performances when a general strike by theater unions in Manhattan closed all the city's major theaters.

2. *Congressional Record*, 78th Congress, 2nd Session (1944), 441–448, appendix A, 2733–2735. Congressional insistence that programs not directly related to acquisition of natural resources needed for the war effort or to defense of the hemisphere be eliminated became sharper in 1944 as congressional committees began preparing appropriations bills. See U.S. Congress, House, Hearings, Appropriations Committee, National War Agencies Appropriation Bill, 1944 (Washington, D.C., 1945), 250. See also Seth Garfield, "A Amazônia no Imaginário Americano em Tempo de Guerra," *Revista Brasileira de História* 29 (2009), 44–50; Justus F. Paul, "Senator Hugh Butler and Aid to Latin America, 1943–1944," *South Dakota History* 8 (Winter 1977): 34–45; Claude C. Erb, "Prelude to Point Four: The Institute of Inter-American Affairs," *Diplomatic History* 9 (1985), 249–269, for discussions of conservative critiques in Congress of U.S. programs in Latin America during World War II.

3. Helen R. Pinkney, "The Division of Cultural Cooperation," unpublished TS, December 1945, in Department of State CU/RG 59, controlled unclassified files, War History Branch Studies, box 10, National Archives, Washington.

4. Spruille Braden, *Diplomats and Demagogues: The Memoirs of Spruille Braden* (New Rochelle, N.Y.: Arlington House, 1971), 263.

5. Benton was also the publisher of the *Encyclopædia Britannica*, and he had been a vice president of the University of Chicago. After leaving his position at the State Department, Benton served as a U.S. senator representing the state of Connecticut. There is one published biography of Benton: Sidney Hyman, *The Lives of William Benton* (Chicago: University of Chicago Press, 1969).

6. Shawn J. Parry-Giles, *The Rhetorical Presidency: Propaganda and the Cold War, 1945–1955* (Westport, Conn.: Praeger, 2002), 31–46. For a contemporary assessment of Benton's approach, see James Eayrs, "New Weapons in the Cold War: A Study of Recent Techniques in International Propaganda," *International Journal* 7 (1952), 36–47.

7. For a full explanation of a "public information" orientation, see Arthur MacMahon, *Memorandum on the Postwar International Information Program of the United States*, Department of State Publication 2438 (Washington, D.C.: GPO, 1945). The goals of a "freedom of information" policy are outlined on xiii, 7–16.

8. Ben Mark Cherrington, "America's Future Cultural Relations," *Annals of the American Academy of Political and Social Science* 235 (September 1944), 79.

9. Archibald MacLeish, "Unesco's Task," *Bulletin of the American Association of University Professors* 32 (1946), 607. In 1948, after the Cold War had definitively divided the United Nations into two opposing camps, MacLeish hoped he could recuperate the broad goals he had proposed for UNESCO two years earlier. In an ideologically divided world where war was always an immediate danger, UNESCO could provide a space where intellectuals from both sides could talk to each other about the larger questions of the purposes of life, the meaning of sacrifice and death, the conditions required for human dignity in an era of global conflict; see Archibald MacLeish, "How Can Unesco Contribute to Peace?" *Bulletin of the American Association of University Professors* 34 (1948), 539–545.

10. Ironically, Huxley proved to be one of the sharpest and most effective critics of the Soviet Union in the early days of the Cold War. Huxley took the lead in challenging the pseudoscientific theory of environmentally acquired inheritance advocated by Trofim Lysenko, director of the Institute of Genetics in the Soviet Union's Academy of Sciences. Debate over how genetic inheritance operated led to publicity over the arrest and execution of Soviet biologists who had not agreed with Lysenko. The debate brought to world attention the oftentimes arbitrary and oppressive conditions of intellectual life in the Soviet Union under Joseph Stalin. See Huxley's book on Lysenko and Soviet science, *Soviet Genetics and World Science: Lysenko and the Meaning of Heredity* (London: Chatto and Windus, 1949).

11. Jacquetta Hawkes and Leonard Woolley, *The History of Mankind*, vol. 1, *Prehistory and the Beginnings of Civilization* (New York: Harper and Row, 1963). On the History of Mankind project, its controversies, and reception, see Clare Wells, *The UN, Unesco, and the Politics of Knowledge* (London: Palgrave Macmillan, 1987), 121–127. Scientific and scholarly publications developed into one of the organization's most intensive and successful activities. Most UNESCO publications were technical reports by international teams examining specific and relatively narrowly focused research questions, while other series presented general histories of different regions of the world. In 1994, UNESCO published the first volume of a seven-volume *History of Humanity*, a project intended to replace the North Atlantic focus of the *History of Mankind* with a series of debates involving hundreds of historians from every part of the world (*History of Humanity: Scientific and Cultural Development*, vol. 1, *Prehistory and the Beginnings of Civilization*, ed. S. J. De Laet et al. [London: Routledge, 1994]). The concluding volume, on the twentieth century, appeared in 2008 (*History of Humanity: Scientific and Cultural Development*, vol. 7, *The Twentieth Century*, ed. Sarvepalli Gopal et al. [London: Routledge, 2008]). Perhaps over many generations, continued UNESCO efforts to synthesize global history will lead to a global scholarly consensus on many important questions, an agreement that could potentially influence the teaching of history in primary and secondary classes.

12. William H. McNeill, "Books Reviewed: *History of Mankind*, Vol. 6: *The Twentieth Century*, by Caroline Ware," *American Historical Review* 73 (1968), 1479. The volume was published in London in 1966 by Allen and Unwin.

13. William Benton, "The Role of International Information Service in Conduct of Foreign Relations," *U.S. Department of State Bulletin* 13 (1945), 589.

14. *Third Semiannual Report of the United States Advisory Commission on Educational Exchange Activities*, House document no. 556, 81st Congress, 2nd Session, 1950, p. 6.

15. Frank Ninkovich, "The Currents of Cultural Diplomacy, 1938–1947," *Diplomatic History* 1 (1977), 227–235; Michael L. Krenn, *Fall-out Shelters for the Human Spirit: American Art and the Cold War* (Chapel Hill: University of North Carolina Press, 2005), 9–49; Louis Menand, "Unpopular Front: American Art and the Cold War," *New Yorker* (17 October 2005), 177.

16. Katherine Dunham and Dino di Stefano, "Program: *Southland*," in *Kaiso: Katherine Dunham, an Anthology of Writings*, ed. Vèvè Clark and Margaret B. Wilkerson (Berkeley: Institute for the Study of Social Change, University of California, 1979), 117–120. Dunham's program was a historical look at the factors shaping African American life, but as African American veterans returned home from the war, lynching was on the rise across the South as segregationists murdered veterans who thought patriotic service entitled them to basic citizenship rights.

17. On State Department–funded cultural tours, see Frank Ninkovich, *U.S. Information Policy and Cultural Diplomacy* (New York: Foreign Policy Association, 1996); Penny Von Eschen, *Satchmo*

Blows Up the World: Jazz Ambassadors Play the Cold War (Cambridge, Mass.: Harvard University Press, 2004); Kenneth Osgood and Brian C. Etheridge, "Introduction: The New International History Meets the New Cultural History: Public Diplomacy and U.S. Foreign Relations," in *The United States and Public Diplomacy: New Directions in Cultural and International History*, ed. Kenneth Osgood and Brian C. Etheridge (Leiden: Martinus Nijhoff, 2010); Danielle Fosler-Lussier, "Music Pushed, Music Pulled: Cultural Diplomacy, Globalization, and Imperialism," *Diplomatic History* 36 (2012), 53–64; Sam Lebovic, "From War Junk to Educational Exchange: The World War II Origins of the Fulbright Program and the Foundations of American Cultural Globalism, 1945–1950," *Diplomatic History* 37 (2013), 280–312. John Brown, a retired Foreign Service diplomat, argues that the State Department never developed a consistent arts diplomacy program during the Cold War; see Brown, "Arts Diplomacy: The Neglected Aspect of Cultural Diplomacy," in *America's Dialogue with the World*, ed. William P. Kiehl (Washington, D.C.: Public Diplomacy Council, 2006), 71–90.

18. The most important work on the Congress for Cultural Freedom remains Frances Stonor Saunders, *The Cultural Cold War: The CIA and the World of Arts and Letters* (New York: New Press, 2000). The *New York Times* revealed the CIA funding of the Congress for Cultural Freedom on 27 April 1966. Other historical studies of the Congress of Cultural Freedom are Christopher Lasch, "The Cultural Cold War: A Short History of the Congress for Cultural Freedom," in *Towards a New Past: Dissenting Essays in American History*, ed. Barton J. Bernstein (New York: Pantheon, 1968), 322–359; Peter Coleman, *The Liberal Conspiracy: The Congress for Cultural Freedom and the Struggle for the Mind of Postwar Europe* (New York: Free Press, 1989); Pierre Grémion, *Intelligence de l'anticommunisme: Le Congrès pour la Liberté de la Culture, 1950–1975* (Paris: Fayard, 1995); Giles Scott Smith, *The Politics of Apolitical Culture: The Congress for Cultural Freedom and Postwar American Hegemony* (New York: Routledge, 2002).

19. Walter Johnson and Francis J. Colligan, *The Fulbright Program: A History* (Chicago: University of Chicago Press, 1965).

20. Harold E. Davis, "Permanent Bases of Inter-American Education," *English Journal* 34 (1945), 208–212; J. Manuel Espinosa, "Exchange of Professors Between the United States and Other American Republics," *Americas* 3 (1947), 535–543; Liping Bu, "Educational Exchange and Cultural Diplomacy in the Cold War," *Journal of American Studies* 33 (1999), 393–415. That there were only four official national languages in the western hemisphere provided a sharp focus for language training during the interwar years. After 1945, with U.S. interests globalized, the languages that needed to be addressed multiplied. Specialization became more practical, replacing a utopian goal of developing a multilingual citizenry. Experts working in particular areas of the world would develop the linguistic proficiencies needed to do their jobs and to provide information to the U.S. institutions that had business to do in those regions. Language training shifted to the university level, where students' career interests guided their choice of a foreign language to study. Language acquisition became a corollary of appropriate expertise rather than the development of global citizenship. Resurgence of interest in French and German fit as well the cultural priorities of a globalized United States with strategic interests focused on the North Atlantic alliance.

21. Ben M. Cherrington to Senator Arthur H. Vandenberg, 27 May 1947, published in Ben M. Cherrington, "Our Unesco Agency," *Phi Delta Kappan* 29 (October 1947), 69.

22. Name withheld to Ben M. Cherrington, 31 May 1947, published in Cherrington, "Our Unesco Agency," 70. On the Smith-Mundt Act and the coalition built to get it passed, see Burton Paulu, "The Smith-Mundt Act: A Legislative History," *Journalism Quarterly* 30 (1953), 300–314; Bu, "Educational Exchange and Cultural Diplomacy."

23. On Communist Party cultural activities, see Augusto Buonicore, "Comunistas, Cultura e Intelectuais entre os Anos de 1940 e 1950," online at http://www.vermelho.org.br/ma/noticia.php?id_noticia=179379&id_secao=11; Carlos N. Coutinho, *Os Intelectuais e a Organização da Cultura no Brasil* (São Paulo: Temas de Ciências Humanas, 1981); Leandro Konder, *A Democracia e os Comunistas no Brasil* (Rio de Janeiro: Editora Graal, 1980); Leandro Konder, *Os Intelectuais Brasileiros e a Cultura* (Belo Horizonte: Editora Oficina de Livros, 1991); Dênis de Moraes, *O Imaginário Vigiado: A Imprensa Comunista e o Realismo Socialista no Brasil (1947–1953)* (Rio de Janeiro: Editora José

Olympio, 1994); Antônio Albino C. Rubim, *Marxismo, Cultura e Intelectuais no Brasil* (Salvador: Centro Editorial e Didático da Universidade Federal da Bahia, 1995).

24. Economic summaries of effects of postwar transition on wages and prices drawn from Laurence Duggan, *The Americas: The Search for Hemispheric Security* (New York: Holt, 1949), 125–131.

25. On U.S. efforts to reform Brazilian labor practices along North American lines, see Eduardo José Affonso, "Para Norte-Americano Ver: Adidos Trabalhistas e Operários Brasileiros (1943/1952)," Ph.D. dissertation, University of São Paulo, 2011, 80–132; for a more general discussion of U.S. labor policies in Latin America between 1940 and 1960, see Robert J. Alexander, "Labor and Inter-American Relations," *Annals of the American Academy of Political and Social Science* 334 (1961), 41–53. On increases in police programs, see Martha K. Huggins, *Political Policing: The United States and Latin America* (Durham, N.C.: Duke University Press, 1998); and Rodrigo Patto Sá Motta, "Modernizing Repression: USAID and the Brazilian Police," *Revista Brasileira de História* 30 (2010), 235–262.

26. Érico Veríssimo, "Fragmento de crônica em inglês sobre protestos no Rio de Janeiro" (1946?), Acervo de Érico Veríssimo, Instituto Moreira Salles.

27. Daniel Cosío Villegas, "La Crisis de México," *Cuadernos Americanos* 32 (March 1947), 29–51. Cosío Villegas's arguments informed an unsigned editorial in the *Chicago Daily Tribune* criticizing Truman's international economic policies, "Utopia, Unlimited" (17 September 1950, p. 24). See Deborah Fitzgerald, "Exporting American Agriculture: The Rockefeller Foundation in Mexico," *Social Studies of Science* 16 (1986), 457–483, for a review of U.S. efforts to improve the productivity of Mexican farmers. Fitzgerald argues that only those farmers already operating on a commercial basis, producing for either national urban markets or markets in the United States and relying on hired farm labor for most tasks, were able to benefit from American aid programs. The majority of Mexican farmers, operating at a subsistence level or on collectively owned land, remained impoverished and unable to secure the loans they needed to improve their yields.

28. Daniel Cosío Villegas, "Concerning the United States," *Revista de América* (Bogotá) 1 (March 1945), 361–365.

29. For a thorough discussion of the congress convened by the Associação Brasileiro de Escritores, see Felipe Víctor Lima, "O Primeiro Congresso de Escritores: Movimento Intelectual contra o Estado Novo (1945)," Ph.D. dissertation, University of São Paulo, 2010; see also Fernando Jorge, *Cala a Boca, Jornalista! O Ódio e a Fúria dos Mandões contra a Imprensa Brasileira*, 3rd ed. (São Paulo: Vozes, 1990), 88–95.

30. Lima, "O Primeiro Congresso de Escritores," 184–196.

Chapter 10

1. Francisco Vidal Luna and Herbert S. Klein, *The Economic and Social History of Brazil Since 1889* (Cambridge: Cambridge University Press, 2014), 192–218, 255–256; Riordan Roett, *The New Brazil* (Washington, D.C.: Brookings Institution, 2010), 41–54; Rafael R. Ioris, *Transforming Brazil: A History of National Development in the Postwar Era* (New York: Routledge, 2014), 51–86, 151–177.

2. Laurence Hallewell, *Books in Brazil: A History of the Publishing Trade* (Metuchen, N.J.: Scarecrow Press, 1982), 235.

3. Hallewell, *Books in Brazil*, 235, 275, 334.

4. Macmillan reported that *Brazilian Literature* sold twenty thousand copies in its first year on the market. For two reviews of Brazilian books published in English translation, see Érico Veríssimo, "Literary Milestone in Brazil: Euclides da Cunha's Fine Study in an English Translation," review of *Rebellion in the Backlands* by Euclides da Cunha, trans. Samuel Putnam (Chicago: University of Chicago Press, 1944), *New York Times* (6 February 1944), Book Review sec., p. 1; Érico Veríssimo, "A Backlands Juliet," review of *Inocencia* by Alfredo d'Escragnolle Taunay, trans. Henriqueta Chamberlain (New York: Macmillan, 1945), *New York Times* (4 March 1945), Book Review sec., p. 4.

5. Érico Veríssimo, "Sempre fui contra o fechamento do Partido Comunista do Brasil" (24 May 1947), Acervo de Érico Veríssimo, Instituto Moreira Salles (hereafter Acervo de EV, IMS). Orig-

inal Portuguese text: acho um bluff colossal afirmar que a Rússia é uma democracia e fico irritado quando os comunista brasileiros apresentam a ditadura Stalinista como um modelo para o resto do mundo.

6. Érico Veríssimo to Julio Teixeira, 7 April 1949, Acervo de Érico Veríssimo, IMS.

7. Érico Veríssimo to Oswald de Andrade, 11 March 1950, Acervo de Érico Veríssimo, IMS. Original Portuguese text: Sou um homem que nessa luta entre dois imperialismos prefere ficar eqüidistante da Casa Branca e do Kremlin.

8. Érico Veríssimo to Dr. J. Braga Pinheiro, Comissão Coordenadora Pro-Anistia dos Presos e Exiliados Políticos de Espanha e Portugal [undated, but 1948], Acervo de EV, IMS.

9. Veríssimo, "Sempre fui contra o fechamento."

10. "Dunham Ban Stirs Brazil," *New York Times* (19 July 1950), p. 22; "Brazil Spurs Racial Act," *New York Times* (24 October 1950), p. 6; "Equality Law in Brazil," *New York Times* (5 July 1951), p. 18; "Katherine Dunham se exhibirá em São Paulo," *Folha da Manhã* (5 July 1950), p. 6; Ricardi, "Katherine Dunham e sua companhia negra," *Folha da Manhã* (13 July 1950), p. 4; "Condenação na câmara dos deputados aos preconceitos de raça e de cor," *Folha da Manhã* (18 July 1950), pp. 1–2; Ricardi, "Katherine Dunham," *Folha da Manhã* (21 July 1950), p. 6; see also *Folha da Manhã* 26 July, 30 September, and 15 December 1950. On enforcement of antidiscrimination laws in Brazil, see Thomas E. Skidmore, *Black into White: Race and Nationality in Brazilian Thought* (Durham, N.C.: Duke University Press, 1993), 212. Elizabeth Bishop discusses the Dunham affair in *Brazil* (New York: Time, 1962), 113–114.

11. Veríssimo wrote about the 1924 rebellion and the march of the Prestes column in *O Tempo e o Vento*, vol. 1, *O Retrato* (São Paulo: Companhia das Letras, 2005; originally published 1951), 7–62. Jorge Amado wrote a strikingly different assessment in *A Vida de Luis Carlos Prestes, o Cavaleiro de Esperança* (São Paulo: Editora Livraria Martins, 1945; updated in 1956).

12. See, for example, Manoel Luiz, "Érico Veríssimo, 'Intelectual de Partido,'" *Horizonte* 2 (January 1952), 20–21; Fernando Guedes, "A propósito de *O Retrato*," *Horizonte* 2 (March–April 1952), 113–115.

13. On Amado's political evolution, see A. M. Miranda, *Cadernos de Literatura Brasileira* no. 3: Jorge Amado (1997), 12–16. For an insightful discussion of the deepening divide between communist and noncommunist writers in Brazil in the 1950s, see Marisângela T. A. Martins, "À Esquerda de Seu Tempo: Escritors e o Partido Comunista do Brasil (Porto Alegre—1927-1957)," Ph.D. dissertation, Federal University of Rio Grande do Sul, 2012, 307–318.

14. Érico Veríssimo, *Solo de Clarineta: Memórias* (Porto Alegre: Editora Globa, 1973), 1:258.

15. Érico Veríssimo, "Conferencia proferida por Érico Veríssimo quando diretor de Assuntos Culturais de OEP para ocasião da abertura da Conferencia Del Niño na Cidade do Panamá em 1955," 1–2, Acervo de EV, IMS. Original Spanish text: Existen en nuestra América muchos millones de personas que viven—si se puede emplear este verbo—en un plano animal más que en un plano humano. Y no conozco una cruzada más noble y grandiosa para los hombres de pensamiento y de gobierno que la de arrebatar a las enfermedades, al analfabetismo y a la miseria esas inmensas masas que viven al margen de la vida procurándoles un mundo mejor, más bello y en el que cada cual pueda tener conciencia no solamente de su cuerpo, sino también de su alma, de su derecho a la felicidad y a participar íntegramente en los beneficios de la comunidad humana.

16. Veríssimo, "Conferencia proferida por Érico Veríssimo," 4. Original Spanish text: el más completo y cruel abandono a poblaciones enteras, sin asistencia médica, sin hospitales, sin escuelas, sin nada. Sinceramente, no veo *mucho* diferencia entre una y otra forma de *irrespeto* a la persona humana.

17. Érico Veríssimo to Herbert Caro, 11 February 1954, Acervo de EV, IMS. Original Portuguese text: As cidades que visitei—Albuquerque, Tucson, Los Angeles, San Francisco, Berkeley, Oakland, Eugene, Seattle, Denver, Colorado Springs, Kansas [City], St. Louis, progridem fabulosamente, são muito confortáveis mas geralmente sem graça, sem imprevisto, sem pitoresco. Fui muito bem tratado, muito festejado, muito "perguntado." As conferencias foram um sucesso quase "teatral." É que eu ia melhorando o meu "ato" de cidade para cidade. Falei com muita franqueza, dourando a

pílula, isto é, entremeiando as informações de piadas; e, com um ar de brincadeira, eu ia dizendo o que queria. Falando para homens de negócios, Babbitts, no Foreign Affairs Institute de Albuquerque, acabei discutindo com os republicanos presentes. O período de perguntas e respostas durou quase uma hora e foi muito agitado. Disse algumas inconveniências durante toda a viagem, coisas que eu "não era suposto" dizer como funcionário da União. Mas disse.

18. Érico Veríssimo to Herbert Caro, 3 September 1954, Acervo de EV, IMS.

19. Érico Veríssimo to Herbert Caro, 6 April 1954, Acervo de EV, IMS. Original Portuguese text: muita besteira, muito discurso vazio. Perdi todo o respeito por esses embaixadores e delegados.

20. The text of the Convention for the Promotion of Inter-American Cultural Relations, Signed at the Tenth Inter-American Conference, Caracas, 1–28 March 1954, is posted on the website of the Organization of American States, at http://www.oas.org/juridico/english/treaties/a-48.html.

21. Activities of the Chicago Pan America Assembly are documented in the papers of Marian L. Larson, Special Collections and University Archives, University of Illinois at Chicago. Larson was the executive director of the group from 1952 to 1973.

22. Érico Veríssimo to Ralph Edward Dimmick, 1 April 1964, Acervo de EV, IMS.

23. Veríssimo, Solo de Clarineta, 1:261.

24. Veríssimo, Solo de Clarineta, 1:271.

25. Érico Veríssimo to Ema and Gino Cervi, 6 August 1954, Acervo de EV, IMS.

26. Veríssimo, Solo de Clarineta, 1:278.

27. Érico Veríssimo to Herbert Caro, 29 June 1954, Acervo de EV, IMS. Original Portuguese text: Como sabes, como deves imaginar, a questão da Guatemala tem trazido a OEA e a União em polvorosa. Meetings a toda a hora. Delegados pálidos em cochiches pelos cantos. Acho todo esse assunto muito sério e ao mesmo tempo melancólico. Discordo da política do State Department. Essa gente jamais aprenderá. Falta-lhes tacto diplomático, savoir faire, experiência. Simpatizo com a causa desse pequeno país que procura sair da sua triste idade media. Está claro que é perigoso fazer aliança com os comunistas, mas o maior perigo não é esse e sim a formação de mais uma ditadura direitista nas Américas com o beneplácito de Washington. Disgusting!

28. Veríssimo, Solo de Clarineta, 1:292.

29. Pablo Neruda to Érico Veríssimo, 19 November 1953, Acervo de EV, IMS. In 1970, Neruda agreed to be included and praised the selection of poems (Neruda to Veríssimo, 1 September 1970), Acervo de EV, IMS. Original Spanish text: friamente extorsionan nuestra economía, planean la represión, destruyen la libertad en el continente, esclavizan a Puerto Rico.

30. Quoted in Érico Veríssimo to Herbert Caro, 30 December 1953, Acerto do EV, IMS. Original Portuguese text: Basta, não acha? Eu não defendo os Estados Unidos dos crimes que o poeta imputa (com perdão da má palavra) a este país. Mas um comunista, um adorador da Rússia soviética não tem direito falar em liberdade de expressão e em justiça.

31. Jorge Amado to Érico Veríssimo, 15 November 1953, Acervo de EV, IMS.

32. Veríssimo recalled the meeting in these terms, but records of the Mexico City meeting show that the U.S. participants were divided. Many attacked the campaign against Arbenz, while others defended it. See Patrick Iber, "The Imperialism of Liberty: Intellectuals and the Politics of Culture in Cold War Latin America," Ph.D. dissertation, University of Chicago, 2011, 289.

33. Doris Meyer, Victoria Ocampo: Against the Wind and the Tide (Austin: University of Texas Press, 1990; first published 1979), 170.

34. Quoted in Meyer, Victoria Ocampo, 212, n. 45.

35. Victoria Ocampo to Gabriela Mistral, 18 September 1951; Gabriela Mistral to Victoria Ocampo, April or May 1952?; Ocampo to Mistral, 21 February 1954; Ocampo to Mistral, 11 July 1954; in Gabriel Mistral and Victoria Ocampo, This America of Ours: The Letters of Gabriela Mistral and Victoria Ocampo, ed. and trans. Elizabeth Horan and Doris Meyer (Austin: University of Texas Press, 2003), 169–171, 187–189, 222–223, 235.

36. Germán Arciniegas, Con América nace la nueva historia (Bogotá: Tercer Mundo Editores, 1992), 56–57; Germán Arciniegas, Cuadernos de un estudiante americano (Bogotá: Ediciones Uniandes, 1994), 567.

37. Germán Arciniegas, "Book in the News: William Benton, *The Voice of Latin America*," *Saturday Review of Literature* (30 September 1961), 17–18; Claudio Véliz, "The Voice of Mr. Benton," *New Left Review* 1 (January–February 1963), 97–98.

Chapter 11

1. Herbert Weinstock to Harriet de Onís, 10 August 1954, Alfred A. Knopf Inc. Manuscript Collection, Harry Ransom Center, University of Texas at Austin.

2. Harriet de Onís to Herbert Weinstock, 26 August 1954, Knopf Manuscript Collection.

3. Herbert Weinstock to Harriet de Onís, 15 September 1954, Knopf Manuscript Collection.

4. On the publishing history of *Los pasos perdidos*, see Deborah Cohn, "Retracing *The Lost Steps*: The Cuban Revolution, the Cold War, and Publishing Alejo Carpentier in the United States," *CR: The New Centennial Review* 3 (2003), 81–108; and Irene Rostagno, *Searching for Recognition: The Promotion of Latin American Literature in the United States* (Westport, Conn.: Greenwood Press, 1997), 48–51.

5. Herbert Weinstock to Jean Malaquais, 12 December 1954, Knopf Manuscript Collection.

6. "To Eden and Back," *Time* 68 (22 October 1956), 116. For other reviews of *The Lost Steps*, see Selden Rodman, "Journey into the Night," *New York Times* (14 October 1956), Book Review magazine, p. 5: "It doesn't quite come off. Perhaps it is because the hero is so very, very much the intellectual that it is difficult, despite the breathlessness with which the three women abandon themselves to him, to be convinced that he is also a man"; Lyn Hart, untitled book review of *The Lost Steps*, *Library Journal* 81 (1 November 1956), 2592: "Not recommended"; untitled book review of *The Lost Steps*, *New Yorker* 32 (10 November 1956), 224: "the descriptions . . . are masterly, to say the least. . . . Mr. Carpentier's prose shines with extraordinary brilliance, but the story he tells—a solemn one—is made absurd by his total lack of humor"; Gouverneur Paulding, untitled book review of *The Lost Steps*, *New York Herald Tribune* (18 November 1956), 7: "a brilliant and unusual novel"; William Pfaff, untitled book review of *The Lost Steps*, *Commonweal* 65 (23 November 1956), 211: "a brilliant and enviable accomplishment"; C. J. Rolo, untitled book review of *The Lost Steps*, *Atlantic* 198 (November 1956), 107: "What is original and exciting about *The Lost Steps* is the way in which action, sophisticated introspection, and powerfully evoked atmosphere are skillfully integrated"; R. W. Flint, "The Undying Apocalypse," *Partisan Review* 24 (Winter 1957), 143–144: "a most *informative* entertainment . . . put to the service of a tired and jejune Lawrentian primitivism"; Dorothy Van Ghent, untitled book review of *The Lost Steps*, *Yale Review* 46 (Winter 1957), 275: "Its grandeur of conception, the splendor of its imagery, the powerful sweep of its energy are qualities of an individual greatness of mind."

7. On Caillois's time in Latin America and its effect on books published in France, see Roger Bastide, "Sous 'La Croix du Sud': L'Amérique latine dans le miroir de sa littérature," *Annales* 13 (1958), 30–46; Silvia Molloy, *La Diffusion de la littérature hispano-américaine en France au XXe siècle* (Paris: Presses Universitaires Françaises, 1972), 178–193; Claude Fell, "La collection 'La Croix du Sud,' tremplin de la littérature latino-américaine en France," *Río de la Plata* 13–14 (1992), 173–189; Odile Felgine, *Roger Caillois* (Paris: Stock, 1994), 197–266, 307–346; Annick Louis, "Étoiles d'un ciel étranger: Roger Caillois et l'Amérique Latine," *Littérature* 170 (2013), 71–81.

8. On Caillois's linkage of politics, ritual, and everyday culture, see Simonetta Falasca-Zamponi, *Rethinking the Political: The Sacred, Aesthetic Politics, and the Collège de Sociologie* (Montreal: McGill-Queen's University Press, 2011). See also Roger Caillois, *Espace américain* (Paris: Éditions Fata Morgana, 1983).

9. Roger Caillois, untitled announcement, *Bulletin de la NRF* 46 (April 1951), 17. Original French text: Dans la collection la Croix du Sud, prendront place les oeuvres les plus diverses . . . les mieux faits pour rendre compte de la formation et du mode de développement des groupes humains et des valeurs humaines dans un continent encore neuf, à peine dominé, où la lutte avec l'espace et avec la nature demeure sévère, qui possède un style de vie particulier, et auquel d'inépuisables ressources permettent un rôle de premier plan dans l'histoire prochaine.

10. Caillois, *Espace américain*, 9–10. Original French text: Isolé par d'immenses étendues d'eau que l'homme n'apprit pas vite à traverser, ce continent demeura longtemps inconnu du reste du monde. Et le jour, qui n'est pas loin, où le monde eut la révélation qu'il existait une terre nouvelle au-delà de l'Océan, il était lui-même vieux et fatigué, en proie à ces difficultés inextricables qui s'accroissent le long de l'histoire.

11. Caillois, *Espace américain*, 11–12. Original French text: Voilà qui marque singulièrement cette contrée parmi les autres: ceux qui devinrent Américains le furent à l'origine de chaque lignée par leur volonté et non par la naissance, formant une race inédite et d'hommes qui avaient un jour rompu avec leur héritage . . . on se trouvait là pour avoir accepté un pari avec soi-même: celui de dé-fier l'avenir en ne comptant que sur ses propres forces.

12. Caillois, *Espace américain*, 25. Original French text: Un sang plus abondant coule plus vif dans les veines des fils, comme s'il gardait quelque chose, non point des fautes ou des timidités des pères, mais de l'audace de leur décision confiante; il semble que la générosité d'un instant continue de marquer . . . [dont] la septième et la dix-septième génération de la lignée nouvelle . . . a gagné une première noblesse et un étrange élargissement de l'être.

13. For a discussion of the promotion campaigns that Gallimard developed for books in the se-ries, see Jean-Claude Villegas, "Aux seuils d'une collection," *Rio de la Plata* 13–14 (1992), 191–205.

14. Washington Lockhart, "El mundo no es absurdo," in Washington Lockhart, *El mundo no es absurdo y otros artículos* (Montevideo: Ediciones Asir, 1961), 9–18, quotes on 15. Lockhart's assess-ment of the Cuban revolution had an equally passionate U.S. counterpart in the sociologist C. Wright Mills's provocative and widely discussed book, *Listen, Yankee! The Revolution in Cuba* (New York: McGraw-Hill, 1960). Mills created a fictional narrator who directly addresses his readers. It was a composite voice of revolutionaries Mills had met in Cuba. Instead of description and analysis, Mills presented an angry emotional tirade that challenged the assumptions of U.S. journalists, like Her-bert L. Matthews, who won a Pulitzer Prize for his reporting on the Cuban revolution in the *New York Times*. Matthews had exposed the venality and brutality of the Batista regime but he remained puzzled about the goals of Castro's movement and its relation to what the Cuban people wanted. The revolution's emotional fervor was puzzling because it seemed to give short shrift to the rational plan-ning Cuba needed to become prosperous. Mills argued instead that the main goal of the revolution was to empower people to take personal responsibility for their collective destinies, a development entirely alien to U.S. citizens, shaped by subordination to the rational organization of labor and con-sumption.

15. "Progresso e ordem" (progress and order) is inscribed in the center of the Brazilian flag.

16. Anaïs Fléchet, "Um mito exótico? A recepção crítica de *Orfeu Negro* de Marcel Camus (1959–2008)," *Significação* 32 (2009), 45, 47.

17. Alfred Knopf to Jorge Amado, 16 July 1963, Knopf Manuscript Collection. In 1952, follow-ing the release of *Time and the Wind*, Érico Veríssimo received a royalty check from Macmillan comparable in size to the check Knopf sent Amado in 1963. Knopf was likely unaware of this, and while Veríssimo's books had sold well, none received the level of attention given *Gabriela, Clove and Cinnamon*. Knopf's comments on how books had done tended toward overstatement. He almost al-ways found sales figures to be "disappointing," even in cases where other evidence indicates a book was selling well. He described reviewers with critical comments as "despicable" and "misinformed." It would be consistent for him to send Amado a congratulatory letter that exaggerated, at least to a slight degree, the scope of his success, particularly given that Knopf would have only general im-pressions of how other publishers' lists had done rather than precise sales figures, which no U.S. publisher made public. "Best-seller" lists provide rough tools rather than exacting measurements of how well books have done. Publishers do not release sales figure data to the public, and even years later it is difficult to know exactly how well individual books did if authors' royalty reports were not saved as part of a writer's papers. The *New York Times*, *Publishers Weekly*, and other journals that prepared "best-seller" lists each surveyed a small number of bookstores with which the periodical had close relations for information on which titles were selling most. They also looked at how many printings a title went through, and they tried to glean information about the size of print runs. Actual

sales numbers of books on the lists could be of widely differing scales. Publishers and bookstores treated "best-seller" lists as advertising tools, and they frequently manipulated information to help generate excitement about a title.

18. Érico Veríssimo to Ralph Dimmick, 4 March 1965; Érico Veríssimo to Luiz Carlos Meneghini, 27 October 1965, 15 November 1965, and 8 August 1966; all in Acervo de Érico Veríssimo, Instituto Moreira Salles (hereafter Acervo de EV, IMS). In 1956, the first dramatic adaptation of Veríssimo's work appeared. Walter George Durst and Cassiano Gabus Mendes made a feature film, *O Sobrado* ("The Big House"), adapted from a section of *O Tempo e o Vento* that focused on the civil war of 1896. The following year, in the United States, Jason Robards and E. G. Marshall starred in an adaptation of Veríssimo's novel *Noite* ("Night"), produced as a live television drama for *The Alcoa Hour*. Veríssimo was unhappy with both productions, despite the impressive talent involved and *O Sobrado* winning the Brazilian film critics' association award for best film of 1956.

19. Veríssimo to Meneghini, 15 November 1965.

20. "Latin American Books from Knopf," full-page display advertisement in the *New York Times* (28 September 1969), Book Review sec., p. 21.

21. More frequent advertisements based on examining the Book Review section of the *New York Times* from 1960 to 1974; information on paperback editions derived from a review of Bradley A. Shaw, *Latin American Literature in English Translation: An Annotated Bibliography* (New York: New York University Press, 1976). Shaw's bibliography notes the number of editions for titles, with the most complete information on when paperback editions appeared. The publisher of the original trade edition of a title seldom released the mass-market paperback edition, but entered into a licensing agreement with one of several houses that specialized in paperback editions, such as Avon, Bantam Books, New American Library, or Signet. Precise sales information for paperbacks was often difficult to recover. Instead of asking for royalty payments, the original publisher typically charged licensing fees for each print run. As a result, some publishers preferred to defer paperback editions until they had determined that they had exhausted the potential for hardback sales. This may have been Knopf's strategy as even *Gabriela, Clove and Cinnamon*, which had robust sales from its appearance in 1963, did not go to paperback until 1974. In contrast, Farrar, Straus and Giroux released paperback editions of Carlos Fuentes's novels within a year, as did Harper and Row for the novels it published by Gabriel García Márquez.

22. From dust jacket of Carlos Fuentes, *The Death of Artemio Cruz*, trans. Sam Hileman (New York: Farrar, Straus, 1964).

23. Tad Szulc, "Visa Denial Bars Leftist's Debate," *New York Times* (7 April 1962), 2; "U.S. Denies Author Visa for Debate," *Washington Post* (7 April 1962), A2.

24. Deborah Cohn, *The Latin American Literary Boom and U.S. Nationalism During the Cold War* (Nashville: Vanderbilt University Press, 2012), 49–50; Graham Kates, "FBI Foiled and Followed Author," *New York City News Service* (21 June 2013), online at http://www.nycitynewsservice.com /2013/06/fbi-foiled-and-followed-author/. A redacted version of the files the FBI compiled on Fuentes is available online at http://vault.fbi.gov/carlos-fuentes/carlos-fuentes-part-01-of-01/view. Explanation for the hold on his visa applications appears in a memo dated 27 September 1965, from director, FBI to SAC [Special Agent in Charge], New York (p. 40 of the redacted file). The memo outlines a plan of action for permanently barring Fuentes from entry into the United States if the FBI could determine that he had participated in anti–Vietnam War protests during any of the visits when the State Department had waived the ban on his entry into the country. FBI sources could not provide the information the agency desired. In 1966, the State Department determined that Fuentes should be admitted into the United States because he was a person of "influence and potential." The FBI put an alert on his name indicating that agents and informants were to watch his activities closely whenever he was in the country, and the agency began compiling evidence that would support permanently banning Fuentes from the United States.

25. Henry Raymont, "Leftist Novelist Is Barred by U.S.," *New York Times* (28 February 1969), p. 39; Henry Raymont, "Refusal to Let Fuentes Enter Puerto Rico Revives Controversy over Immigration Policy," *New York Times* (3 March 1969), p. 11. In 1970, after Senator William Fulbright

brought the issue up in Congress, Secretary of State William Rogers instructed State Department consular staff that Fuentes was to receive a waiver whenever he applied for a visa to enter the United States. In 1978, the State Department issued Fuentes an H-1 so he could teach at U.S. universities. With his ongoing right to live and work inside the United States, issuing a waiver for him to enter the country was no longer needed. The FBI, however, continued monitoring his activities until 1987.

26. Emir Rodríguez Monegal highlighted the importance of Fuentes's business arrangements in *El boom de la novella latinoamericana* (Caracas: Tiempo Nuevo, 1972), 22–30.

27. Carlos Fuentes, prologue to Margaret Sayers Peden's English-language translation of *Ariel* (Austin: University of Texas Press, 1988), 13–14, 20–22.

28. In addition to its program for supporting translation and reception of contemporary Latin American literature, CIAR had a gallery where staff and guest curators mounted four to seven art exhibitions each year, as well as a program for promoting contemporary music from Latin America. A goal of the art program was to help Latin American artists find a gallery in New York. See Chapter 13 for further discussion.

29. Luis Harss and Barbara Dohmann, *Into the Mainstream: Conversations with Latin-American Writers* (New York: Harper and Row, 1967); Rita Guibert, *Seven Voices: Seven Latin American Writers Talk to Rita Guibert*, trans. Frances Partridge (New York: Knopf, 1972).

30. On the launching and development of the CIAR program, see annual reports of the Center for Inter-American Relations, 1968–1973, Americas Society Archives, New York City. See also Elaine De Rosa, "Center for Inter-American Relations: A Decade of Translation Service," *Translation Review* 2 (1978), 37–40; Irene Rostagno, *Searching for Recognition: The Promotion of Latin American Literature in the United States* (Westport, Conn.: Greenwood Press, 1997), 102–115; Alfred MacAdam, "The Boom and Beyond: Latin American Literature and the Americas Society," in *A Hemispheric Venture: Thirty-Five Years of Culture at the Americas Society, 1965–2000*, ed. John A. Farmer and Ilona Katzow (New York: Americas Society, 2000), 179–205; María Eugenia Mudrovcic, "Reading Latin American Literature Abroad: Agency and Canon Formation in the Sixties and Seventies," in *Voice-overs: Translation and Latin American Literature*, ed. Daniel Balderston and Marcy E. Schwartz (Albany: State University of New York Press, 2002), 129–143; Cohn, *The Latin American Literary Boom*, 145–192.

31. Mudrovcic, "Reading Latin American Literature Abroad," 129–130. Sábato's book did not appear in English until 1981.

32. Johan Heilbron, "Toward a Sociology of Translation: Book Translation as a Cultural World-System," *European Journal of Social Theory* 2 (1999), 429–444.

33. Emir Rodríguez Monegal, "The New Latin American Literature in the USA," *Review: Latin American Literature and Arts* 1 (1967), 3–13, quotes on 3.

34. Henry Raymont, "Latin Writers Stirring Up U.S. Publishers' Interest," *New York Times* (15 April 1969), p. 41.

35. "Books: Journey Without an End," *Time* (24 March 1967).

36. John Ashbery, "A Game with Shifting Mirrors," *New York Times* (16 April 1967), Book Review sec., p. 3.

37. José Donoso, *The Boom in Spanish American Literature: A Personal History*, trans. Gregory Kolovakos (New York: Columbia University Press, 1977), 24; José Donoso, *Historia personal del "boom"* (Buenos Aires: Sudamericana, 1984), 28.

38. Donoso, *The Boom in Spanish American Literature,* 13. Spanish text: Encontrábamos estatismo y pobreza (Donoso, *Historia personal del "boom,"* 20).

39. Donoso, *The Boom in Spanish American Literature*, 21. Spanish text: podían representar con dignidad las cualidades de su continente . . . identificándose con los niveles más obvios de sus luchas (Donoso, *Historia personal del "boom,"* 26).

40. Robert J. Clements, "Latin America's Neglected Literature," *Saturday Review* 48 (22 May 1965), 60–61.

41. For a discussion of the tension between literary autonomy and political commitment in the novels of Mario Vargas Llosa, see Efraín Kristal, *Temptation of the Word: The Novels of Mario Vargas Llosa* (Nashville: Vanderbilt University Press, 1998), 3–24.

Chapter 12

Note on chapter title: Veríssimo completed the sentence with: "before it had seemed to me an invention of communist propaganda." Érico Veríssimo to Daniel Fresnot, quoted in Daniel Fresnot, *O pensamento politico de Érico Veríssimo* (Rio de Janeiro: Graal, 1977), 55. Original Portuguese: AGORA EU ACREDITO NO IMPERIALISMO AMERICANO, que antes me parecia um pouco invenção da propaganda comunista (capitalization in original).

1. In 2011, the Brazilian Congress established a National Truth Commission to documents human rights violations between 1946 and 1988. Accumulated findings of the Brazilian National Truth Commission are online at http://www.cnv.gov.br, including a three-volume report detailing its findings. On training in interrogation methods in the United States, see Comissão Nacional da Verdade, *Relatório* (Brasília: Comissão Nacional da Verdade, 2014), vol. 1, 141–149, 329–336, 352–354, 574; Simon Romero, "Leader's Torture in the '70s Stirs Ghosts in Brazil," *New York Times* (4 August 2012). Recently declassified State Department documents related to the systematic use of torture and summary executions during the dictatorship are discussed in Peter Kornbluh, "Brazil: Dictatorship-Era Torture Techniques and Secret Executions Revealed in Declassified U.S. Documents," *National Security Archive* (8 July 2014), online at http://www.globalresearch.ca/brazil-dictatorship-era-torture-techniques-and-secret-executions-revealed-in-declassified-u-s-documents/5390565.

2. For concise analyses of the changing directions of the dictatorship, see Thomas E. Skidmore, *The Politics of Military Rule in Brazil, 1964–1985* (New York: Oxford University Press, 1988); and Maria Helena Moreira Alves, *State and Opposition in Military Brazil* (Austin: University of Texas Press, 1985). On censorship, see Alvaro Gonçalves Antunes, *Cultura Amordaçada: Intelectuais e Músicos sob a Vigilância do DEOPS* (São Paulo: Arquivo do Estado, 2002); Maria Luiza Tucci Carneiro, *Livros Proibidos, Idéias Malditas: O DEOPS e as Minorias Silenciadas* (São Paulo: FAPESP, 2002); Creuza de Oliveira Berg, *Mecanismos do Silêncio: Expressões Artísticas e Censura no Regime Militar (1964–1984)* (São Carlos: EdUFSCar, 2002). Caetano Veloso, one of the leading figures in the Tropicália movement in the 1960s and a prominent musical recording artist, described his imprisonment, torture including the use of execution threats, and exile in his memoirs, *Tropical Truth: A Story of Music and Revolution in Brazil* (New York: Da Capo Press, 2003), 197–201, 215–263, 291–292. On the military's treatment of musical artists, see also Christopher Dunn, *Brutality Garden: Tropicália and the Emergence of a Brazilian Counterculture* (Chapel Hill: University of North Carolina Press, 2001), 109–118, 143–150, 164–166.

3. For an articulation of the dilemmas Veríssimo saw as he wrote *O Senhor Embaixador*, see Érico Veríssimo to Enio Silveira, 17 November 1964, Acervo de Érico Veríssimo, Instituto Moreira Salles (hereafter Acervo de EV, IMS). For a thorough study of Veríssimo's critique of U.S. foreign policy and style of global governance in *O Senhor Embaixador* and *O Prisioneiro*, see Carlos Cortez Minchillo, *Erico Verissimo, Escritor do Mundo: Circulação Literária, Cosmopolitismo e Relações Interamericanas* (São Paulo: Editora da Universidade de São Paulo, 2015), 207–262.

4. Thomas Lask, "Books of the Times: Absolute Power and Absolute Corruption," *New York Times* (1 April 1967), 29.

5. Érico Veríssimo, *O Senhor Embaixador* (São Paulo: Companhia das Letras, 2005; originally published 1965), 382. Original Portuguese text: Para vocês, liberais burgueses, liberdade é algo que pode existir fora do contexto da vida e do bem-estar do povo. Uma jóia que se guarda e não se usa por ser uma relíquia de família. Jóia falsa, na minha opinião. Inútil. . . . A liberdade não pode ser um fim em si mesma. É um *meio* de proporcionar uma vida melhor para a maioria. Se ela não conseguir esse objetivo, de nada valerá.

6. Veríssimo, *O Senhor Embaixador*, 407–411.

7. Carlos Fuentes to Herbert Weinstock, undated, ca. 1966, Alfred A. Knopf Inc. Manuscript Collection, Harry Ransom Center, University of Texas at Austin.

8. For Fuentes's reflection on his reaction to Castro's support for the Soviet invasion of Czechoslovakia, see Carlos Fuentes, "Cuba's Paradise Lost: Fed Up with Fidel Castro? Join the Club," *Los Angeles Times* (20 April 2003), sec. M, p. 1.

9. In 1980, as a result of Gabriel García Márquez's lobbying, the Cuban government permitted Padilla to leave Cuba. He moved to the United States, where he was a fellow at the Woodrow Wilson International Center for Scholars in Princeton, N.J., and a visiting professor at U.S. universities.

10. Gabriel García Márquez to Plinio Mendoza, 28 October 1968, quoted in Gerald Martin, *Gabriel García Márquez: A Life* (New York: Knopf, 2009), 338.

11. The distinction Donoso made between "entertainment" and "pleasure" draws upon a critique of utilitarian thought with a deep tradition in Latin American intellectual life. In *Motivos de Proteo*, published in 1909, José Enrique Rodó identified separation from the practical demands of everyday life associated with work and family as essential for personal renewal. The "pleasure" one feels when contemplating abstract ideas provides an emotional and intellectual release from the narrow specializations that reduce people to functions of an institution and its practices. As one learns, pleasure invites expansion, reinventing oneself, becoming noble by trying to reach for the ideal embodied within one's interests. It stimulates openness to more advanced states of being toward which a person can aspire. "Entertainment," on the other hand, is a commodified form of diversion that ensures that rest time and work operate within an identical logic. The soul withers because, lacking genuine leisure time to refresh the imagination, it cannot see alternatives to its current life, or room for renewal and growth. In a world dominated by the logic of existing institutions, people lose sight of the ideal, which is never found in what currently exists. See José Enrique Rodó, *Motivos de Proteo*, § 107, in José Enrique Rodó, *Obras completas*, ed. Emir Rodríguez Monegal (Madrid: Aguilar, 1967), 439–445.

12. José Donoso, *The Boom in Spanish American Literature: A Personal History*, trans. Gregory Kolovakos (New York: Columbia University Press, 1977), 124; José Donoso, *Historia personal del "boom"* (Buenos Aires: Sudamericana, 1984), 83.

13. Jorge Edwards, *Persona non grata: Versión completa* (Barcelona: Seix Barral, 1982); Jorge Edwards, *Persona non Grata: A Memoir of Disenchantment with the Cuban Revolution*, trans. Andrew Hurley (New York: Paragon House, 1993).

14. Edwards, *Persona non Grata: A Memoir*, xi.

15. Edwards, *Persona non Grata: A Memoir*, 212; Edwards, *Persona non grata: Versión completa*, 337. Spanish text: Tengo que explicarle lo que le sucede a un chileno de buena fe, que no ha escatimado su simpatía a la Revolución Cubana, y que llega hoy a Cuba. . . . Un chileno lee en la realidad de hoy de Cuba una de las posibilidades del porvenir de su país. Ahora bien, para hablarle con absoluta franqueza, creo natural que este futuro, tal como puede descifrarse en la realidad cubana de hoy día, no le guste. Tampoco les habría gustado ese futuro a ustedes si hubieran podido anticipar, en 1959, lo que sería Cuba en 1971.

16. Marifeli Pérez-Stable, "Persona non Grata: A Memoir of Disenchantment with the Cuban Revolution," *Political Science Quarterly* 109 (1994), 726; John H. Turner, untitled review of Jorge Edwards, *Persona non grata*, *Chasqui* 4 (1974), 84–86, quote on 86.

17. Sec. 502B of Foreign Assistance Act, 1974, 22 U.S.C. 2304, P.L. 93–559. The State Department retained authority to defer suspension of aid. With the advent of the "war" against drugs, Congress authorized new forms of police assistance that contributed to remilitarizing law enforcement in most countries receiving financial and material supplies. See Michael Stohl, David Carleton, and Steve Johnson, "Human Rights and US Foreign Assistance from Nixon to Carter," *Journal of Peace Research* 21 (1984), 215–233; Clair Apodaca, "U.S. Human Rights Policy and Foreign Assistance: A Short History," *Ritsumeikan International Affairs* 3 (2005), 63–80; Rhonda L. Callaway and Elizabeth G. Matthews, *Strategic U.S. Foreign Assistance: The Battle Between Human Rights and National Security* (Burlington, Vt.: Ashgate, 2008), 41–45.

18. The phrase comes from a letter in 1954, after Veríssimo had taken up his post at the Pan American Union. He wrote a friend: "I am becoming very disappointed with the Americans, principally with the personnel at the Department of State, so inept in the skills of international politics. This country is losing a unique opportunity to bring the world to a more decent and just place. Preoccupied with fighting communism, they are veering to the right. And as a result of this stupidity, this lack of comprehension, true liberals are in a terrible position, *between two fires*. . . . These fools will never be able to understand other peoples, they believe that the rest of the world was fashioned after the image of the United States and that what works in this country will work as well for everybody else" (Érico Veríssimo to Lúcia Machado de Almeida, 27 July 1954, Acervo de EV, IMS). Original Portuguese text: Ando muito decepcionado com os americanos, principalmente com este pessoal do *Department of State*, tão inábil em matéria de política internacional. Este país está perdendo uma oportunidade única para conduzir o mundo para rumos mais decentes e justos. Preocupados com combater o comunismo, vão rumando para a direita. E como resultado dessa burrice, dessa incompreensão, os verdadeiros liberais ficam numa posição terrível, *entre dois fogos*. . . . Estes bobalhões, que jamais poderão compreender os outros povos, creem que o resto do mundo foi feito à imagem e semelhança dos Estados Unidos e o que serve para este país servirá também para os outros.

19. Érico Veríssimo to Osório Lopes, 10 February 1966, Acervo de EV, IMS.

20. "Macmillan, Inc. History," *International Directory of Company Histories* (Farmington Hills, Mich.: St. James Press, 1993), 7:284–291.

21. Alfred A. Knopf to Érico Veríssimo, dictated 27 July 1972, transcribed 1 August 1972, Acervo de EV, IMS.

22. Lucille Sullivan to Érico Veríssimo, 6 March 1969 and 1 February 1970, Acervo de EV, IMS.

23. Laurence Hallewell, *Books in Brazil: A History of the Publishing Trade* (Metuchen, N.J.: Scarecrow Press, 1982), 462–463; Renato Ortiz, *A Moderna Tradição Brasileira* (São Paulo: Brasiliense, 1988), 3–17. An important part of the plan to modernize the publishing business was a treaty with the United States for Cooperation for Technical, Scientific and Educational Publications, signed at the beginning of 1967. The U.S. Agency for International Development provided Brazilian publishers with translations of U.S. books for use in Brazilian schools at every grade level, as well as assistance with production costs, acquisition of illustrations, copyright clearances, editing, and distribution. Publishers who participated had virtually cost-free access to content that they knew had guaranteed sales.

24. Irene Hirsch and John Milton, "Translation and Americanism in Brazil, 1920–1970," *Across Languages and Cultures* 6 (2005), 234–257; John Milton, "The Importance of Economic Factors in Translation Publication: An Example from Brazil," in *Beyond Descriptive Translation Studies: Investigations in Homage to Gideon Toury*, ed. Anthony Pym, Miriam Shlesinger, and Daniel Simeoni (Amsterdam: John Benjamins, 2008), 168–170.

25. Brazilian literary critic Antônio Cândido has discussed the importance of *Incidente em Antares* for the Brazilian public when it appeared and the encouragement the book gave to younger writers about how to address issues that the dictatorship hoped to banish from public discussion in "A Nova Narrativa," in Antônio Cândido, *A Educação pela Noite, e Outros Ensaios* (São Paulo: Editora Ática, 1989), 199–215, with emphasis on 208–209.

26. Érico Veríssimo, *Incidente em Antares* (São Paulo: Globo, 1995; first published in 1971), 233. Original Portuguese text: Já que estamos mortos e não somos personagens da comédia humana, posso ser absolutamente franco.

27. Knopf to Veríssimo, 27 July 1972.

28. Richard Pattee, untitled review of *A Century of Latin American Thought* by W. Rex Crawford, *Catholic Historical Review* 30 (1945), 488–489.

Chapter 13

1. For recent reinterpretations of Tamayo's work, see Juan Carlos Pereda, ed., *Rufino Tamayo: Trayectos = Trajectories* (Mexico City: Museo Tamayo, 2012); and Diana C. Dupont, ed., *Tamayo: A Modern Icon Revisited* (Santa Barbara, Calif.: Santa Barbara Museum of Art, 2007).

2. See, for example, William Rubin, "Matta," *Bulletin of the Museum of Modern Art* 25 (1957), 1–3, 15–17, 20–22, 36.

3. On the development of Camargo's career, see Mônica Zielinsky, ed., *Iberê Camargo: Catalogue Raisonné* (Porto Alegre: Fundação Iberê Camargo, 2006); Lygia Arcuri Eluf, ed., *Iberê Camargo* (Campinas: Editora da Unicamp, 2013); Iberê Camargo, *No Andar do Tempo: Nove Contos e um Esboço Autobiográfico* (Porto Alegre: L&PM Editores, 1988).

4. Hilton Kramer, "David Von Schlegell at a Happy Standstill, Nonmoving Sculptures at the Royal Marks, Other Current Shows Are Summarized," *New York Times* (21 May 1966), 20.

5. Todd Florio, "Deconstructing 'Modern Cuban Painting' and Reconstructing the Canon" (2009), 2, 11–12, unpublished paper, on line at https://nyu.academia.edu/ToddFlorio; Todd Florio, "'Modern Cuban Painters': Promulgating Modern Cuban Modernism," MoMA Research Papers, #255 (2009).

6. The authoritative study of Gómez Sicre and the visual arts program he directed is Claire F. Fox, *Making Art Panamerican: Cultural Policy and the Cold War* (Minneapolis: University of Minnesota Press, 2013). Fox details the publication and exhibition program that Gómez Sicre developed. The book focuses on the tension in cultural projects associated with the Organization of American States between ideals of promoting pan-American citizenship and the postwar renaissance of Latin Americanism across the political spectrum. Gómez Sicre was committed to building a continental culture that was fully equal, one in which Latin Americans were not seen as in need of North American assistance to better their lives. Assumptions of inherent U.S. superiority within the United States continually frustrated his efforts and pushed him to focus on developing cultural networks between Latin American countries.

7. José Gómez Sicre, "Trends—Latin America," *Art in America* 47, no. 3 (1959), 22.

8. José Gómez Sicre, "Nota editorial," *Boletín de Artes Visuales* 9 (January–June 1962), 3; José Gómez Sicre, "Al Lector," *Boletín de Artes Visuales* 20 (1970), 3–4. In 1965, Gómez Sicre secured funding from Esso (the predecessor of ExxonMobil) for an exhibition of work by artists under the age of forty. Esso bought the work selected for its corporate collection, but subsequently donated what it had acquired to the Lowe Art Museum in Miami. See José Gómez Sicre, "Al Lector," *Boletín de Artes Visuales* 13 (1965), 2–4; and José Gómez Sicre, "Salón Esso de Artistas Jóvenes," *Boletín de Artes Visuales* 13 (1965), 20–25. Gómez Sicre assisted other U.S. corporations in acquiring contemporary art from Latin America, with important acquisitions reported in the *Boletín de Artes Visuales*.

9. Gómez Sicre, "Al Lector," *Boletín* 13, 3–4.

10. For an introduction to pop art in Brazil and Argentina, including evaluation of the relationship of work from those countries to international pop, see Darsie Alexander et al., eds., *International Pop* (Minneapolis: Walker Art Center, 2015).

11. No reviews were published in the *Washington Post* or the *New York Times*. A review of art journalism databases indicates that between 1946 and 1992, two reviews appeared in art journals and one review in *Time* magazine.

12. For a discussion of the group's founding, see Luis Camnitzer, José Guillermo Castillo, and Liliana Porter, "El New York Graphic Workshop comenzó a funcionar en1964," in *The New York Graphic Workshop* (Caracas: Instituto Nacional de Cultura y Bellas Artes, 1970), 1–10. For the goals of exhibitions, see Luis Camnitzer, "Art in Editions: New Approaches," in *Art in Editions: New Approaches* (New York: Pratt Center for Contemporary Printmaking, 1968), 1–7; quote from Luis Camnitzer, "Febrero 6, 1969: El New York Graphic Workshop se reúne para analizar y discutir la experiencia de la exposiciónen el Museo de Bellas Artes de Caracas," in *Luis Camnitzer, Liliana Porter* (exhibition catalog, Santiago de Chile: Museo Nacional de Bellas Artes, 1969), 3 (original Span-

ish text: del context dado por el museo, la galleria, la colección [museo individual] y el libro); Luis Camnitzer, "El New York Graphic Workshop," *Revista del Instituto de Cultura Puertorriqueña* 5, no. 10 (2004), 1–37.

13. Luis Camnitzer, "The Idea of the Moral Imperative in Contemporary Art," *Art Criticism* 7 (1991), 21.

14. On the issue of "Latin American conceptualism" in relation to North American and European "conceptual art," see Miguel A. López and Josephine Watson, "How Do We Know What Latin American Conceptualism Looks Like?" *Afterall: A Journal of Art, Context, and Enquiry* 23 (2010), 5–21.

15. Luis Camnitzer, "La colección latinoamericana del museo Guggenheim," *Arte en Colombia Internacional* 37 (September 1988), 31–32.

16. Freire's book first appeared in Portuguese in 1968. The English-language translation was published in New York by Continuum in 1970. The book sold well, and translations of six other Freire books appeared in the United States over the next twenty years. He was the only nonfiction writer from Latin America to reach large numbers of U.S. readers during this period (see Table 3 in the Appendix).

17. A shorter letter protesting the exhibit, signed by eighteen artists, appeared in the *New York Times*, "Art Mailbag: Dressing the Wounds for Derain, Reinhardt, and Latin America" (8 October 1967, p. 25).

18. Neruda's continuing cooperation with CIAR angered Luis Camnitzer. In 1972, he wrote another artist that Neruda had given poetry readings in New York City and his visit ended with a reception for him at CIAR. Camnitzer wanted to protest the event but decided against it. A more positive form of protest, he thought, would be to organize an artist boycott of the upcoming San Juan Biennial of Latin American Prints, with each artist submitting an autographed map of Puerto Rico with the legend "Puerto Rico Free and Latin American" (Luis Camnitzer to Lorenzo Homar, 16 April 1972, Documents of 20th-Century Latin American and Latino Art, Museum of Fine Arts, Houston).

19. For an authorized history of the CIAR art program, see José Luis Falconi and Gabriela Rangel, eds., *A Principality of Its Own: Forty Years of Visual Arts at the Americas Society* (New York: David Rockefeller Center for Latin American Studies, 2007).

20. Americas Society, *Annual Report 1987*, Americas Society Archive, New York City. In 1985, the Center for Inter-American Relations merged with the Americas Society, an organization that David Rockefeller had started in 1965 for more general educational and philanthropic purposes.

21. El Museo del Barrio started in 1969 initially as a venue where Puerto Rican culture could be celebrated, particularly the culture of the people who lived in the neighborhood between Harlem and the Upper East Side where the museum was located. In the 1980s, the museum expanded its program to do regular programming of Chicano and other Latino artists in the United States, as well as work from Latin America.

22. Luis Camnitzer to Lorenzo Homar, undated but early spring 1970, Documents of 20th-Century Latin American and Latino Art. For a discussion of how anti-CIAR protests expanded to other issues, see also Camnitzer "El New York Graphic Workshop," 12.

23. Aimé Iglesias Lukin, "Contrabienal: Latin American Art, Politics and Identity in New York, 1969–1971," *Artl@s Bulletin* 3, no. 2 (2014), 68–85.

24. Grace Glueck, "Show Is Suspended as Artists Dissent," *New York Times* (20 March 1971), 13.

25. Luis Camnitzer, "The Museo Latinoamericano and MICLA," in Falconi and Rangel, *A Principality of Its Own*, 216–229.

26. In an oral history interview, Stanton Catlin stated bluntly that CIAR fired him without any advance warning, in "Oral History Interview with Stanton L. Catlin, 1989 July 1–September 14," interview by Francis V. O'Connor, Archives of American Art, Smithsonian Institution, available online at http://www.aaa.si.edu/collections/interviews/oral-history-interview-stanton-l-catlin-5454.

27. The classic formulation of this thesis can be found in Frederico Morais, *Artes plásticas na América Latina: Do transe ao transitório* (Rio de Janeiro: Civilização Brasileira, 1979). Morais ex-

cluded Mexico from "América Latina," arguing that its geographical proximity to the United States and the integration of its economy into a broader North American market separated Mexican writers and artists from developments in other countries in the western hemisphere while making them active participants in U.S. cultural movements.

28. Beverly Adams, "Latin American Art at the Americas Society: A Principality of Its Own," in Falconi and Rangel, *A Principality of Its Own*, 32–33.

29. I concur with Odd Arne Westad's argument in *The Global Cold War: Third World Interventions and the Making of Our Times* (Cambridge: Cambridge University Press, 2007) that the Cold War involved a struggle between two opposing revolutionary societies, both determined to use their power to transform the rest of the world. Westad presents the core distinctions between the opposing conceptions of revolution in chapters 1 and 2, pp. 8–72.

30. Néstor García Canclini, *Hybrid Cultures: Strategies for Entering and Leaving Modernity* (Minneapolis: University of Minnesota Press, 1995), 64–65, 52. Published in Spanish originally as *Culturas híbridas: Estrategias para entrar y salir de la modernidad* (Mexico City: Editorial Grijalba, 1990).

31. García Canclini, *Hybrid Cultures*, 65.

32. Quoted in Andrew J. Bacevich, *American Empire: The Realities and Consequences of U.S. Diplomacy* (Cambridge, Mass.: Harvard University Press, 2002), 40–41.

33. On the development of the Organization of American States since 1970 and the expansion of its human rights conventions, see Mônica Herz, *The Organization of American States (OAS): Global Governance Away from the Media* (New York: Routledge, 2011); and Rubén M. Perina, *The Organization of American States as the Advocate and Guardian of Democracy: An Insider's Critical Assessment of Its Role in Promoting and Defending Democracy* (Lanham, Md.: University Press of America, 2015).

34. See note 1 of Chapter 12.

35. Paulo Coelho Filho, "Truth Commission in Brazil: Individualizing Amnesty, Revealing the Truth," *Yale Review of International Studies* (February 2012), online at http://yris.yira.org/essays /440; Ricardo Nazer A. and Jaime Rosemblit B., "Electores, sufragio y democracia en Chile: Una mirada histórica," *Mapocho* 48 (2000), 222–225.

Chapter 14

1. Ernesto Che Guevara, *Notas de viaje* (Barcelona: Ediciones B, 2002), 158. Original Spanish text: Creemos, y después de este viaje más firmemente que antes, que la división de América en nacionalidades inciertas e ilusorias es completamente ficticia. Constituimos una sola raza mestiza que desde México hasta el estrecho de Magallanes presenta notables similitudes etnográficas. Por eso, tratando de quitarme toda carga de provincialismo exiguo, brindo por Perú y por América Unida.

2. *The Motorcycle Diaries*, Walter Salles, director; José Rivera, screenwriter (Focus Features, Spotlight Series, DVD 25942), chapter 16, "Salute to a United Nation." In the appendices of *Notas de viaje*, a letter from Guevara to his mother (6 July 1952) contains a brief reference to his having swum across the river while staying at the colony in order to overcome his fear of water (*Notas de viaje*, 189). In his account of his birthday celebration, rather than he crossing the river to join the patients, a group of patients who are musicians cross over to serenade him with their accordions and guitars (185). Alberto Granado's diary of the trip, published as *Con el Che por Sudamérica* (Havana: Letras Cubanas, 1989), made no mention of the toast at all and focused instead on the dancing that evening, particularly a joke Granado played that led to Guevara trying to dance the tango to a samba tune, a moment incorporated into the film (200–203). Granado's diary has an entry from another day that mentions in passing Guevara having swum across the river (211).

3. Alberto Granado, *Con el Che de Córdoba a la Habana* (Córdoba, Argentina: Op Oloop Ediciones, 1995), 48. Original Spanish: ratificación práctica de conocimientos teóricos. Far from being a political neophyte, Granado had long been an activist against the government of Argentina. In

1943, he was imprisoned for his activities organizing a student strike against a military coup led by people he considered pro-Nazi. On the student strikes, Granado's "clandestine life," and his arrest, see 18–25.

4. Granado, *Con el Che por Sudamérica*, 31–32, 123.

5. Guevara to his mother, 15 July 1956, in Ernesto Che Guevara, *Otra vez: Diario inédito del segundo viaje por Latinoamérica* (Barcelona: Ediciones B, 2001), 177. Original Spanish text: Para toda obra grande se necesita pasión y audacia en grandes dosis.

6. Guevara, *Notas de viaje*, 170–171. Original Spanish text: El porvenir es del pueblo y poco a poco o de golpe va a conquistar el poder aquí y en toda la tierra. Lo malo es que él tiene que civilizarse y eso no se puede hacer antes sino después de tomarlo. Se civilizará sólo aprendiendo a costa de sus propios errores, que serán muy graves. . . . En sólo dos fracciones antagónicas, estaré con el pueblo . . . inmolado a la auténtica revolución estandarizadora de voluntades.

7. The passage of the Immigration Reform Act of 1965 may well be the event that most clearly revealed the end of pan-Americanism in the United States. The act, which removed barriers to immigration from Asia and otherwise made it easier for people from other countries to gain residence in the United States, imposed immigration quotas on the members of the Organization of American States. In some cases, particularly Mexico, the new quotas were far below the numbers of people who came to the United States to work. Neither migration patterns nor labor markets changed, but those who came to the United States to work had become "illegals," subject to arrest and deportation. Putting caps on immigration from Latin America to the United States was a turning point in inter-American relations that went against the ideal of thinking of "Americans" from all countries as forming a single community with shared interests. For a history of immigration policy at the U.S.-Mexico border, see Michael Dear, *Why Walls Won't Work: Repairing the U.S.-Mexico Divide* (New York: Oxford University Press, 2013), 50–70.

8. Original Spanish: Una revolución sin tiros? Ni modo.

9. Granado, *Con el Che Guevara por Sudamérica*, 129. Original Spanish text: ¿Salir a desfilar sin armas para que nos caguen a palos? Ni loco. Yo no salgo si no cargo un bufoso.

10. Paco Ignacio Taibo II, *Ernesto Guevara también conocido como el Che* (Mexico City: Planeta, 2003), 10. As Taibo showed in his biography, Marxist-Leninists in Latin America before the Cuban Revolution, and at times after, viewed Guevara's romantic and bohemian revolutionary theories as a "petty-bourgeois deviation."

11. Granado, *Con el Che por Sudamérica*, 154. Original Spanish text: Verdad que la unión hace la fuerza, pero tiene que ser la fuerza de la gente que trabaja. Si alguno hubiera dicho que no iba a meter pico y palo, la unión hubiese roto, y seguro que eso habría pasado si en lugar de ser una caravana de camioneros, campesinos y algún loco suelto como nosotros, hubiera aparecido un par de profesionales como los que hemos conocidos en estos días.

12. Quoted in "Concluding Remarks," in Craig Calhoun, ed., *Habermas and the Public Sphere* (Cambridge, Mass.: MIT Press, 1992), 478.

13. On the role of U.S. media enterprises in constructing a transnational American cultural market, see the work of Néstor García Canclini, *Hybrid Cultures: Strategies for Entering and Leaving Modernity* (Minneapolis: University of Minnesota Press, 1995), published in Spanish originally as *Culturas híbridas: Estrategias para entrar y salir de la modernidad* (Mexico City: Editorial Grijalba, 1990); Néstor García Canclini, *La globalización imaginada* (Buenos Aires: Paidós, 1999); Néstor García Canclini and Carlos Moneta, eds., *Las industrias culturales en la integración latinoamericana* (Buenos Aires: Eudeba, 1999), in particular essays by Carlos Juan Moneta, "Identidades y políticas culturales en procesos de globalización e integración regional" 21–34, for an effective analysis of the challenges that the market poses for concepts of national unity, and García Canclini, "Políticas culturales: De las identitades nacionales al espacio latinoamericano" 67–94; Néstor García Canclini, *Latinoamericanos buscando lugar en este siglo* (Buenos Aires: Paidós, 2002).

14. On the development of telenovelas and of the television industry in Latin America, see Livia Antola and Everett M. Rogers, "Television Flows in Latin America," *Communication Research* 11 (1984), 183–202; Elizabeth Fox, *Latin American Broadcasting: From Tango to Telenovela* (Luton,

England: University of Luton Press, 1997); Ana M. López, "Our Welcomed Guests: Telenovelas in Latin America," in *To Be Continued . . . Soap Operas Around the World*, ed. Robert C. Allen (London: Routledge, 1995), 256–275; José Marques de Melo, *As Telenovelas da Globo: Produção e Exportação* (São Paulo: Summus, 1988); Sérgio Mattos, "Un perfil de la television brasileña: 40 años de historia (1950–199)," *Communicación y Sociedad* 16–17 (1993), 45–74; Nora Mazziotti, *La industria de la telenovela: La producción de ficción en América Latina* (Buenos Aires: Paidós, 1996); Heriberto Muraro, *Invasión cultural: Economía y comunicación* (Buenos Aires: Legasa, 1987); Omar Souki Oliveira, "Brazilian Soaps Outshine Hollywood: Is Cultural Imperialism Fading Out?" in *Beyond National Sovereignty: International Communication in the 1990s*, ed. Kaarle Nordenstreng and Herbert Schiller (Norwood, N.J.: Ablex, 1990); Everett M. Rogers and Livia Antola, "Telenovelas: A Latin American Success Story," *Journal of Communication* 35 (1985), 24–36; John Sinclair, "Dependent Development and Broadcasting: The Mexican Formula," *Media, Culture and Society* 8 (1986), 81–101; John Sinclair, "The Decentering of Cultural Imperialism: Televisa-ion and Globo-ization in the Latin World," *Intercom* 16 (1993), 120–134; John Sinclair, "Mexico, Brazil, and the Latin World," in *New Patterns in Global Television*, ed. Elizabeth Jacka and Stuart Cunningham (New York: Oxford University Press, 1996); Joseph D. Straubhaar, "Brazilian Television: The Decline of American Influence," *Communication Research* 11 (1984), 221–240; Joseph D. Straubhaar, *World Television: From Global to Local* (Thousand Oaks, Calif.: Sage Publications, 2007); Aluíziova R. Trinta, "News from Home: A Study of Realism and Melodrama in Brazilian Telenovelas," in *The Television Studies Book*, ed. Christine Geraghty and David Lusted (London: Arnold, 1997); Tuula-Liina Varis, *International Flow of Television Programmes* (Paris: UNESCO, 1985).

15. See, for an example of how they publicized their film *Neruda* when released in the United States by emphasizing the importance of their work for understanding current problems, Rory Carroll, "Gael García Bernal and Pablo Larraín: 'Trump Has the Nuclear Codes but We Have a Camera,'" *Guardian*, U.S. edition (9 December 2016), on line at https://www.theguardian.com/film/2016/dec/09/gael-garcia-bernal-pablo-larrain-donald-trump-we-have-a-camera.

Index

Acknowledgments

The initial concept and themes of the book emerged out of a series of graduate seminars I offered between 2003 and 2011 on comparative intellectual history of the Americas and "U.S. Intellectual and Cultural History: Global Contexts." Research support from the University of California, Berkeley, provided from the Committee on Research and the Department of History, supported the extensive travel needed for exploring archival sources. Funding from the university allowed Samuel Redman and Alice Goff to work as graduate research assistants, pursuing aspects of my project that intersected with their fields of study. Sam collected the data on art exhibitions and publications in the United States, while Alice prepared a bibliography on U.S.-German competition in South America during the first half of the twentieth century.

In 2010, I spent a semester at the Catholic Pontifical University (Pontifícia Universidade Católica) in Rio de Janeiro as the Fulbright-PUC Rio de Janeiro Distinguished Chair of American Studies. I cannot imagine better guides for my stay in Brazil than Danilo Marcondes de Souza Filho, Angela Randolpho Paiva, Margarida de Souza Neves, the History Department chair at the time, and Marcantonio Pamplona. My research assistant at PUC-Rio, Leonardo Pradela, deserves special mention. He was an undergraduate at the time but already working at the level of an accomplished graduate student. He has since done graduate work at Columbia University. Visiting professorships at the federal university in Niterói (Universidade Fluminense Federal) and the University of São Paulo deepened my connections with Brazilian scholars, as did invitations to give talks coming from many different universities. Over the years, I have had the chance to talk with many wonderful scholars on both sides of the equator as well as both sides of the Atlantic who shared their perspectives with me and provided opportunities to present material from the study to their colleagues and students.

There are so many people who have helped me in the course of writing this book that I cannot possibly name them all. Early in the project several long discussions with Ellen DuBois were particularly important for helping me define what I wanted to do, as was a conversation I had with Ian Tyrell. As my work developed, I owe special thanks to Ana Maria Mauad, Paulo Knauss, Ricardo Santhiago, Fernando Cássio, and Ana Carolina Maciel for the help they provided. Marilena Pessoa, my Portuguese professor in Rio de Janeiro, assisted me in making the talks and articles I wrote in Portuguese reasonably understandable. In 2009, the personal papers of Érico Veríssimo arrived at the Instituto Moreira Salles in Rio de Janeiro, where for the first time they were available to scholars to peruse in their entirety. Manoela Purcell Daudt D'Oliveira and the staff at IMS were extraordinarily helpful. I have been at few archives that were as comfortable places to work and think. Katherine P. Smith read the last two versions of the book, correcting errors, offering comments and critiques, and challenging me to think more about how to tell my story in a more direct way.

This is the second book that I have published with the University of Pennsylvania Press in the Arts and Intellectual Life in Modern America series. Robert Lockhart, the press's senior editor for American history and American studies, and Casey Nelson Blake, the series editor, gave me generous, insightful, and in-depth readings of a very long manuscript at a precarious moment when I needed to give it more reasonable shape. Bob and Casey proved to be the engaged, knowledgeable readers that writers hope to find in their editors.

*   *   *

Earlier versions of material in this volume appeared in two articles: "Fotografia de Boa Vizinhança: Uma Norte-Americana no Brasil, 1941–1942," *Cadernos do CEOM, Centro de Memória do Oeste de Santa Catarina: Patrimônio, Memória e Identidade* 40 (2014), 71–84, and "Érico Veríssimo, um Embaixador Cultural nos Estados Unidos," *Tempo* 19, no. 34 (2013), 147–173. I presented an early version of the material on William Carlos Williams and *In the American Grain* at el Centro Cultural, Universidad Autónoma de Baja California, Mexicali. I presented an earlier version of the material on Walter Salles and *The Motorcycle Diaries* at a colloquium the Department of History at UCLA organized on the "U.S. in the World" and at an annual faculty workshop at the American Studies Program at the University of California, Berkeley.